Stories from an Ancient Land

Asian Anthropologies

General Editors:
Hans Steinmüller, London School of Economics
Dolores Martinez, SOAS, University of London

Founding Editors:
Shinji Yamashita, The University of Tokyo
J.S. Eades, Emeritus Professor, Ritsumeikan Asia Pacific University

Recent volumes:

Volume 12
*Stories from an Ancient Land:
Perspectives on Wa History and Culture*
Magnus Fiskesjö

Volume 11
*Aspirations of Young Adults in Urban
Asia: Values, Family, and Identity*
Edited by Mariske Westendorp,
Désirée Remmert, and Kenneth Finis

Volume 10
*Tides of Empire. Religion, Development,
and Environment in Cambodia*
Courtney Work

Volume 9
*Fate Calculation Experts: Diviners
Seeking Legitimation in Contemporary
China*
Geng Li

Volume 8
*Soup, Love, and a Helping Hand: Social
Relations and Support in Guangzhou,
China*
Friederike Fleischer

Volume 7
*Ogata-Mura: Sowing Dissent and
Reclaiming Identity in a Japanese
Farming Village*
Donald C. Wood

Volume 6
*Multiculturalism in New Japan: Crossing
the Boundaries Within*
Edited by Nelson Graburn, John Ertl, and
R. Kenji Tierney

Volume 5
*Engaging the Spirit World in Modern
Southeast Asia*
Edited by Andrea Lauser and
Kirsten W. Endres

Volume 4
*Centering the Margin: Agency and
Narrative in Southeast Asian Borderlands*
Edited by Alexander Horstmann and
Reed L. Wadley

Volume 3
*The Making of Anthropology in East and
Southeast Asia*
Edited by Shinji Yamashita, Joseph Bosco,
and J.S. Eades

For a full volume listing, please see the series page on our website:
https://www.berghahnbooks.com/series/asian-anthropologies

STORIES FROM AN ANCIENT LAND

Perspectives on Wa History and Culture

Magnus Fiskesjö

berghahn
NEW YORK · OXFORD
www.berghahnbooks.com

First published in 2021 by
Berghahn Books
www.berghahnbooks.com

© 2021, 2025 Magnus Fiskesjö
First paperback edition published in 2025

All rights reserved. Except for the quotation of short passages
for the purposes of criticism and review, no part of this book
may be reproduced in any form or by any means, electronic or
mechanical, including photocopying, recording, or any information
storage and retrieval system now known or to be invented,
without written permission of the publisher.

Library of Congress Cataloging-in-Publication Data

Names: Fiskesjö, Magnus, author.
Title: Stories from an ancient land : perspectives on Wa history and culture / Magnus Fiskesjö.
Other titles: Perspectives on Wa history and culture
Description: New York : Berghahn Books, 2021. | Series: Asian anthropologies; 12 | Includes bibliographical references and index.
Identifiers: LCCN 2021022441 (print) | LCCN 2021022442 (ebook) | ISBN 9781789208870 (hardback) | ISBN 9781789208887 (ebook)
Subjects: LCSH: Wa (Asian people)—China—Yunnan Sheng—Civilization. | Wa (Asian people) —Burma—Civilization.
Classification: LCC DS731.W32 F57 2021 (print) | LCC DS731.W32 (ebook) | DDC 951/.350049593--dc23
LC record available at https://lccn.loc.gov/2021022441
LC ebook record available at https://lccn.loc.gov/2021022442

British Library Cataloguing in Publication Data

A catalogue record for this book is available from the British Library

ISBN 978-1-78920-887-0 hardback
ISBN 978-1-80539-737-3 paperback
ISBN 978-1-80539-920-9 epub
ISBN 978-1-78920-888-7 web pdf

https://doi.org/10.3167/9781789208870

Contents

List of Illustrations	vii
Preface	ix
Acknowledgments	xii

Introduction
Sources, History, Issues   1

Chapter 1
Gifts and Debts: Fieldwork in the Wa Lands   29

Chapter 2
Naming Oneself, Naming the World   52

Chapter 3
Rice Beer and the Making of Wa Sociality   73

Chapter 4
Mining, Hierarchy, and the Anti-state Wa   92

Chapter 5
Slavery as a Threat to the Ideology of Kinship   123

Chapter 6
War, Headhunting, and the Erasure of Wa History   142

Chapter 7
Barbarian Ruse: Playing with the Fears of the Civilized   175

Chapter 8
Disease and Death in the Peripheral Situation   193

Chapter 9
Hope against Hope: Border Prophets and Foreign Saviors   223

Chapter 10
The Power of the Exotic: Negotiating the Future   249

Epilogue
Dark Clouds Gathering   267

References   271

Index   309

Illustrations

Figure 0.1	Map of the Wa region. By Nij Tontisirin Anantsuksomsri.	2
Figure 0.2	Fields and forests near the village of Yong Ou. Photo by the author, 1997.	3
Figure 0.3	Buffalo and human figure in the rock paintings at Cangyuan. Photo by the author, 1998.	7
Figure 1.1	Hillside irrigation canal digging ordered by Chinese officials. Village of Yong Ou. Photo by the author, 1997.	34
Figure 1.2	Map of the neighborhood of the Yong Ou ancestral center. By Nij Tontisirin Anantsuksomsri.	37
Figure 1.3	Coffee and excitement at the farewell party in the author's room. Village of Yong Ou. Photo by the author, 1998.	40
Figure 1.4	Mourners at a funeral in Yong Ou. Photo by the author, 1997.	41
Figure 1.5	Women at work thatching the roof while the men finish the body of a new house, in Yong Ou. Photo by the author, 1997.	43
Figure 2.1	Blae Ge Jen, conducting a *hlax doh* sacrifice outside his house in Yong Ou. Photo by the author, 1998.	55
Figure 3.1	At a gathering in Yong Ou, the host is waiting for a guest to finish his share of rice beer. Others wait for their turn; in the background, one man is making his libation to the ancestors. Photo by the author, 1997.	80
Figure 3.2	The author learning to drink Wa rice beer, sporting a betel bag. Yong Ou, 1997.	84
Figure 4.1	Wa gentleman showing a family heirloom: an ancient bronze drum. Cangyuan County. Photo by the author, 1998.	93
Figure 4.2	"Map of the Kawa area" indicating the autonomous central Wa country, as well as the Wa peripheries. From Fei Xiaotong 1955, 105.	95

Figure 5.1	Wa girls posing on a *ngrah* veranda, in their best clothes in local style, to celebrate the New Year in Yong Ou. Photo by the author, 1997.	125
Figure 6.1	"After the battle, the Wa descend to the camp for a conference." From Prestre 1938; this may be the only photo of Wa warriors on the warpath. Note the crossbow (*ox ag*).	143
Figure 6.2	A drum shrine with four drums and one bamboo head post (*njouh*), from the village of Matet in central Wa country. "Sketched by Lt. C. E. Macquoid, 1st Lancers, Hyderabad Contingent" (Macquoid 1896).	147
Figure 6.3.	Bamboo head posts (*njouh*) at a village in Yong Ou circle, in the winter of 1957–58 (Winnington 1959).	148
Figure 6.4	Skull avenue at a village near Mengtung. Ling Shun-sheng, 1935–36 (Academia Sinica collection, Wa-071; courtesy of the Institute of History and Philology, Academia Sinica, Taipei).	149
Figure 6.5	A tiger rack, *ndaig' a vi*—here with a leopard. Line drawing by Jidapa Janpathompong, based on Xu Zhiyuan (2009: 54); the only known photo of this display.	170
Figure 8.1	Consuming the sacrifice. Photo by the author in Yong Ou, 2006.	194
Figure 8.2	The *hlax doh* sacrifice. Photo by the author in Yong Ou, 2006.	205
Figure 8.3.	Interpreting the chicken bone oracle. Village of Yong Ou. Photo by the author, 1997.	206
Figure 8.4.	Portraits of Wa State leaders, posing while administering vaccinations. Photo by the author in Wa State, 2006.	212
Figure 10.1	Wa dancers at the Shenzhen theme park. Photo by the author, 2015.	258
Figure 11.1	The future of the Wa people. Schoolchildren in Wa State, Burma. Photo by the author, 2006.	270

Preface

This book is laid out in ten chapters, in which I seek to offer a new and nuanced picture of the Wa people and their history. I also have a more universal agenda, concerned with an old question: To what extent can we humans on Earth take charge of our own destiny? As we shall see, this question is very much actualized in the Wa struggle to determine their own fate, despite the powerful forces that try to make them passive recipients of a set destiny as a marginalized periphery.

Above all, I hope to convey that the Wa have a rich civilization of their own, and a rich history of struggling to take charge of their own destiny. I can make only a few limited contributions here toward presenting and discussing the richness of their story. There is so much more to tell, for example, about Wa music, much of which remains unrecorded, and many other aspects of their culture and history. Others will help in these endeavors. I emphasize these goals here not least because incorrect stereotypes abound in many older but still dominant writings about the Wa. My book is also intended as a contribution toward disarming, debating, and countering some of those persistent misunderstandings, especially in the discourse of self-appointed civilized people who look down upon the Wa.

In Western and Chinese literature, the Wa are often mentioned above all for their fierce warlikeness in the past, and especially for their "headhunting." Especially in Chinese publications, but also in the Western ones that inherit the British colonial perspective, such aspects are emphasized as signs of a certain primitiveness of the Wa, which by extension is taken to explain most of what there is to know about them. I disagree. I believe, instead, that war and headhunting are relatively late and recent phenomena in Wa history—and I argue, as part of a larger rethinking of Wa history, that the headhunting must in fact have been borrowed, quite recently, from the Chinese state (chapter 6).

All this is also linked to another oft-mentioned issue: opium. While opium has been phased out of Wa agriculture in recent years, it is true that it was once hugely significant, and other kinds of drug production do continue in the region. From my perspective, what is interesting is not so much the opium production and handling itself (which I mostly leave out, but see Fiskesjö 2000) but that the opium, too, made its appearance in the Wa lands relatively recently, and that the very history of big-time Wa opium production for export to the land of the "civilized" rather fatally undercuts the flawed view of the Wa as a primitive people hopelessly stuck in a static past.

As we shall see, in fact, the Wa were never as isolated as they have been made out to be, and historically they themselves engaged the world outside in sophisticated ways. Their history is also world history, and the question of what it means to be in charge of our destiny seems to stand out more sharply in their case. In this sense, too, I believe we all have something to learn from them.

The chapters of the book deal with both history and the present day, and they are arranged with this in mind. It will be okay for readers to jump around as they please, but the introduction provides an overview that is meant both as a guide and as a broad review both of Wa history and of the present-day situation. Then, chapter 1 introduces my own experience and position as an ethnographer venturing into Wa country, including how I came to learn about the Wa understanding of themselves as caretakers of the world.

The chapters that follow are not strictly chronological but rather thematic. Chapter 2 explains how the Wa name themselves according to their own social dynamic, and how the Chinese have been trying to rename, and redefine them. Chapter 3 addresses how Wa inclusive sociality is forged through shared drinking (and eating) and introduces the concept of "participant intoxication."

After these accounts, which attempt to illuminate several striking aspects of Wa society as it was in the past and continues today, chapter 4 presents a political anthropology of the independent Wa of the past, examining how they struggled to prevent mining-generated wealth from leading to a hierarchy or state and disrupting their much-cherished egalitarian system. Chapters 5 and 6 continue this thematic exploration, first of Wa "slavery" and how it has been misunderstood in relation to kinship and morality, and then of Wa warfare in the context of history and how Wa "headhunting" in reality is no primitive phenomenon but was very likely borrowed recently from Chinese state practices of trophy taking, judicial punishment, and terror spectacles (in ways quite different from what some of the Chinese tales have to say about this issue!). These three chapters all speak to the core issue of how the Wa sought to shape their own society despite the external pressures pushing for hierarchy and for the commodification even of their own people, and to write their own history despite their lack of a writing system.

In chapter 7, I discuss the fear exhibited by many foreigners toward the "barbarian" Wa, and I also suggest how the Wa deployed the fear engendered by their violent practices as part of a strategy to maintain their independence.

In chapter 8, I present my understanding of the indigenous Wa ideas about how to deal with disease and death, and recount the catastrophic consequences of the forced relocations of the new era, which have severely disrupted traditional Wa ways of engaging the landscape of their living homeland.

In chapter 9, I examine the long history of border prophets and foreign saviors, which at times have appeared as a different kind of hope, especially in destitute areas exploited by external powers.

The last chapter moves to the present-day spectacle put on in Chinese theme parks and elsewhere of the Wa as an exotic, alluring, and still-dangerous people. I discuss how, paradoxically, some elements generated within this starkly "Orientalist" framing is transformed by new generations into a source of pride, and how this suggests a different kind of hope for the future of their people, even after the loss of their independence and autonomy after the 1950s.

Acknowledgments

First of all, I want to thank the people of the ancient Wa lands, along the China-Burma border, where most of my research has taken place. I may not have the right words to convey it—and there is no word for "thank you" in "my" Wa dialect—but let me try to explain. I have had the good fortune to experience firsthand the civilization of the Wa people. They are people of striking dignity, remarkable courtesy, and formidable generosity and hospitality toward strangers. When I first went to the Wa country, I was not sure how dangerous it would be; I too heard the usual rumors of severed heads, smuggled drugs, and other such things. But as it happens, over the years I have never once felt threatened in the company of Wa people. On the contrary, I came to enjoy a great sense of safety, ease, and comfort, among their people. I realized that the dangers that figure into the many rumors about the Wa are mostly imaginary, and that actually, the machinery of state power might be more of a danger. The vast majority of Wa people are warmhearted, friendly, and helpful even in the midst of scarcity, poverty, and illness. I found that even at the most impoverished and distant house, I would be sure to find fellow human beings that would treat me with great decency. I miss their company, and I am grateful not just for how people shared food, drink, and conversation with me, but also for them allowing me to share their gracious presence, the memories of which I will treasure all my life. I take my hat off to the Wa people, in both China and Burma, and I dedicate my writings to them.

This book has been long in coming and many people helped along the way. I want to thank the faculty and my fellow students at the University of Chicago, where I discovered anthropology in the early 1990s—truly an experience of being born again. Early on, as I began imagining the exciting possibility of ethnography, I ventured to the late Valerio Valeri that there probably would be nothing left to study in China. Rejecting this, he asked me to look up the dissertation of a former student, Charles McKhann (1992). I had to come back to ask about the spelling of Chas's name; but finding and reading his work on the revival of Naxi rituals made me realize how wrong I had been. Even with the atrocities and the regimentation that swept China in the twentieth century, people will still try to rebuild, and create themselves anew.

Later, in 1995, while helping to prospect for an archaeology project, I visited the Wa mountains. In the end, the US-Chinese archaeological project never received permission to proceed, but the trip became my own first encounter with the Wa people. At one point, after climbing up to one of the ancient rock art sites in the Wa area (Wang Ningsheng 1985), I found myself coming down a mountain slope and noticing a small Wa boy herding buffalo. Hoping he might understand Chinese, I said hello and then asked him about the buffalo: "What do you call those in your language?" He told me, "*grag*." He then paused, and asked me: "And you, what do you call it in *your* language?" While returning the favor, I was mightily impressed with that bright response. I still think of that boy, his inquisitive mind, and also his attention to reciprocity (on which more in the coming chapters).

Back in Chicago, reading up in the library and finding out how little ethnography had been possible until this time in the Wa lands, I found myself fired up with the motivation to return there for ethnographic fieldwork. And I did go again, first for field research in 1996-1998, and again for shorter visits in 2006 and 2013. I am grateful to the late anthropologist Wang Zhusheng (2001), my host at Yunnan University in Kunming, as well as many others, including Ai Gad Yaong Rūng, who also helped me arrange for my long-term fieldwork. In Kunming, the formidable Chinese anthropologists Yin Shaoting and the late Wang Ningsheng shared invaluable experiences and rich insights from working among the Wa in previous decades. I will always cherish the inspiration from these Chinese scholars, especially their fierce integrity, intellectual independence, and profound scholarship. I also thank the many other scholars and students around the world who have helped me go further, through commentary, dialogue, and debate. Many, though not all, are referenced in the text that follows. At Cornell University, I must mention Yu Yu Khaing, Lecturer in Burmese, and San San Hnin Tun, our former Lecturer in Burmese (and French), as well as Kyaw Myo Lwin, for help with translations and transcription of Burmese materials. I am grateful to Dr. Nij Tontisirin Anantsuksomsri for her excellent maps, and Jidapa Janpathompong for the splendid tiger rack drawing.

I would also like to express my thanks to the Wenner-Gren Foundation for Anthropological Research, the China Times Cultural Foundation, the Pacific Cultural Foundation, the University of Chicago, the Charlotte W. Newcombe Foundation, and Cornell University (including the Southeast Asia Program) for support towards my research.

I am also deeply grateful to the libraries and librarians who have helped me, especially those at the University of Chicago, Cornell University, and Yunnan

University, as well as at the British Library and its old and new India Office collections in London. Needless to say, all errors are my responsibility.

I thank my family and friends for their encouragement throughout, not least Loke and Zhen. My mother and my father always supported even my farthest journeys, and I am sorry that they did not get see this book in their lifetime, yet they did hear my interim reports.

Some of what follows is revised from previous publications, as well as from my 2000 dissertation. I thank the publishers for permission to use portions of certain texts, as indicated.

Lastly, I wish the best for the next generation of scholars who will be fortunate enough to visit and study the remarkable people of these mountain lands, including the Wa and their shining civilization.

INTRODUCTION

Sources, History, Issues

The ancient homeland of the Wa people is located between today's Burma (Myanmar) and China, in a region of upland Southeast Asia sometimes known as Zomia (Schendel 2002; Scott 2009) or as the Southeast Asian massif (Michaud 2006), overlapping with the fabled Golden triangle.[*1]

The broad extent of the ancient homeland of the Wa is indicated by how Wa languages are spoken in a broad, north-south "Wa-ic corridor," in between the upper Salween and Mekong Rivers, which today run through Burma and China, respectively.[2]

Today, the bulk of the Wa population lives in the mountains and mountain valleys east of the Burmese city of Lashio; north of the old Shan realm of Kengtung; and west of the Chinese tea town of Puer, or Simao. Many of these named modern towns are in areas historically populated by Wa-speaking people, and today some Wa also inhabit these cities, although they are dominated by Burmese, Shan, and Chinese people.

In recent history, Wa country was rather wealthy, and their land was one of the most densely populated in its neighborhood. I will have much more to say about these surprising facts. Today, the Wa people number about one million and share the region with less numerous peoples who speak closely related northern Mon-Khmer languages and who have also long inhabited these lands (the De'ang; the Bulang, etc.), along with more recent arrivals who speak other languages—including the Shan (or Tai, who are known as Siam in the Wa language); the Chinese and the Burmese; as well as the Lahu, a Tibeto-Burman-speaking people arriving from the north in recent centuries (and on whom more will be said in

---

Endnotes for this chapter begin on page 24.

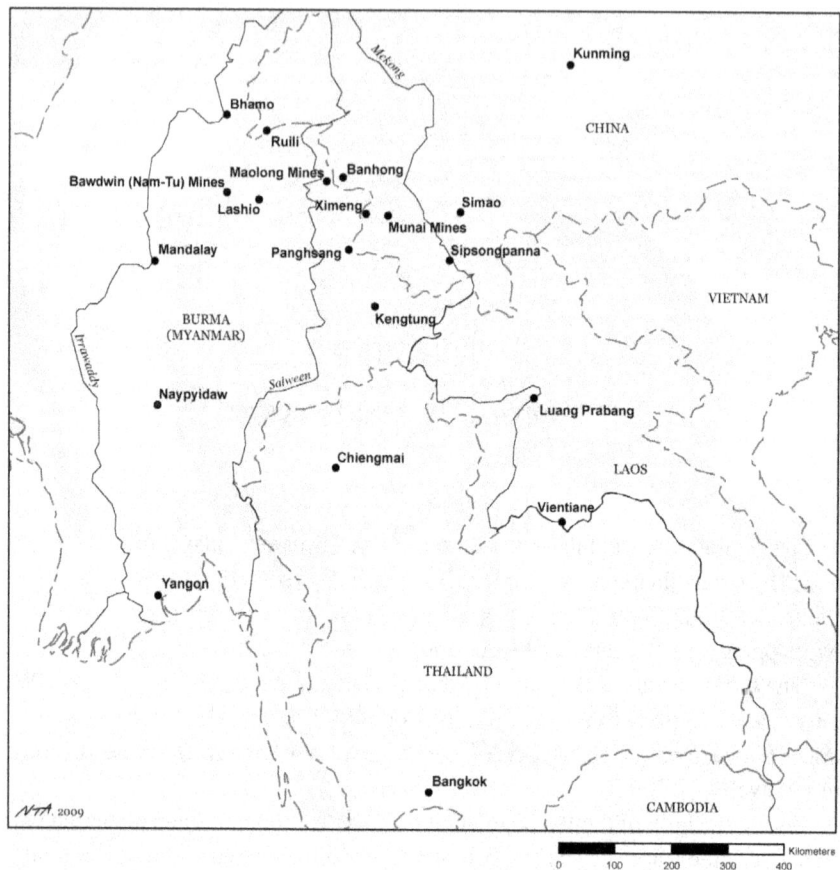

Figure 0.1. Map of the Wa region. By Nij Tontisirin Anantsuksomsri.

chapter 9). Interestingly, all these neighboring peoples traditionally recognize the Wa as the prior inhabitants of the region, something that agrees with widespread Wa oral traditions about themselves as indigenous to the area and living there prior to all others.

These Wa lands were once heavily forested but have been heavily denuded, especially over the last century. Originally, the Wa claimed both uplands and valleys, but they are now mainly in mountains crisscrossed by smaller rivers and valleys. They originally lived as self-sustaining forest farmers, rotating their fields on mountain slopes and growing rice, millet, and many other crops.

In the past, the Wa were also hunters, but the importance of hunting has greatly diminished in recent times. They have also long been engaged in trade with other people in the region. It was in the eighteenth and especially since the nineteenth century that they developed trade in major export items such as opium, as well as

Figure 0.2. Fields and forests near the village of Yong Ou. Photo by the author, 1997.

the yields of mines of various kinds. For centuries, and continuing alongside the development of these export industries, the Wa lands were self-governed. They did not have a state or a king, but maintained their autonomy under arms (using guns, crossbows, fortifications, and so on), remaining autonomous at every level, from the person, to the clan, to the village and its "circles," and uniting across any and each of these internal boundaries only against external threats (just like in the Nuer's "ordered anarchy," see chapter 4). Obviously, this didn't mean that the Wa were isolated, as they engaged in wide-ranging trade and contact with neighboring peoples (chapter 4). Even Chinese observers in the early twentieth century recognized the remaining central Wa lands as "politically and economically independent" (Fang Guoyu 1943d: 1–3), and the Wa were not directly governed by other powers or states until after the middle of the twentieth century.

In the last years of the nineteenth century, the British and Chinese first initiated an attempt to delineate a border between each other's empires. This project was abandoned, several major wars intervened, and in the 1940s an international border was eventually agreed upon between British Burma and the modern Chinese Republic. However, no such border could be demarcated between Burma and China until one was negotiated in the early 1960s, this time between Communist China (the People's Republic) and newly independent Burma.

This new international border was installed without consulting the Wa people, and it split the formerly independent Wa areas in the middle, dividing their ancient territories between the new modern nations of China and Burma, respectively. Since this time, approximately a third of the million or so Wa people are citizens of China, and the remaining two-thirds citizens of Burma. Today, most Wa are able to travel more or less freely in their own ancient lands, across the border and beyond.

The Wa are formally recognized in both Burma and China as an ethnic minority officially entitled to limited autonomy. On the China side, Ximeng and Cangyuan Counties are recognized as demographically dominated by the Wa. In accordance with the Chinese political system, ethnic Wa hold government posts there, while much of the real power is held within the Chinese Communist Party, which maintains a parallel hierarchy of power and reigns supreme in China. The Wa also figure nominally, as a minority, in the official names of the adjacent counties of Gengma and Lancang; and through the presence of so-called Benren (original) people, who are closely related to the Wa but lost their language in the course of Chinese expansion and colonization over the last few centuries. The Benren are also present in the Chinese counties of Zhenkang and Yongde. In addition, there is also a Wa diaspora in the more remote cities of China, Thailand, Burma, and beyond.

On the Burma side, the ancient Wa areas are today recognized as Burma's Special Region 2, frequently known in English as the Wa State and in Chinese correspondingly as Wa Bang. The word *bang* refers to something less than a fully sovereign entity, similar to one sense of the English word "state." The Wa State, headquartered in Panghsang (Pangkham or Pang Kham) close to the Chinese border, also has ethnic Wa leaders. In contrast with the Wa in China, the Wa State also has its own armed forces, the United Wa State Army (UWSA), which was created in 1989 after the demise of the China-sponsored Communist Party of Burma (CPB) that had used these lands as its base area.[3]

The Wa State in Burma is demographically dominated by ethnic Wa people who mainly speak the Wa language in its various dialects. Four languages are officially taught at the Panghsang high school: Wa, Chinese, Burmese, and English. Shan (Tai, or Dai) languages are also used in and around the Wa State and in China. However, the commercial as well as political, military, and other links to China are very strong in the Wa State. For example, there is widespread use of Chinese currency, and of the Chinese language, which in reality dominates both in schools and as a market lingua franca.

For these reasons, it is common to hear people in Burma suggest that it has already been "taken over" by China or that the Wa "are Chinese," yet the Wa are culturally distinct from the Chinese, and UWSA leaders have stated repeatedly since 1989 that they recognize that their area is part of Burmese territory. The debate between Burma's government and the ethnonationalistic leaders of the Wa State inside Burma has instead been, and continues to be, about what form of autonomy this area should enjoy within Burma (Myanmar). At the time of writing, despite flare-ups of military confrontations, the tenuous ceasefire between the Burmese and Wa military first agreed upon in 1989 is still largely holding, even as the UWSA has declined to join the formal agreements that Burma's army has signed with other ethnic insurgent groups.[4]

Ordinary Wa themselves, in their own language, often simply call their lands *hag a diex A Vex* (the lands of the Wa).[5] In the past, this land was not a state, nor did it have permanent borders, which is a feature of the modern nation-state. At present, Wa people are ambivalent about the implications of all this. They do note the current political reality of the modern nation-states of Burma and China and the undeniable fact that the Wa lands are now split between Burmese and Chinese territory. However, this understanding coexists with ancient traditions asserting as another undeniable fact that these are ancestral lands of the Wa, who claim to have lived here since the beginning of time. In an important strand of Wa mythology, this is conceptualized as the famous *Sigang lih*, or "emergence [*lih*] from within the earth," which marks the emergence of humanity. This emergence is often understood literally, of people arising from the ground, the location of this phenomenon sometimes identified as a cave-like place near Blag Dieh, just inside Burma, across from Ximeng County in China. There, in remote antiquity, the autochthonous Wa emerged first; other peoples such as the Burmese, Chinese, American, Indian, and so on only emerged subsequently. That is why, some say, these people now live farther afield in the world.

I will return to these issues in several chapters. Here, in the following, I offer an overview of the sources on Wa. They are presented thematically and chronologically, as a guide, and they also set the stage for the ensuing chapters while providing some of the information that can be mined from them about the Wa.

Sources of Wa History and Culture: Overview

The sources for the study of Wa history and culture include archeological remains like the ancient rock art in Wa country, which I'll discuss further below. Most important, of course, are the Wa people themselves and their rich oral traditions, which include their own accounts of their own history and of their region, as well as Wa-language writings, Wa music, and other arts. Other available sources include Chinese written documents, which extend at least back to the late 1200s when the Mongol world empire reached this region, and even further back. There is also a large and more recent corpus of Chinese literature, including documents from the substantial Chinese government-sponsored investigations of the Wa areas undertaken in the 1950s and 1960s. In addition, there are Burmese chronicles as well as Burmese scholarly writings; Shan chronicles; and British documents, many of them composed by colonial government officials in British

Burma in the period up until the late 1940s. There are also writings by various foreign Christian missionaries who likewise, directly or indirectly, contributed to knowledge about the Wa. And, there are more recent studies of Wa linguistics, ethnography, and other aspects made by scholars from places as varied as Britain, Thailand, Japan, the United States, and Europe.

Wa Archaeology

Relatively little archeological work has been undertaken in the Wa lands thus far. One major exception is the research on the fascinating rock paintings found in the Cangyuan Wa Autonomous County, now a part of Yunnan Province, China (Wang Ningsheng 1985, 1992, 1997: 208–47; also Malinee Gumperayarnont 1987).

This rock art, which may be several thousand years old, is not practiced today, but echoes of it can be discerned in the rich woodcarving art adorning Wa houses, which survived into the 1950s and still exists in the collective memory, as well as on a smaller scale in the carved *lei* bamboo beer cups (see chapter 3). Rock art motifs are also today often copied in contemporary art and used in advertisements, especially when exploited by Chinese entrepreneurs in the tourism industry.

The rock art consists of paintings, not carvings, and shows an array of human figures, cattle or buffalo, and houses on poles that evoke traditional Wa dwelling styles. Farming does not seem to be depicted at all: the images perhaps reflect an era when farming was less important or even nonexistent, and people lived by herding livestock, gathering, and hunting. The ancient paintings are found on rock faces at several dozen sites. Rural Wa people often attribute them to the gods or to distant ancestors; many Wa scholars and officials are keen to identify them with the ancestors of the Wa people, but there is no conclusive proof of this—even if it is indeed very possible that they are right. The main area with rock paintings is on the northeast fringes of present-day Wa country, but in areas that were almost certainly dominated by Mon-Khmer-speaking people in recent centuries, if not millennia.

Ongoing and future archaeological research at Cangyuan, Gengma,[6] and elsewhere may reveal more about the connections between rock paintings and Neolithic and other archeological sites. There may still be undiscovered rock art sites, and the potential for this kind of research is vast.

This is also the case with other historical-archeological sites, such as ancient fortified settlements, which remain poorly understood and largely unexplored, mainly because it has seemed so unexpected and unlikely to Chinese and Burmese archaeologists that the "primitive" Wa would be able to build fortifications. A future archaeology of such fortifications could link them to those of recent Wa villages and thus might reveal more about both the historical processes that engendered them and how they relate to the still obscure but clearly very old his-

Figure 0.3. Buffalo and human figure in the rock paintings at Cangyuan. Photo by the author, 1998.

tory of the Wa and other Mon-Khmer-speaking people in this region.[7] There are also other, similar kinds of ethnoarchaeological challenges, notably explored by the late Wang Ningsheng.[8]

The same goes for the spectacular ancient bronze drums that are found throughout the Wa area, which are different from the famous log drums, but like them also connect the Wa with the history and archaeology of a much wider region of Southern China and Southeast Asia.[9]

Wa-Language Sources

The Wa everywhere have rich oral traditions, but there are also many texts written and published in the Wa language. Myths about Wa autochthonous origins are one of the most salient parts of these traditions. Some of these traditions have been paraphrased in both British and other publications, including in Scott and Hardiman (1983 [1900]; 1983 [1901]), Scott (1918), and Obayashi (1966), and in numerous retellings in Chinese of varying quality. One good example of Chinese-recorded Wa oral traditions is the bilingual Wa-Chinese rendering of an origin myth recorded rather meticulously in 1957 (*Wazu shehui lishi diaocha* II: 158–209).

More recently, Wa and other scholars have recorded additional such myths more meticulously, and directly in the Wa language (e.g., Nyi Ga 1988; Chen and

Wang 1993; Chen 2001; etc.). Wa proverbs and other materials were collected by the Chinese linguist Wang Jingliu (1992; 1994) and analyzed by Justin Watkins (2013a). Many more publications in the Wa language, including more transcripts of oral texts, are gathered and referenced in the highly valuable website of the Wa Dictionary Project housed at the School of Oriental and African Studies (SOAS), London (Watkins et al. 2006), a project that also has produced the best available dictionary of the Wa language (Watkins 2013b).

Wa Voices: 1947 and After

One famous and oft-cited direct quote of a Wa voice from before the advent of modern ethnography (and before modern publishing in the Wa language) is found in the records of the 1947 Frontier Areas Committee of Enquiry, which interviewed ethnic Wa leaders. This committee had been set up by the British colonial government to prepare for the new constitution of the Union of Burma. Burma's independence was declared a year later.

The Wa interviewees may not have fully shared the British conception of what these meetings were meant to accomplish. Some participants were styled as Shan *sawbwas*, princes or kings, and some as direct representatives from autonomous Wa country, called "Wild Wa" in the British colonial vocabulary. The Wild Wa are quoted as stating their preference for total independence and brushing off other queries with the words, "We are wild people" (Burma Frontier Areas Committee of Enquiry 1947; Lintner 1994: 72–73). The exact circumstances of these statements are not known, and it is possible that the translators "framed" this part of the conversation to reconfirm their own view of the "Wild" Wa.

However, the Wa stance for autonomy and the independence that it reflects is unmistakable. In the very same year, 1947, in a much less widely known incident, Wa people also sent the very same message to China, stating their preference for self-rule. In 1947, the young Chinese Republic's national government had requested a Shan frontier principality to also bring Wa delegates to the Chinese national parliament in Nanking (now Nanjing) to confirm their status as Chinese citizens. The Wa, still engaged in their centuries-old balancing act between their own autonomous Wa lands, the neighboring Shan principalities, and the Chinese and Burmese states, refused to attend. Instead, they sent word that "the Wa will govern the Wa mountains" (*Gengma, Menglian, Shuangjiang* 1962: 29).

It is rare, in the various sources, to find such direct statements quoted. Even today, outsiders often presume to speak for the Wa, or put words in their mouth. Overall, this is an unfortunate and unavoidable consequence of the Wa historical situation as a periphery of powerful states that have encroached upon their lands, divided the Wa on two different modern states, and installed them as "minorities" therein.

Wa Writings

Since the middle of the twentieth century, the Wa are increasingly able to write and publish in their own language on both sides of the new border imposed on their old homeland. They did not have a writing system until one was created for them in the 1920s and 1930s by American Baptist missionaries, active in the vicinity from about 1900 to 1950. These missionaries primarily worked on the peripheries (see chapter 9), not in the central, autonomous Wa areas; they were concerned above all with the translation of their own scriptures for missionary purposes and did not encourage independent Wa writing. Apart from Bible translations, there are very few Wa writings from this early period (though some information about the Wa in this period can be gleaned from missionary documents). As we shall see, the Wa, like other people of the mountains, also have their own stories about possessing writing in the past—in the Wa case, writing was invented by a mythical culture hero, Glieh Neh.

Unfortunately, in the 1950s, Chinese authorities devised and imposed a second, separate system using different sound values, and this is the system in use for materials printed in China. For the Wa today, still largely illiterate, the confusion caused by several writing systems continues to impede the spread of native literacy. Partly because of this, Chinese and other languages are more widely taught in schools—even in Burma's Wa State. On the China side, despite laws that guarantee education in minority languages, literacy has been fostered almost exclusively in Chinese.[10]

Neither of the Wa writing systems (both inherently workable) have been effectively promoted, and most schools in China and many in parts of the Wa State in Burma today teach Chinese only, often with Chinese-trained Wa teachers. Most Wa are illiterate, and few children attend school.

Most Wa texts are composed in the key dialect of Yong Soi (Aishuai), an old trading center located just inside Chinese territory, in Cangyuan County. The dialect is also known as Parauk (Praok, Baraog). Other dialects remain important as spoken languages,[11] and this naturally also complicates the spread of literacy. Despite the various obstacles, a large number of Wa-language school textbooks and other materials (language and writing primers, children's books, and other materials) have been compiled in Wa, often in the alphabet used on the Burmese side (in the orthography revised from the early missionaries' system) and to a lesser extent in the system imposed in China.

Many such texts have been printed in Chieng Mai, Thailand, and elsewhere, and these are circulated and used in schools in the Wa State in Burma. This occurs even as the Wa State authorities themselves also publish Chinese-language journals, documents, and Chinese-styled gazetteers (that is, officially sanctioned local histories compiled on the Chinese model), where all but the title is in Chinese (e.g., *Miandian Wa Bang Mengmao Xian zhi/Phuk lai Been Meung Mau* 2002; the title says, in Chinese, "Gazetteer of Mengmao County, Wa State, Burma"; interestingly, its Wa title omits the Chinese terms for Burma [*Miandian*] and Wa State [*Wa Bang*]).

Both Chinese-Wa bilingual works and wholly Wa-language works have also been published in China. This literature also comprises a wide range of publications on aspects of Wa culture, mythology, and history, as well as school textbooks in both scripts, and Chinese-Wa dictionaries (which for the most part are superseded by and mentioned in the Wa Dictionary Project).[12]

This also includes a new literature by Wa who are literate only in Chinese or who prefer to write in Chinese, not in their own language. As one example, and as an introduction to this genre, see Mark Bender's study (2011) of the contemporary prolific Wa poet and author whose Chinese name is Buyi Yilu. This genre also includes autobiographies of Chinese-trained ethnic Wa officials, who similarly never learned to use their own alphabet and typically write only in Chinese.

Some Wa scholar-authors trained in Chinese have chosen to also write and publish in the Wa language. These China-based Wa scholars include Nyi Ga or Wei Deming (1988, 1999, 2001); Chen Weidong (1993); Zhao (2000); Zhao Mingsheng (2013); Zhao Furong (2005); Guo Dachang and others [1992–97] on Wa herbal medicines, and many others. There may also be Wa authors expressing themselves in Shan or Burmese, and online, too.

Chinese Sources

Parts of the region to the north and northeast of the historical Wa lands were first brought under imperial Chinese control or influence already two thousand years ago, as the Chinese penetrated what later was to become their Yunnan Province ("South of the Clouds") (Yang Bin 2009a). Ever since then, and to some extent even earlier, China's southwestern frontier has been the subject of much Chinese historiography, gazetteer compilation, and travel writing by Chinese scholars and officials.

More substantial early accounts dealing indirectly with Wa areas include the ninth-century *Man shu* (Book of the Man [southern barbarians]), by Fan Zhuo (ca. CE 860). Chinese scholars believe that there is a continuity from what these records call the *Pu-Man* (Pu [southern] barbarians) to the Wa and related Mon-Khmer-speaking peoples, such as the Bulang (Blang) and the Benglong (today's De'ang, or Palaung), and that this can be traced onward, through the Chinese Song dynasty era (tenth to twelfth centuries) and the Mongol imperial era (thirteenth to fifteenth centuries), and up until today. There is a large Chinese scholarly literature debating such identifications under the heading of "nationalities history" (*minzu shi*, the history of ethnicities).

This literature often overlooks the problem, especially serious in the gazetteers, that materials from other books and earlier versions of the same titles are recycled without specific references, explicit quotes, or renewed fact-checking. The aim of these local histories is not to ascertain facts but to compose a picture of a place that can serve to situate this place into the grand narrative of China.[13]

Yet at the same time, there are tantalizing possibilities that these older records (of people known in Chinese as the "Wang," "Wangjuzi," "Puzi," or "Puman") are indeed referring to the Wa (or Mon-Khmer-speaking brethren and ancestors of theirs) who used to live farther north in what is now China (Yunnan) but were either engulfed and assimilated or driven south by the early "secondary states" that developed in the region (Dian, Nanzhao, Dali), and then again by the later Chinese empires as they conquered, engulfed, colonized, settled, and assimilated this region, which the Chinese renamed as Yunnan.[14] Chinese gazetteers will often say about Yunnan places that they are located "in an ancient [e.g. former] barbarian land" (*gu Man di*); even current Wa oral traditions also tell of how some of their brethren fled toward the south, from areas farther north (see chapter 3).

Some historians, Chinese and others, have suggested that "the Wa" once served in the army of the Nanzhao kingdom.[15] A source in Chinese (the oldest written language in this region) says that after it successfully invaded Upper Burma in the late eighth century, Nanzhao armies seized "over a thousand households of Wangjuzi and Wangwaiyu people from Yongchang [in the west, nearer Pyu Burma], . . . redistributing them near the [capital] city . . . in order to keep the roads and the thoroughfares peaceful," and some of these "Wangjuzi" barbarians became shock troops of the Nanzhao army.[16] Certainly the Nanzhao state, as well as its successor the Dali state, created its own dependent peripheries and also made use of young men from subjugated peripheral and stateless peoples as soldiers—itself an old pattern, which keeps repeating itself.[17]

From the Wa perspective, states like these secondary formations, as well as the later Tai-speaking Shan states (which I will discuss below), have evidently served both as adversaries and as a first buffer against the penetration of the (waxing and waning) Chinese imperial behemoth. The *Ming History* recorded that "Shunning, originally the land of the Pu Man [the Pu southern barbarians] . . . never was connected with China before the Song" and "not even the houses of Meng [of Nanzhao] and Duan [of Dali] could control them."[18]

But the empire pressed on when possible. Continued Chinese efforts to subjugate Yunnan's aboriginal people are chronicled in the monumental *Yongchang fu wenzheng* (Collected documents on the prefecture of Yongchang [eternal prosperity]), edited by Li Genyuan (1941), which includes materials on how representatives of some of the subjugated "Pu Man" ancestors of the Wa in Yunnan were also installed as *tusi*, or intermediary "native chiefs,"[19] attached to the Chinese imperial bureaucracy at places given purposeful names like Shunning (which in typical Chinese fashion means "submissive tranquility").

Yet since empires wax and wane, these cycles sometimes also brought about situations in which Chinese immigrants were nativized, instead of serving to assimilate the barbarians, as one Ming-era historian lamented for the so proudly named Yongchang district.[20]

The Chinese empire also suffered major setbacks at its Southwestern frontier, as in the disastrous and costly military defeats in the 1760s wars with Burma. These were fought near the Wa lands, and perhaps even inside them.[21]

In late imperial times (eighteenth to twentieth centuries), when Chinese penetration increased further, the Wa are referred to as "Kawa"—probably because the Chinese were interacting with them through Shan middlemen, who appended the Tai term for "unenlightened" mountain people (*Khaa*). This point was not realized until the twentieth-century modern ethnographic efforts. The Chinese name Kawa was changed to Wa, and the earlier Chinese distinction of them as being a people divided between "raw" (wild, independent) and "cooked" (tamed or subjugated), (Ka-)Wa, was also scrapped.[22]

Until the 1950s, the Wa were seldom described firsthand—they were mainly discussed through hearsay, and from a Chinese perspective. Numerous Chinese and other traders in opium, salt, and other items had already ventured into Wa country and must have known quite a bit about the Wa. But these Chinese and other traders very rarely wrote anything themselves, though they are sometimes quoted in passing, and anonymously, in Chinese and British documents. But one can also read between the lines. The writings include explicit hints of Chinese involvement in the origins of headhunting (chapter 6), and also of Wa involvement in Chinese (and Wa) mining, often run by private Chinese entrepreneurs whom the Chinese state struggled to control and who themselves tried to work through local Wa middlemen (chapter 4; cf. Pasquet 1989)—a pattern of for-profit triangulation that continues today across the region and also involves the Burmese military and other players.[23] Chinese sources do include gems such as the account of purportedly "the first Chinese ever to venture into the (core) Wa lands," Zhang Chengyu (1941 [1891]; also see chapter 7), a Chinese spy-observer accompanying an early British expedition in the winter of 1890–91 (following the British annexation of Upper Burma in the 1880s).

Chinese writings about the Wa really began to proliferate at the time of the border confrontations between the British and Chinese empires and their boundary commissions of 1898–1900 and 1935–37 (both were failures, and the project delayed until the early 1960s).[24] These developments provoked more interest in this frontier region from assorted patriots and nationalists, and also prompted scholarly investigations, including those by ethnologists and ethnohistorians influenced by Western ethnology such as the eminent Fang Guoyu (himself an ethnic minority scholar from northern Yunnan) and Ling Shun-sheng. Both visited the fringes of Wa country in the 1930s and 1940s. Recently, a photographic archive with more than four hundred photos from this period in the Wa lands was discovered in storage at the Institute of History and Philology, Academia Sinica, Taipei. The archive has gradually been made public as part of the institute's digital treasure house (searchable mainly in Chinese).[25]

During the same prewar period, there was also an explosion of opinionated works by patriotic Chinese writers protesting British imperialism and arguing for Chinese ownership over the region. Beginning in the early 1950s, when the new Chinese Communist government sent troops to consolidate the frontiers of the Chinese nation-state in preparation for renewed negotiations with new Burma over their mutual border, yet more Chinese studies materialized. These were compiled even as the Communists continued their civil war with remnants of the defeated Kuomintang (Republican) troops lingering in and near Wa country (see below).

Most importantly, a large-scale Wa ethnography project was launched by the Chinese government in 1956–58. The intent was to support Chinese control of the area and advance planned social and economic "reforms." This intensive research on the Wa also covered areas later confirmed as Burmese territory in the China-Burma border agreement of 1961, thus becoming today's Wa State. The investigations of social and cultural conditions, as well as any historical information that could potentially bolster Chinese claims, were recorded in large files of handwritten materials now held in various closed archives. The records were then edited as seven volumes printed "internally," not meant for public circulation but mainly for officials planning the annexation of the Wa region (the *Kawa zu diaocha cailiao* [Kawa nationality research materials], volumes 1–4, and volumes 5–7 instead issued as *Wazu diaocha cailiao* [Wa nationality research materials][26]). Then these texts were once again condensed into four volumes for official publication (*Wazu shehui lishi diaocha* [Investigations of the society and history of the Wa nationality]), which include the bulk of the seven-volume-set content but omit the direct political aims of the day. One participant in the 1956–57 investigations recently published a personal account (Xu Zhiyuan 2009), with valuable firsthand photography not included in the reports. Similar photography collections from the Wa country of the 1950s and 1960s have been published by Wang Ningsheng (2010b) and Li Jiarui and Li Yaoping (2011). Other personal accounts by military officers and others have also shed light on the Chinese takeover of formerly independent Wa lands (Zhang Shiliang 1992, Wang Jingliu 2007, etc.).

Similar accounts have described how the Communist Party of Burma (CPB), with Chinese support, took over the Wa lands left to Burma. From 1968 to 1989, the Maoist-inclined CPB used the Wa lands as a base while fighting against the Rangoon government.[27] The CPB also drafted Wa men as foot soldiers and interfered with local society, enforcing their ideologically driven policies to destroy old Wa society—according to some, even more vigorously than the Chinese Communists did. This involved the symbolically devastating demolition of drum houses and Wa log drums, which had been the ritual-administrative focal points of independent Wa society. They also destroyed the once-powerful autonomous Wa warfare capabilities, which was overcome by superior weaponry and denounced as "primitive headhunting" (chapter 6). However, lacking success in its own main mission in Burma, the CPB itself turned to opium before it finally collapsed in 1989 (Lintner 1990; 1992, 303–5).

On the Chinese side, state-sponsored scholarship continued with serious linguistic and ethnographic research that built on the 1956–58 materials. This has included work by a subsequent generation of sophisticated Chinese scholars, including Luo Zhiji (1995, etc.), Wang Ningsheng (1985, 1989, 1997: 208–47, 2001, 2006, 2010a, 2010b), Li Yangsong (1983a [1957], 1983b [1957], 1983c [1957], 2006); Wang Jingliu (1992, 1994, etc.), Li Daoyong (1996, etc.), and later, after the first waves of government-sponsored efforts, new scholars like Qu Ming'an, Guo Rui, and others. Special mention must be made of Yin Shaoting, the extraordinary researcher and scholar who is the author of numerous studies on traditional farming methods among minority groups around Yunnan, including the deep history of Wa agriculture (Yin 2001).

The failure in China to promote even the Wa writing system created by the Chinese government (largely due to the discriminatory stigma attached to the Wa language and culture), has also caused many of the Chinese-educated Wa to neglect their own alphabet and not write in their own language. Even many well-meaning Chinese scholars and amateurs hoping to record songs, stories, etc., have been reduced to using Chinese transliterations[28] for the Wa words in recording such texts (or even to direct paraphrasing in Chinese, without making any attempt at all to record the original Wa). These practices have resulted in the loss of vast opportunities to record folklore traditions accurately. The early state ethnographers, who did not yet have access to the Wa writing system being devised, used the international phonetic alphabet for some transcriptions, with results that are accurate but inaccessible for a wider Wa public, as they might have been if written in one of the existing Wa scripts.

Since the 1980s, there are also many new local gazetteers and scholarly articles concerned with ethnology, especially with Chinese-led development, a favorite theme. More recently, especially over the last decade, China's move away from socialist rhetoric and policies has generated new genres of written publications, VCDs (video compact discs), DVDs, television programs and films, and even websites on the Wa (on the films, see further below). These genres thrive in close connection with a new tourist industry that indulges in Wa exotics, seeking to profit from domestic tourists intensely attracted to an image of the Wa as somehow primitive and untamed—some are also attracted to casinos in and near the Wa State. In a profound historic irony, tourist exoticism often involves making replicas of the very same log drums and headhunting paraphernalia that the Chinese and Burmese Communists previously sought to destroy. But the most interesting question for the future is doubtless if and how Wa people themselves can assert more control or influence over at least some parts of this new torrent of representation and spectacle, against many odds (chapter 10).

Burmese and Shan Sources

To the west of Wa country is Burma and Burmese civilization, historically centered on a Buddhist Cakravartin throne with claims to universal rule and a conception of expansive civilization that would equal and rival China's imperial claims and pretensions.[29] Across the region, both inside the historical Wa lands and in their immediate vicinity, there was also a galaxy (Tambiah 1976, 1985) of Shan princes who acknowledged subservience and tributary duties to either Burmese or Chinese overlords, or both. From the Chinese perspective, regardless of their largely Buddhist heritage, these princes were all subservient to China from the moment they were invested with Chinese titles under the so-called *tusi* (native-chief) system of the empire governing by such proxies. But nearly all Shan states on the China-Burma frontier were also at some point tributaries of Burmese kings, and they considered themselves part of Buddhist civilization, at least since the adoption of Buddhism. Some Wa, too, historically turned Buddhist under the influence of the Shan and remain Buddhists to this day (Liu 2009; Chit Hlaing 2009; see also chapter 4).

Most of the Buddhist Shan states generated chronicles in their own writing systems, some dating as far back as the thirteenth century. They include much information on confrontations with the indigenous "Lawa," which broadly refers to Mon-Khmer speakers that include the Wa ancestors inhabiting the region prior to the arrival of the Shan.[30] This is famously reflected in the legends of Shan conquest and Lawa (Wa) submission recorded in major Shan centers like Kengtung, Chieng Mai, and many other Tai-speaking polities where these legends have also periodically been reenacted in court rituals, such as when aboriginal Mon-Khmer-speaking people are cast in the role of the conquered, the displaced, and the humiliated, as in the traditional coronation ceremonies of Kengtung.[31]

This discourse, which may represent a Shan idealization of history but also must reflect war and conflict, is also found in several smaller Shan states now annexed by China, including Menglian, next to the central Wa country. The village Yong Ou, where I did my fieldwork, is today in ruins, but a shadow of its former power and glory. In the past, however, it exercised diplomatic intermarrying with this Shan polity of Menglian, which was set up by Shan in-migrants long ago. The Wa permitted their stay, on condition that they were sealed by marrying a village leader's daughter to them, locking them into a tributary relationship that obligated them to pay dues to the Wa, as some Lahu also did (see Kataoka 2013, and chapter 9).

This relationship is remembered by both Shan and Wa, independent of Chinese interventions, and according to one Menglian Shan tradition, which resonates with corresponding Wa traditions, the very first Menglian chief (sometimes said to have been the first Menglian *tusi*, established in 1404) was such a Wa woman. Such arrangements, with the Wa as wife-givers and the Shan in the position as wife-takers is also reported from elsewhere in the old Wa lands (such as at Gengma, etc.), and continued at Menglian up until the demise of the Shan polity there after 1949.[32] When the Menglian Shan chief or prince married such a Wa woman, there were spearing sacrifices of both buffalo and elephants, the elephant tusks representing the never-ending relations between the two peoples.[33]

In other places, the Shan and other newcomers have similarly sought accommodation among the original inhabitants, including paying respect to their gods. This kind of regard for the lingering potentialities of the various Mon-Khmer peoples and their deities is found in Thailand, Laos, and also among smaller Shan polities in China's Yunnan Province.[34]

Shan chronicles also include separate texts compiled by Shan monasteries. These are of formidable interest even when focused mainly on the genealogy of local ruling Shan dynasties or more purely on local monastic history. Many Shan chronicles are being annotated and republished, sometimes in facsimile, and some have been translated from Shan into Chinese and/or English (e.g., Sao Saimong Mangrai 1965, 1981; the *Menglian xuanwu shi*, Terwiel 2003; Yin and Daniels 2005, 2010, etc.).

Historical records in Burmese are also very rich—even though Burma's royal courts (like imperial China's) were historically further removed from the Wa than the Shan princes. Still, much like the Wa presence in Chinese records, the Wa occupied a significant place in the Burmese imagination regarding frontier people, and Burmese Wa lore to some extent parallels the Chinese image of the Wa as fierce barbarians. For example, Burmese traditions speak of the supposedly unconquerable fierceness of the Wa. Even the great king Bayinnaung (1551–81) is said to have sent an army against them, which never returned (Tinker 1956: 331).

Earlier in history, the Wa also appear among those borderland peoples who were captured and kept as slaves by the Burmese. There are inscriptions in Pagan, the ancient Burmese capital, dated as early as the twelfth century, where Gordon Luce identified both Wa settlements, written as "Lawa villages," and listings of pagoda slaves.[35] (Early Burmese records use the term Lawa, but in the colonial period, there is a shift to the current usage "Wa," following British colonial usage).

Much more research remains to be done on these materials. Overall, the Burmese literature on the Wa, published in the course of the buildup of the new modern Burmese nation-state which incorporated part of the Wa lands, is more limited than the comparable Chinese output. But for both Burma and China, the definition and description of minorities as components of their nation-state has been a key part of the new modern-state project. Thus, we also find records of the Wa in Burmese government publications, such as in the overviews of all 135 "races" of Burma, in the Wa entries in the encyclopedia *Myan-ma sweh-soun-jan* (1954–), and in ethnological studies such as those by U Min Naing (1967). There is also a recent book-length Burmese study of the Wa by the anthropologist Tin Yee (Daw Tin Yee), published in both Burmese (1999) and English (2004).

Similar to the British and the Chinese before them, the new Burmese government and military, after regaining independence from Britain in 1948, also conducted expeditions to the Wa and to other borderlands and compiled reports intended for use in attempts to extend government control, send Buddhist missionaries, build roads, and so on. Sai Kham Mong (1996, 1997) is an interesting introduction to this period (if heavily biased, based as it is on the work of the British colonial officer James George Scott and other British views, plus Burmese documents). The report discusses one of the worst problems encountered by newly independent Burma: the spillover of remaining troops from the losing side in the Chinese civil war, the Kuomintang (KMT) who took up bases just inside Burma in 1950 to launch intrusions back into China, at times using bases in the Wa lands.[36] The Burmese military was forced to try to dispel or at least contain them, but the KMT remnants lingered on until 1962, themselves taking up the narcotics trade to finance themselves. The Burmese saw that these developments brought the danger of increased long-term Chinese influence (and as mentioned above, these fears came true in the 1960s and 1970s with the Maoist-styled Communist Party of Burma). Sai Kham Mong describes how the Burmese military for these reasons launched "flag marches" to the Wa lands, starting in 1955, which included interesting encounters with Wa chiefs and arguments with them over the propriety of food, drink, and opium use.[37]

The Wa very much remain in the general Burmese public imagination, along lines similar to China: older ideas about mountain wild men are now mixed with modern-nationalist ideas about the majority Burmans as the nation's master race (Walton 2013). Burmese government publications as well as news reports frequently discuss the Wa in terms of the future of the ceasefire, the military confrontations, the continuing negotiations between the Burmese army and the United Wa State Army, and to some extent the collusion between drug producers, exporters, and Burmese wealth.[38]

In the genre of government-sponsored investigations, we must mention the highly interesting report *Wa-do hta-ni* ("About Wa people of Burma: A study" by Than Sein Thit et al, 1962), compiled after a one-time 10-member expedition which included four members of the Myanmar Literature Association, launched after the 1960–61 border demarcations with China. One of the authors, Mya-Wa-Ti Ye Khaung, echoed exactly my own sentiment when he wrote, on his return: ". . . it has been said about Wa people that they are frightening, disgusting people, and that they are barbarians with no history and no culture of their own. In reality, Wa people have very pleasant manners and traditions. The more knowledgeable [you are] about their culture, the more sympathetic it will seem."

Contemporary Burmese literature continues to explore imaginaries of the Wa. Wendy Law-Yone's recent English-language novel (2010) about a mountain girl calls her a "Lu," thus avoiding direct identification of the Wa as the source of the author's inspiration (Law-Yone and Bow 2002), but still builds on the fantasies of the Wa as, until recently, a primitive people of headhunters (and cannibals) (2002: 91):

> Head-hunters. I'd thought I'd heard the last of that shameful name-calling. They had teased me about it enough in the Daru village. "*The Wild Lu chop off heads, the Wild Lu chop off heads; the Burmese chop down coconuts but the Wild Lu chop off heads. Then they drink the blood like coconut juice, slurp slurp slurp.*" Why had they said such horrible things? I never once saw anyone chop off anyone else's head, and what was a coconut, anyway? It was only in Rangoon that I saw my first coconut.

British Colonial and Other European Accounts

Britain completed its conquest of the realm of the Burmese monarchy by deposing the last Burmese king in late 1885. But Burma's borders were not fixed to the last inch, as in modern nation-states, and as the British wanted. Like the Burmese before them, the British entered into multiple confrontations with a succession of Chinese governments over who should hold sway over these borderlands.

Realizing the potential wealth of natural resources like forests and mining, the British sought to delineate borders and to extend their control (provoking counteractions from China), even over the central Wa country, the so-called Wild Wa or Wa State in British parlance. But this area never came under British administration despite several attempts to take it over. British rule only extended to mixed Shan-Wa areas just west of the Wild Wa, much like Burma's had in the centuries before the British colonial period.

Thus, when the imperial census was extended to Burma, the Wa could not be counted. Even so, ever since the 1880s, and to some extent even earlier, the British produced numerous reports and studies of both the "administered" and still "un-administered" Wa lands. Many of these papers, including both unpublished and once-secret documents, can be consulted in the British Library as part of the India Office Records. They document everything from troubles between the Shan states and the Wa, to Chinese frontier affairs involving the Wa, and to British reconnaissance and surveying in the Wa lands, also including Wa history (Harvey 1933; Barton 1933; Sadan 2008).

Special mention must be made of the writings of one particular British colonial administrator of the Shan states, James George Scott, who was particularly fascinated with the Wa and quite sympathetic to them, while at the same time maintaining a decidedly colonialist perspective. Scott first entered autonomous Wa country in 1893, made repeated visits, and became a self-declared expert on the subject. He was also an avid photographer, whose collection is also now in the British Library. Because of the dearth of reports on the Wa, his many books (including the *Gazetteer of Upper Burma and the Shan States*, with J. P. Hardiman, published in 1900–01) long served as the major if not the only reference on the Wa in much of Western literature.[39] Even Japanese writings on the area made during the Japanese occupation of Burma in 1942–45 mostly summarize British sources, above all Scott.[40]

The British reoccupied Burma in 1945 but relinquished their colony shortly thereafter. They organized a Frontier Areas Committee of Enquiry, but, as mentioned, Wa involvement was ambiguous. The Wa were also absent from the historic Panglong Agreement signed in February 1947 to provide a framework for a unified Burma comprising Burmese and "Hill Peoples." An inconclusive debate is said to have ensued within British officialdom regarding just how to include the Wa under formal Burmese and Shan jurisdiction (Tinker 1983–84). In the end, Britain left as its empire crumbled, but London preserves a publicly accessible record of many aspects of Wa history, especially for the period 1880–1950.

One key British writer on the Wa postdates this period, namely Alan Winnington, a leftist journalist stranded in China after reporting on the Korean War from the North's point of view.[41] In the late 1950s, the Chinese state news agency took him on a tour of the newly annexed Wa lands as a witness that could be relied upon to praise the changes introduced by Chinese rule. And this he did, in his unique book *The Slaves of the Cool Mountains: The Ancient Social Conditions and Changes Now in Progress on the Remote South-Western Borders of China* (1959). Most of its pictures and notes come from the same area where I did my own fieldwork. It stands as a fascinating testimony, and at the same time is deeply problematic in its absence of reflection on the self-assumed superiority of the author's Chinese hosts.

Before the British, the Wa show up in the famous *Lusiades* (the *Os Lusiadas*) by Camões (ca. 1572), or so it is said. But this clearly belongs with a certain kind of travelogue hearsay of forest wild men that continues through the ages (chapter 7). There are many other examples of this genre, including Chinese as well as latter-day British (Marshall 2002, traveling in the footsteps of J. G. Scott) and French travelers (Merleau-Ponty 2003).

Foreign Missionaries' Writings

Missionaries from several Christian denominations came into contact with Wa people during the late nineteenth century and the first half of the twentieth (chapter 10). Western Christian missionary activities were disallowed by both Burma and China after the 1950s, yet have continued sporadically and clandestinely (Brandt Smith 2012, and others).

Early missionaries in the broader Wa region included American Baptists (the Young family, the Buker brothers); Protestant-interdenominational China Inland Mission workers, publishing in the journal *China's Millions* or through other venues; Swedish Pentecostal missionaries; and also Catholic missionaries from the Pontificio Istituto Missioni Estere. With rare exceptions, no missionaries ever wrote about local events or made any ethnological observations except those directly related to their proselytizing. Most saw only the peripheries of Wa country. However, the American Baptists, after failing to convert any Buddhist Shan in the Kengtung area, did eventually make thousands of converts among the Lahu and also among their Wa neighbors—again mainly the so-called "tame" Wa whose exploited position made them fertile ground for Christianizing endeavors.

Baptist missionary writings and correspondence of great interest are accessible at the American Baptist Historical Society (in Valley Forge, Pennsylvania). In particular, Harold Young and Vincent Young both grew up in the region and spoke Lahu and Wa fluently. Their intimate knowledge of the area shines through in their writings. However, because of these missionaries' conception of indigenous culture as an obstacle to be overcome, their writings are mainly valuable for the study of the missionaries' own proselytizing and only indirectly as a guide to Wa culture. Still, as in other parts of the world where marginalized and oppressed people yearn for some kind of salvation from their circumstances and are therefore more easily swayed by foreign influence, the missionaries' biased records can still illuminate the general circumstances of the people targeted for conversion.

Recent Scholarship

Scholarly research in the Wa areas long remained difficult or impossible, and much of the literature reviewed so far was largely produced on the sidelines of colonialism and military interventions. The lack of Wa ethnography was lamented by many prominent ethnologists in older generations, such as Karl Gustav Izikowitz, Rodney Needham, and Robert Heine-Geldern.

In the 1970s, Jonathan Friedman undertook a major study of the region (1998 [1979]) from afar, challenging the famous work of Edmund Leach (1970 [1954]) and developing a new Marxist-inspired theoretical approach that went beyond the Kachin discussed by Leach to address what he saw as underlying processes affecting all the mountain peoples of the region, including the Nagas and the Wa (see chapter 4, and below).

Since the 1990s, new Wa ethnography and other research has become more feasible. The generally more peaceful and open conditions have enabled foreign scholars to go beyond the earlier re-reading of older materials and bring new questions to the field. I myself began ethnographic fieldwork on Wa ethnohistory in the mid-1990s (chapter 2). Many other foreign scholars from a variety of nations and disciplines have also worked in the area. Scholars, aid workers, and others have investigated interrelated issues regarding Wa political and economic history, current affairs, Wa Buddhism and indigenous Wa religion, linguistics, folklore, and other cultural aspects. Not all can be mentioned here, but what follows takes note of some recent work, indicating how more scholars over the last few decades are beginning to explore the rich field of Wa studies.

Studies of the Wa language include the work of eminent linguists such as Gérard Diffloth and Justin Watkins. Among those carrying out ethnography among the Wa, Liu Tzu-k'ai (Liu Zikai) of Taiwan has done extensive studies of Wa house culture, Wa Buddhist ritual, and other topics, employing a productive linguistic-anthropological approach (Liu 2009). Wa architecture and other elements of Wa traditions also figure in the highly valuable ethnographic record assembled by Torigoe Kenzaburo and his collaborators.[42] Other ethnographers include the French anthropologist Bernard Formoso (2001, 2004, 2013), whose studies include drums and headhunting in Wa history as well as Wa textiles; the late Ronald Renard, who wrote on the UWSA (2013; Renard previously worked on the historical relations of Tai- and Mon-Khmer-speaking peoples); the noted Burma scholar Chit Hlaing (F. K. Lehman), who studied the relation between Wa and Shan/Tai Buddhism (2009); and Klemens Karlsson, whose studies include research on Kengtung (2013). Ma Jianxiong, of Yunnanese-Chinese origins, has done important ethnographic-historical work on the Lahu people, neighbors of the Wa, and on their close relations with the Wa (Ma 2007, 2012a, 2012b, 2013a, 2013b, etc.; on Lahu-Wa relations, see also Anthony Walker 2009, 2014). The Wa State is largely left out in this book (except for the discussion of forced relocations, in chapter 8); among other scholars writing on the Wa State are Bertil Lintner (2021 and many other titles), Andrew Ong (2018a, 2018b, 2018c), Hans Steinmüller (2019, 2020), Dominique Dillabough-Lefebvre (2019), and several others, with more forthcoming.

The dearth of studies on Wa music, a most fascinating field, must be lamented. While undertaking field research in rural Wa areas, I was often struck by the beauty of Wa songs, especially the formidable and hauntingly beautiful Wa funerary wake songs, but also many other kinds of music. Perhaps musicologists and music lovers will explore and record this music, which also invites comparative study across Southeast Asia, in particular with the traditions of other Mon-Khmer people. This is especially the case for the Khmu (Kammu) of Laos, whose music (Proschan 1999; Lundström 2010) displays striking parallels, despite the great distances between the Khmu and the Wa. There's been some research on the enormous Wa log drums that were used for long-distance communication.[43]

There is a large literature on the long history of opium and the production of other illicit drugs in the region, which often mentions the Wa. Historically, many Wa grew opium (cf. chapters 4, 5; more in Fiskesjö 2000), yet they were not the only ones: nearly all powers and polities have been involved, including (as mentioned above), Chinese nationalists, Burmese Communists, and, before them, Britain as a colonial power (after conquering Burma, the British empire expanded opium production under its own control), as well as the Burmese military.[44] The most interesting point here is how the opium economy affected the independent society of the Wa (chapters 4 and 5).

Some of the literature on opium, and on the synthetic drugs produced in the region especially since the beginning of the twenty-first century, derives from recent international efforts to suppress this production—(which I do not focus on in this book, but see chapter 8). These efforts include the drug-economy substitution programs of recent years, managed by the United Nations International Drug Control Program (the UNDCP) as well as by the national governments of Burma and China, and by the Wa State authorities. In 2005, after a five-year drawdown begun in 2000, the Wa State announced that opium production in its territory had been terminated, notwithstanding considerable economic hardship caused to those farmers who had relied upon it for their livelihood.[45] At the same time, many observers of narcotics issues suspect that synthetic drugs are now increasingly manufactured there.[46] Yet the narcotics issues remains intractable, and while military men in the Burmese army may previously have profited both indirectly and directly from the trade, Meehan (2011) argues that in Burma a new situation has been created in which state military power itself feeds on the perpetual "suppression" of narcotics.[47] Opium production either seems to have shifted location or has been supplanted by synthetic drugs manufacturing.[48]

One related and ambitious work on the economy and politics of the region, which has garnered much attention in the last few years, is James C. Scott's *The Art of Not Being Governed* (2009), which discusses the Wa as one of many "Zomia" mountain-region people avoiding state rule. One of the great accomplishments of the book is the way it redirects attention to the Southeast Asian uplands and rekindles the 1970s debate[49] over how to understand upland-lowland interactions, including the structural inequality and endemic violence long affecting the region. Though he does not engage Friedman's alternative perspective (1998, 2011), Scott (no relation to the "Scott of the Wa hills" of the late nineteenth and early twentieth century), also drew on Edmund Leach and his work (1954), but he sought to highlight the historical agency of the mountain peoples which was largely absent in Friedman's work. However, Scott saw it as expressed mainly in the mountain peoples evading the state, though for the Wa this only works some of the time: it is true that some Wa historically were indeed refugees, escaping Chinese pressure, similar to the Lahu or the Hmong; but what stands out about the Wa is their striking armed autonomy based in heavily fortified settlements from which they refused to budge—and where they maintained a strict commitment to egalitarianism (see chapters 3–5 on these key issues).

The political anthropology of the Wa, which is at stake in these ongoing debates, also involves the Thai scholar Cholthira Satyawadhna's admirable work (especially her voluminous 1991 dissertation; also 1990a, 1990b), which compares the historical situation of several Mon-Khmer-speaking (or Austroasiatic, the term she prefers[50]) people, and reexamines crucial gender issues in innovative fashion.

Museum Exhibits and Film

There are Wa exhibits in only a few of museums around the world. One permanent exhibit is in the National Museum of Myanmar in Rangoon, where the Wa are grouped with other people in a Hall of Ethnic Culture. In China, there are exhibits in three museums in Kunming, the capital of Yunnan Province. The most substantial is in the Yunnan Nationalities University Museum, where a full-size Wa drum house has been reconstructed; another is in the Yunnan Nationalities Museum, which opened in 1995; some materials are in the new Wu Mayao Museum of Anthropology at Yunnan University. In the United States, the Denison Museum in Granville, Ohio, holds examples of exquisite Wa textiles, and the California Academy of Sciences in San Francisco holds a small collection of Wa objects obtained from a 1940s Wa chief, including a sword and a shield. These were exhibited in the 1990s under the (questionable) heading "Weapons of Wa: Symbols of a Royal Past."

Chapter 10 discusses the new theme parks in China that cater to tourists enticed by the exotic appeal of Wa culture, and it also mentions the flood of cheaply made VCDs and DVDs made in recent years, in a very similar themed spirit of exoticizing the Wa for commercial purposes. Not least in the Maoist-Socialist era, feature films were also made that project the Chinese official interpretation of the "liberation" of formerly autonomous indigenous people such as the Wa—an example is the pompous 1978 feature *Kongque feilai Awa shan* (Peacock flying to [the] Awa mountain). More documentaries and films featuring the Wa have been made since the 1980s by various scholars, amateurs, and new filmmakers.[51]

One notable early documentary film was made as part of the 1950s documentation efforts. Entitled *The Kawa* (1958),[52] it was a highly political film, portraying the Wa as sorely in need of Chinese aid for the sake of progress. But in the ethnographic spirit of the day, it also includes and tries to analyze scenes of everyday life in the 1950s—scenes later photographed by the British Communist journalist Alan Winnington (see chapter 7). Some of the film was shot in the same area where I did much of my fieldwork, in Ximeng County, and when I discussed it with Wa people, one man remembered that at the time, as a little boy, he watched his mother throw mud at the lens to avoid being filmed. Watch for that, he said; however, this scene has been edited out of the final cut.

Notes

* This introduction draws in part on my 2013 article "Introduction to Wa Studies," *Journal of Burma Studies* 17(1): 1–27.

1. For more maps, see the Wa Dictionary Project, Watkins et al. 2006 ("Maps of the Greater Wa-Speaking Area").
2. See the map of the "Wa Corridor" in Diffloth 1980: 5; on the Wa languages, see Diffloth and Zide 1992; Watkins 2002, 2007, 2009, 2013a, and, in particular, 2013b; and Watkins et al. 2006; also Shorto 2013; and on all the Mon-Khmer languages, Yan Qixiang and Zhou Zhizhi 2012 [1995]; Shorto et al. 2006.
3. On the UWSA, its political wing the UWSP (United Wa State Party), and the post-1989 Wa State, see Kramer 2007; Renard 2013, 2016; Lintner 2003; Paoli et al. 2009: 130–39; also Dalton 2000; on the CPB also Lintner 1990, 1992, 2003, and below.
4. On the background and the current situation, see, for example, Kramer 2007, 2009a, etc.; Woods 2011; Davis 2014; Lintner 2017a, 2017b, 2018; Ardeth Maung Thawnghmung 2017. One reason for this long-term suspended nonwar may be China's influence over the UWSA and its interest in maintaining something like the useful "frozen conflicts" engineered by Russia in its own neighborhood in recent years.
5. Here I use the alphabet devised for the Wa by Chinese authorities, modified to reflect the dialect of the Yong Ou area in Ximeng County on the border with Burma, where I have done much of my field research. On Wa writing, also see below.
6. See the report on the *Gengma Shifodong* (the Stone Buddha Cave at Gengma), issued by the Yunnan Institute for Cultural Relics and Archaeology (2010).
7. See Fiskesjö 2001—an attempt to place the recent fortress-villages of the Wa people, traces of which can still be seen in many villages, with the region's deep history of fortification, defense structures, and warfare (as seen in the early history of moated and walled settlements in both Southeast Asia and China).
8. See above all the works of Wang Ningsheng (1989, 1997, 2001, 2008, etc.; also Kong Lingyuan 2013; Cai Kui 1984, etc.); on the ethnoarchaeology of Wa ceramic traditions, see Longacre and Li 1999.
9. On Wa bronze drums, see Hu 1985; Wang Ningsheng 1989; Fiskesjö 2000. The best works on bronze drums as a regional tradition are Caló 2013 and Bernet Kempers 1988.
10. On Wa writing, and on how the missionaries' somewhat imperfect system was adapted to fully represent the sounds Wa language, see Watkins 2013b, which builds on the valuable website of the Wa Dictionary Project established in part to help explain and

overcome problems caused by the duplicate writing systems ("Writing of the Wa Language," Watkins et al. 2006). The website also lists and presents many publications in the Wa language, including more transcripts of oral materials. I myself use a slightly modified Chinese-derived orthography to reflect the dialect of the area of study in today's Ximeng Wa Autonomous County, an ancient Wa area within China's borders.
11. Hopple 1988; Zhou et al. 2004; also Yamada 2013.
12. Watkins et al. 2006; Watkins 2013b; see also note 10 above.
13. The best discussion of this enterprise, which dominated the time of officials assigned to remote locations during the imperial era, is Lin Kai-shyh's 1999 dissertation. This continues even today.
14. The Nanzhao state was roughly contemporaneous with the Chinese Tang dynasty (618–907 CE). It can be said to have succeeded the Dian; and its later successor state, Dali, persisted until it was overrun by the Yuan Mongol empire. On Nanzhao origins, see Blackmore 1967; Backus 1981; on the geography of Nanzhao and its neighbors, Ma Changshou 1961; You Zhong 1980; Fang Guoyu 1994; Yang Bin 2009b. On Yunnan's history overall, see Yang Bin 2009a.
15. C. K. Ting 1921: 64; Ma Changshou 1961; also Parker 1893: 340 on the so-called Wang-tsa soldiers (both male and female, with helmets clad with cowries), mentioned in accounts of the Nanzhao kingdom, and who may also have been "Wa." The assumption may be shaky, but the geographical correlates given west of the Mekong are suggestive (see the discussion in Luo Zhiji 1995: 58ff.).
16. *Man shu*, chap. VI (Luce trans. p. 57); when some Wangjuzi soldiers were captured by the Tang army, they would not talk even when tortured (*Man shu*, chap IV, p. 39; cited in You 1985: 295–96).
17. This appropriation of conquered "wild" people as soldiers recalls the recent, similar British use of Kachin and other people in Burma, and they also hoped for the future recruitment of Wa men as "light infantry" (Scott 1906). In even more recent history, Wa men were recruited into the Burmese Communist Party insurgent army (Lintner 1990, 1994) and the regular Chinese People's Liberation Army.
18. The oft-repeated Chinese phrase is *Song yiqian bu tong Zhongguo*. Here I cite the *Ming shi* (*juan* 330, *liezhuan* 201, "The *tusi* of Yunnan: Shunning"), quoted in Gong Yin 1988.
19. On the *tusi* or native-chief system of imperial-era China, see Wade 2015; also Gong Yin 1992; Herman 1997, 2007, Tapp 2005: 167ff.; Took 2005; Ma Jianxiong 2007; Giersch 2006, 2013, and below. For more on the Shan states and *tusi* offices in the Wa region, see Fiskesjö 2000 (chap. 2.2, "Defeat and Displacement in Myth and History").
20. Zhuge Yuansheng, in *Dian shi* 1994 [1618]: 166ff.; on such fluctuations in the fortune of an expanding and then contracting empire, see also Fiskesjö 1999a; Wang Ningsheng 2010a; and the general theory presented by Friedman 1998 [1979].
21. Luce 1925; Dai 2004, also Fiskesjö 2000, chap. 2.2.
22. I have written on these general ideas elsewhere (Fiskesjö 1999a; also 2009, 2011, etc.), and now plan a separate book on these issues.
23. Kramer and Woods 2012. This Wa pattern isn't unique in the region's history: see Friedman 1998, and for comparison the discussion by Sadan (2013), on how the Kachin (known as the Kang, in Wa) historically were recognized by Burmese authorities as enjoying the right to give concessions for the exploitation of underground riches.
24. On these border demarcations, there is a large literature: See extensive citations in Fiskesjö 2000, as well as Tinker 1956, 1967; McGrath 2002; Ma Jianxiong 2012b, 2013a; and many others.

25. See instructions listed under "Institute of History and Philology," in the references.
26. On the Chinese name change from "Kawa" to "Wa," see above and chapter 3.
27. Unfortunately, the CPB records, which would have been of great interest (including, as they would have, reference to CPB conduct in Wa areas), were apparently destroyed during the anti-CPB revolt of 1989 (Lintner 1990).
28. This is extremely sad, for all that has been lost. However, note too that it builds on a very old tradition in Eastern Asia of the secondary use of Chinese characters for transcribing languages without a script of their own (and which haven't borrowed one from Indic traditions, as is common across Southeast Asia). The Tai-speaking Zhuang people of Guangxi are a prime example (Holm 2013).
29. On the dynamic, interacting system of the Buddhist Burmese state (or, empire), and the smaller, interdependent Buddhist Shan kingdoms or principalities, as well as mountain peoples, see Tambiah 1976, 1985; Lehman 1963, 1967a, 1967b; Sunēt Chutintharānon 1990; Friedman 1998; Lieberman 2003; Scott 2009; and many others (incl. Fiskesjö 2000, chap. 2.2). For overviews of Burmese history, see Luce 1925, and more recently Aung-Thwin and Aung-Thwin 2012.
30. The term "Lawa" may also serve to capture a wider range of ethnolinguistic affiliations (cf. Diffloth 1980: 6; Watkins 2009).
31. Sao Saimong Mangrai 1965; Sao Saimong Mangrai (1981: 201–4, 230; 284n45), citing the *Jengtung State Chronicle*; see too Tin Yee 2004: 35-36. Harvey (1957: 128) suggests that without the presence of the Wa as the original owners of the land, the Kengtung royal installation ceremony was considered incomplete. Bernatzik, who visited briefly in 1936–37, also mentions (1955: 209) an "annual"(?) Kengtung Shan ritual in which a Wa man is made to carry insignia of power and sit on a throne, but then is triumphantly driven away. Scott and Hardiman (1983 [1900]: I:517–18, and 1983 [1901]: II.1:392–402 [esp. 396–97]) also mention the Kengtung installation ritual and describe the ceremonial driving out of the Wa as a "founding event." See also Heine-Geldern 1976 [1914]: 33—citing Scott and Hardiman. Scott and Hardiman (1983 [1901]: II.1:389–90) mention the first Buddhists as immigrants who were preceded in the area by "Kha" people, with whom, at first, they shared their food, but later conflicts developed. In the translated *Jengtung State Chronicle*, the conquest involved fending off Wa (Lua; Lawa) attempts at subduing the Shan as they began to migrate into the area (1981: 223–24), and the conquest is also gloriously defended against continuous Chinese pressure for submission (1981: 230–31, 255; also Scott and Hardiman 1983 [1901]: II.1:397–98). Scott and Hardiman also describe King Mangrai's original conquest of the Kengtung area, justified as the imposition of Buddhism on a savage land. The invasion is first driven back twice by the Wa, but it succeeds with the aid of Lawa spies recruited from already subjugated lands around Chiengmai and a mock invitation to certain nearby Wa to come and share food at the newly established residence of a Shan "priest" (Scott and Hardiman 1983 [1901]: II.1:395ff.). Telford (1937: 92–93, 167) said the conquest happened in 1243, but the dates are disputed (see Fiskesjö 2000, chap. 2.1, also on the related stories from Chieng Mai, Thailand). On Kengtung (Jengtung), see also Aroonrut Wichienkeeo 2002; Karlsson 2013. Note also the separate traditions of the Kammu in Laos, who were the original owners of the lands to the south of Sipsong Panna and of the Muhei salt wells but were driven away to Laos (Svantesson et al. 1981: 96).
32. The first wife (*zheng qi*) of the last Menglian *tusi*, Dao Paihong, is also said to have been a Wa woman known as Danyang Manleng (perhaps her origin), whose Wa name was Nan Han Gui. She has lived in Burma since the demise of Menglian, but she visited in 1986 (field notes II:19–21, from a visit to the former *tusi* compound in

Menglian on 27 November 1996, one of the few Chinese-style *tusi* compounds still standing). For more on these relations see Fiskesjö 2000, chapter 2.1.

33. The Asian forest elephant was formerly common in the valley, but it survives only in two protected areas in Sipsong Panna and at Nan'gunhe on the northern edge of Wa country, near Banlao, Banhong, and Mengding (Fang Guoyu 1943a: 195). Elephants figured as tribute payments and as the vehicles of war up to about the time of China's Ming dynasty, but afterward become rarer. The rhinoceros, once common, is also extinct.
34. The late Chinese ethnologist Zhu Depu described traditions of this kind from many places (Zhu Depu 1993, 1996; for a brief review of Zhu's work, see Fiskesjö 1999b).
35. Raymond 2013: 223n1, citing Luce 1969–70: 1:24, 31, 112, includes details on an inscription in Bagan's Dhammayangyi temple dated to CE 1165–66; and Luce 1985: 1:14–15. Raymond (2013) also discusses illustrated catalogs of Burmese borderlands peoples, painted and compiled in the nineteenth and early twentieth centuries. For more on the Burmese literature on the Wa, also refer to Pasquet 2010.
36. There is a sizeable literature on these Kuomintang soldiers in Burma (later in Thailand), and their activities as part of the US-Chinese Cold War. Lintner (2003: 248–49, 418n92) cites his interview with former CIA agent Bill (William) Young on how they installed a "radio spy station" at Vingngün, in Wa country. See too Shackley and Finney 2005: 200ff.; McCoy 2003; and Lintner 1992.
37. Sai Kham Mong 1996: 212.
38. Tin Nyunt 2016. See also news sites such as the *Irrawaddy*, *Mizzima*, and *Frontier Myanmar*.
39. It was the only source for Frazer's oft-quoted, fanciful summary of Wa headhunting in his famous *Golden Bough* (Frazer 1911: 7:241–43).
40. On Scott's life, see Mitton 1913, 1936; Marshall 2002; also Scott 2009; and Cholthira 1990b. Scott's many photographs are now also in the British Library.
41. For more on Winnington, also see chapter 9.
42. Torigoe and Wakabayashi 1998; Torigoe, Wakabayashi, and Kawano 1983; Torigoe 1993; these works contain admirable ethnographic accounts of Wa architecture, agriculture, and so on, and also explore possibilities of cross-continental links to ancient Japanese culture, which are less persuasive to non-Japanese scholars.
43. See Zhao 2000; Oppitz 2008b; Wang Jingliu 1990; Formoso 2001, 2013; also Chen Didan 1985; Davis 2014; and Fiskesjö 2000.
44. Chouvy 2009 (see also the author's website, www.geopium.org), Maule 1992, 2002; Wright 2014; on the deep history of opium and the continuing intractable problems of heroin and synthetic drugs, see also McCoy 1992, 2003; Lintner 1992, 1994, 2003 (esp. 263ff.), 2010, 2014; also Sai Kham Mong 1996: 213–15; on the Burmese military involvement, see Bernstein and Kean 1996, and others below.
45. See sources cited above, as well as Lintner 2010; Takano 2002; Bouan 2001; Wechsler 2004; Dalton 2000; Lone 2008; Chin 2009; Milsom 2005, 2012; Kramer and Woods 2012; Kramer et al. 2014; and others. On the history of the Chinese Communist government's efforts since the 1950s, see Zhou 2004 (even though there is no mention of the Wa).
46. *Economist* 2018; International Crisis Group 2019.
47. Lintner (2010) pointed out how the United Nations, made up of national governments as it is, has long overlooked the role of Burma's military and government (in either ignoring or even in allowing and profiting from the trade). Paoli et al. (2009: 139) mention that the US government has noted this suspicion—and the absence of evidence for it.

48. Kramer et al. 2009; Jensema et al. 2014; etc.
49. Including in a special issue of the *Journal of Global History*, cf. Fiskesjö 2010b; see chapter 5.
50. The term "Austroasiatic" refers to the larger language family to which Mon-Khmer languages like that of the Wa also belong.
51. See, for example, Chen Didan 1985 and Yang Rui's films on Wa topics, including *Crossing the Mountain* (2009); cf. Frangville 2014.
52. It was recently reissued in Germany (Institut für den Wissenschaftlichen Film, 1997); see too Yang Guanghai 2009 (reminiscences by one of the main directors of these films).

1

Gifts and Debts

Fieldwork in the Wa Lands

Sometime in the fall of 1996, after arriving in the Wa lands where I would undertake field research over the following two years, I learned that before I even got there my interlocutors had decided I was indebted to their people in a serious way.* This judgment was based in Wa history and in a certain Wa conception of world history, according to which they see themselves as the first people on earth and as the guardians of humanity's ground zero.

In this chapter, reflecting on the conditions and circumstances of my fieldwork, I attempt to account for these fundamental conceptions of the place of the Wa in the world, which shaped their view of me and my research. The challenge of how to understand and relate to these judgments constituted the main ethical challenge in my fieldwork—it was emotional, too, though the main emotional challenge was dealing with the diseases, deaths, and burials of people I came to know (see chapter 8).

Slowly I came to understand that grasping the meaning of this debt challenge would form the only viable basis and framework for dealing with and understanding various mundane but nonetheless important everyday challenges, such as how to share food and drink, how to interact and talk with people, how to show reciprocity in offering help and material gifts or payments, how to resolve puzzles around theft and borrowing, how to negotiate subjects that seemed taboo, and so on.

The Wa at the Center of the World

According to stories I was told during my research, as in similar versions recorded by previous fieldworkers in Wa country, the history of humanity on earth begins

---

Endnotes for this chapter begin on page 50.

right in the heart of the Wa lands. Human beings first emerged through a hole in the ground onto the surface of the earth. This event is called the *Sigang lih*, that is, the emergence (*lih*) from the primordial hole, *Sigang*. In the area I worked, now Ximeng County on China's border with Burma, many Wa assert that this same aperture is still evident at Blag Dieh, which is now on the Burma side of the international border established in 1961 that cuts through the core of the old Wa country.

In current retellings of this origin myth, as I heard them, the Wa people emerged first, and other members of the human family came later. These "others" include key neighbors of the Wa, namely the Siam (the Shan, or Dai in Chinese parlance), the Gui (the Lahu), the Houx (the Chinese), the Man (the Burmese), and any others, who are typically mentioned last, if at all, when people explain this. The latter include Indians, who, along with Europeans, Americans, and every other people not included in this Wa shortlist, are mostly called Grax (on whom more will be said in chapter 7). On the Myanmar side, similar stories have humanity emerging from a dragon's egg, the Wa first, but with a slightly different set of late-coming neighbors (the Palaung, the Kachin, etc.; Tin Yee 2004: 37–38).

The Wa, having emerged first, settled the lands around humanity's ground zero. In this understanding, this is why the Wa live in these most ancient lands, and also why foreigners (both Asian and non-Asian) live so far away: when we (the others) came out, we had to move on, since the land at ground zero was already settled by the Wa.

This origin myth must be related to the logic of itinerant forest agriculture (swiddening, or shifting cultivation), which many Wa consider to be their primordial way of life and which they practiced for centuries, until recently. Basically this involves rotating fields in the forest, where hill rice and other crops would be grown; afterward, the newly cleared fields would be left fallow for many years.[1]

In the more distant and now idealized past, when land was plentiful, anyone arriving in an area already settled by others would move on and settle into virgin forest. This ancient logic has, in my view, been redeployed by the Wa in their account of their more recent history over the last few centuries as a history of encroachment by outsiders—who are seen as "returning" to encroach on the original Wa lands.

The story is also one of increasing population density, which together with the menace from external powers provoked intense and sometimes deadly conflicts over land and resources in the Wa region.[2] Nevertheless, until the 1950s, the core Wa areas held out against the Chinese, Burmese, and Shan states in the region as an autonomous area whose inhabitants cherished these origin myths—and also refashioned them for new purposes. As outsider-scholars, we may surmise that this Wa origin myth was elaborated to justify a present-day or recent historical

Wa claim to their lands, which they have long occupied. Today, however, these lands have been appropriated formally by the two modern territorial nation-states of China and Burma, and informally by so many Chinese entrepreneurs planting cash crops or opening mines in the name of "development."

For the Wa, however, the key aspect of the myth is the mixed blessing of having been the first on earth. In the views of many local people I spoke with, the Wa are still paying heavily for this fate, because as the original owners of "ground zero," they have to care for the deities and other spirit-beings of their mysterious land, nurturing them on behalf of all others. Thus, the Wa speak most importantly of the *muid' eei eix gon A Vex* (the *muid'* [supreme deities] that we Wa feed). The deities are "fed" (*eei*) or "nurtured" by Wa people, who make sacrifices to them (*yuh si niee*, "make sacrificial ritual") on behalf of the rest of humanity.

Everyone else—all the latecomers—got off lightly by escaping this fate. In the words of several Wa people I spoke with, outsiders do not even know how to sacrifice any more (*ang li raong tei yuh si niee*). Outsiders live easily in their present lowland dwellings (*nqieh*, downhill, "in the valleys") where they have been able to enrich themselves, whereas the Wa remain saddled with their formidable and thankless burden.

Thus, while this conception of Wa history reaffirms their position as the first settlers and historical owners of this land—as mentioned, this is something that everyone in the immediate neighborhood (Shan, Lahu, Chinese, and otherwise) traditionally does acknowledge—today it is also highly significant in that it casts the Wa in a position of responsibility that creates a relationship of indebtedness with outsiders. In my interpretation, this is a new idea modeled on old notions of propriety, which go back to an earlier era of forest farming when today's permanent territoriality was still unheard of. This is the key aspect we must pay attention to, before we dismiss the *Sigang lih* as so much primitive nonsense.

In this old tradition, the eldest son is supposed to remain in the settlement and nurture his elders as well as the village's associated spirits (including elders transformed into spirits after death). Younger siblings typically go off into the world either as new settlers or, especially in recent centuries, as tradesmen or migrant workers (chapters 5, 10). This ancient formula is now used to explain and present an argument that also involves present-day relations with ethnic others. Thus, the Wa are the *Ai* (elder brother) of humanity, while other peoples are the younger siblings (*Nyi, Soi*, and so on, in the birth-order naming system of the Wa; see chapter 2), who owe their Wa seniors respect. Just as a younger sibling, after returning from afar with exotic riches, would (in the Wa view) owe some respect to his elder siblings who stayed behind and held the fort, it follows that all present-day descendants of latecomers on earth are fundamentally indebted to the Wa.

Indebted Outsiders

This indebtedness includes not just me, a late-arrival Swedish ethnographer, but obviously also the Chinese, the British, and all others who in recent history have turned around and "come back" to Wa country to claim more than their fair share of the forests and riches that remain there. This violates propriety: it is not fair and not right, since it is the younger sibling peoples who owe the Wa, not the other way around. Of course, today, because of the formidable firepower of the modern Chinese state and its unquestionable grip on administration and resource extraction in the Chinese-owned parts of these old lands, such views cannot easily be expressed about Chinese people, at least not to their face. They also would not understand—they have never heard of the Wa area as the ground zero of humanity, and they are much too mired in their own view of themselves and their investments and profiteering to bring development to a backward area. The same is true, albeit in a different way, for the Wa lands that have become part of Burmese territory.

While the origin myths cast the Wa as the rightful owners of the land, today people can at most make empty gestures lamenting their losses. I recall Wa people pointing out past borders on the horizon and explaining the extent of the now-defunct sovereign Wa polities (*jaig' qee*, or "realm") to which they once belonged: "Our *jaig' qee* reached from that mountain ridge over there . . . to those forests over there . . ." and so on.

Those boundary lines were never recognized by the neighboring states, and these old "realms" are now overrun, both conceptually and concretely speaking, by outsiders. Today, entrepreneurs farm fast-growing trees, tea leaves, sugar cane, and other cash crops on the native lands, then ship the bulk of the extracted profits to the outside—in effect turning the formerly proudly independent Wa into peasants like any others on a subjugated periphery.[3]

And so, the revamped origin myths circulate today in unequal competition with state-propagated conceptions of the Wa as but one of many backward "minority" nationalities that make up the Chinese and the Burmese nations—conceptions that enable outside investments where profits are all exported to be described as in aid of "development." In Chinese-controlled Wa territories, this means that both Han Chinese entrepreneurs and people belonging to the managerial class of Chinese-trained town-dwelling cadres are automatically justified in their "leadership" of the supposedly backward Wa. These are the formidable impositions that the older Wa origin myths compete with. Yet even so, the myths still sustain an interpretive framework within which the present-day situation of exploitation as well as the recent calamities of history can be understood on Wa terms.

Anthropologist fieldworkers and other foreigners entering the Wa lands must realize that, as in similar situations elsewhere, they inevitably enter the picture as part of an ongoing competition between different interpretative frameworks and conflicts of interest. From a Wa perspective, they would be seen as outsiders indebted to the Wa, not the other way around, no matter the amount of outsider "aid" and investment.

Agents of the Chinese state are typically—like colonial officers throughout history—frustrated by the apparent lack of gratitude on the part of many Wa for all the "investments" made in their land. This is something often pointed out to me by Chinese officials, who wished for me to commiserate. The situation of such state agents has been compounded by the many false starts of post-1950s Chinese development schemes in the Wa lands and a repetitive wrongheadedness that often evokes the classic pattern of "seeing-like-a-state" development failures (Scott 1998). Such grand "gifts" to the Wa by outsiders are themselves revealing; take, for example, the 1970s scheme to make the Wa shift to wheat-growing on former highland opium lands, a plan that failed for both environmental and cultural reasons. The idea was to have the Wa shift their diet to noodles and bread, which they were reluctant to do—not least because they grow dry hill rice not just as a staple food but also to produce the socially all-important Wa rice beer (see chapter 3).

By coincidence, hilltop lands have been overrun from the 1950s onward by an invasive weed, *Eupatorium adenphorum* (a one- to one-and-a-half meter tall plant with origins in Central America). Its Chinese name is *Zijing zelan*, but it is colloquially known as *Gaifangcao* or *reeb gaifang* (liberation grass) in Wa. Cattle don't eat it, and it hampers forest regrowth (about the only place it does not grow is in shady forest). Only marginal success has been achieved in combating it—as well as the notion that it arrived with liberation, which in Communist parlance was supposed to have brought bounty, not misery. To be fair, it is known in Wa both as *reeb gaifang* and *reeb feiji* (airplane grass, an indication that it appeared around the same time airplanes were first seen), but the concept of liberation is tainted, nonetheless.

The Chinese also, since olden times, favor canals and terraces built for growing irrigated rice, which they see as inherently superior to swiddening, regardless of the local conditions. As Scott (2009) has argued, one reason for this is the fixed, easy-to-inspect nature of terraces, as opposed to the mobile swidden lands shifted around in the mountains by the farmers. Irrigation canals and terraces are often seen in Wa areas today, as well as traces of failed such projects that also dot the landscape. Irrigation can work in some places that enjoy natural streams, but many hill sites are simply not suited for such agriculture and are better suited for the astute rotation systems of swiddening (Yin 2001, 2009). I saw many traces of half-baked projects for irrigation ditches dug across the hills, intended to transport water to new rice paddy fields, but not lined by concrete and lacking any other means of preventing the water from sinking into the ground.[4]

Figure 1.1. Hillside irrigation canal digging ordered by Chinese officials. Village of Yong Ou. Photo by the author, 1997.

Once, in 1997, I myself took part in one such ill-fated project of hillside irrigation canal digging ordered by local Chinese officials. The command to assemble villagers for this work was transmitted only days earlier to the Chinese-appointed village chief (a gentle man whose appointment was based on his former service in the Chinese army manning antiaircraft guns at a Yunnan airport). He then asked all able-bodied villagers to come out in force, bring their hoes and spades, and engage in this project. Since I too had already become a familiar figure in the neighborhood, I too was allowed to join. I helped dig with a spade while observing how the endeavor was carried out in a cheerful spirit even though many realized, and said plainly, that it was a complete waste of time and labor. It was done in recognition of the fact that "we live in the Chinese era" (*oud eix nqu Houx*), in which the Chinese authorities can impose anything, as a matter of course, and typically do not ask for the opinion of local farmers, who are regarded as ignorant and, in the case of the Wa, undeveloped and in sore need of tutelage.

The Context of "Development"

The approach reflects the top-down socialist-style development that dominated the Chinese-ruled Wa lands from the 1950s, and especially the 1960s, and up until the 1990s. In the 1990s, this government-led effort was joined by private entrepreneurs who own their investments (in agroforestry, cash crops such as tea and sugar cane, mining ventures, and so on), though in the Chinese state-sponsored interpretation it is all still justified as "development" benefiting the Wa on either side of the international border.

For the rural Wa, formerly independent warriors not ruled by any government, the reality is that neither state nor private "development" schemes can be opposed. Above all, they are backed by overwhelming military force. Everyone knows of the 1958 catastrophe, a minor war in which the initial Chinese policy of respect for local social institutions was abandoned in favor of pushing Chinese-led transformations.[5] The Communist authorities first sought to confiscate Wa firearms and then to suppress the resistance that followed. Several local people were shot dead, and many fled to what would later become Burmese territory. Locals who fled and took refuge in the old Wa territory now recognized as part of Burma are still trickling back to their old home villages. *Wu ba nian* (the year 1958) thus carries an ominous meaning.

Since then, in the areas where people have lived under direct Chinese rule (albeit supposedly under a system of semi-autonomy), people often emphasized to me that it is necessary to *hngied a gah*, or "obey" (literally, listen to the words of) the authorities as imposed on the locals. This means not just lining up for corvée-style canal-digging experiments but also becoming peasant workers on cash crop plantations while never openly questioning the state-guaranteed ownership regime that makes these new arrangements possible. Yet, like oppressed peasants elsewhere, people will negotiate even this kind of predicament (Scott 2009). While diluted and scattered by economic migration, the Wa still have their collective memories and mythologies of how this land was once owned by them, through the Wa *jaig' qee*, the kinship-based "circle" of village settlements that made up the backbone of the political-economic organization of independent Wa society.

Showing Up in Wa Country

Against this background, I hope the reader can better understand the context of power inequality and competing narratives into which I treaded warily as an ethnographer. I even had to accept that it was not strange if I myself, on arriving in the central Wa country that had come under Chinese rule since the 1950s, was even taken for a Houx, a "Chinese."

Let me explain. Even though I look rather more like the Scandinavian I am (although with brown hair and green eyes), due to the Chinese conquest and domination of this Wa country this designation as Houx (Chinese) was by no means as far off the mark as it may seem. Because of recent history, since the earlier British retreat from Burma after World War II, Westerners had been rare in the area, as had the Indian traders who used to come to the Shan states and the Wa lands (and some Indians in British legions that penetrated Wa areas in the late nineteenth and early twentieth centuries, as the British unsuccessfully tried to expand their control of colonial Burma into the Wa lands).[6]

Many older Wa remembered the exceptional visitor Alan Winnington, the British Communist journalist stranded in China by his own government after the Korean War, when he reported from the North Korean side. The new Communist government in China sent him on a tour of newly liberated peripheral areas of the Wa, the Yi, and others (Winnington 1959; see also chapter 7). I was even compared to Winnington from time to time: older people observed that I looked a bit like him; I always carried a notebook, just like him; and I also had a camera—the only difference was that "his camera had three legs."

At the time of his visit in 1957–58, Winnington would have been designated as a Grax, the old Wa term, and so, the elders who remembered him also wanted to designate me as a Grax, not a Houx. As my grasp of the local Wa dialect improved, I discovered that in fact ever since my arrival there had been a long-running local debate over both my identity and my purpose. A majority of younger people thought I must be a Houx: I was obviously neither a "Gui" or Lahu, the Tibeto-Burman people who had migrated into the region since the nineteenth century, nor a Siam (Tai-speaking Shan, from the Buddhist valley kingdoms surrounding the Wa lands), and I was not "Man" or Burmese, so "Chinese" was the closest fit. The elders' revival of the term "Grax" was one of an almost obsolete ethnonym-without-referent, something that brought grudging respect for those who remembered this category. This seemed to reassert the viability of native systems of classification and reinforce a sense of Wa identity. It also highlighted the futility of ever thinking I could be a fly on the wall. Impossible.

Some younger people still insisted I was really a Houx, and I do not blame them. After all, I initially arrived from the Chinese county town, with Chinese arrangements and Chinese permission, accompanied by a Chinese official; I spoke Chinese, and, like most Chinese, I could not speak Wa. While I had been studying Wa with tutors in Kunming for several months, my knowledge was still at a preliminary level, and the standard Yong Soi dialect taught in Kunming differed from that of the Ximeng area where I pursued most of my fieldwork. It was only slowly that I learned to speak the local A Vex dialect of the old Yong Ou *jaig'qee*, spoken in parts of China's Ximeng and in adjacent Burmese territories. And either way, whether as a strange-looking Houx or as a Wa-speaking Grax, I would necessarily be regarded as part of the general framework outlined above—as a foreigner returning to the Wa lands, the ground zero of humanity.

But what then was my purpose, as a stray "returnee" from some distant, unheard-of place? As I consistently tried to explain in my slowly improving Wa, my native land was Sweden, and I was a student at a university in the United States, in a place called Chicago—a school of sorts where we cultivated an interest in the cultures and histories of other people around the globe. I said that my peers and I would return there from our ethnographic forays around the globe to report to each other on such matters. By extension, I said, we hoped this would promote global understanding and peace. This was my anthropological credo.

My interlocutors interpreted these propositions in light of historical experiences with outsiders who had ventured into the Wa lands and, in some cases, appropriated their land and its natural resources. The Chinese, Burmese, and British had used military and other efforts to impose control and force changes in Wa society that sought to put them under foreign rule. This was, in turn, seen as part of larger patterns of global injustice and ingratitude toward the Wa. No one had heard of ethnography or anthropology, apart from the Chinese state ethnographic efforts in the 1950s to investigate local society, but that was obviously carried out with the purpose of furthering "reforms" and integration, so it was inevitable that my presence would be explained along similar lines.

Early in my fieldwork, after temporarily settling into Yong Ou—a place chosen because I knew it was once an important Wa center—I wandered about, introducing myself, learning the language, and trying to be a patient observer. I followed the advice that my professor Marshall Sahlins had offered on the eve of my departure. When I half-jokingly asked him, "So, I'm leaving for 'The Field'—

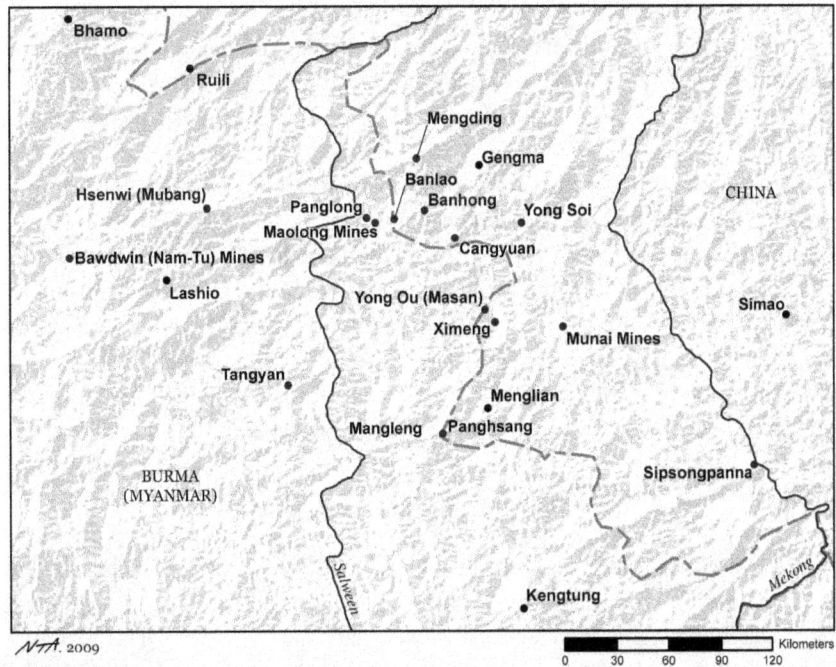

Figure 1.2. Map of the neighborhood of the Yong Ou ancestral center. By Nij Tontisirin Anantsuksomsri.

what's your final advice for me?" he replied without missing a beat, "Don't ask any questions the first two months."

I took this literally, sticking to finding my way in the social landscape but postponing many of my questions. Sahlins's advice was very useful, because it instilled in me an appropriate measure of humility as an anthropologist venturing into Wa country with limited knowledge of its history, culture, language, and morals—of who was who, and what was what. Questions must build on knowledge and on reflection drawn from experience, but I had little of either of these. Ethnography requires a kind of dedicated humility toward others that cannot be rushed, but on the contrary demands slowness. The resulting experience was one of "radical" fieldwork, which changed my life profoundly, and I'm still in awe of it.

One such early day when I was wandering about, a group of women and children were resting on an *ngrah*, an elevated bamboo veranda typically attached to every house and used for drying clothes and other household tasks. They waved for me to come over and invited me to sit with them. I was determined to purposely do nothing except listen, learn the language, and learn about the people without pushing my research agenda yet. A slightly awkward conversation got under way. My Wa was already coming along, thanks in no small measure to Robbins Burling's *Learning a Field Language* (1984), the wonderful tongue-on guide to language learning through reciprocal interaction. We were speaking in Wa, yet there was still much I did not understand. Although nowadays schoolchildren are taught in Chinese, in this area only some of the younger people could speak a language other than their local Wa dialect. Some older folks knew the Wa lingua franca, as well as Chinese, Burmese, or Shan, albeit typically somewhat limited in each.

Soon, a thirtysomething woman started talking to me, and I struggled to follow. It turned out that the words I was missing were not too difficult to have explained by gestures: one was *a miux* (dream); another was *si nieed* (gun). She was telling me and all the other women that she had had a dream the night before in which I walked around the village with a big rifle, going from house to house and shooting everyone inside. To bring home the point, she vividly expressed this with gestures suggesting how, in her dream, I had gone about the killings. I was taken aback and hardly knew what to say, even though the atmosphere was friendly, cheerful, and not in the least hostile. I simply tried to say that I had no gun and no intention of doing any such thing.

I often pondered the significance of this incident. While it tells of the forthrightness and cheerfulness of Wa people, including of their strong, outspoken, and independent women, it also evokes the Wa perspective on their world and the historical background of war and misery that came before me. This history, I slowly came to understand, never seemed very far from the lived experience of the people in the area, even though most had not seen war since the 1958 Chinese suppression of local resistance. Refugees from that time kept coming back to try to claim land in their old village, reminding everyone of these cataclysmic events. They would also bring new stories of the ongoing wars in Burma, where the Wa State (the UWSA) keeps some twenty thousand men under arms and has been engaged in fighting with other insurgent armies in the region.

Add to this the long-standing insight that wars might also be instigated by faraway powers[7]—from the quarters of those ungrateful lowlanders/latecomers that would come back and menace the Wa—and it becomes easier to understand one theory about the purpose of my stay that seemed almost like a corollary to the woman's dream: I was a harbinger of violence to come, a scout of some faraway power (the United States, perhaps) intent on invading Wa country. This also does not seem far-fetched if one considers that the United States has actually indicted the top ethnic Wa leaders of Burma's Wa state as international narco-criminals, news of which has prompted much speculation.

Likewise, Burma's military leaders (who have not yet been indicted) have frequently used the imagery of the US bombings and invasions of Iraq and other countries as props in their own domestic propaganda. All such actions may engender rumors, even in areas with geographically and socially limited TV and internet access. As if to underscore the gravity of these concerns, people frequently and pointedly asked me to convey to whatever faraway powers whence I had come the message that "the Wa want peace, not war." There, I have tried once more to convey this important message.

Ethnographic Interaction and "Participant Intoxication"

As my Wa language skills improved, my ethnographic endeavors developed to include going places, meeting people, and attending and participating in both farming and other work, as well as events. Ultimately, I was able to get to my agenda of interviewing people about history, including difficult topics such as headhunting warfare, and there were people who understood and took seriously my professed interest in Wa culture and history. It was a long process, and I was asked myriad questions about my family and myself, as well as about my country of birth, my country of residence, and many other things besides the difficult questions about what my ethnography and anthropology was intended to be. This "questionnaire" was never completed. The discussions continued on my memorable last night, when I threw a party that lasted until dawn at my lodgings in the spare room of a small Chinese-built school (Figure 1.3).

People continued to discuss, in my presence, why I had been there, and what the real or hidden purpose was behind my asking so many questions, talking to so many people, and going to so many places in the area. There was no conclusive agreement on this issue, as if the assembled men (for this night it was mostly men)

Figure 1.3. Coffee and excitement at the farewell party in the author's room. Village of Yong Ou. Photo by the author, 1998.

seemed to reserve their right not to be surprised if everything I had said turned out to be lies.

Given everything discussed so far, I cannot blame them. At the same time, I feel honored that so many did find plausible my explanation of my presence. I was also very pleased to hear that there was at least agreement that I had conducted myself properly during my stay (or, more correctly, stays, since my prolonged visits to the village and its immediate region continued over about two years during 1996–98, with interruptions for travel in other Wa areas and elsewhere, plus later return visits).

The question of propriety was a highly important issue: people reminisced about "small" things, like how I had brought liquor and cigarettes to funerals and how I had tried to learn how to act and speak properly toward the dead and the bereaved on such occasions, which loom very large in the Wa social context (see also chapter 8).

In hindsight, I can see more clearly that these several aspects are intimately related. In a practical sense, my proper conduct in accordance with Wa ways ensured my access as an ethnographer to many settings and interlocutors. Only by conducting myself with respect toward the Wa—through participation in the symbolically important and highly complex aspects of sharing rice beer and betel nut in everyday settings, as well as more highly charged ritual settings—did I earn a social standing as a person of decency with whom one might talk, and who would

Figure 1.4. Mourners at a funeral in Yong Ou. Photo by the author, 1997.

be permitted to attend such private functions. These gestures and observances on my part were important for the local people, even though the explanation for my presence remained hard to understand and could seem obscure or spurious to some. These gestures were also fundamental to my project, which included listening in earnest to people's explanations of their perspective and seriously considering the implications of what I was told, even if it could at first seem incredible as presented (stories about humanity's emergence from a hole in the ground, and so on). This did not mean accepting at face value whatever I was told—as every anthropologist must, I was working out my own analysis and conclusions—but grasping the significance of Wa perspectives on things was indispensable both for understanding Wa history, for negotiating the ethics of my own research agenda on sensitive issues related to this history, and for making my own judgments.

In my mind, I sometimes compared my situation to that of David Schneider when he insisted on having permission from the chief of the Pacific island of Yap for his fieldwork there. It was granted, albeit with a big laugh, while the chief pointed to the multiple American warships anchored in plain view just off the coast. The United States obviously had the means to bully Yap locals into anything, so the chief and his colleagues thought his request for permission for ethnographic investigations was rather funny (Schneider and Handler 1995). Yet Schneider's move established that even under circumstances of domination (shared by both Yapese and Wa), as an ethnographer one must respect both the locals *and* one's own autonomy, not just for show but as a matter of principle. As in my case, Schneider's signaling of this ethical stance could not be more than the starting point of the negotiations of all the ethical issues that, inevitably, arose *after* this beginning.[8]

Wa house dances (*n'groh nyiex seroh*) held when a new house is built are another instructive example. These events last through the night, until dawn. It is seen as essential for the hosts (both those who arranged for the building of the house and those set to live in it) to host an open house and insist that everyone dance the house dance. This applies especially to the traditional bamboo-floored houses on stilts (now disappearing since the Chinese are insisting on "modern" concrete or mud bricks, even though such houses pose a far greater risk in the case of earthquakes). Stilt houses are expected to be built in a day, and are made from wood poles and structural beams, with thatched roofs, flattened bamboo walls, a *ngrah* veranda, and bamboo floors with built-in wooden fireplace boxes.

Around these new fireplaces everyone dances in circles, singing auspicious songs about the merriment of starting a new life in the house, happily connected to everyone else in the living community. Visitors are encouraged by the hosts to dance as hard as possible, and sometimes the house shakes and floors and walls break.

Only local residents or relatives living elsewhere can attend such a dance, and it is a serious taboo violation if an unknown outsider or foreigner should show up. The Wa would explain this to me merely by saying explicitly, *Tueh eix nah* ("This, we taboo"). Even visitors from afar who might be legitimate dance participants because of a kin relation to the house builders must also avoid appearing suddenly, uninvited and unexpected. Naturally, the question of my eligibility arose in such situations, and it was only after I had been in the area for many months and participated extensively in other aspects of ordinary social life that I was admitted as a guest at these special dances. I was then not admitted reluctantly but wholeheartedly and fully, and I was expected to take part entirely, as a decent person would. Admission was not unconditional: no sitting on the sidelines. This was a time when the cheerful community tested the strength of its social bonds as well as that of the bamboo floors and walls.

On these occasions, no other outsiders would be present; indeed, no other outsider or foreigner would usually stay overnight in rural Wa villages. Government officials from the county seat—about an hour and a half by jeep from the village of Yong Ou where I spent the most extensive periods of my fieldwork—would occasionally show up during the day but almost invariably return by night to one of the nearby towns where they live and work.

Yong Ou, an old Wa center and ancestral village at the core of the former system of branch villages, was devastated in the 1950s annexation and then demoted under Chinese rule, so that one of its former branch villages became the local

Figure 1.5. Women at work thatching the roof while the men finish the body of a new house, in Yong Ou. Photo by the author, 1997.

village office seat (*cungongsuo*). This meant officials would practically never stay overnight at Yong Ou, which lacked official places to sleep. The only building that was not a Wa household was the concrete and brick schoolhouse built some years earlier (in which, by lucky coincidence, there were five rooms, only four of which were occupied by teachers, so that I could make my quarters inside the last one). The schoolteachers, all under twenty years of age, included two non-Wa teachers who were never interested in the dances, although they would have been eligible to attend. One was an ethnic Lahu woman from a nearby village, the other a Han Chinese woman from central Yunnan doing a stint in the village with a view toward relocating back to Han areas later on. Visitors from Wa communities in

China or Burma, often relatives returning home, could stay the night with their local hosts in their houses and could also show up at the dances. Had I not decided to give myself ample time to sink into the community and to respect local mores, I could never have experienced these events and would have had much less ground to stand on when addressing the wider topics of historical ethnic relations that concerned me most.

One persistent aspect of my fieldwork was the Wa rice beer, of enormous social importance, which is discussed further in chapter 3. Homemade rice beer—in competition with imported, much more harmful Chinese hard liquor—is the lubricant of Wa society and is drunk on any social occasion, not just ceremonial events but also in the everyday context of evening drinking with neighbors and relatives. The beer is consumed with sets of complicated, culturally specific rules that I also had to learn and accept, or I would have been treated with suspicion and exclusion like other outside visitors who might refuse to share the rice beer on account of its being dirty or because of some other prejudice.

Because of the key role of rice beer, my ethnographic work inevitably involved what I have called "participant intoxication." This is the ethnographic field method of drinking with your informants because your research depends on, and even consists of, properly joining in with your hosts as a local person would. This can be likened to conventional "participant observation," but with the added element of rice beer. If choosing to participate in drinking the beer, the ethnographer must also face the consequences either way, including putting down one's guard and giving one's trust, as well as gaining the trust of one's companions.

The chewing of betel (*bao*), like the smoking of tobacco (*sub*), is another important "social lubricant" in everyday Wa life as well as on ceremonial occasions.[9] The main difference is that the raw materials and utensils are carried around by individuals, and no other preparation is necessary other than each person preparing their own wad for chewing—and being sure to engage in the sharing of the multiple ingredients that the personal bags will hold. Until the catastrophe of 1958, people used elaborate, ornate bags suspended from the waist for their betel ingredients. In recent years, people have turned to using discarded plastic bags and small medicine jars instead. Hearing about the nostalgia for the old betel bags, I bought cloth and decorative cords and asked a few elderly women to help me recreate a betel bag of old. I relished engaging in the language of social betel exchange, where one sits around to borrow different supplies and reciprocates with those that others are missing. Betel chewing is tasty, but it can be dangerously intoxicating and can even make you faint if you use too much fresh tobacco leaf in the wad.

There is also cigarette and cigar smoking, which is similarly important socially. However, having never been a smoker, I self-consciously rejected it. I was selective in embracing food, drink, and betel chewing as media of social interaction, because tobacco could be sidelined as a matter of personal preference if only one had enough decency to engage in the proper sharing of food, drink, and betel.

Of course, little of these exchanges could have been accomplished without proficiency in the Wa language. For me, learning to ask for food, to accept and eat it properly, and to be ready to offer something appropriate in return at some other time was key to both decency and survival. The same issues of propriety and reciprocity also surfaced in exchanges of material help, such as with tools. Occasionally someone might ask for my tape recorder or camera, using the logic of "You have one, I don't" (and implicitly, "If you are a decent person, you better share it with me"). This was an extreme case of the logic of foreigner's indebtedness that I had to wrestle with. Yet it was really no different from when a local schoolteacher kept "borrowing" my things without asking, a common practice that nevertheless annoyed me. Due to my own ingrained cultural background, I had to struggle not to think of this as plain theft—which of course also exists as a cultural category, yet is defined in different local terms.

I tried instead, as much as I could, to give away other goods that could be properly presented as reciprocal gifts. These consisted of not just food and betel but also photos—I became the local photographer, developing pictures and having them encased in protective plastic in nearby Chinese towns—and medicine, where possible. Here I relied on my meager background as a medic in the Swedish navy and on the precious practical handbook *Where There Is No Doctor* (Werner et al. 1992). Still, the limits of my abilities to help the sick and dying in the context of an abysmal lack of proper healthcare became the most painful part of my fieldwork. I spent much time struggling to understand, and come to terms with, this dreadful situation (see chapter 8, on disease and death in the Wa lands).

One incident throws into further relief the significance and the difficult challenge of the process of learning to be a decent person in relations with local people. The ethnographer is inevitably forced to navigate delicate situations and sometimes choose sides, and to take stands against others. In April 1998, an elderly man who had become something of an old acquaintance sought me out to invite me to an event he was planning for the following day: a "sweeping of the tombstone" (*sao mu*, a Chinese loan word) for his prematurely dead young son, who had passed away years before. The practice of marking tombs with inscribed stones and sweeping them in April was a new one, copied from the Chinese and taken up only since the 1990s. All this was of course tremendously interesting for me to witness. I had already attended a number of funerals in the old local style, wherein the grave is made in the garden of the deceased and without any permanent marker, as well as those done in the new style copied from the Chinese, in which the grave is made on higher or prominent ground so as to last permanently, marked by a tombstone.

On the following day, we assembled as agreed at the house of a relative, who was preparing all the necessary offerings and gathering everyone to go to the tomb. We were almost ready to solemnly file out of the house when suddenly a jeep arrived, stopping on a nearby road and discharging several people who came looking for us. Among them was a Han Chinese researcher, an anthropologist from Beijing. This young scholar was conducting research on Wa demography and had heard about my presence from local officials. She had arranged transportation through the local government in the manner common among researchers in China, something that could perhaps be termed "jeep ethnography," since it involves riding in government jeeps to communities singled out for research (using impromptu translators and, backed by the power of the Chinese administrative apparatus, gathering up informants for surveys and interviews).[10] She seemed decent, and at any other time it would have been interesting to talk with her about her research. Yet in this case, we could only awkwardly await their departure. I thus became party to an effort to expel these visitors by way of passivity and inactivity, effectively "boring" them out of there, offering only a modicum of food and drink, as if to signal that there was going to be no welcome party. It also turned into another test of my own patience.[11] I could perhaps have walked away with this woman and had a conversation elsewhere, but I felt unable to do so, due to the heavy sense of reciprocal duty I felt toward my hosts, who of course had priority. In this particular case, the visitors left after several hours of awkward conversation, and we proceeded to complete the tearful ceremony as planned.

Wa people under Chinese rule often end up in this kind of situation, with officials and administrators showing up at inopportune moments, forcing locals to resort to various ways of "boring" them out of there—although with the arrival of cell phones in the area since the mid-2000s, such visits are often no longer surprises.

During my fieldwork, local Wa people occasionally designated themselves as particularly authoritative sources on Wa culture (most often understood as *hlag oud eix gon A Vex*, "how we Wa are," literally "the way of being of us Wa people") and history (*nqu ga*, [life in] "former generations"). Sometimes neighbors and peers were dismissed by such self-declared authorities as know-nothings or even fakes (here often using the immensely popular Chinese loan word, *jia*, for "fake"). This could sometimes be rather annoying to me, since my task then became to fight back emotional reactions within myself and to persist in navigating, politely, between potential informants without offending anyone. I knew that I had to work to keep doors open as I continued to learn about the meaning of rhetorical genres, about who was who, and about whom I should talk to about the issues I was interested in. As I slowly came to understand Wa social life, by taking part in it, I became increasingly adept at arranging meetings with people when they might be able to speak to me without undue interference in their daily lives, or in their farming and household labor, and with just enough (but not more) of the ubiquitous rice beer and other drinks.

As in every society, not everyone was a self-declared expert. Some people instead preferred to defer to those with better gifts of memory, rhetoric, or ambition. When the occasion arose, I endeavored to speak with such persons on their terms, without pushing the various agendas for research that I might have taken up with someone more interested in interacting with me (or even in monopolizing my engagements and favors). Instead, I would try to remain quiet and humble in the manner of my early days in the area. Indeed, slowing down and suppressing expectations is a method that has never failed me, not least since I could of course never aspire to becoming a full-fledged "expert." I knew I would never attain the incredible mastery and expertise that some of the most talented Wa persons displayed, being thoroughly versed in the Wa language with its rich oral traditions, all committed to memory, in a way that always humbled me as someone enslaved to pen, paper, and computers.

Sometimes patient self-restraint would serve me well with quiet, unassuming people. In one memorable instance, a very quiet man who would almost never speak up in a group demanded to see the photos that I had shown several other acquaintances but which he had not yet seen. These were pictures taken by Winnington (1959) in this very same area, in the last years of the 1950s, and also pictures of similar Wa settlements found in the works of James George Scott (1911, etc.), the British colonial administrator of the Shan States of Burma. By my second year of fieldwork, I had enough confidence speaking Wa to show these historical photos and ask for comments about what they depicted. In this case, my interlocutor asked me point-blank if I had taken these pictures myself "at the time of the *Sigang lih*"—that is, back in the early days of the beginning of humankind. He had theorized for himself that I might be a time traveler who had sought his way back to the Wa lands from an earlier time. I said no, and explained that I was not present then.

The incident prompted me to reflect deeply on conceptions of time and space, and it humbled me in the same way that the incident involving the dream of my shooting the villagers had. I came face to face with the reality that local people might hold views far outside my expectations, even if my expectations had matured considerably over two years of trying to understand local affairs and the range of local understandings, and sophistication. Beyond such "culturalist" expectations of how "Wa people" would understand things, people also have their own individual proclivities.

Some meetings with exceptionally valuable interlocutors, a small number of elderly men and women who are now all dead—may they rest in peace—were arranged in field huts in mountain fields far from the village. My interlocutors would relocate there for one or several nights in order to work the fields and not have to make the arduous round-trip journey on foot back to the village every day. During dark evenings in such distant field huts, there would be no one else but the farmer, his or her next of kin, and me, with nothing to do except talk to each other in an atmosphere where the ethnographer might have a better chance of directing, to some extent, the course of the conversation. In the village, any attempt at such conversation was likely to be interrupted by impromptu visitors out for a stroll (*lou li*), looking for a place to socialize around rice beer and launch into the intense, sweet fireside conversations (the *a peag*, marvelous sessions of spirited small talk), and sometimes singing (*nqox*), that at this time still characterized the TV-free Wa evenings. Such occasions offered an entirely different window of opportunity—often much more difficult to follow, since it is doubly hard to understand native speakers engaging with each other at full intensity, reveling in the use of puns and other rich elements of their language, than it is to seek out someone for an interview where one might gain more control over the conversation.

I would also sometimes be asked to explain life in other countries, or to give my opinion on things, as I was queried on one occasion whether I believed the theory suggested in the children's school that Earth actually goes around the sun. This unfolded while guarding a fire and waiting for dawn to break, so that a traditional one-day mutual-aid house construction project could get started. Again, I was impressed by people's open-mindedness, and I explained what I knew about space exploration, and the photos of Earth taken from the moon, which confirm that we are going around the sun, and the moon around us.

Television, Culture, and Tradition

In the late 1990s, the future decline of the marvelous Wa conversational tradition was barely detectable, but I should have seen it coming. When traveling to visit other Wa areas that lay within the reach of hypnotizing television transmissions, I had already sat in houses where folks were glued to the dizzying poor-quality Chinese TV screens and had stopped talking to each other in the traditional manner, unable to speak to me because of their hypnotized state—much as in *Ginger e Fred*, that famous Fellini movie. At best, the spirited Wa-style *a peag* was relegated to very late hours, the time when light from the fireplace is fading and only the elders would still be awake, brewing tea instead of beer.

In 2006, on one of my return trips to my 1990s fieldwork sites, I noticed a significant change. Many people now had TVs, even where there was still no TV broadcast signal, and were using them to watch VCDs (video compact discs) and DVDs. In the 1990s, the only TV screens were those of the occasional shop owner who bought or rented Hong Kong kung fu movies in a nearby Chinese town and brought them back to the village to show to children on his house TV screen, for a small entrance fee. In Yong Ou, such appliances were powered by electricity that the village had acquired only a few years earlier, in exchange for selling a forest to Chinese loggers. By 2006, many people had bought their own TVs and disc players and were able to watch Chinese-made presentations that depicted the Wa as wild and exotic. The dancing, drumming, and so on was repackaged material drawn from a world that had ended in 1958, when many of the practices and traditions associated with independent Wa society were prohibited or fell into disuse. This revival came to me as another shock. Now it was I who began to feel like a person from the past, an elder not used to seeing these novelties. I had to struggle to contain my feelings about how such staged, exoticizing versions of Wa culture distorted the Wa past and Wa traditions.

Such feelings were wrong. Here was a new tradition of local people taking in and obviously enjoying these versions of themselves, even though they were staged by the Chinese, and perhaps even, to some extent, because this staging implies a recognition of sorts from the dominant power. The staging of Wa culture did not seem to bother anyone, even as both the elderly, middle-aged folks, and even the young will state the obvious: these are inaccurate descriptions of Wa dances and other aspects of their culture. At the same time, the VCD/DVDs serve as a prompt for reminiscing about and discussing what such dances and other scenes were actually like. And people appeared to relish the great vigor that these staged performances were choreographed to convey.

This derived, in part, from the longstanding Chinese imaginings of the Wa as fierce barbarians (Fiskesjö 1999a, 2002; also, chapters 7 and 10). Perhaps it's taken as a compliment by young Wa people because it evokes past Wa martial strength and power. This could account for at least some of the popularity of the discs, which even outsold the kung fu films from that now-distant era of the 1990s. There might be a mutually reinforcing admiration for that imagined vigor—perhaps even imagined as Chinese fascination and recognition for the enduring power of the Wa—which by extension bolsters a sense of self-worth and pride among younger Wa viewers.

Still, as an outside observer I cannot deny my mixed feelings. My sadness for the many people, now dead, who told me about the proud past of their people and about the devastating blows to that society is mixed with admiration and apprehension for the strange and unexpected setting in which new generations of Wa now attempt to revive their pride and write a new chapter in their history, albeit one in which their language is often that of foreigners. Whatever happens, the developments engendered by the VCD bonanza, the staged festivals, and the theme park versions of Wa culture must become part of a new and different Wa research agenda in the future, to take into account how the Wa reformulate and re-present themselves and their culture on a global stage (cf. chapter 10).

Notes

* This chapter draws in part on my contribution "Gifts and Debts: The Morality of Fieldwork in the Wa Lands on the China-Burma Frontier," in *Red Stamps and Gold Stars: Fieldwork Dilemmas in Upland Socialist Asia*, ed. Sarah Turner (Vancouver: UBC Press, 2013), 61–79.

1. On Wa swidden agriculture and its decline in the face of population pressure and economic change, see Yin 2001; also Li Genpan and Lu Xun 1985 (on pre-1960s agriculture); for more references on swiddening generally, Cairns 2007, 2013. "Swidden" is an old English term revived by Izikowitz (1951; also, Sprenger 2006). Ever since the post–World War II era, a battle has raged between those who, like him, saw swidden agriculture systems as an ingenious invention and an example of valuable indigenous knowledge, and those who embraced a development view, in which swiddening was a "slash-and-burn" practice, both backward and destructive.
2. On these issues, see chapter 4. For a sampling of Chinese views of the *Sigang lih* story as cultural tradition rather than living myth, see Na Jinhua 2009.
3. See Kramer and Woods 2012; Woods 2011, 2016, 2018.
4. These are thus very different from the traditionally bamboo aboveground aqueducts used for village drinking and cooking water, which is piped in from the hills.
5. This was a policy shift away from accommodation with local elites and toward overthrowing them—the effects of which were seen most dramatically in Tibet, where Tibet's leader, the Dalai Lama, was forced to flee to India. This drastic policy shift does not seem to have been studied comprehensively in terms of its origins, and the consequences for "autonomous" ethnic areas. It is linked, of course, to Mao's disastrous shift to a "Great Leap Forward," at about the same time (Dikötter 2010). Also see the epilogue.
6. See the introduction, and chapter 8.
7. Apart from the most recent Chinese army invasion, people might also remember KMT soldiers and CIA mercenaries from the World War II/Cold War period, and they would also have been aware of fighting involving the UWSA in Burma at the Burmese-Thai border, including skirmishes with the Burmese army and competing drug cartel forces (see introduction).
8. This also highlights the divergence between anthropological fieldwork as a never-ending process of learning and negotiation and the legalistic, institutional ethics framework of US universities, where obtaining a signature on a form is often conceived as the finalization of consent (*American Ethnologist* 2006; Metro 2014, also Fiskesjö 2020a).
9. The Wa are not alone in this (see Rooney 1993; Reichart and Philipsen 1989; Achaya 1994: 48ff.; see also Reid 1985, on how betel has been replaced by tobacco in Indonesia). The Wa are at the northern frontier of betel use in Southeast Asia; betel is a tropical plant that does not grow high in the mountains, and the Wa import it from the lowlands, mainly from Burma. On historical Wa betel use, see also Li Yangsong 1983a [1957]; Scott and Hardiman 1983 [1900]: I:2:344–45.
10. This contrasts with the Chinese ethnographers of the 1950s and 1960s, who were on a mission to delve into local society and who spent extensive time in these communities—in some cases years—for academic study and writing (for example, Luo Zhiji [1995], a very accomplished woman fieldworker and scholar); or Wa scholars trained in Chinese academia, such as Wei Deming (2001). But it is striking how brief and thin fieldwork usually is in the contemporary Chinese social sciences. Undoubtedly, the reason is epistemological: many Chinese scholars do not value in-depth fieldwork,

or indeed in learning any language (which they rarely do; instead, they often use the dominant Chinese without reflection).
11. Which was already under stress by the threat of getting thrown out of the place at a moment's notice because of the slow pace of my work, which seemed even more incomprehensible to local township bureaucrats than to the local Wa themselves. Why would anyone need to stay more than a week in such a backward place?

2

NAMING ONESELF, NAMING THE WORLD

This chapter is about how Wa names work, and how the culturally distinct Wa naming system serves as a foundation of the identity and presence of the Wa people in this world.* Because I also introduce the patriclans, the backbone of the Wa kinship system expressed in Wa naming, I will also briefly discuss the drums and the drum shrines in the care of these clans.

As it is with people anywhere, the personal name is most fundamental to a person's identity. Every child is named in order to become socialized as a person. Naming a child is one of the key instruments people have to make and recognize persons both as individuals and as members of a society, and by natural extension as one of the agents of society's reproduction.

The power to assign a name to a child typically rests with its parents, but as elsewhere around the world, the range of potential choices is also restricted to that which works within the specific cultural framework of naming. Naming one's children is thus also, on the level of languages and ethnicities, about organizing and maintaining oneself as a people, by defining oneself and one's relation to others, on one's own terms. This is why this chapter discusses both how an individual Wa person is named and how the Wa name themselves as a people, as well as how they define the world on their own terms. It's also why I will discuss the Chinese attempts to rename the Wa. In situations of inequality, such as in today's Chinese-dominated Wa lands, the power to select and assign names often becomes a key venue of confrontation. In these unequal struggles, one side tries to dominate or even erase the other by renaming and redefining them.

The most paradigmatic example of such domination by naming is of slaveholders throughout history changing the name of newly purchased slaves to show them and everyone else who was the new master. Another example of dominant

---

Endnotes for this chapter begin on page 69.

imposition of names is the requirement and imposition of surnames by modern state authorities in many places around the world to increase control over the populace; in situations of ethnic and cultural diversity, the imposition of new names will be in the dominant language, as local names are translated for the sake of "legibility" (Scott et al. 2002). Below I will also discuss how this process has played out in Wa country in the second half of the twentieth century and in the twenty-first century.

The Wa Naming System in Its Social Context

In the Wa setting, memorized genealogies of the personal names of successive patriclan ancestors remain highly important today. These genealogies once served as a historical memory of heroic moves across the landscape, linking the names of newly claimed places with each associated ancestor. They also give form to the memory of historical wars and to the refugee waves that occurred when former Wa lands were lost.

In the remembered genealogies, as the Wa became more sedentary and ceased migrating as they once had, the connections faded between forefathers and the places they lived, and genealogies instead began to serve mainly to affirm the possession of already settled land, and also to highlight the depth of the Wa presence now mythically traced back to the very origins of humanity, the *Sigang lih*. Even today, adults in central Wa country are expected, and most are able, to recite their own patriclan (*ntoung*) genealogy (*ndax*, "track") with the personal names of male ancestors. It is thus very important that each account properly traces each patriclan all the way back to the *Sigang lih*, the primordial event of humanity's emergence out of an aperture in the ground. This simultaneously reaffirms the origin myth and also gives each person a place within this narrative.

Historically, hundreds of such named *ntoung* are known from central Wa country,[1] which was divided on *jaig' qee*, Wa "realms"[2] made up of the ancestral village that was its original seat, and groupings of kindred villages established by clansmen in a process that combined fissioning with entrenchment. The clans themselves most likely formed and multiplied in that very process of territorialization. There are stories that refer to an ancient time without clans, when the Wa used only birth-order terms, and I speculate that these may refer to an era centuries ago when unlimited virgin forest land could be appropriated for swidden farming, and people could move through it freely (and alone, without necessarily encountering or confronting other people). But that kind of free expansion came to an end. The clans may have been created to manage a fixed territory, in turn producing a new context of social self-reproduction through the patriclan framework.

The data that I cite and discuss here derives mainly from what I learned about one particular realm (*jaig' qee*), that of Yong Ou, known in Chinese and Lahu as "Masan" and located in the "Big" or "Wild" Wa lands incorporated into new China in the 1950s. Today it lies immediately next to the new international border, which actually cuts directly through the realm. Its founder, Ou, is said to have set up an ancestor-village here seventeen generations ago. His name, literally "mute," also carries the senses of "dull," in the sense of "not easily thrown off balance." The multiple layers of meaning, as I understand them, suggest the traditional ambivalence surrounding *ai*, the elder brother, often expected to be less entrepreneurial than subsequent younger siblings who may venture into the unknown. But the other side of this coin shines brighter: he stays in his home, in order to serve important ritual functions on behalf of his kin. When the origin myths personify the "Wa" as *ai*, the "elder brother" of humankind as a whole, it is as humanity's supreme sacrificer-guardian.

Having arrived in search of promising forest lands, Ou stayed on, and he was reportedly joined by another man, A Meang (literally, "chief"). These two men became the ancestors of two of the most important local intermarrying patriclans, "Yong Ou" and "A Meang." Note that "Yong" in Wa means "village," and its very use in the formation of many clan names also suggests that the migration-settlement founding pattern was one of the ways in which clans and their names were first created.[3]

As the founder-village of Yong Ou grew into a realm or "circle" (the British term), it was elevated into a ritual ancestor center called Yong Ou Dax or Yong Ou Ting (the "Ancestral" or "Great" Yong Ou), with at least ten patriclans represented among its residents: Siu'ei, Yam, Muid Nku, Npoung Ki, Yong Glaih, Gon Qeim, Krim, and Si Ku, plus A Meang and the still-revered Yong Ou founder-clan. When recited, the *ndax ntoung* (genealogy) of one of these might sound like the following, from the late Blae Ge Jen,[4] a village elder in Yong Ou and member of the Yong Glaih clan residing there, who died only recently:

> Jen; Jen Van; Van Leid; Leid Sian; Sian Kri; Kri Soux; Soux Ki'eid; Ki'eid Lan; Lan Hou; Hou Boi; Boi Gan; Gan S'reng'; S'reng' Hong; Hong Peh; Peh Nge; Nge Ki'eim; Ki'eim Gang . . . daom eix dao Sigang [we come from the Sigang]![5]

The repetition of each name of paternal ancestors is a mnemonic device, which builds on the structure of the genitive in the Wa language, thus "Jen Van" means Van's Jen, that is: "Jen, son of Van."[6] This helpful device also is used as the short answer to the everyday question "Jen who?" ("Jen *pui*?" as in, "Now, which Jen are you talking about here?"). The true, full answer really would be the complete *ndax ntoung* above (the entirety of which is a Wa person's "full name"); but the

Figure 2.1. Blae Ge Jen, conducting a *hlax doh* sacrifice outside his house in Yong Ou. Photo by the author, 1998.

short form "Jen Van" is an abbreviation that is also used frequently in everyday life, to identify the speaker as "Jen, son of Van." Because the patriclan exogamy framework continues to govern kin relations today, these genealogies continue to be maintained even across the Wa lands annexed into China and placed under Chinese domination. This is true even though the patriclans have lost the political functions they once held in the past era of self-rule, when each such clan mattered beyond marriage taboos. For example, each clan was once associated with the ritual management of one of the village drum shrines, located at the endpoints of the water aqueducts built to lead water into the village-fortress.

Patriclans, Log Drums, and Drum Shrines

In a small village there might only be one drum shrine (*nyiex kroug*), but in big ones like Yong Ou there were multiple such shrines, which served as highly important focal points for various rituals and feasts; they also served as a means of communication, especially in wartime (such as in case of danger, or attack). Each drum shrine would take on special significance if the event in question concerned a member of the clan that built and cared for their particular shrine. (In the case of pan-village matters, as discussed in chapter 6, the shrine of the clan of the *O lang*, the ritual chief or high priest of the village, might become the focus instead of one of the other clans.)

The shrine was a simple structure: an open shed without walls covered with a grass roof (or occasionally with a roof made of interlocking bamboo tubes cut in half). The drum (*kroug*) was housed underneath. Its creation and installation was a lengthy process, from the selection and felling of the right giant tree, through the intriguing hollowing out of the tree's interior to make for the extraordinarily far-reaching sound of the drum, to the moment it was dragged home in the company of throngs of villagers. It was then made to "wait" for three days before being brought in through one of the village fortress gates. I won't cover all these topics here.[7]

I hasten to point out here that the Chinese burning of these log drums and drum shrines in the 1950s and 1960s should really be understood as underscoring their original importance as focal points of Wa social power organized around the clan kinship system. Compare how bronze drums were targeted for destruction by Chinese imperial armies during the Chinese conquest of what is now Southern China precisely because they too were the focal points of local political structures and therefore of resistance to the empire.[8]

The genealogies organized by clan obviously also serve as stores of personal names that might be recycled in later generations, but I should note that Wa clans do not seem to ever have "owned" personal names exclusively, as documented in other ethnographic contexts. Clan loyalty mattered in the past and still matters today, not least in terms of marriage options, but Wa kinship is also a framework for social relations in which power, under an ideology of fierce egalitarianism, is rather placed in the hands of each autonomous adult person, expressed not least in how naming remains the prerogative of parents.

Ethnonymy

We must underline again that the fabled *Sigang* aperture—expounded in origin myths, ubiquitous in everyday parlance as the endpoint that every genealogy is traced back to—signifies the legitimating claim that the Wa rightfully possess the lands where they live today. The Wa appeared first on earth and stayed around where they had emerged; non-Wa latecomers on earth had to move farther away (to China, America, etc.), and such modern-era outsiders moving into Wa lands to appropriate its riches are intruders. In the past, such definitions helped overcome internecine conflicts and unite the Wa. They form claims that combine the mythic and the "anti-mythic"[9]: in myths, otherworldly forces are credited with setting the basic conditions of existence (such as, that people eat cattle, and not vice versa); anti-myths explain the history, power, and influence of this-worldly fellow humans, as well as injustices such as the unequal distribution of the possession of writing systems, modern machinery, and weaponry, the loss of ancestral lands, etc.

The ideas about clans and their origins still form the bedrock of Wa self-identification as an ethnic identity, the systematic ethnonymy of names a society entertains for the known universe of other ethnic identities, including both self and others ("autonyms" vs. "exonyms"). Like personal names, each ethnonymy is never just a neutral catalogue of names for Others but is in itself a collection of fascinating instances of referential practice, packed with sediments of etymology and history. In Wa perspective, and parlance, the salient kinds of non-Wa foreigners are usually noted in the order of their appearance on history's stage: the Siam (e.g., Tai-speaking Shan), the Gui (e.g., Tibeto-Burman speaking Lahu or Muhso, nineteenth-century immigrants), the Houx (e.g., Chinese of different kinds, such as Muslim Chinese caravan traders whose long history in the region explains why Houx is occasionally mentioned ahead of Gui), the Man (Burmese), as well as (in some versions) the Kang (Kachin/Jingpo, known only in the northern Wa country) and Grax (Indo-European traders arriving through Burma from distant India, and any other Westerners: see the introduction, and chapter 1).

Ethnonymy is meaningful classification in social context,[10] and the Wa case also highlights how ethnonymy, as a complete set (both the autonyms used to define communities themselves and exonyms used for others), forms part of an autonomous ordering of the world, which both identifies the self in relation to others and, at the same time, creates a workable world map that aids in navigating it. Founded on a powerful historical narrative reinforced by memorized name genealogies, the Wa ethnonymy is linked with the patriclan framework within which Wa name themselves and their persons, both on the level of "a people" constituted in practice by the clans and of clan members, that is, individual, autonomous Wa persons. Nowadays, probably due to the post-1958 disruption of Wa autonomy and social order (which I will discuss further below), lacunae frequently appear in the famous genealogies—usually somewhere in the less salient, hard-to-remember middle. But the most recent string of forebears is nearly always remembered, along with the crucial early sequence that connects with the primordial beginning of humankind and qualifies each Wa person as sharing, through the clan, in the potency of that narrative. This applies both to men and to women, who are often as eloquent as men are in remembering their lineage. For all the emphasis on patriliny, women's personal names have a strong presence (e.g., they are listed first in references to couples), and women have strong voices in Wa society even though its descent as well as the mnemonic framework for recalling it is organized through patriliny.[11]

Wa Personal Names

The macro level of ethnonymy and the micro level of personal naming are strikingly linked through the identification of the Wa in their role as *ai*, oldest sibling of humanity's family. The importance of birth order extends in the main form of personal naming, under which children in each nuclear family are enumerated by nine birth-order terms that combine with the name of the weekday of the birth to form the name of a person. This core "name type" of the Wa given name (here using the terminology of Macdonald's [2009] groundbreaking theory) consists of two parts: a birth-order designation, and a weekday name (or, a substitute given name). This arrangement seems to apply across Wa country, with only slight geographical variation.[12] Other Wa name types include nicknames, which are discussed briefly below, posthumous names for the recently dead, and kinship terms that often can either replace or accompany given names in everyday speech. The clan names, important as they are as an organizing structure, aren't used in everyday speech. They figure mostly in the background and serve as an actively used name type only on serious and formal occasions internal to local Wa society, and not historically in foreign relations (which, as we shall see, matters in the convoluted story of how Chinese surnames were imposed on the Wa, when clan names were also explicitly deployed in the Chinese rendering as part of everyday personal names).

Let me first focus on the standard personal name, which is binomial, combining two parts. First, the birth-order term—by virtue of birth order, sons are known by one of the following nine terms for boys only: *ai, nyi, soi, sai, sam, laog, niu, meig', uig'*. Daughters are known by one of the terms for girls only: *yiex, ei, og, ui, am, eib, iad, ou, uig'*. The last name on both these lists, *uig'*, also means "the last." However, if one has more than nine children of either sex (as has actually happened in the past), number ten again is either *ai*, or *yiex*, respectively. The second part of the personal name consists of the name of the day of the week on which one was born. In Yong Ou, the Wa week has nine days,[13] named *brag, hrax, naom, raong, goum, s'rom, riex, miong, o*. These names of the days of the week double as basic building blocks of personal names, and thus we have the two-part names. Examples of classical-sounding, ubiquitous Wa names are Ai Naom and Nyi Raong for men, and Yiex Goum and Og Miong for women.[14] (These names surely denote *with* connotation, namely the connotation of Wa identity.)

A certain flexibility in the system allows for not always using the two parts together. For example, in my case, born on a day assumed to have been "Riex," and me being the middle child but the eldest son of my parents, my Wa name becomes Ai Riex. In everyday situations, I might be called either the full "Ai Riex" (which is slightly formal), simply "Riex" (especially by familiar people of my age), or simply "Ai."

The latter would often be politely used, in common fashion, by people who don't necessarily know my given name or even birth-order position ("Hey, Ai, where are you going?"). If more conversation follows, people might follow up with questions like, "That's it? You're an *ai*? Or is it *nyi*?" Local people are treated in the same way, especially since Wa villages may comprise several hundred people (it used to be more: in many places, settlements are but shadows of their once formidable size with thousands of inhabitants in one fortress-village), so few can know the formal names of every single person, especially not of the children.

Among the Wa, kinship relations, especially clan membership, are well known by all. These elements serve as the main framework for social relations, the tabooing of sexual relations between members of the same patriclan, etc. Kinship terms may often be appropriate in place of personal names, as when young people address a person of the previous generation: if an older man is an agnate, a member of one's own clan, one calls him *geeing* (uncle; also an alternate for "birth father"), or for a woman, *mex* (aunt; also means "birth mother"); for an older man from another clan, i.e. a potential affine, one uses *boux* ("maternal uncle"), or for a woman, *ting* ("maternal aunt"), leaving out their personal names. Elders can be addressed minimally as *dax* for men or *ya* for women; these terms can also be used as a prefix, together with the given name. As mentioned, in death the person is spoken of with the honorific prefix Blae (and Ge, which together means something like "The late . . ."), plus the given name.

Note that it is precisely for lack of patriclan affiliation that a foreigner cannot participate fully in Wa society. The lack means that in my own case, for example, there is no answer to the important question, "Riex who?" The foreigner is nobody's kin, and my own Wa name remains little more than a matter of convenience, and a joke of sorts—which by contrast highlights the enduring importance of the clan system for the "anchoring" of ordinary Wa persons, male and female, even though the clan names are seldom used in everyday life.

Among people of the same generation, personal names are mainly used in everyday address, and they are mandatory when referring to a couple, then always starting with the woman's given name (as in, for example, "Brag *ha* Kam"). Women who have become mothers, when they are a topic of conversation, are also often spoken of in the third person, by the given name or weekday name only, plus the suffix "*ha*," for example, "Huan *ha*." When addressed in person, one uses the peculiar and very convenient Wa dual pronoun *ba*, "you two," which is also used for mother and (small) child, and also for a mother, even if her child isn't present.

In the case of people older than oneself, personal names can also be combined with kin terms, again dropping the birth-order part of the binomial autonyms (as in "Geeing Van," Uncle Van; or "Box Jen," maternal Uncle Jen). When the audience is multigenerational or when one is speaking across a generational boundary, teknonymy is also widely used (though not mandatory). It can involve grandparents (e.g., *dax* Naom Gin, "Gin, grandfather of Naom") but mainly is used for fathers or mothers with the given name of their first, or oldest, living child. For example, *mex* Hrax, "the mother of Hrax," leaves out the mother's personal name, and one can only be sure that she is not herself Hrax because children are rarely if ever given the same weekday name as either parent, even if they are born on the same weekday.

This circumstance is but one of several that can actually prompt the giving of a name other than a weekday name. Names (*ngai*) are given right after birth by the parents themselves, or by an older clan member present on the occasion (on the associated ceremonies, see too Tin Yee 2004: 70-75). Names are usually retained over a lifetime, except in cases where the child encounters accidents or disease (the result of evil spirit attacks). In such cases, village oracles will often declare that the name is taboo (*tueh*) and should be changed (*vai*, which conveys the sense of "repair"), and they will suggest making the required sacrifices for warding off spirit attacks (see chapter 8).

In such situations, it is again usually the parents that decide on a new name. They may, following traditional practice, choose a name that advertises to the evil spirits that the child is someone they wouldn't want. In this case, common words like *diag* ("throw-away") and *nbri* ("dirt") are used for boys' names; *brah* ("leave aside" or "leave behind") and *gam* ("[rice] chaff," e.g., "unwanted"), etc., for girls. Some are used for both sexes, like *s'reng'* ("disdain," as in the disdain or disgust one may feel for something unclean; or it can mean "to avoid, out of disgust," as in the oft-heard moral exhortation, *Po s'reng' nah kod* [Do not disdain/avoid old people because you think they are unbecoming]).

Even the verb *vai*, "change," can be used: Vai ("changed") can be such a new, substitute name. And this kind of name substitution is quite common, especially the first few examples (Diag, Nbri, Brah, Gam; also Vai, etc.). Strange as it may seem, these carry no stigma at all. Every member of society is aware of what is really the intended audience. An interesting variation is when birth-order names are shuffled to fool the spirits (one can even rename boys using girls' birth-order names, and vice versa). The name is a name, it is a label to go with you, but it is not the totality of who you are.

Moreover, instead of weekday designations, other given names may be substituted by the parents. Some names will be recycled, some invented anew, whether at birth or in response to misfortune. Like weekday names, they are used in combination with a birth-order term. They often lack explicit lexical meanings, but parents choose them for ease of pronunciation and pleasant sound. Examples of names other than weekday names used in Yong Ou in recent memory include, for men, Kiad, Vui, Ven, Man, Hah, Hian, Jang, Dang, Diam, Song, De, Nte, Nge, Teh, Leang, Li, Tu, Bai, and Gou; for women, Huan, Heim, Heng, Hang, Ham, Peh, Pen', Puad, Mah, Ah, Briad, Kruad, La, Loid', S'rie, Suan, Jang, and Guoi. (Unlike the weekday names, few of these names are "unisex").

As mentioned, some of these conferred names follow historical ancestors, and one then talks about the naming as a case of *plug ngai*, "filling in the name." Others are chosen explicitly to resonate with birth-order designations or to appear alongside fathers' names in the inevitable recitations of genealogies. Thus *ban* ("grove," or "stand" of a plant) was once chosen for the son of a certain Riex—itself not just the name of a weekday but also the word for banyan tree, thus Ban Riex ("Ban, son of Riex," which sounds like "Banyan tree stand," evoking a positive image and at the same time serving to name a person the culturally proper way).

Is it getting complicated? Yes—and this is testimony to the point I flagged early on: this is indeed a culturally distinct naming system. Sometimes, there is humor or irony involved: a father named Sen recently had one daughter beyond the limit set by the Chinese government, and therefore faced penalties for what the Chinese call *chao sheng* (excessive births). She was named Qao; thus every time she is mentioned as his daughter ("Qao Sen," Sen's daughter, Qao), this "excess" (*chao sheng*) is recalled.

Occasionally, such seemingly whimsical names revert to traditional names when the child meets with disease, requiring a name change. Thus, a boy named Lu (Chinese for "road," after his mother gave birth on the road), was later renamed using the ancestral Qi. This also exemplifies the widespread present wavering between the Wa repertoire and the now-fashionable adoption of Chinese words as Wa names (fueled by the resigned—but practical—insight that "We now live in *nqu* Houx [the 'Chinese-dominated era']").[15]

Names that refer to an event or circumstance at the time of birth include Pi, "forgotten" (the name of a man whose father died before he was born); Kuad, "cold" (evoking the weather on the day of his birth); Kan, suggesting a difficult birth; etc. However, many seemingly meaningful names, even those explicitly recommending a wariness toward evil spirits (as in Kui, "careful," "slow"), are not always acknowledged as such. When asked, people will typically emphasize the freedom of the parents to do whatever they like; only the name must sound good to the ears. But this surely involves not only phonetic but also social and cultural values, and this unspoken standard also covers other names with obvious lexical meanings but unclear implications. For example, Soux ("dog"), rarely used today but figuring in several Yong Ou genealogies, and in some areas Lig ("pig") have served as names. One scholar (Li Daoyong 1992: 337) suggests these names are applied with the express intention for the children to grow up quickly, like these animals do, but I found it difficult to confirm this.

Nicknames, invariably descriptive, are attached to given names (e.g., Nbrah Hled, "Nbrah the Deaf") but never replace them. The famous Ou ("dull" or "slow") is sometimes thought to have been a descriptive nickname that stuck; others say it was given to harmonize nicely with the name of his own father, O, to produce the melodious "Ou O" (Ou, O's son).

In instances of adoption, yet another kind of name change has also historically occurred. The names of children purchased in this trade, occurring mainly within

Wa country, seem to have been left unchanged except in the case of disease or other trouble (see chapter 5). However, in headhunting warfare, children might be spared, taken as war captives, and renamed. In the 1940s, one such boy was captured, adopted into a clan, and given the new name Pun ("captured"), memorializing the defining event and marking him as a perpetual newcomer. (Eventually, this new name was undone under Chinese rule when he returned to his ravaged home village and reverted to his previous name.)

All in all, the key point about Wa naming is that the Wa, like many other peoples around the world, have historically constructed a highly complex and astoundingly rich, yet at the same time flexible and highly viable, *system* of naming in their own language, and this has obviously formed a crucial part in their society's self-reproduction.

Renaming of the Chinese Other: Historical Precedents

The Wa lands were once far "beyond the pale" of Chinese civilization, but as in the past, wherever there is Chinese rule, Chinese names are assigned. In addition, China's version of modern territorial nation-state ideology (Scott's *Seeing like a State*) dictates that Chinese names are to be given to every person, and thus even the Wa must now be classified, named, enumerated, and processed into the sort of statistics that the state machinery relies on for taxation, population control, and so on.[16]

Earlier, in imperial times, Chinese officials on these distant southern frontiers would at most issue Chinese names to native elites, including the local lieutenants known as *tusi* (native chiefs).[17] These imperial proxies would get *xing* (Chinese surnames, of which only a limited range is available) as well as *ming* (personal names, reflecting the particular individuals' service to the empire and linking them directly with Chinese imperial power and civilization). Because of the potential benefits of rising above fellow non-Chinese natives, and attaching oneself directly to superior sources of political, military, and commercial power, there were also many spurious claims to Chinese ancestry—as when self-interested *tusi* would claim to be *not* natives but descendants of Chinese soldiers deserving recognition for conquering their "barbarian" lands.[18]

Unlike the modern nation-state situation in which every single citizen is meant to be counted, most imperial-era Chinese renaming seems to have been limited to such local elites. However, indigenous populations might also switch to Chinese naming practices, and even lose their language entirely, in areas where they have become marginalized minorities in their own lands due to heavy immigration of Chinese settlers. Such processes were at work even after the native chief system began to be dismantled from the early 1700s onward and more indigenous peoples instead came to be governed directly by "regular" officials—who further promoted Chinese naming as part of the process of registering new subjects for taxation and control.

Many non-Chinese peoples, even those nominally governed by a *tusi*, would of course still not be affected by any such naming impositions but simply would continue to name themselves according to local practice, in non-Chinese languages. In the case of the Wa, who were mostly beyond Chinese domination up until the 1950s, Chinese names were not used at all before the modern period.

Before the 1950s, Chinese as well as Burmese presence in the vicinity of the Wa was sporadic, consisting of, for example, opium and salt traders, mining adventurers, and military expeditioners. Few Wa knew any Chinese or Burmese, and officials from those governments dealt with the Wa mainly through intermediaries (mainly Shan, and Lahu). This is revealed in the older Chinese ethnonym "Ka-wa" or "Ka-la" for the Wa, using the Shan (Tai) terms "Wa" or "La/Lua" plus the prefix *Khaa*, which refers to non-Buddhist, "primitive" people, "natural slaves." "Ka" wasn't dropped from Chinese until the 1950s, when government anthropologists charged with classifying and renaming the non-Chinese peoples of China came to realize its separate meaning.[19]

After their 1949 victory in China's civil war, the Communists imposed direct control over imperial China's former peripheries to an extent only hoped for, but never realized, by Republican-era governments (1911–49). Chinese troops were sent to Wa country as early as 1951–52, but they were withdrawn from some occupied Wa areas ceded by China to Burma when the international boundary was finally agreed upon and installed in 1960, dividing the Wa lands.[20] In 1958, conciliation collapsed, and a minor Wa-Chinese war in the central Wa country sent waves of Wa refugees into Burma. There has been no challenge to Chinese rule since. Within China—as in the Burmese parts of the Wa lands, later taken over by the Chinese-supported Burmese Communist Party and by the China-aligned Wa State—much of the Wa social order was disrupted: the crucial drum shrines and the associated clan-based forest, land, and water management systems were destroyed or abandoned. Chinese institutions were imposed by army-backed "work teams," which featured government ethnographers preparing for subordination and integration into the Chinese state and economy. As a prerequisite for inclusion into the new state structure, non-Han peoples were reclassified as "minority nationalities"; their native institutions of power and wealth were analyzed and targeted for "reform." Only since the 1980s has the transformation of Chinese state management of rural areas permitted a partial restoration of self-governance, religious practices, etc.

Collecting and recording the names of each person was critical for this project of a "modern-scientific," "multinational" nation-state under Chinese command. But how would Wa people be named and their names written in Chinese?[21] At the outset, "minority" policies expressly included respect for local customs, including naming, and real linguists and anthropologists participated in the research. This explains why, initially, scientific Chinese reports list ethnic Wa names in phonetic transcriptions using Chinese characters—awkward, but it's at least an attempt to account both for clan and personal names. Wa clan names (*ntoung*) were often placed first, in Chinese fashion, while Wa people (including both illiterate villagers and Wa writers educated in missionary traditions) tend to place them last, likely because of how the Wa themselves emphasize the given personal names (and the persons), as well as reciting genealogy, but not the clan names (which are missing from the genealogies).

This practice of demanding to know the clan names and recording them as if they were surnames was observed by knowledgeable Chinese ethnographers who were to some extent sympathetic to the locals in their charge, and who were also mindful of choosing neutral or positive characters from Chinese sets ordinarily used to transcribe foreign names. It was, however, soon abandoned in favor of the historical Chinese practice of assigning Chinese-style *xing* (surnames) and *ming* (given names).[22] One reason for this was the education level and chauvinist outlook of state, party, and military officials who would not learn Wa, and who envisioned a totally Chinese-speaking future. The difference between different Chinese officials has been in how fast this assimilation would arrive: From the 1950s onward, most Chinese Communist officials and the state-employed ethnographers, saw their overall task as ensuring a peaceful but steady expansion of Chinese control; this general policy was disrupted by the more aggressive interventionism of 1958[23] and by the so-called Cultural Revolution and its "Political Frontier Defense" episode in 1969–71 (Schoenhals 2004).[24] Local Wa people remember this period as a dark time, when some Wa were incited by the Chinese to denounce and attack other Wa, and many died.[25] Today we are apparently seeing a new, similarly dramatic policy shift (see the epilogue).

Either way, imposition of the Chinese language, in the shape of spoken Yunnanese dialect and written standard Chinese, was and is generally perceived by government officials as modernization through Sinicization, as a Chinese "Manifest Destiny." I heard this echoed in many private comments by contemporary officials, who would insist—off the record, mindful of the still official policy of respecting the minority nationalities as entities to be recognized and respected—that the Wa language must be destined to die out, eventually, and be replaced by the inherently superior Chinese language.

This widely shared idea of a Chinese "Manifest Destiny" meant that after the initial period of transcription of Wa names into Chinese, mostly done by diligent scholars, the Chinese administration and school officials who took over later eventually shifted toward assigning Chinese names, as in imperial times—but for everyone.

Initially, however, in the Yong Ou area, the Chinese occupying force took pragmatic cues from local Lahu who lived in close association with the Wa, whose men the Lahu would call "Ai," and the women "Na."²⁶ These terms were copied in official Chinese transliterations and used as surnames (!) for Wa people instead of clan names. But, unfortunately, "Ai" used as a Chinese surname soon causes an unmanageable proliferation of duplicates, as if the Wa were all "surnamed" Ai and Na,²⁷ and this confusion became a contributing reason why Chinese names later began to be assigned. Now the Wa would be organized in line with the time-tested Chinese administrative model of a one-syllable ordinary Chinese surname, plus a Chinese personal name (*ming*, in either one or two syllables; some attempts were still made to transcribe into Chinese the basic Wa birth-order position plus weekday name and use that as a Chinese *ming*).

Because of the stark differences in Chinese and Wa phonetics, representations of Wa in written Chinese cannot be accurate. They can't, for example, account for either the initial consonant cluster or the final consonant of the ubiquitous weekday name Brag—instead, three Chinese words awkwardly make "Bu-la-ge" (alternatively reduced to "Bu-la" to conform with the normative two-character limit and dispensing with the Wa final "-g"); similarly, the common name Hrax in this mode is written with the character for *la* (obscuring the initial and omitting the glottal stop expressed in the Wa orthographies as "x"); Naom as "Na" or "Nao"; Raong as "Long"; Goum as "Gao"; and so on. This is the sad mess of ambiguous transliterations that nowadays can be found in tax and population registers, on Chinese national ID cards, etc.

The wholesale assignment of Chinese surnames started in earnest after 1958, when Chinese policy shifted decisively from conciliatory to activist. The surnames generally derive from the limited sets acceptable for Han Chinese, and they have been successively imposed for every Wa person on Chinese territory who is now identified as yet another Zhang, Wei, Li, Chen, Yang, Xiao, Tian, or Zhao (which are among the most common). The surname precedes transliterations of Wa personal names (for adults and others who never attended Chinese school), or a *ming* with typical, explicit Chinese meanings, like those often assigned to Chinese-schooled Wa by their teachers (say, for example, Chen Xueming [Chen "Study Bright"] or Li Jianhua [Li "Build China"]).²⁸ Such Wa persons now have fully "Chinese" identities, and if they belong to the ranks of cadres or businessmen living in county seats, who emulate Chinese ways in many respects, then they may speak Yunnanese Chinese instead of Wa at work and at home, and the complete disuse of Wa naming and decisive departure from Wa identity may already be a reality.

One can also say that at least two distinct types of Wa people were created: those who are Sinicized in almost everything except a formal identity (but with some memory of descent from Wa ancestors, and who self-identify as Wa even though they cannot speak the language), and those who continue living in rural areas and preserve Wa kinship and naming practices. Those in the latter group speak Wa as a primarily language even as many of them, too, take on Chinese as a secondary language and adopt Chinese names alongside their Wa names, and whose young generation nowadays often travels east to China's industrial cities for work (see also chapter 5).

This situation, with successively Sinicized officials and city dwellers and predominantly subordinate general populations of ethnic Wa in the countryside, has direct parallels across the border in the Wa State of Burma. Chinese language is spoken and Chinese currency used in the marketplace; official publications are often only issued in Chinese; place names sometimes appear in Chinese rather than Wa; and state leaders (under Chinese influence, compounded by the failure to promote Wa writing as well as the legacies of historical fragmentation) are often publicly known mainly by their Chinese names, complete with *xing* and *ming*. (When Burmese people today sometimes conclude that the Wa "are Chinese," they are overstating it, but they are not totally off the mark.)

Chinese *xing* have not been assigned altogether randomly. The Chinese recognition of the existence of Wa clan affiliations, the mistaken equivalence of clan names with surnames, and the cohesion of Wa clans have all contributed to certain historically contingent consistencies. For example, when Yam clansmen were registered, the Chinese surname Yang seemed close at hand because of the phonetic proximity. After several decades, the association of Yam with Yang is beginning to be taken for granted by clan members themselves. Absent any such instant similarity, certain clans now still have come to associate themselves with particular Chinese surnames—even when it varies by locality. Various clans may also get the same surname: at least twenty-three central Wa clan names have been subsumed under the ubiquitous "Zhang," which also happens to be one of the most common surnames in China, whose bearers number in the hundreds of millions.

Wa naming is still the default system in rural areas, where few people are bilingual. But decades of Chinese schooling has now already created a situation where many rural persons see themselves as having two sets of names. Even before the recent wave of work migration to eastern Chinese cities, this binomial reality has come to seem more and more natural. As time goes by, propositions like, for example, "We in the Siu'ei clan, we *xing* Li" come to seem self-evident, signaling the beginning of the end for the Wa patriclans as cornerstones of an autonomous generative framework. After a few generations, the process creates the illusion that a fixed Chinese *xing* is but a translation, when in reality it indexes an already effective social transformation. The next steps might be the abandonment of Wa kinship, genealogies, and even land claims they embodied, or the emulation of the cadre-class practice of complete Sinification.

The change from autonomous Wa clan rule to Chinese governance (where subjects are named, counted, taxed, and controlled) can thus be seen as a default transformation accompanying the demise of autonomous social structures in the face of conquest and overwhelming resettlement, among other things. This can be traced not least in the Shunning, Zhenkang, and Yongde Counties north of the central Wa lands, where the immigration of Han Chinese into areas formerly dominated by Mon-Khmer speakers has a centuries-long history (see the introduction to this book). Settlers in some remote areas melted into local cultures, but many remained Chinese and claimed land for themselves. They would not entertain the sort of respect and fear of the old ghosts of the land once displayed by the Shan when immigrating into the region. These settlers, in contrast to the fleeting Shan galaxy of Buddhist principalities, were in a position to demand Chinese law and order.

Traveling there in the late 1990s, I realized that local Chinese still acknowledge the local Wa people there as *benren*, "autochthonous people," which is used as if it were the name of a minority people. Some of these Benren[29] still speak Wa and retain elements of their culture; in terms of power relations, however, they have wholly lost the native structures that previously governed their social life, and they came to live like landless peasants of Chinese landlords. In the 1950s, they unexpectedly encountered Communist government land reforms and received recognition as Wa, an officially acknowledged ethnic minority. This was unexpected because of the preceding centuries of subjugation, in which no such recognition had been forthcoming other than in the shape of discrimination. It was accepted, and in the new atmosphere of ethnic revival since the 1980s, some Benren are even seeking to "retranslate" themselves as Wa, by finding and reviving Wa equivalents to their current Chinese names, revealing further the central relationship between naming and power.

The End of Wa Naming?

After journeying briefly to these northern former Wa areas, including especially Zhenkang County, and having returned to central Wa country where I was doing field research, I related what I had learned about the Benren to my long-standing interlocutors there. Some of what I had to say was no surprise: these "Wa" or Benren must be the people of the widely known stories about terrible past wars when many Wa were forced to flee south from those northern lands. According to these stories, some of the Wa forged ahead, reaching what is now central Wa country, leaving their brethren behind but cutting forest plantains (*ge muah*)[30] along their path for the benefit of stragglers who would follow the path to catch up. However, when the stragglers finally did come along, the plantains had already shot up again by so much that the stragglers figured they would never catch up, and so they decided to stay behind. These, then, became the Benren, and it is no wonder that they were compelled to "Sinicize" in the ways I described.[31]

But one point of my account deeply offended several knowledgeable community members (who, I must add, had never traveled to Zhenkang themselves). This was my claim that Zhenkang "Wa" had no *ntoung* (patriclans). If so, I must be mistaken in claiming that they were, indeed, Wa. Perhaps they claimed to be Wa, and even spoke something I heard as Wa, but without *ntoung*, how could they be Wa? I countered that those Wa had once traveled down the same road that the Wa in the central Wa country were now traveling: although there are still Wa *ntoung* with attendant marriage rules, and even if the role of the clans is being revived in some aspects of agroforestry management, would not the Chinese names people are adopting alongside their Wa names and increasingly regard as part of their identity not lead to giving up the *ntoung* altogether, in the future? "Never!" was the answer.

Perhaps indeed the Wa, in their "peripheral situation," can continue a dual system under which they name and govern themselves to a limited extent, even while they are simultaneously named again, so as to be governed from the outside—this remains to be seen. Alternatively, a distinction of more Chinese-like and more "Wa-like" Wa may emerge in the short term, much like is already happening in Chinese-ruled Wa areas today.[32]

The social arena on which Wa persons are realized—where one becomes Wa and where Wa ways are continuously reproduced and creatively refashioned by the very persons formed within those same viable, generative sets of sociologics—depends for its sustainability on some measure of cultural if not political autonomy as its foundation. The naming system's viability and the right to name oneself are obviously among the most salient expressions of this autonomy, reaffirmed every time the name for one's own people is reiterated—even when it merely figures as a silent foundation, as with the named clans absent from most explicit forms of address and barely figuring as a name type but which create the true Wa person, in the view of most people in the central Wa lands. The link to land claims is still seen as crucial there, as the Wa make up the overwhelming majority and their stake in the territory continues to be meaningful.[33] From the perspective of these Wa in the old central Wa lands, if the "remaining" minority Wa (Benren) in the north are named only in Chinese, it is a sure sign that they are reduced to guests in their own land, as a subset of Chinese.

Perhaps such reductions are the ultimate goal of the modern state policies for the assimilation of everyone. Because of the high stakes involved in the naming of persons, kin groups, ethnicities, or other social entities and their associated claims, they will quickly become a focus for external forces challenging the autonomous structures where the power to name is lodged. Even when externally imposed names merely appear to duplicate and coexist with indigenous naming practice, seizing the power to define what are "official" names has crucial importance, since it is key to controlling food production and trade, armaments, freedom of movement, etc., as well as, more importantly, harnessing and exploiting (re)named land and its natural resources.

At Yong Ou, people can point out vast lands recognized in the past as controlled or "owned" by their *jaig' qee* realm; under the Chinese-configured economy of representations, much of the land and its resources are exploited by state agroforestry and other industries. No licenses are paid: it is clear that the once-powerful *jaig' qee* Yong Ou is not only obsolete today but also actively obscured. Its name is ignored, to block its claims, and the Wa of these areas have in fact been reduced to the classic "peripheral situation" (Turner 1986).

It remains to be seen whether the Wa as a whole (including the majority Wa areas in Burma, now under heavy Chinese influence) will indeed become a subset of the Chinese, or if some different kind of accommodation will be found. One curious hint appears in the fact that domestic animals in central Wa country nowadays often have Chinese names, given partly in jest, as if jokingly, and partly in mockery. The Wa have a limited range of *kreng ei* (*kreng*, "belongings"; *ei*, "to raise"): dogs, pigs, chickens, buffalo, and cattle. Nowadays, with the exception of chicken, these are all given names in Chinese: Xiao Hua, "Little Flower," etc. (the chicken's turnaround is perhaps too rapid for them to be given names).

This Wa "Sinification" of their own animals may seem oddly out of line,[34] but it mirrors the Wa anti-myths that poke fun at powerful outsiders while also recognizing the overwhelming powers that the Wa must negotiate. Granted, in the world we live in, the main characteristic of human-animal relations is, after all, that animals are dominated by humans and work for them, and they are even killed and eaten by them. But as the origin myths already recognized, things could very well have been the other way around.

Notes

* This chapter draws in part on my 2009 contribution, "The Autonomy of Naming: Kinship, Power and Ethnonymy in the Wa Lands of the Southeast Asia-China Frontiers," in *Personal Names in Asia: History, Culture and Identity*, ed. Zheng Yangwen and Charles J-H Macdonald (Singapore: NUS Press), 150–74.

1. Luo Zhiji (1995: 223) suggests there were 125 such clans just in what is now the Wa Autonomous County of Ximeng; see also Luo et al. 1986, and Xiao Zegong 1990.
2. Twelve British colonial-era writers called them "circles," the Chinese more recently use "tribes" (*buluo*), a term derived from older Western and Japanese anthropology.
3. See Luo Zhiji 1995: 225ff., 232ff.
4. Both "Blae" and "Ge" are honorific terms attached to the names of recently deceased elders, as they ultimately vanish and become unnamed, threatening ancestor spirits (*ge meang*).

5. Wa field notes, 1997: XV:81.
6. The patronym we encounter here may look like "a kind of surname" (cf. Watkins et al. 2006, "The Wa System of Personal Names"), even if it is not—it isn't permanent, and shifts with each generation.
7. For more on the wooden log drums, see the references in the introduction, note 43; on their association with war and headhunting, see chapter 6; on the contemporary fate of these exotic drums, including their appearance in the Chinese ethno–theme parks, see chapter 10.
8. Bernet Kempers (1988: 390–91) noted several such instances, including one account describing how, in 1573, Chinese imperial forces killed sixty bronze drum-owning "rebel" leaders in Guangxi Province and captured a total of ninety-three of their bronze drums, reportedly used to summon the warriors of the local communities—just the way that the Wa log drums would also have been used.
9. See Da Matta 1971, and especially Turner 1988.
10. Bruck and Bodenhorn (2006: 8–10) note that Claude Lévi-Strauss, in his discussion of names in *The Savage Mind*, left behind the more nuanced insights of Marcel Mauss on how names simultaneously identify and classify (Mauss 1985 [1938]).
11. For a comparative view of Chinese women's namelessness and incomplete personhood, see Watson 1986.
12. The terms I quote here are those used in Yong Ou. See also the comparative chart "The Wa System for Personal Names" in the Wa Dictionary project at SOAS (Watkins et al. 2006). A full comparison of Wa, Shan, Lahu, and Burmese naming remains to be carried out. In Burmese, too, part of weekday names are regularly used to form given names (I thank San San Hnin Tun, earlier at Cornell University, for pointing this out; see also Brac de La Perrière 1999). Certain Wa terms including "Ai" are shared with the neighboring Shan, whose naming system also deploys birth-order terms in personal names but is otherwise different, due to the marked hierarchies in Shan society (Ai San 1992). Wa and Shan (and the Burmese) are very old neighbors (cf. Liu 2009), and mutual borrowings and influences have certainly occurred but are comparatively less evident in central Wa country and more so on the Wa peripheries, which are generally overrepresented in Chinese publications on Wa customs.
13. The names of Wa weekdays differ with the locality, as does the length of the week (from seven to ten days). Local events are divined based on the local calendar, but just as elsewhere in the region one also keeps track of the ten-day Shan week in order to catch the larger marketplaces running on a five-day cycle (as is still done today, even as the "Chinese" Gregorian calendar is also gaining currency).
14. When birth-order terms and weekday names become "name tags" in personal names, they are appropriately capitalized as proper names.
15. Few scholars have studied this shift or the intermingling of Wa and Chinese naming and the clash between Wa and Chinese naming *systems*, which I discuss below, in the next section. For example, Zhao Furong (2005: 83) says only that the use of Chinese-sounding names is a widespread fashion, but without further discussion. As elsewhere, he seems to be taking as a yardstick the peripheral Wa, not the central Wa.
16. On the reconfiguration of non-Chinese peoples as "minority nationalities" in the new Chinese nation-state, replacing earlier imperial-era designations as barbarians, see Fiskesjö 1999a; 2006; and 2011b; also Tapp 2002; Leibold 2007; Yang Bin 2009b.
17. See the introduction.
18. One of the best publications on this complex process of conflicting and shifting loyalties and identities across China's southwest is Faure and Ho 2013.
19. Fiskesjö 2006, 2011b; on the term *Khaa*, see also Chit Phumisak 1992; Proschan 1996.

20. For a Chinese scholarly summary and perspective on this period, see Luo Zhiji 1995 (esp. 416–47); for a Burmese perspective, quite similar in the view of the Wa as backward and sorely in need of outside intervention, see Sai Kham Mong 1996, 1997.
21. Note that even though an alphabet already existed for the Wa language, it seemed too closely associated with its missionary inventors for the Communist Chinese regime, and Latin letters were also unfamiliar to most Chinese—even though a new alphabetic transcription system of their own language (the pinyin system) was also being introduced at this time. In addition, an unfortunate central policy was adopted that any minority writing system must adhere closely to the sound values set in the pinyin system—thus, unfortunately, a second Wa writing system was created on the China side (see Yan Qixiang 1981; Zhou Zhizhi 1992; also see the introduction), yet it was only halfheartedly promoted. The ensuing confusion has slowed the growth of Wa literacy.
22. On Chinese naming conventions, and the importance of the surname (*xing*) as an organizing device, see Scott et al. 2002; Ebrey 1996; Alleton 1993; Yuan Yuliu 1994; Zhang Lianfang 1992; Blum 1997; Nari Bilige 2000; as well as Zheng Yangwen 2009. One of the most penetrating recent monographs on naming among ethnic minorities in China and their interdigitation with Chinese practices is Chen Meiwen 2003.
23. This involved the suppression of resistance and a push for "social reforms" to break down existing social formations. It was a policy shift that affected all of China's peripheries ranging from the Wa lands to Tibet, but which have so far not been studied together by China scholars.
24. During the Cultural Revolution, Maoist Chinese Communists pushed straight up to the borders to root out any "class enemies" and push for further instant change of "backward" non-Han peoples, with total disregard for local conditions and nominal autonomy. In the words of Mao's powerful wife Jiang Qing: "Why do we need national minorities anyway? National identity should be done away with! . . . If you follow socialism, why worry about ethnicity?" (cited in Gladney 1991: 138, 203).
25. During the "Political Frontier Defense" of 1969–1971, in the Wa Autonomous County Ximeng and three neighboring counties, 718 people were persecuted to death ("dying from unnatural causes") and 3,950 households were wholly or partly confiscated (Schoenhals 2004: 44).
26. On Lahu naming, see He Jiren 1992; and on Lahu-Wa naming interaction (but *cum grano salis*) Zhao Furong 2005: 82–91. Zhao explains that the Lahu "Na" originates with a female deity and is customarily used in women's names and often coupled with a birth-hour (!) name. The corresponding male term is "Ja"; it is not clear why the Lahu wouldn't apply it to the Wa.
27. This was as Winnington (1959: 133) heard it in 1957.
28. In some cases, these special assigned Chinese surnames carried particular meanings—for example, the Bao of the singular Wa chiefs of Banlong, who are said to have "protected" (in Chinese, *bao*) China against British aggression in the 1930s. In areas closer to the imperial center, it is more common to find "irregular" Chinese-style surnames marking even assimilated people as different, as in the case of the Tujia who have largely lost their language (Brassett and Brassett 2005).
29. On the Benren, see also Zhao Mingsheng 2013, who gives their current number as forty thousand in these three Yunnan counties: Zhenkang, Yongde, and Tengchong.
30. The different species of wild plantain are very important in Wa country because they are the main staple food for domestic pigs: they are cut in the forest, and the trunks or stems are carried home, sliced, cooked lightly with water in a huge pot, and then offered to the pigs. They grow extremely fast (but, somehow, attempts to grow them inside the villages are not always successful).

31. These stories probably do reflect in part the historical explanation for the presence of scattered remaining populations of Mon-Khmer speakers in otherwise Chinese-dominated Zhenkang, etc.
32. This might be similar to the case of Hmong distinguishing "Chinese Hmong" among themselves, based on the transformation of burial customs (cf. Tapp 1989: 161ff.)—but the Hmong, though also stateless, have a much farther spread, a much more powerful international presence, and an increasingly elaborate global identity (Tapp 2010).
33. Note the insightful comparative discussion of land and resource claims in ethnic minority context by Sturgeon (2005). On the relationship between naming and land claims, see also Parkin 1989.
34. Though probably not. Bloch (1998: 193–95, "Why Do Malagasy Cows Speak French?") discusses how people in Madagascar speak to their cows in French, the language of the former colonial power. Moreover, the Hadza of Tanzania speak to their dogs in Swahili, the dominant national language. In neither case do we learn if they also name their animals in the languages of the powerful, but it is a strong possibility.

3

Rice Beer and the Making of Wa Sociality

It does not take long for a visitor to Wa country to be invited to share homemade rice beer.* This social practice is very important in Wa society. It is a process of making and expanding sociality through the sharing of rice beer, as well as other drinks and food (discussed below), with the rice beer by far the most important.

Sharing rice beer usually involves a single bamboo mug (called a *lei*) that is passed among the party. If outside visitors are used to drinking from individual glasses, they may be afraid to drink from a communal mug. This forces a choice: Will the visitors accept the established Wa cultural and social norms or not? If they refuse to share in the prescribed manner because they are appalled by the imagined or real uncleanliness of the bamboo mug, they are confirmed as outsiders. Thus, rice beer is a tool for ascertaining who belongs and who is an outsider. Among those who do belong to the local community or are visiting from another Wa community, practically none of them would ever refuse an offer of rice beer. Beer thus helps create and govern social life, in intricate ways—who drinks with whom is also a measure of respect, and closeness.

The central role of rice beer was unknown to me until I actually arrived in Wa country and joined in social interaction. For a foreign ethnographer like myself, the rules of drinking rice beer compelled me to join in "participant intoxication," a term that I have introduced not just as an extension of the conception and methodology of classic "participant observation" in anthropology but also as a contribution to understanding the place of drinking in the dynamics of sociality and ethnicity.[1] This chapter describes and analyzes Wa rice beer and its place both in local society and in the regional dynamics of unequal ethnic relations. It also mentions how the self-defined civilized neighbors of the Wa see them as filthy primitives, the opposite of civilized cleanliness—to a large degree because of

---

Endnotes for this chapter begin on page 89.

the rice beer. Conversely, such civilized discourse has itself been borrowed into the Wa imagination, forming part of a dialectics of mutual imaginations that then distorts the close historical interdigitation of the Wa heartland and the economic and social spheres of China and beyond.

The precise way of growing and preparing ingredients, brewing, and sharing the beer varies from place to place. We must recall that there was no unified Wa State in the past. Wa autonomy was based in each community by itself. Each community was heavily armed, loosely associated with other similar polities, and fiercely egalitarian. This was much like what Evans-Pritchard (1940) described as the "ordered anarchy" of the Nuer people in the Sudan region.[2] British colonial officers had no word for this kind of stateless sovereignty, so they called them "Wa states" (or, "statelets" subdivided into "circles"). The mountainous terrain made it difficult for outside powers to try to capture and directly control the Wa, and only in the 1960s, after several joined but failed efforts by the British and Chinese empires, was an international border imposed that divided the ancient Wa country between Burma and China (see chapter 2). All the self-ruling Wa communities bolstered the outsider's impression of how dangerous the Wa were, especially by means of the Wa spectacles of violence, especially the Wa headhunting warfare of the late nineteenth and early twentieth centuries.[3] This also laid the groundwork for cultural distinction between different Wa "circles," which not only counted a different number of days in the week but also drank their beer slightly differently.

Hill rice, which is used both for food and as a main ingredient for the rice beer, remains a key agricultural pillar in all the Wa lands. Until the recent opium ban in the Wa State in Burma, announced in 2000 and implemented in 2005, food crops there were supplemented by opium and other cash crops like tea and sugar cane, as well as by taking up irrigated rice, which itself is more common on the Chinese side where opium has been prohibited since the 1950s. (Synthetic drugs continue to be produced in Burma.) The Wa in China also sell rice to the Wa State, but rice beer can't be made from it.

The historical Wa heartland was deeply connected to the region beyond. By the nineteenth century and perhaps earlier, trade in opium, mining products, and other exploits generated considerable wealth and also power (see chapter 4). The geopolitical setting was unusual: Wa autonomy was real, so it was nothing like the classic "peripheral situation" of subjugated, exploited marginal areas (Turner 1986). It also does not quite work to see the Wa heartland mainly as a refuge for people escaping oppressive and exploitative states (as James Scott's "anarchist" history of the region [2009] suggested as a driving motive for all the many peoples in the "Zomia" region, who may have arrived in the mountains through such an act of escape). I think the egalitarian and "primitive" but wealthy and powerful Wa society can be better explained in the terms first proposed by Jonathan Friedman in his structuralist-Marxist analysis (1998 [1979][4]), in which he theorizes it as a "predatory" polity arising at the edge of empire because indigenous and traditional forms for political hierarchization were stifled by the neighboring states—something that would also explain the deep-seated Wa anti-state egalitarianism.

At the same time, as will be further discussed in chapter 4, Friedman's model also has problems. It is powerful when it comes to explaining the entrenchment in fortified mountain fastnesses, etc., and the awe-inspiring militarization of the egalitarian Wa. It also helps explain their wealth. But it nevertheless bypasses the historical agency of the people in question,[5] and therefore can't explain their actions to counter any permanent privilege or hierarchy—as when fellow Wa attempted to hoard mining profits and become mining kings in the late nineteenth century, but were blocked from doing so (chapter 4).

The strange society of the central Wa lands must be interpreted simultaneously as an outcome of process and circumstance and as the determined actions of the people there, doing their best in their situation to uphold their own morals of honor and autonomy. And the forging of mutual sociality achieved through the sharing of rice beer was actually a key part of this. In many ways, the beer took on a much deeper significance than I imagined.

Wa Rice Beer: Production and Social Use

Rice beer is a favorite daily drink among the Wa. It is not just a social drink but also a thirst quencher, and it can also serve as food—a nutrition-rich supplement during daytime farming labor. Rice beer figures in almost any social encounter and must be part of every ritual or festive occasion, such as funerals or the home sacrifices held to alleviate illness (chapter 8), or on other social occasions for mutual aid, such as when friends and family are invited to help plant fields, build houses, and so on.

Rice beer is known as *blai*. This is also the default word for "alcoholic drink." To clarify that one is talking about Wa rice beer, the term "beer proper" (*blai num*) may be used, but the term is mainly used in north-central Wa country. One can also say "Wa beer" (*blai* A Vex), which differentiates it from Chinese-style distilled liquor (called *blai* Houx), which in recent years has also gained ground.

The Wa word *blai* should be translated as "beer," despite the fact that it isn't malted and brewed as most beers are[6] but instead is fermented and infused. The bubbly brownish drink that results is never transparent, but otherwise looks and tastes much like good beer. This production method is distinct from both rice wines and hard liquors; in fact, no wines made from either grapes, rice, or other fruit are made in Wa country. Before the 1950s, locals distilled grain liquor, also in Yong Ou (the area where much of my field research took place, straddling the China-Burma border), but this continued only up until the recent broad influx of commercial Chinese hard liquor.[7]

Similar kinds of water-infused rice beer are made locally across Burma and northeastern India,[8] and across Zomia.[9] The raw materials and production processes are largely similar across this whole region. However, utensils and drinking methods may differ. For example, Mon-Khmer-speaking people in highland Laos or Vietnam share the rice wine through multiple straws in the same large wine jar.[10]

Water-infused rice beer is "an alcoholic beverage made by fermentation of cereals" (Terwiel 1992: 131). Among the Wa, the main raw material is *ko*, a kind of millet that is interspersed with hill rice (*hngoux*) as it is grown, or planted on the ridges of irrigated rice fields, and *maong*, a kind of hillside buckwheat. The *maong* is a filler; sometimes maize (*vuong*) is also mixed in as a filler. The making of rice beer is called *bloug blai* ("cooking" beer) or *yuh blai* ("making" beer). When I asked for a description of the process, this is what I was told:

> We [*eix*] put a pot [*kang*] of water on the fire and pour in the *ko* millet. We cook it [in the water] and then dry it on a mat [*n'gui*, made of woven bamboo], and after the grain has dried completely, we mix in some yeast [*a seix* or *a seix blai*]. We then store it in a basket [*kra*] for at least three days. When it's sour [*nex*, fermented and sour], then it's ready [*hmom*]. We then pour some of it into an infusion container [*loh*, made from a section of thick bamboo], and pour in fresh water. We let it sit for a little while and then suck it out [*doud*]. That's the first round [*nbeng*]. After finishing that first round, if we pour in more fresh water [into the *loh*] we then call it *ge qieh* [watery, weaker beer].[11]

The powdery commercial Chinese brewing yeast known as *a seix* Houx is nowadays often bought for use in villages. Its taste differs from *a seix* A Vex, "Wa-style yeast," which is homemade from fermented rice that has been soaked in water until it becomes soft (which takes a day or so, but sometimes overnight is enough). It's then mixed with rice chaff (*gam*), fermented, and sun-dried as small, whitish cakes. These are broken and powdered before use, and as mentioned, are mixed with the partly sun-dried, already-cooked *ko* and *maong*. The mix stays in a sealed basket fermenting for at least three days, but if the basket is tight enough, it can be kept there up to six months or more. If it is completely dry and sealed when first stored, the taste is said to improve with age. Its smell and taste determines when the fermentation is complete. The *blai* is scooped up and put into the *loh* container, and then fresh water is added. This is the infusion, which creates a bubbly beer, ready to enjoy from a *lei* bamboo mug.[12]

The fermented mix of *blai* can also be eaten directly before it is infused. "Ang meix eih blai?" (Won't you eat some beer?) is the cheerful question one can hear when this "beer" is offered by hand—a happy occasion. One can also bring the fermented mix to the field or eat it at home, as children often do instead of candy (which is historically unknown).[13]

The large infusion container, *loh blai*, is made from one segment of large, very thick bamboo, either harvested wild or planted in the vicinity of the village. Bamboo is a ubiquitous, hardy, multipurpose material which is used for almost everything in Wa country, from house frames and water pipelines to feeding troughs for pigs and stools for sitting indoors or on the verandas. To make the *loh*, one cuts a fifty- to seventy-centimeter segment from the extra tall and thick bamboos that are typically grown in huge, proprietary stands near the village, each planted and owned by a certain man.

When the *blai* infusion is ready after a few minutes, the beer is sucked out through a straw (*hraig*). Formerly, Wa used bamboo pipes and grass straws for this, but nowadays they use a rigid bamboo pipe usually connected to plastic tube (*hraig suliao*, "plastic straw," a Chinese loan word). The beer, emerging because of the pressure difference, is not poured directly into the all-important *lei* (drinking mug) but into an intermediate-sized pitcher called a *glag*—today this is often a plastic bottle, also used to carry beer into the fields.[14] The "classic" bamboo version of a *glag* has one small opening for pouring beer into the *lei* and a small air hole on the other side of the top.

Next, the rice beer is poured into the *lei*, which also is made from a natural section of bamboo that uses the natural horizontal segment plate as its bottom. *Leis* are made from thinner bamboo, about as thick as an arm. It's a special rice beer utensil, not appropriate to use for any other drink. The *lei* is often elaborately carved with abstract patterns, and is thus one of few remaining spaces left for such carvings.[15]

The *lei* belongs firmly within the household where it was made; although a household may have several *lei*, it uses only one at a time. However, hosts of large gatherings (funerals, weddings, etc.) can deploy more than one *lei* and circulate them simultaneously.

Forging Sociality By Way of Inclusive Drinking

Drinking always involves a minimum of at least two people, typically one host and one guest, and is profoundly social. It is the most common expression and embodiment of Wa social relations, more so than the more restricted family commensality, or the like. The only other comparable social practices are tobacco smoking (*doud* [smoke] either Burmese cigars, *si lid*, or Chinese cigarettes, *sub*), betel (*bao*) "eating" (*eh*, chewing), or even tea (*la*) drinking, which each differ in important ways from the shared rice beer. Tea has a long history, and is itself hugely important at funeral wakes, at the legendary late-evening fireside *a peag* conversations, etc., but it is not shared directly between people like rice beer.[16]

It is true that betel chewing also involves sharing. There is set of ingredients, that are often shared. Most are imported and kept in personal pouches, and people lend these to one another with any ingredients they may lack, to build their own betel wad.[17] But, betel wads themselves are not shared, nor are cigars or cigarettes. Homegrown rice beer, on the other hand, simultaneously nurtures and intoxicates, providing a means of producing society through joint drinking from a single cup. The movements of this trace the forging of ideal social relations, starting with a host and a guest, and proceeding onward to include entire communities as well as outsiders. Wa rice beer "construct[s] the world as it is" and, I would also say, "the world as one wishes it to be."[18]

In the local community, nearly every social interaction outside of the circle of one's immediate kin requires rice beer. Even the most casual visitor must be offered some. If there isn't any at home that can be prepared, it is felt to be very bad and improper. In such cases, both the failed host and would-be guest might even leave together in search of *blai* at the house of a friend, relative, or neighbor.

After dusk has fallen, when there is no more light for farming or other outside work, one can see people "out for a stroll in the village" (*lou li nung yong*), hoping to be invited in somewhere to have some *blai*. If someone from a household notices them, by sight or by sound, and as long as there is *blai*, they must invite the wanderers in. A small drinking session can attract further neighbors and passersby, eager to join such occasions, for drinks and conversation (*a peag*). Guests may have various other pretexts for visiting (perhaps to arrange for help planting fields in the coming days). The pretexts for stopping by the homes of others are often predicated on the relationship of drinking together, which in turn builds the sociality on which mutual aid is based. If a would-be host shows reluctance, he'll be frowned upon and avoided; if the sociality of drinking is disrupted, mutual aid on other matters may suffer too. Any host who is, for whatever reason, unable or unwilling to treat impromptu visitors is often forced into a white lie: "Ah, we're out of *blai* . . . let's go and see if we can find some elsewhere."

In small, everyday drinking sessions, the host will typically invite people in— usually "up," *hog*; traditional houses are raised on stilts, so guests will be asked to "Step up, come into the house!" (*hog nung nyiex*). The host sits down with the guests at his fireplace[19] and asks his children to fetch *blai* from the household's storage basket and fresh water for the *loh* container, which is usually tied against the wall. If no children or other suitable helpers are available, the host will fill the *loh* himself. When the *blai* is ready, and a first round transferred to the *glag* pitcher, the host will pour the first *lei*.

But he does not hand it to the guest. He first pauses to gently pour a sip or two of the beer on the floor (or on the ground if outdoors). The house floors traditionally are made from bamboo planks that have been split and flattened, so the beer enters the ground. This is actually a sacrifice, called *n'groug ge meang* ("recognizing" the ancestor spirits, *ge meang*). He may remain silent while doing so, but often addresses the *ge meang* with a minimal greeting, "Ge meang beix!" (Ye ancestor spirits!), alerting them to the offering.[20]

Then he will lift the *lei* to his mouth and take just one sip. He'll lower it and wipe the wet beer from the rim of the mug with the palm of one of his hands (usually the left, if holding the mug with his right hand). It is a peculiar, always identical movement, the palm pressing along the rim with the fingers spread and pointed outward. When finished, he hands the *lei* to the main guest (or as the case may be, the only guest). In informal settings, this can be done with only one hand, but the *lei* must never, ever fall or spill. If it is a more formal occasion or an emotionally charged setting, the host will instead use both hands in another very common and standardized gesture. While securing the mug by pressing it between the palms of both hands, he opens all his fingers wide on both hands and, leaning toward the guest, slowly and gently presses the *lei* into the open, receiving hands of his guest. As they come together, their hands clasp (*mi'an diex*) around the mug, and the transfer is complete. This is the most polite and formal way of handing over the beer, and the great care shown in the gesture is meant to link the two drinkers together in caring for each other. This move is not easy to learn, but it is a way of showing mutual respect: it requires an attentive focus on one's drinking partner, creating a deep connection.[21]

The guest is now expected to take only a first sip. This first *lei* is still the share (*groux*) of the host, a key concept here: since it still belongs to the host, it is his responsibility, and it is also his duty to share it with the guest. A polite guest, on receiving the mug, will also pause to pour a little beer on the ground for the ancestor spirits. He will usually do so without speaking, especially if he isn't close kin. It isn't the place of a visitor to be the first to alert the ancestor spirits there—even though the *ge meang* are not individuated but roam collectively, so that they are in effect omnipresent (see chapter 8).

Now the guest takes his sip (called a *qim*, taste, a "sipping from another's share"). He then wipes the *lei*, handing it back to the host, who only then will finish his share. He is supposed to empty this first *lei* himself, to conclusively demonstrate that the beer is good (that nothing is wrong with it in any way; that it isn't poisoned).

Shaking out the last drops on the floor, the host fills the *lei* again, now handing it directly to the first guest. This is the share of the guest, who is similarly obligated to first drink a sip (after first pouring out some of the share for the ancestor spirits, as is always proper with one's first share, for one's own sake and for everybody else's). But he must then hand the *lei* back to the waiting host, so that the host may taste the guest's share. While the host waits for this, he often sits with one hand raised in the air, half open, his elbow resting on his knee, gently signaling that he is waiting for his sip, his *groux*. This equally common and very formalized bodily gesture, or pose, is also used on festive occasions while waiting for one's share of food. It suggests a relaxed confidence about social relations—that one feels safe in the assumption that the drink or the food is coming, that one is entitled to decent treatment, a share like the others.

Having taken a sip of the guest's share, the host returns the *lei* to the guest so that the guest can finish it, after he first treats any other people present to a sip if he chooses to do so. Every adult person present will receive his or her share in turn, each getting a full *lei* handed over by the host or his *gon si mang*, "the one who serves" on the host's behalf, if there are many guests present. As mentioned, if there are only two drinkers, the host and *gon si mang* roles naturally coincide.

All who receive a *lei* will follow the set pattern of the first pair of drinkers. They will also expand on it by offering the *lei* to other guests in the same way, pairing up with them one at a time, beginning with the host family's senior members (husband, wife, elders), then moving on to others, like senior guests who are particularly deserving.

Anyone still expecting their share—or waiting to have it returned from someone they passed it on to—also holds his or her body in the posture of beckoning, meaning, "I'm here, I'm still expecting my turn." Having received one's own proper share (*groux*), they wipe off their *lei* and invite someone else to have a sip from it, uttering the formulaic invitation, "Ax ha!" (Let's drink, us two!). The word *ha* means to "go," and *ux* is the unique Wa dual pronoun that means "we"

Figure 3.1. At a gathering in Yong Ou, the host is waiting for a guest to finish his share of rice beer. Others wait for their turn; in the background, one man is making his libation to the ancestors. Photo by the author, 1997.

in the special restricted sense of "us two" (as opposed to *eix*, "we, more-than-two")—a pronoun incidentally missing in many languages but extremely useful in Wa social life.[22]

Competent guests may expand on this basic pattern with selections from the more elaborate invitations that also exist, such as those that appear in the lyrics of the house-warming songs of the classic all-night dances in new houses, which all highlight the values of sharing. They often laud "the *lei* passing to one's fellow," which will hopefully continue to happen innumerable times in such new households.[23]

Guests are expected to busy themselves by making offers of a *qim*, a sip, to the hosts or other guests as a matter of course. However, this offer is often rebuffed by symbolic protests: "You drink your share, that's your share! We've had ours!" (*Niaex meix, moh grox meix, hei niaex yix grox yix!*). These are "fake" but polite protests meant to suggest a concern that guests get their fill of beer and not fall short because they are too polite or formal. Conversely, these protestations also have the effect of praising the person offering sips as generous with his share. This indicates that the guest is a generous and therefore decent person.

The process of polite sharing, with all the gestures and expressions that surround it, both create and reinforce drinkers' mutual recognition as worthy members of their community. This occurs between hosts and guests, between two guests, and between people among a crowd of guests, who pause to interact in recognition of each other, two by two.[24]

Hosts are of course also indebted to the guests, who in effect offer them the stage on which they can perform their generosity and decency. Hosts and guests produce each other's social worth, and adolescent youth (men and women alike) become adult subjects in learning to properly share rice beer. Ever since they were babies, they will have received small sips of beer; also, by the time they are teenagers, they will have served as *gon si mang* (family waiter) many times, learning how it all works.

When there are large crowds, such as at funerals and weddings, several bamboo *lei* might be circulating among the guests, and a number of ambulatory *gon si mang* might also serve beer, all on the host family's account. Often there is no time to exchange the *lei* between many drinkers, as would usually be done, but basic principles are still upheld. Special rules do apply: Above all, two "traveling" *lei* should never cross each other's path (it's spelled out as: *po dox lei a bleid'*).[25] That would risk breaking the path of mutual recognition between two autonomous humans (the *ax* pair) who might be in the process of drinking together, and such social disruption is inappropriate because it interferes with the wishes of those engaged in this most central of personal rituals.

Such a rule also sustains the exceptional case of *blai li'eid* (or *blai qim*), which is beer "sent around" long distances across big crowds, with each person only taking one sip instead of holding onto the *lei* until it is empty. This is a rare exception to everyday patterns that happens only on grand occasions, such as funerals or weddings. It still reinforces the production of sociality that the sharing of beer accomplishes on special, larger occasions, at which a community is reaffirmed not just two by two, but through longer "chains" of drinkers.

One can never allow the *lei* to spill or accidentally fall onto the ground. When such disruptions occur, as they inevitably will, the cause is not believed to be drunkenness or carelessness but the offender's supposed failure to give some beer to the *ge meang* ancestor spirits, which are always present (although invisible). These then take revenge by angrily striking the *lei* out of the offender's hands. Idealized social relations are given as the appropriate interpretive framework for any accident, rather than considering the event a momentary mishap.[26]

As mentioned, rice beer drinking differs somewhat across the Wa area. What I have offered above is a description of the practices in central Wa country as exemplified by the inhabitants of the Yong Ou realm. Having painstakingly learned these manners, I was sometimes surprised by different procedures in other locations. In Wenggake, also in the Ximeng County in China, the carved bamboo *lei* is much taller, and thinner. When two people drink together, they don't temporarily "own" their share and hand it to third persons for a sip, like Yong Ou people do. Instead, each person finishes a mug, and only when finished, the invited paired-up drinker asks a third person to form a new pair with him (using the short, *ax*!, meaning [let's drink this!] "the two of us"), so that a chain is formed.

Other places have different ways still. But it remains true everywhere that Wa social relations are fashioned by means of the *blai*—more so than almost any other Wa form of social connections, and in largely similar ways.

Boundary Making, Competitive Drinking, and Wa Ethnic Identity

Wa rice beer also serves as a vehicle of internal competition. The competitive building of reserves of social prestige based on the generous provision of drinks as part of feasting is known from around the world, so this is no surprise here.[27] There is also no contradiction here with what I wrote earlier about how the egalitarian Wa society of the independent past frowned upon hierarchies of power—this by no means precluded or prevented competition for social prestige. Such competition was done by way of the classic "feast of merit" tradition in this part of the world (Stevenson 1943; Lehman 1989; Friedman 1998 [1979]), and involved the lavish treatment of local guests to food and beer.

After the loss of autonomy in the 1950s, as well as the wealth that Wa people were able to generate under it, large-scale feasts became a thing of the past. The truly grand community-wide buffalo sacrifices and feasts, often using animals bought or requisitioned from outside the central Wa country, can no longer be held today. Still, occasions such as funerals and weddings continue to provide a fertile arena, if a smaller one, for hosts to try and outshine fellow villagers in measures of social prestige.

In many places around the world, this kind of competition engenders tactics of coercion,[28] and this is true here too—such as when hosts half-jokingly insist that guests must finish their share. A foreigner such as myself easily becomes the target here, not least because my social standing is ambivalent and bears testing.

And yet, the deep Wa egalitarian ethos always tempers such competition, and any coercion. It dictates respect for individual preferences and decisions. For example, while few people will decline an offer of rice beer, it can happen, and it can be accepted. This is so especially when the relationships in question are long established, and also when someone seems vulnerable, because of illness or for other reasons. Elderly people especially are generally entitled to decline a second round, and they may even ask a younger person to finish their share—a move that is also almost never refused by the person asked.

One particular incident in my own experience comes to mind. A very old lady—rumored to be the oldest in her village, happened to be sitting together with me on the sidelines of a wedding packed with people. While the parties of the wedding recounted the past relations of their lineages joining in the wedding, she turned to me, a newcomer. She hesitated, probably worried that I wouldn't understand or know to go along with what she was about to offer me. With her advanced age, she dispensed even with the standard host admonitions. Leaning forward, handing her *lei* to me, she simply urged me, "Niaex!" (Drink!). I had accepted her *lei*, and she made a brisk, upward-thrusting hand gesture that means, "And finish it off!" She then addressed me as the odd foreigner: "Eix niaex, moh eix A Vex" (We drink: We are Wa), proudly reiterating the Wa commitment to a completely open hospitality, inclusive even of complete strangers like myself.[29]

The beer's intoxicating power is, of course, also of central importance. If the host can get his guests drunk, it obviously serves to show the host's generosity, and wealth. And getting drunk together, in the measured ways of Wa beer drinking, also cements the relationships of those involved (cf. Netting 1964). Although drinking may provoke fights that really have their origin in preexisting discord, it was more striking during my fieldwork how extremely rare such incidents were. Drinking sessions were mostly characterized by amiable conversation and joking. Wa rice beer can get you drunk, but it is mild, and even on the rowdiest occasions revelers would somehow still avoid getting intoxicated to the point that they could not make it home. Instead, the light intoxication on *blai* may count as the "controlled collapse of everyday work" (Mitchell 2004: 191). This benign effect applies only to the homemade Wa rice beer; commercially promoted hard liquor with higher alcohol content is something different (see below).

Figure 3.2. The author learning to drink Wa rice beer, sporting a betel bag. Yong Ou, 1997.

When the drinking involves outside visitors, the stakes are altered. If it is Wa people from neighboring areas, they mostly know how to drink and behave politely, or they can quickly learn the local variations on this theme. They know to pay attention to such local mores, to fit in, and to avoid committing any *faux pas*. They will show delicate restraint and get only appropriately drunk, submitting to the host's good will, but only halfway, within limits. The same is true for other ethnic "neighbors" that have had long-standing contacts with the Wa, such as the Lahu, Shan, and even some Chinese.[30] Their mode of participating while also striving to maintain an escape route resembles the anthropologists' ambivalent stance—although they are different in other ways.[31]

Especially since the Chinese state took over the Wa lands in the 1950s, rice beer has also come to be used to demarcate "ethnic" boundaries. As I mentioned earlier, the moments when Wa hosts offer outside visitors rice beer are probing moments demanding a decision from hesitating outsiders. Wa people themselves would in principle never refuse an offer of rice beer, except in situations of severe discomfort or illness, or of open enmity (e.g. over grudges of suspected serious theft, or the like—in the past, if their enmity really rose to such an intensity, it could provoke violence or even local war). Foreigners, however, lacking in socialization into Wa politeness, and with only hazy ideas of what it would entail, must decide whether to meet the Wa challenge and engage with them on their terms—of Wa autonomy, based in honorable recognition, as recognized in the distinctly Wa spirit that permeates the rice beer drinking. Ignorance of the real or claimed rules for drinking can never be more than a fleeting excuse; the moment a guest declines on such grounds also marks when they become defined as a non-Wa outsider, one who does not accept the rules of mutual respect on equal terms, as defined in *blai* drinking, and who therefore may potentially try to throw out equality and impose their own rules.

Such suspicions on the part of the Wa may well be justified. As they sought to incorporate the Wa lands into British Burma, frustrated British imperial officials would observe that in the Wa area, "nothing could be done without drinking, and nothing could really be accomplished when drunk."[32] This, then, left only a brief window of opportunity for them to try to accomplish something—the "something," of course, being the negotiation and introduction of British plans for dominance and exploitation, all of which the Wa would rather avoid.

Incidentally, British officials were amused by the obsession among Wa "savages" for sharing beer, but I find no evidence that they also shared it. This condescending attitude was not fundamentally different from that of the Chinese—although the early Chinese Communist advances in the 1950s were couched in the revolutionary rhetoric of "friendship" and of "sharing everything with the masses"—even filthy, primitive beer. Each in their own way, the British and the Chinese imperialists believed they could gain something by initially *pretending* to accept Wa ritual.

Thus, when taking over the Wa lands in the mid-1950s, the Chinese started out by signaling respect for local customs, sometimes by sharing the beer. This was a conscious policy reflected in Chinese propaganda, which deployed images of soldiers sitting with Wa farmers, smiling to suggest they're gladly drinking the *blai* offered to them (Ch'en 1964). But it was mostly about posing, to endear them to the Wa and defuse suspicions. It presumably also built on their knowledge of older confrontations, where even armed outsiders were treated peacefully if they accepted customary symbolic gifts of peace and shared rice beer (as occurred with the 1930s League of Nations border demarcation delegations and their armed troops).

But the Communist Party policy soon shifted from reconciliation to confrontation, as they aimed to demolish autonomous Wa political institutions.[33] As part of this project, Chinese authorities in the Maoist era actually prohibited Wa rice beer for approximately twenty years. The exact dates are unclear: this much-resented affront is remembered by some people, but without precise dates. The dogmatic Chinese rationale was that beer making was a "waste" of food grain. The Chinese insisted that wheat be cultivated and that it be used for making noodles, which represented progress much like irrigated rice. As such, it simply had to replace the lower-yield *ko* that is used for rice beer. The Chinese authorities forced the Wa to experiment with growing wheat, mainly on the high-altitude fields formerly used for opium. But, like various intermittent irrigation schemes, it was only partly successful, and in most places has been abandoned.

Only from about 1980 were the Wa allowed to grow *ko* again, and since then, the *blai* made a comeback across the land. The shift can be explained by the progressive abandonment of socialism and the relaxation of intrusive Mao-era micromanagement and scrutiny of economic life. This shifted the Wa away from the Communist experiments with Peoples' Communes to what we have today—something more like the classic "peripheral situation." Later, although Wa farmers were once again allowed to make rice beer, the renaissance of Wa-style social life remains predicated on the de facto carving up of the ancestral *jaig' qee* territories that have been appropriated for state-directed uses. In recent years they are being be carved up again, for new plantations of tea, coffee, sugar cane, agroforestry, etc., with the profits often going to distant Chinese entrepreneur-investors who enter into alliances with the new city-based local Chinese (and Chinese-Wa) elites. The rural populations, who were once proud warriors, have mostly been reduced to peasants laboring for others on what was once their own land, and across the region, micromanagement of subsistence farmers is back, as well (Lau 2020).

In this new situation, the role of Wa rice beer in defining outsiders has taken on curious new forms. To the extent that the colonialist mythology of benign Chinese tutelage is upheld, Chinese officials do still know they ought to share rice beer with locals, who will offer it to them if they venture into rural areas. However, this clashes with their strongly held convictions that the Wa are filthy primitives, and their beer is among the worst expressions of this filth and primitivity. In fact, not just the Chinese but even many of the Chinese-trained Wa cadres in the county towns will see the *lei* offered to them as the epitome of native backwardness. They will think of the contents as bacteria-infested filth. (And indeed, it is true that the *lei* is never washed, only wiped off "clean" with unwashed hands before it is dried on the rack above the fireplace.)

Sometimes, new local elites are barely able to control their sense of disgust, as they, politely or not, will turn down *blai* offered to them when visiting rural areas in their jurisdiction. This avoidance is inspired by the Chinese-derived idea of dirt and cleanliness, which is closely correlated with the Chinese imaginary of a primitive/civilized divide. Such invitations also form an uncomfortable challenge to state power: in an official's mind, he probably should not accept such gestures from the peasantry in his charge. Usually officials talk down to the people, ordering them around. Thus, in such settings, refusal is so common that it has become expected, and the impulse to offer them beer has died down.

Several decades into direct Chinese rule, rural Wa know well that they are seen as filthy. To some extent, this resonates with older understandings: within Wa society, elders are aware that they are both respected and also regarded as unseemly. They may even be feared, as soon-to-be-dead *ge meang eim* (living ancestor spirits). When offering younger people a sip of their beer, elders often preventatively admonish them by using the phrase *po s'reng' nah kod* (don't look down on the old, as if they were dirty). This hard-to-translate phrase, especially the phrase *s'reng'*, expresses the worry that "strong and healthy" younger people (*ba nbrax*) will resent the old and infirm to the point that they no longer honor them on equal terms as autonomous living beings—and perhaps they will honor them only in death, when the elderly regain strength as potentially revengeful ancestor spirits. Also, many Wa regard themselves and their people as a whole as the guardian elders of humanity. This is because their people were, ostensibly, the first to emerge onto the surface of the earth (chapter 2). And so, we can say that the contempt (*s'reng'*) for the once-powerful Wa that is displayed by now-powerful Chinese officials and Chinese-trained ethnic Wa officials actually mimics this same relation.

There are even echoes of this strange parallel in the Wa responses to the civilizing narratives, in which the Wa are painted as relishing a role as the filthy barbarians on the wild margins of civilization. The Wa saying *prex a vi, som A Vex* (the food of the tiger [is like the] meal of the Wa) seems like an ironic commentary on their traditional lack of chopsticks and porcelain, eating instead like the last tigers in the forest, with their hands—although usually they'll bring plates made of banana-tree leaves (in the past, some had wooden plates) (Fiskesjö 2007).

Also, because of how the Wa beer is frowned upon as dirty and primitive, the "threat" of rice beer hospitality can be deployed by them as if it, too, were a deterrent—keeping officials away. Back when British and/or Chinese military columns entered Wa country (in the 1890s, 1920s–30s, and in the 1950s respectively), it is possible that the Wa already offered beer as a "weapon" deployed to attempt to hold up, delay, frustrate, or even neutralize these dangerous outsiders who had penetrated deep into Wa country. These outsiders obviously did not intend to assimilate to Wa social norms but instead would try to impose their own—along with a new hierarchy. The British and the Chinese may have believed that they were manipulating the ignorant Wa, but the Wa still had ways to defend themselves.

Foreign Liquor as a New, Dangerous Challenge

Like so many other places mired in the "peripheral situation," Wa country is now awash in hard liquor. This type of drink is much more potent than homemade rice beer, and thus more socially disruptive. Its disruptiveness doesn't so much stem from its foreign origin—in the Wa setting, its consumption is, in principle, governed by the same rules as rice beer, but a *lei* cannot be used. Drinkers usually share a porcelain cup instead, or they may switch to the Chinese custom of one cup per person. Rather, the disruptive power of hard liquor is a consequence arising directly from the dismantling of Wa autonomy and its supporting social institutions. The intoxicating force wreaks havoc, and is addictive, because the old social institutions can no longer prevent the descent into alcoholism as they prevented opium addiction in the past: in the early twentieth century, when Wa opium production was prevalent, any Wa drifting into addiction would be confronted by throngs of relatives showing up at his house to warn him and put a stop to his descent. In contrast, while the Chinese authorities today may prohibit opium and heroin, they are invested in the trade of hard liquor, which is accepted as perfectly legitimate all over China but which can, in reality, also bring addiction and illness. And today, no Wa social institutions exist that can watch its members for drug abuse.

The link between distilled liquor alcoholism and the reality of the peripheral situation is evident around the world. In Chinese-ruled Wa country, it also involves the history of conflict between Chinese officials and foreign missionaries. Seeking to expand their influence on the Wa peripheries, foreign missionaries converted some Wa and Lahu and required them to deny their old gods and abandon liquor and opium. Many obliged, and this threatened Chinese liquor profits, clashing directly with Chinese interests. In 1923, American Baptist missionaries faced a Chinese official at Menglian bent on halting the spread of Christianity. He forced people to reestablish "native spirit altars," destroyed churches, and interrupted services, then forced those attending to kneel down and have Chinese liquor forced down their throats.[34]

The autonomous Wa also distilled their own hard liquor in the past, or they purchased it from Shan or Chinese sources. They incorporated it into their social life, and even into common sacrificial rituals. When offered to the ancestor spirits, it is described to as *blai Houx blai Siam* ("Chinese liquor, Shan liquor," regardless of whether the real origin was Shan, Chinese, or homemade).

Although the Chinese opium buyers may be long gone, the Chinese liquor market is expanding aggressively, flooding nearly every Wa village. The trade has official protection and involvement, just like the opium trade once did. The inherent corruption in the market often involves substandard and poisonous liquor that can harm or kill people; along with alcoholism, it also produces impoverishment, exploiting peasant savings.

Chinese scholars who understand the situation have sometimes argued behind the scenes for curbing liquor sales (anonymous, personal communication), but the attempts seem futile. Similarly, cigarette tobacco, also harmful to human health, has replaced opium as Yunnan's most profitable cash crop. It is similarly backed by powerful interests that ignore health concerns.[35] Today's liquor and tobacco companies are firmly supported by the Chinese state, which is of course due to the large state tax revenues, and also by how these items mark the status of Chinese identity. This must be why Chinese authorities in Xinjiang, Western China, today force native Muslim shopkeepers to stock cigarettes and liquor, even though many of the natives regard such items as inappropriate. Such practices recall the reprehensible ways in which Chinese liquor was forced on rural people across Southwest China.

There is no escape from the current exploitation of the classical peripheral situation in which many Wa and other peoples now find themselves. It will simply have to be negotiated, painstakingly and painfully. In the arena of autonomous rice beer drinking, passing the *lei* still continues to help locals build strong communities—even while traditional Wa homegrown beer is altered by the commercial yeasts, turning away some drinkers due to the headaches the new brewing ingredients cause, as well as to the altered taste. Foreign liquors or even more potent substances (drugs) are increasingly consumed today, to "bridge the gap" between the older elusive ideals of sociality and plenitude and the new, harsh realities of monetized social life (Mitchell 2004: 194).

Many young Wa leave to become migrant laborers in China and beyond. The role of the *lei* itself, left behind in the village as the idle anchor of a Wa sociality, now takes on a new meaning. The people leave, but the rice beer *lei* stays behind . . . beckoning with its own promise of satisfaction and security in a community potentially resurrected once more.

I recall how I obtained firm promises from several long-standing interlocutors and drinking partners of getting a souvenir *lei* made for me. Before I left, I anticipated my own nostalgia for that sense of belonging in the welcoming warmth of people gathering around a *loh* of *blai*. I knew that for me, a Chinese-made tourist *lei*, sold in a Chinese county town, would not suffice—I did not want that as a souvenir. But, despite the promises, I never received a *lei* to take with me. It was probably exactly because of my advertised intent of disappearing with such a *lei*, away from the social context into which I had been so graciously invited, that I could never have one. The rice beer *lei* is made to anchor Wa sociality, or even figure at the core of a reformulated cultural identity, so it simply could not be allowed to depart.

Notes

* This chapter draws in part on my 2010 article, "Participant Intoxication and Self-Other Dynamics in the Wa Context," *Asia Pacific Journal of Anthropology* 11(2): 111–27.
  1. There is a large anthropological and sociological literature on social drinking: Douglas 1987; Wilson 2005; Dietler 1990, 2006; de Garine and de Garine 2001; Fournier and D'Onofrio 1991; Marshall 1979, 1982; Washburne 1961; Mitchell 2004; and more.
  2. See also the intriguing developments of Evans-Pritchard's Africa-based theory in Baumann and Gingrich (2004), and chapter 10.
  3. On the political history and headhunting warfare of the Wa, see chapters 5 and 6 (also Fiskesjö 1999a, 2000, 2009).
  4. Friedman 1998 [1979]; also compare Friedman 2011; Fiskesjö 2014; and chapter 4. For related discussions on insular Southeast Asian societies, see, for example, Gibson

1980; Healey 1985—also the broad discussions of autonomous politics in Gibson and Sillander 2011.
5. An agency that was emphasized by Scott 2009, and rightly so.
6. On the brewing process in modern industry, see Briggs, Hough, and Stevens 1981–82.
7. Li Yangsong 1983a: 99; 1983b: 148–49. In addition to the Chinese, the neighboring Shan and Kachin also have long traditions of distilling liquor (Scott and Hardiman 1983 [1900]).
8. Kerketta 1960; Achaya 1994; Teramoto et al. 2000, 2002; Kumar and Rao 2002; Midya 2004.
9. On Zomia, see above, and the introduction. On rice beer across the region, see Hutton 1969 [1921]; Burkill et al. 1935; Izikowitz 1951; Ling Shun-sheng 1957; 1958; Frake 1964; Condominas 1977; Dove 1988; Terwiel 1992; Ivanoff 2000; Zheng 2000; Le Roux 2002; Barclay 2003; Salemink 2003; Pearson 2009. On Wa rice beer also see Tin Yee 2004: 12-14).
10. Izikowitz 1951; Condominas 1977.
11. Fiskesjö, Wa field notes, VI:126–27, IX:2–3, XIII:185–88.
12. Fiskesjö, Wa field notes, XIII:187. Terwiel (1992: 132ff.) reviews quite similar techniques used in Assam and Burma, and Hutton (1969 [1921]: 97–98) describes the rice beer of the Angami Naga (similar to the Wa in certain other respects, but not linguistically), which they call *zu*, a Tibeto-Burman term also used by the Chin (Lehman 1963: 57) and by other Nagas (Terwiel 1992: 142) in Burma, and in Northeast India.
13. Once, I bought some mango fruit to offer to the children of an interlocutor. But they rejected it ("Too sweet!").
14. The alternative would be to carry a full *loh*, but infusion in the field is avoided because the water there may not be from the usual trusted sources inside the village (or from bamboo-aqueducts running from safe sources near the village; today these are sometimes replaced by steel pipes).
15. After the 1950s catastrophe, the large-scale carvings on the wooden boards on the short ends of houses—especially that of the so-called Big House of the traditional *o lang* chief, an office now suspended and existing only in popular memory—came to an end, and this art form is largely dead. Wa art also does persist in the woven shoulder bag designs (Formoso 2001), but many nowadays are mass-produced and sold back to the Wa by the Chinese.
16. For more on tea among the neighboring Mon-Khmer-speaking people, see Li Quanmin 2008, 2010 (on the De'ang or Ta'ang people); Hung 2013 (on the Bulang).
17. For more on betel and betel chewing, see chapter 2.
18. Douglas 1987: 8, 12. In this context note Kathryn March (1998: 71) on the anxiety hiding inside such happy expectations, even as one celebrates the generative power of yeast and the women's enabling care (in Nepal).
19. In the past, three fireplaces were maintained, one for domestic foods, one for wild foods, and a third for "cooking" rice beer and entertaining guests (Fiskesjö, field notes, XIII:65–72).
20. The *ge meang* are the spirits of the dead, who have joined a collective existence under this name. An elderly living person may be called *ge meang eim*, "living *ge meang*," suggesting that he will soon join this collective of the dead, who are omnipresent and who want their share too (chapter 10).
21. This and other movements are illustrative examples of Mauss's "techniques of the body," patterns of movement that must be learned in a real setting, within the proper sociocultural framework (Mauss 2006; also Bloch 1998, the chapter "Things That Go without Saying"). (When teaching, I sometimes use the example of Wa rice beer

drinking as part of a first introduction to anthropology. It is profoundly human and profoundly distinct at the same time).
22. Compare Taiwanese aboriginal drinking duos joining their lips at the rim of the same vessel (Barclay 2003: 84ff.).
23. After years of constant use, the *lei* blackens from being held and caressed, and from the smoke on the *n'grex* rack (where it rests when not in use). But it is never washed.
24. This gesture resembles the peculiarly Swedish custom of drinking across the table at events like parties or weddings: two people sitting far apart will catch each other's eye, raise their glasses to each other from a distance, and silently drink (without inviting others to join), then briefly rejoin their mutual gaze, thus creating a special, exclusive moment of recognition between the two drinkers, even in a large crowd.
25. Fiskesjö, field notes, VI:54.
26. I once spilled my *lei* and was immediately told that I "must" have forgotten to greet the *ge meang* when I was given my share at the outset.
27. For comparative examples, see Netting 1964; Karp 1980; Marshall 1982; Rehfish 1987; and de Garine and de Garine 2001. On the archaeology of competitive feasting as an engine of social transformation, see Dietler 1990, 2006; Fung 2000; and Jennings et al. 2005.
28. Cf. Dove 1988; March 1998: 48ff.
29. On these issues of hospitality, see also Shryock 2008.
30. On drinking styles in "multicultural" contexts see Room 2005. Terwiel (1992: 130ff.) discusses Tai-speaking Ahom in Assam using rice beer to distinguish themselves from Hindus. Non-Hindus in Nepal also do this (March 1998).
31. The anthropologist has an agenda: its name is analysis. Krasdolfer (2006: 304) suggests that many anthropologists only pretend to accept local food and drink, purposefully alternating this with refusal, so as to maintain their privileged distance to achieve their agenda. My method of "participant intoxication" is different.
32. Quoted in Scott and Hardiman 1983 [1900]. Compare Salemink (2003) and Pearson (2009) on how missionaries and soldiers have manipulated Vietnamese highlanders' hospitality.
33. Especially from 1958 onward (Fiskesjö 2000: 364–73)—not just in the Wa lands but also in Tibet and elsewhere along China's ethnic frontiers.
34. William Young, letters from Bana Village, Mong Lem, China, 15 October 1923, p. 2 (American Baptist Foreign Mission Society, Records, 1817–1959, in FM 264-4-9) and 27 March 1924 (in FM 264-4-10).
35. This includes Burma's Special Region 2, which is so economically integrated into China that Chinese currency dominates completely—alongside Chinese cigarettes and liquor bought with that currency.

4

Mining, Hierarchy, and the Anti-state Wa

Against most outsiders' expectations, the land of the Wa was wealthier and more densely populated than neighboring areas before it was divided between the modern nation-states of China and Burma (see figures 0.1 and 1.2, maps with major mining sites noted).*[1] Today, these rather sparsely populated highlands are the exploited peripheries of the region's more heavily populated, valley-based nation-states. But this has not always been so.

The concept of "wealthy Wa" would seem to run counter to the mantra of "primitive Wa poverty" repeated endlessly in much of the literature written by condescending outsiders, who prefer the view that the Wa must have been poor in the past, when they wore little or no clothes. This may be true, but they forget that some wore silver headgear and bracelets at the same time, and weren't necessarily abstaining from clothing out of poverty.[2]

The high population density, and wealth, in the historical Wa country once surprised the British as they (unsuccessfully) sought to incorporate the Wa areas into their Burmese colony in the late nineteenth and early twentieth centuries. The British noted the conspicuous jewelry and other confounding signs of wealth, which indicated that the Wa were "much more prosperous than [people] on our side" (Harvey 1933: 91, referring to other, already subservient margins of the former Burmese state conquered by Britain as a colony).

The British had come face-to-face with the peculiar, autonomous polity of the Wa, which existed before the 1950s. Locally, in the parts of the Wa lands that were taken over by China, Wa people tell stories of how they preserved their family and personal jewelry well into the late 1950s and 1960s, when most if not all of it was lost in the "class struggle" imported from Mao's China that destroyed Wa institutions, turned Wa against Wa, and scattered the wealth of many households. The

---

Endnotes for this chapter begin on page 119.

Chinese searched these households for real or imagined signs of social distinction, material or personal, and many people were killed (see chapter 3).

Some such wealth still remains hidden and guarded years after those events. Once, in about 1998, while sitting in the home of an elderly villager in a remote location, I happened to ask the man if he had ever seen one of those fabled bronze drums of olden times.[3] His unexpected response was, "Sure! I have one here." He lifted up his bed and pulled out an ancient drum from underneath for me to admire (Figure 4.1, below).

If we know about the past wealth of the Wa, it will immediately seem less strange that many Wa people themselves, even into the present, have insisted that their land is an important center, not a periphery. I have already mentioned how certain origin myths recount how humanity emerged out of the ground in the middle of Wa country, and that the first people on earth were the Wa, who settled at this ground zero of human history. The ancestors of the Burmese, Chinese, Shan, Americans, and so on emerged only later, and had to settle farther away. Based on this scenario, many Wa have identified their land as the center of the world, and their people as the "elder brothers" of humankind, with special responsibilities on its behalf (see chapter 2).

I believe these myths obviously help to bolster Wa land claims, and this kind of "updating" of origin myths to deal with present-day challenges is not unique to the Wa (cf. Turner 1988a, 1988b). But one cannot simply dismiss these myths as self-serving concoctions, not just because they represent Wa attempts to define

Figure 4.1. Wa gentleman showing a family heirloom: an ancient bronze drum. Cangyuan County. Photo by the author, 1998.

their situation and their relations with outsiders but also since most ethnic neighbors of the Wa (Shan, Lahu, Chinese, and so forth) unanimously take it for a fact that the ancestors of the Wa were indeed present before all others. There are other indications that Mon-Khmer-speaking ancestors were, in fact, in the area first, or at least "first" in a relative sense, in the last millennium, or even the last millennia.[4]

The Wa claims to centrality and importance might still seem outrageous from the perspective of the Chinese or Burmese empires and kingdoms with universal presumptions, or even those of their smaller Shan Buddhist "client states" historically flourishing in the neighborhood of the Wa (Chit Hlaing 2009: 24). In almost any Chinese setting, the Wa claims are sure to elicit the famous proverbial dismissal of the king of Yelang, who reportedly dared to compare his smaller realm, located in today's Yunnan and Guizhou, with the vast Chinese empire, thus the saying "Yelang *zi da*" (or, "Yelang thinks he's big"). That kingdom was indeed later incorporated into the empire; yet recent research has shown that it, too, was actually rather more powerful and significant than the Chinese accounts sought to portray it, and the proverbial drumbeat dismissing the Yelang as a joke certainly must be read as a tendentious Chinese interpretation.[5]

While the Wa were even more distant from historical Chinese power centers than the Yelang, they are both examples of how people in centers of civilization such as China and Burma forge imaginary descriptions of their peripheries as backward and hapless. This tendency is integral to civilization as ideology (Friedman 1994), and it frequently leads to glaring discrepancies between historical fact and civilizing fantasy, as with the Yelang—and the Wa.

These discrepancies become especially apparent in the variation between the discourses of the flag bearers of civilization (officials, historians, and the like) and those recoverable from people less invested in the ideological *project* of civilization, like no-nonsense merchants who are not invested in state ideology in the same way, and therefore more realistic. One good example of this is the inclination of Chinese merchants to refer, as they did historically, to the powerful, wealthier, and better-armed central Wa as the "Big Wa" instead of using the official Chinese "Raw" (*sheng*, or "Wild," *ye*) Wa, which implied inferiority (Fiskesjö 1999a)—the merchants also referred to the already marginalized Wa as "small" (instead of "cooked" or "tame" as in the discourse of civilized orthodoxy; more on this in chapter 7). The Chinese sociologist Fei Xiaotong (1955: 105) also recognized and was able to visualize the reality of the autonomous Wa center, surrounded by ethnic Wa peripheries dependent on either the central Wa or the state societies beyond them.

This chapter investigates how the powerful and wealthy autonomous Wa—whom Chinese merchants pragmatically recognized, but who later surprised the British—depended not just on the geographical advantage of their mountains

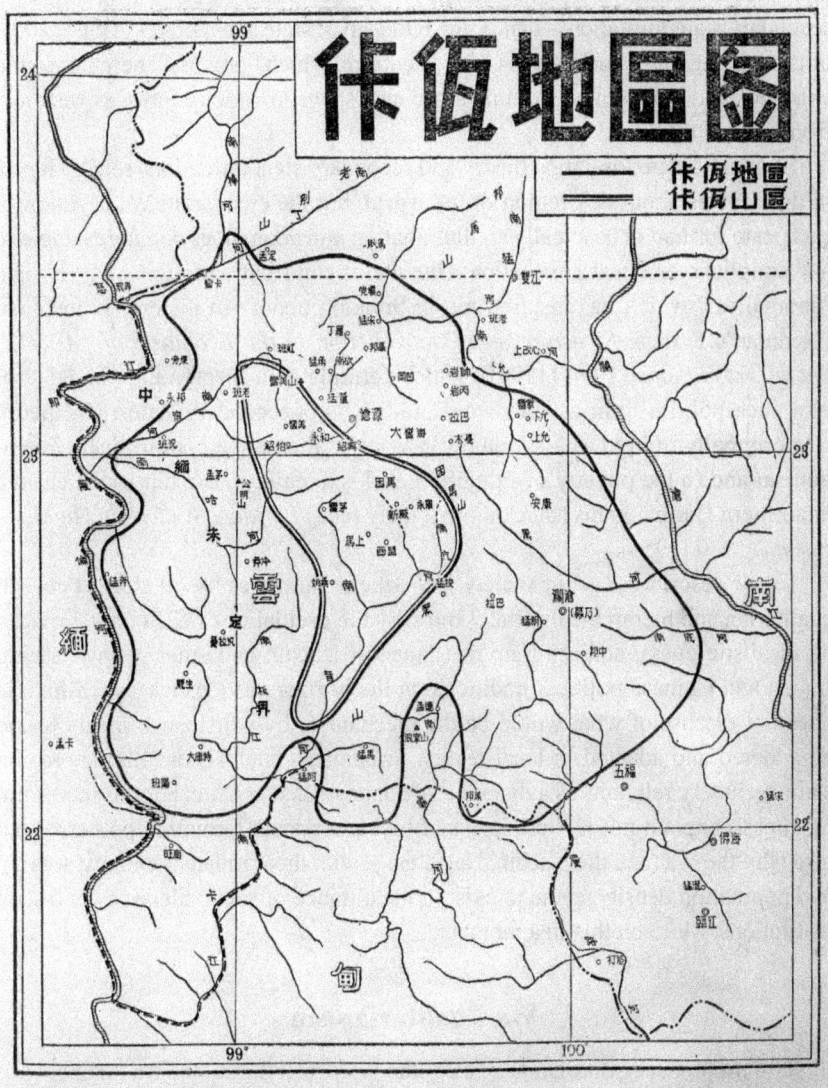

Figure 4.2. "Map of the Kawa area" indicating the autonomous central Wa country, as well as the Wa peripheries. From Fei Xiaotong 1955, 105.

but also on their manipulation of marketable resources and goods, as well as the politics of their society. Here I mainly discuss these issues in terms of mining and largely pass over other key items, such as cotton[6] and opium, though I will return to the issue of opium at the end of this chapter.

One key difference between the Wa and kingdoms such as the Yelang (or for that matter the small Buddhist Shan states in the Wa region) is that the Wa for the most part had no kings, no army, and no state. They did not engage in Yelang-style secondary state formation—that is, the build-up of state apparatuses in the shadow of preexisting ones, such as the Chinese empire, which "provoke" new states into existence and which in turn mimic those new states in various ways, as we know from around the world.[7]

Strangely, state formation theory and secondary state formations seldom figure in the debates about this region of the world, but the egalitarian Wa negation of such state formation is actually an illuminating and anomalous counterexample to any simplistic or linear conception. One major contribution to the study of such "anomalies," which has inspired me in thinking about Wa history, is Jonathan Friedman's *System, Structure and Contradiction in the Evolution of "Asiatic" Social Formations* (1998 [1979]), which formulated a theory, and "model," of how such polities form as "predatory polities," not secondary states. His theory was originally offered as a structuralist-Marxist alternative both to linear evolutionism and to the poverty of Edmund Leach's attempt to explain social change in northern Burma, in his (much more widely read) *Political Systems of Highland Burma* (1970 [1954].)

Leach describes Kachin society in northern Burma as "oscillating" between egalitarian and hierarchical ideals.[8] But why the oscillation? Leach only provides an idealistic guess, conjuring up the image of Kachin and other peoples seeing Indian and Chinese political traditions on the horizon, as ideals to reach for. He does not discuss of what would be the mechanism by which such ideals would be adopted and adapted in local reality. Friedman's analysis of "Zomia" region state-periphery relations as a dynamic social process was a much more successful attempt to explain not just primary and secondary state formation processes but also why the Wa (and the Kachin, Naga, etc.), with their armed autonomy, wealth, and population density, came to exist in the absence of social hierarchy and state institutions. More on this in a moment.

Wa Egalitarianism

First, more on the egalitarian politics of the Wa. Until the end of Wa autonomy in the 1950s, every man, and generally also every woman, in the central Wa country was regarded as independent and autonomous in themselves, according to an ethos that strongly emphasized equality and was bolstered by codes of honor and moral norms. These also regulated institutions such as marriage, which persons could only establish through patrilineages other than their own. Such patrilineages, or clans, had certain prerogatives—for example, each would manage their own sacrificial drum and water aqueduct pipeline into the village. People would also unite beyond these clans to defend their shared villages and, in larger conflicts, the genealogically connected networks known as *jaig'qee* (Wa "realms"), or even, when necessary, Wa country in general.

But personal and local autonomy was always retained and exercised as far as possible, contributing to frequent internecine quarrels governed by internal laws of conflict. Everything happened under an aegis of "ordered anarchy" similar to that practiced by the politically segmentary and kingless Nuer people in the Sudan, famously described by Evans-Pritchard.[9] The British were disappointed on this score, not just in the Sudan but in the Wa lands too, in their search for leaders to engage or to enthrone as puppets. Here is James George Scott's frustrated account of his 1893 search for a rumored great chief, conducted on foot in the core Wa areas (the land of the "Wa Hai" or Wild Wa in the Shan description, whom British intelligence relied on):

> We went slightly out of our way in order to meet Sung Ramang, the great *O-lang-la* of these parts. His capital contains 306 houses, and over 30 villages, each numbering more than a hundred houses, were said to acknowledge his authority and Hpaya Möng Hsaw assured us that Sung Ramang wished for British protection, or at any rate wished to have something to allege against Chinese aggression. Except, however, that we visited the place, showed that we were friendly and scrupulously paid for all supplies, we took very little by our visit. It was absolutely certain that the *O-lang-la* was in the village; indeed no one whatever, not even the women, left the village; but Sung Ramang could not muster up the courage to declare himself. Five persons were successively presented to me as the Chief, but all in turn declared that it was not so, not even the temptation of a many-bladed knife was effectual. Yet we walked all over the village, we sat for some time in the Chief's house, and almost certainly spoke with him, without a knowledge which of the crowd he was. Much of this was due to the undoubted fact that the Wa Chieftains inspire no awe and not much respect among their subjects. . . . Sung Ramang has entirely built up his own power and is said to have derived his good fortune from the possession of a nine-tailed dog. When an allusion to this notable animal failed to arouse the pride and disclose the owner, I gave up the attempt in despair . . . I am inclined to doubt Sung Ramang's absolute authority over his thirty villages. That he is recognized as the most powerful chief in the neighborhood is certain, but it is as a chief of a confederation rather than as the sole lord.[10]

"Take me to your leader!" The British wished to find a local lord, someone reliably powerful enough to be effectively coopted for imperial purposes. But Scott himself also, at the same time, vaguely realized that the idea of such an exalted figure could "inspire no awe" among the egalitarian independent Wa.

Several kinds of leadership positions did in fact exist among the autonomous Wa, but all with limited authority. The hereditary, more ancient position of *o lang* (mentioned by Scott, above) was a spiritual authority, associated with pan-village rituals. In secular affairs, the *o lang* and everyone else were seconded by the *a meang* (officials), nonhereditary individual leaders or chiefs rising to contingent challenges of war and foreign affairs. None of them had the power to order fellow Wa around, and none of them could take the wealth of the community and concentrate it in their own hands.

How should we understand anti-state Wa politics and its resemblance to Nuer "ordered anarchy"? More concretely, how should the relatively powerless "chiefs" of the obsessively egalitarian yet also wealthy Wa be understood? Are these the shadow remnants of chieftainship whose growth into permanent authority, kingship, and state structures (primary or secondary) could not be sustained even as Wa autonomy solidified, however precariously and in nonhierarchical mode?

In his book on these issues, first published 1979, Jonathan Friedman argued that the "anti-chiefs"[11] of the Wa, the Nagas, and other peoples in the region are the consequence of an inevitable formula of "social devolution" forced by circumstance, especially the circumscription by outside powers, blocking the growth of indigenous chiefs.[12] However, I believe it is also possible that, at the same time, such chiefs served as part of a historical agency that intentionally weakened chiefly power so as to ensure mastery of the Wa situation on behalf of the community as a collective, and that this was done purposefully to avoid the road of secondary state formation whereby powerful local chiefs enrich and elevate themselves based on local resources and by way of trade with neighboring powers. This is my argument, which acknowledges Leach, Lévi-Strauss, and especially Friedman's critique, as well as Scott's recent work, but also attempts to go beyond them all.

I have already suggested that it is possible to identify the Wa and Naga social forms with the conscious refusal to be drawn into the processes of state formation. This would agree with James C. Scott's insistence (2009: 113ff.) on the active agency of the mountain people—though he emphasizes this as an aspect of evasive action to seek refuge from the state. This does not square with the fearsome Wa digging into their mountain fastnesses.

To shed more light on these questions and build an argument about Wa wealth and politics, this chapter reviews the history of Wa autonomy with a special focus on the manipulation of mining resources in the central Wa area while it remained autonomous (until the mid-twentieth century). To repeat, this was no secondary state formation—rather, it was the opposite of state formation: its rejection. There was no Wa king, and no army other than the armed people themselves.[13] The Wa center was also quite unlike Wa areas that had been subjugated and dominated by others (such as by the Shan or the Chinese) as in the classic "peripheral situation" (Turner 1986; Nugent 1988). Those areas also had no powerful chiefs of their own, only headmen that served as liaisons with the powers that be—much like village headmen do today: their work is mainly to relay the commands of the Chinese or Wa State authorities.

The fiercely egalitarian Wa center of the past contrasted with an incipient Shan-styled Wa "kingship," which twice arose on the outskirts of Wa country in the era before modern nation-states: once in the mine-rich Wa areas of Banhong (the so-called "Hulu kings"), and once at Mangleng (the "Mang Lün" Shan-style chief mentioned by Scott in the quote above as one of Scott's allies and informants). In the following, I talk about mining in the historical central Wa lands in relation to these two cases of would-be "kings." I largely pass over the dependent Wa peripheries and refer only very briefly to the post-1989 centralized government of the Wa State on the Burma side. The Wa State is a very different story: it has many trappings of state power built on the Chinese model (a hierarchical structure, a formal army, a Communist Party, and so on) which were completely absent in the past.[14] (Its area was once the western part of Wa territory and includes the Mangleng area, while Banhong has ended up in China. See figures 0.1 and 1.2).

Subterranean Riches of the Wa Hills

The rich mineral resources in the Wa area include silver, gold, iron, and tin, and rumors about them have a very long history. Since ancient times, precious minerals and gems from the region have appeared in Chinese accounts as tributes brought from the southwestern margins of the empire. Such rumored riches have served, both symbolically and materially, to fuel the building of the Chinese and other states. Mineral wealth was a major motivation for incorporating today's Yunnan Province (which includes part of the Wa lands) into the body of the Chinese state, which began over two thousand years ago (Yang Bin 2009a). Such territorial ingestion was often preceded by tribute relations that ensnared and transformed local society (Yao 2016), and as we shall see, forward parties of Chinese miner-entrepreneurs often inserted themselves into such processes, in their own interest.

The pattern is broadly comparable to the case of the British, who were taking over Burma in the late nineteenth century and who also became attracted by rumored riches in the Wa lands. They, too, saw divergences between commercial-entrepreneur and strategic-imperialist interests. At first they focused on rumors of a Wa "gold tract" south of Ximeng (Möng Hka) that may have been identical to the "Shwe Thamin Chaung" (Golden Deer Stream) that a royal Burmese army had once attempted to reach but found themselves blocked by "Wild Wa" resistance.[15] Around 1890, one Chinese traveler in the area reported local gold lore, as well as fears of British intrusion.[16] The British too surveyed the area but found no "gold tract," and thus temporarily retreated. Then, with the British annexation of Burma in the nineteenth century, a race developed between the twin empires of Britain and China, a mimetic race based in the desire for control of these underground riches, real or rumored. Meanwhile, the independent-minded Wa still attempted to chart a route preserving their independence.

The Maolong Mines and the "King" of Banhong

In the Wa region, the once famous but now largely exhausted Maolong silver mines stand out in history. They cover about fifteen square kilometers of once disputed territory in the northernmost Wa country, now just inside Burma. Large-scale silver mining was carried out here between about 1650 and 1800. The site became one of the most important silver mines of the Chinese southwest and was increasingly important as a Chinese source of both silver, copper, gold. At times, Yunnan yielded half of the empire's silver. Many people arrived from China's interior for mining work, while private merchant-entrepreneurs were often permitted to run silver mines for profit, without the state subsidies granted to other mines.[17] Most such mines were within Yunnan, but some were in areas that had never been under Chinese administration, and remained so: Maolong was "the biggest to the south of China."[18] Bawdwin was another large silver mine even farther into Burma (and outside of the Wa area). In 1855, at the time of the outbreak of the Muslim-Chinese imperial mining wars in Yunnan, which severely disrupted the trade (Barton 1933: 124–25), as many as ten thousand Chinese miners were still present at Bawdwin.

Significantly, whereas at Bawdwin the Chinese miners paid dues to the Burmese sovereign (Daly 1891: 6:23), the Maolong site was located in a self-administered Wa area outside the limits of both Chinese and Burmese sovereignty and also removed from the control of local Burmese or Chinese Shan client kingdoms. Thus Chinese miners at least initially paid dues to the Wa (and possibly continued to do so into the twentieth century).[19]

The earliest discovery and exploitation of ores may have been done by the Wa themselves, before Chinese entrepreneurship, but indigenous written records are lacking. "Mao-long" may originally be a Wa name, though it is often taken as another example of the Sinicization of a Shan name—like so many Chinese place names in this region. (Chinese traders and officials often first encountered and dealt with the literate valley-based Shan Buddhist polities here, and subsequently, through them, nonliterate people such as the Wa.) The first syllable in "Maolong" (also Mulung, or Molung) may derive from *me*, Wa for "silver" (cf. Pasquet 1989:

62), while *long* is the common Wa word for "upper." These "Upper Silver" mines may relate to two other famous silver mines near Ximeng, Munai and Xinchang, located inside the old Wa country.[20]

Chinese sources carry little trace of any Wa initiatives. Instead, they ascribe mining entrepreneurship to Chinese investment and tutelage. They typically suggest that mining at Maolong was started in 1644, after the downfall of the Ming dynasty, by Ming-loyalist refugee general Li Dingguo (1620–62), who arrived there with thousands of soldiers to mine silver, gold, copper, and iron.[21] In one story recorded from the area (Wang Jingliu n.d.), a silver nugget found by two Wa men was carried by their mother in a cotton basket to the Shan market town of Mengding. Li Dingguo and his soldiers saw it there and identified it as silver, and began operations after receiving permission from the Wa Banlao polity and the Mengding Shan prince, who would all share the profits.

Chinese sources thus suggest there already was a Banlao "king" (*wang*) known to the Chinese. This king in turn was part of a Hulu (gourd) kingdom, composed of a group of five or more related Wa hereditary chiefs, including one at Banhong—which subsequently became the more important in the group.[22] In fact, the position of *wang* may have been inaugurated when the Chinese mining general identified his interlocutor as such and obtained his permission—and it may have become hereditary because the Chinese paid respects to the "royal" descendants.

However, the origin of Hulu kings also precedes this Chinese creation of convenient counterparts. Chit Hlaing (2009) has discussed these kings, their titles, their relation to Shan and Burmese Buddhist conceptions of rulership, their partial conversion to Buddhism, and the influence of Shan culture (on dress, village architecture, etc.), possibly all of which emerged before there were any mining operations.[23] The Banhong chief and other "kings" had styled themselves as Shan-like *cao fa* ("kings" or "princes") or *cao meng* ("rulers of the land," a lesser title), with Shan regalia and so on, converting their own "subjects" to Buddhism and prohibiting Christianity (Xiao Zisheng et al. 1986: 8).

Yet as we shall see, all this may have been a spectacle, drummed up for outsider's consumption. Like many other originally non-Buddhist highland peoples, these Wa were at risk of drifting into the orbit of such princely Shan states, or even being conquered by them (compare Kengtung, mentioned in the introduction, once owned by the Wa but then conquered by a Shan prince). They were susceptible to becoming tied up as suppliers of tribute and labor to Shan kings, as happened in many other places. But what seems to have happened here is that these Wa deflected such Shan attempts to dominate them by seizing on their own geopolitical advantage to set themselves up as Shan-style princes, on the model of those same threatening Shan states, so as to be able to compete with them.

There are many reasons for religious conversion, but here it was probably about sharing in Buddhism's universal appeal, and thus set the stage for competition on equal terms (Chit Hlaing 2009: 20–21). However, later on, and especially with the confrontation between the British and Chinese empires (and the Chinese Republic), the Banhong dynasty, as we shall see, eventually ended up as a vassal of China instead, and the Chinese state apparatus overtook the appeal and potential of this Shan model of Buddhist kingship.

Note that the unique position of the Banhong Wa, with their mines, stands out particularly in comparison with the peripheral Wa areas engaged by American Baptist missionaries in the early twentieth century, such as in Lancang County, where there were no mines that could be controlled by the Wa. There, no Wa "kingdoms" appeared, and the conversion to a foreign religion proceeded (as usual, and similarly to the appeal of non-Christian indigenous prophets) in the "hope against hope" of patronage and protection in a peripheral situation of dependency, landlessness, debt, and oppression (see chapter 9). The missionaries, tellingly, kept complaining internally of the superficiality of Wa faith, while the Chinese authorities, incredulous of the missionaries' stated motives, repeatedly suspected the missionaries of being involved, like everyone else, in for-profit mining (see chapter 9).

The contrast between the Wa converting to Christianity or syncretic millenarianism in a situation of powerlessness, on the one hand, and the respect demanded by the more powerful central Wa and the Buddhist Banhong Wa, on the other, is stark. This is illustrated in British glimpses of Banhong from 1900 and 1929:

> In 1900 the Chinese even with an escort of 100 rifles dared not take our Boundary Commission surveyors into Panghung [Banhong] but turned back at its border . . . they did not administer Panghung, but stopped short at the western border of Mengting [Mengding]. Rev. R. B. Buker AMB [American Baptist Mission] says he has never heard of the Chinese daring to enter Panghung. In March 1929, the deputy Ma Lien-wei could not visit Panghung without sending gifts and waiting for permission to enter. In October 1929 the escort of 60 rifles which under the orders of the Yunnan government took Draper (& Barton) to visit the mines, halted at the Panghung border for three consecutive days while waiting for its chief to accepts its gifts and grant permission to cross his territory; while crossing it . . . the whole escort was in a state of nerves, men sleeping in their boots, for terror of the Panghung Wa (& these are not wild Wa, but comparatively tame).[24]

Chinese Mining Entrepreneurs and Their Politics

British sources offer revealing glimpses of this sort, but in the more voluminous Chinese sources, the history becomes significantly and interestingly distorted.

Even contemporary Chinese scholars portray Li Dingguo as a forerunner of Wa-Chinese friendship (Gong Yin 1982: 88–91). For example, much like the Communist mythology concocted around Mao's twentieth-century People's Liberation Army, Li's seventeenth-century ragtag soldiers are supposed to have opted to "eat grass roots and tree bark" rather than take food from the Wa who, supposedly, as "primitive" swiddeners, hardly had food for themselves (this despite their "kingdom").

In these Chinese tales, Li Dingguo is even said to have become deified among the Wa, alongside the famous miner-entrepreneur Wu Shangxian and a Chinese Buddhist monk who supposedly instructed the Wa in growing " the five grains, . . . build[ing] houses, and abolish[ing] headhunting," and who converted the Wa of Banlao and Banhong to Buddhism. A local Chinese saying even suggests that it was Li and Wu who taught the La-jia (Buddhist Wa) "to work iron, to use wood, and build houses" (Duan and Zhao 1991).

The Wa do indeed have their own rich traditions of agriculture[25] and house building. The motive in denying this is obviously to impose (mostly for Chinese consumption) a value hierarchy that relegates Wa to primitiveness on civilization's ladder while elevating Chinese agriculture and technology. In reality, Wa headhunting, as well as its framing as a primitive custom, is a relatively recent phenomenon, born out of exactly the kind of conflicts discussed here—its juxtaposition with other supposedly primitive aspects of Wa existence denies or "overwrites" Wa history (chapter 6). This move defines the Chinese engagement with the Wa as a civilizing mission while also purposefully omitting the Shan intermediaries, and the Burmese, already engaged in their own (Buddhist) civilizing mission.

But the Chinese civilizing mission may actually have been exercised mostly at a distance—by officials, literati, and (later) modern patriots—whereas Chinese mining entrepreneurs on the ground probably seldom campaigned for it. In order to maintain peace and maximize profits, they would interact pragmatically, even respectfully, with Wa natives. We do know that such entrepreneurs did fall in line whenever they dealt with Chinese officials—probably playing both sides.

Wu Shangxian, who revived the mines in the 1740s, is a prime example—including of the mortal dangers involved in this game. His case also offers further insights into the nature of "Hulu kingship." Wu is said to have had supernatural talents for finding hidden silver ores and became very wealthy within a few years, living in his own Maolong "palace," the remains of which the British agent Barton saw in 1929 (1933: 61–62). Like Li Dingguo, Wu actually started by obtaining Wa permission: "Under license of the Wa king Panghsu [Bangzhu] of the big Mu mountain, who ruled five Wa circles, between Mengting and the Salween" (Barton 1933: 49; 117–18). In 1935, Fang Guoyu, the patriotic Yunnan historian, visited the area and found a 1743 tablet recording how the "Hulu king" granted Wu the right to run the mines.[26]

In 1746, Wu embarked upon a foolish diplomatic adventure, heading a delegation of three "Kawa" (Wa)[27] leaders and a representative of Gengma (one of the most important nearby "Chinese" Shan *tusi* polities[28]) to the provincial capital Kunming. Wu pressed for tributary status for one "Hulu king" (Bangzhu), whom he had offered to pay for his lease. The Wa king had refused, he claimed, and instead proposed to enter the fee as tribute to the Chinese empire and thus acquire status as a tributary polity (a potentially profitable position of alliance). While tributary status also required formal submission to the Chinese state, such requests were brought by many who sought acceptance as trading partners within the Chinese system, or as Chinese-appointed "native chiefs"—some of whom were not "native" at all, but Chinese from the interior, posing as natives to reap more profits from their frontier trade. This, as Pasquet (1989) suggests, may have been Wu Shangxian's objective. The mission may have been entirely his own initiative, an attempt to fool his Wa hosts by way of some other tale. Regardless, it indicates clearly the structural interrelationship of the actors involved.

Some Chinese in the region already knew of the Wa (as shown by earlier accounts[29]), but the Wa had not hitherto figured in imperial (Qing dynasty) calculations. In 1746, Yunnan's governor general reported to the imperial throne in Beijing that the origin of the "Hulu king of the Kawa" was unknown, that his territory bordered on the (autonomous) "Raw Kawa," and that the polity had "never since antiquity had relations with China," but also was not subject to Burma.[30] The court accepted a nominal tributary status for the "Hulu king," but with reservations that signaled the beginning of the end for the volunteer intermediary Wu Shangxian:

> [The Emperor's] Council report upon a proposition of the Viceroy that the offer of the K'awa Hulu Prince [wang] Pengchuh be accepted: This prince says that the Maolong silver mines are within his territory and that a large number of Chinese are working there and offer to pay a royalty or rent, which he the [Wa] prince cannot venture to receive: he offers to pay this rent as tribute. The Council think[s] that the expression of loyalty on the part of a prince far beyond our limits is sufficient without our accepting his tribute, and advise that the Viceroy be instructed to preach him a homily in this sense and send him back to his lair.
>
> But Wu Shang-hsien and his companions have no business to surreptitiously cross the frontier to work mines and the Viceroy should be called upon to report who is responsible for this carelessness. . . . Yunnan has no agricultural wealth, and depends upon its minerals for the sustenance of its poor population. Though the barbarians have mines, too, they don't know how to work them, and the presence of Chinese here is advantageous to both. The prohibition to cross the border has always been understood

not to refer to traders, so long as they do not trade in contraband goods. There are now between 20,000 and 30,000 persons there engaged in mining or trading peacefully, and no disturbance has taken place for over a hundred years. Though the Hulu Prince may be a barbarian beyond the vivifying influence of civilization, his offer of tribute is a genuine piece of loyalty, . . . he might well be allowed to pay in half the royalties (Rs. 33,000) offered by him, as was done with the Sawbwa[31] of Meng Lien in the case of the Munai mines,[32] keeping the other half to himself. The Council approves, but adds that the Viceroy should at the same time watch the frontier more carefully.—Sanctioned.[33]

Pasquet relates the court's debate over Wu Shangxian's machinations, and whether they would allow the Chinese-run mine to deliver tribute in the name of the Hulu. The "viceroy" argued that the region's economies were interdependent and that the empire would gain from resources drawn from barbarian lands. The court, unimpressed, prohibited subjects from working mines outside its control. The imperial Chinese authorities were wary of entrepreneurs venturing beyond the limits of their administration: it risked the loss of technological know-how, increased threats to social order, and raised other concerns of imperial overextension (Golas 1999: 418ff.). Indeed, later, the devastating Panthay Muslim wars in Yunnan (1856–73) began over conflicts with immigrant Chinese attempting to appropriate mines already worked by local Muslims.[34] Moreover, many imperial soldiers sent to these southern regions perished from disease, not fighting, and for this reason the 1765–70 Burma campaign was "the most disastrous frontier war that the Qing dynasty had ever waged."[35]

In 1746, prudence reigned, and all border trade not under direct state control was curtailed (Barton 1933: 113). The Wa were left in place, mainly because they, too, were beyond control: "All through this dynasty they [the Wa] have not been crushed as they extend into foreign territory, and it was feared that foreign troubles might ensue."[36] Wu Shangxian, the self-appointed spokesman, was detained and died in a Kunming prison, though only after first accompanying, in 1750–51, another tributary mission to Beijing, this time from Burma. Tribute was accepted, but Wu again was rejected as mediator. Then, with Wu gone, the silver ran out; the Maolong mines were declared closed in about 1800, as was the once-important Munai mine.

At Maolong, vast mountains of lead-rich slag remained, but their economic potential was not realized until the British stirred again in the early twentieth century, in turn provoking renewed Chinese interest. Wa exploitation occurred in the intervening period, and there is fragmentary evidence suggesting that Wa interests diverged from those of the Chinese. Indeed, more than a century after the Chinese disengagement, when Britain and China began eyeing the lead-rich slag, the Wa were still granting concessions, using the lead-rich slag to manufacture bullets both on their own and through Chinese contractors (Barton 1933: 2).

The Wa polity of Banhong, near Maolong, retained its independence but already was slowly drifting into the Chinese state system. In 1891, Banhong aided China in quelling a dispute between minor Shan polities in the area, and its *wang* was recreated with a Chinese low-ranking *tusi* title (*tudufu*), and a Chinese surname (Hu).[37]

Meanwhile, control of the mines apparently shifted temporarily to the nearby Wa polity that the British called the "statelet" of Yungpang (Yongbang), which was closely connected with nearby Panglung. The latter was a settlement of Chinese Muslim refugees from the nineteenth-century Panthay wars in Yunnan, and a new factor in the local power balance, especially after the Wa-Panthay War of 1926–28 in which the better-armed Muslim traders won their own emancipation from tribute obligations to the local Wa and later overcame a Wa boycott.[38] However, even if power was shifting away from Wa natives and their "Hulu kings" to "bandits" such as the Panthay—and to the reformed Chinese state looming in the background (in the shape of Yunnan's semi-independent governor, Long Yun, who pushed for interventions responding to British advances)—the Wa clearly still remained in control of the mines, until the 1930s. In 1929, Barton interviewed Yao Hsiang, a military representative of the Chinese Republic at Mengding, who remarked candidly on the Maolong mines:

> Whatever their position with regard to Mupang[39] or China, [the mines] still are very definitely in the hands of the Wa and can only be visited, not to mention worked, with the Wa's consent, but the Wa's [sic] are quite keen on having them worked by a private concern, and not by the Chinese government. (Barton 1933: 57–58)

Clearly, the Wa were in charge of their own mines. An opportunity of sorts existed for British overtures, but it was not exploited successfully. In 1920, a British mining expert named Oberlander (Xiao Zisheng et al. 1986: 9) noted the enormous old lead-rich slag heaps only 120 miles east of Lashio. This rekindled the interest of the British, whose Burma Corporation was now working the Bawdwin mines. Previously, it had not mattered much to either Britain or China that it had been impossible to define their border in the independent Wa area (the first attempt, in 1898–1900, was a failure partly because of Wa resistance), but now the rediscovery of Maolong stirred new interest in "the obstinate Wa and their slag-heaps."[40]

This culminated in a British military intervention, the 1934 Banhong incident, which was also a failure due to the resistance of Wa and others.[41] In China, this incident is generally defined as glorious Wa patriotism on China's behalf. British sources do speak of "Chinese forces . . . supported by bandits and tribesmen,"[42] but the "tribesmen" were diverse: according to one Chinese account, the British also "bought" the service of certain "treacherous, Wild Kawa, . . . given to killing for heads and robbing villages," who would never "allow the border areas to have peace."[43] Evidently, the Wa once again—like so many others in danger of becoming mired in a peripheral situation—were being manipulated, but they themselves also sought to manipulate a situation that closely evoked past patterns.

The key Chinese figure in repelling the British and subduing anti-Chinese "Kawa disturbances" (other, self-interested Wa actions) was Li Xizhe, a modern reincarnation of the more ancient Yunnanese-Chinese soldier-entrepreneur. Li was a former salt miner and modern patriot whose irregular operations were sanctioned by the Chinese Republic, which had succeeded to the empire's concerns. Li prevailed, using modern weaponry, and reportedly lavishly rewarded his Wa allies, including Banhong, with salt and cloth. Then, setting himself up as their spokesman, he invoked an anti-British alliance of eighteen Wa leaders and composed a patriotic declaration in their name—in Chinese.[44] Banhong's chief Hu Zhonghan (Hu "Loyal to Han [Chinese]," bearing a name bestowed by Chinese officials[45]) figured prominently, now with the modern title of "plenipotentiary" (*zong'guan*). Before the hostilities, he purportedly insisted to the British that China must be consulted, which may make sense given his Chinese affiliations and the long history "hosting" Chinese miners. However, given the contradictory assessment of the Chinese military representative at Mengding, cited above, this may also be a tendentious Chinese representation supporting the official Chinese recognition, redefinition, and strategic investment in "their" own Wa "kings."

In any case, this anti-British Banhong incident was soon dwarfed by World War II, when fighting involved Japan, China, Britain, and the United States, and the ensuing Chinese civil war spilled over into the Wa area itself. This was the beginning of the end of Wa independence, terminated by socialist China in the 1950s in the Wa east and in the west in the 1960s by China's ally, the Burmese Communist Party. Today the eastern Wa lands have become a classic extractive periphery of China. In the postsocialist situation of today's China, Chinese businesses and state enterprises as well as numerous mining entrepreneurs and investors are even active in the Wa State in Burma, beyond Chinese territory. The situation is new in some respects, as the UWSA's state-like structures are derived in part from the Chinese Communist model (chapter 8), but it can still be argued that the historical pattern of mutual manipulation known from Banhong and elsewhere has reappeared in new form, with Wa State hosts/owners entertaining Chinese clients/entrepreneurs eyeing Chinese and global markets for both licit and illicit goods.

The question remains as to whether the defunct Banhong and other Hulu "kings" developed substantial powers over their own people, or if they mainly deployed a spectacle of, first, Shan-style rulership and, later, Chinese-style officialdom, which mattered in relations with outsiders but not at home. The latter would support Scott's suggestion (2009: 113ff.) that such political forms are derived from the outside to be deployed as an occasional ruse, part of a strategy to evade state interference and incorporation. And indeed, these kings differed little from their fellow men, supposedly their subjects. An astonished Fang Guoyu (1943c) noted that the woman pounding rice for dinner at the royal Banhong household was the king's own queen, as in any Wa house. This he had not expected at a "court" that had been granted Chinese state tax revenues sufficient to employ forty soldiers. Fang's visits occurred in the 1930s, after the infamous incident had pushed Banhong further into the Chinese orbit, but still, even at this time, there is little evidence that its "king" was owed allegiance by fellow Wa as superior to them in any way. On the contrary, the rising Chinese influence at Banhong raised alarms among the Wa in general, as suggested by their cited preference for excluding Chinese state authorities from mining exploitation.

Chit Hlaing (F.K. Lehman) writes of Banhong institutions as "Buddhism manqué," and their political institutions may be described as statehood *manqué*. They may have reflected a conscious performance of some of the trappings of statehood, where this served the long-term purpose of safeguarding Wa independence, here supported by profitable mining concessions (a strategy ultimately overpowered by Chinese schemes). This interpretation is further supported by the curious discrepancy of the dual versions (in Chinese and Shan) of another ostensibly patriotically pro-Chinese tract handed in on behalf of the Wa to the League of Nations commission in 1936. The Chinese version says that while the Wa may be "stupid" (*yu*), they reject the British. On the other hand, the Shan version (it is not clear who penned it, but it may reflect Wa views more directly) demands that the commission chairman "order the British to withdraw their forces," but at the same time it refers to what it says is the "common saying" that "the Wa have bowed neither to Burma nor China" (Senior Commissioner, n.d. [mid 1936?]).

Wa Mining at Mangleng and Beyond

The other case of Wa-controlled mining, at Mangleng, is less famous than Maolong and the associated Banhong incident. Mangleng was farther away from Shan and other competition, located in the midst of supposedly "Raw" or "Wild" Wa of south-central Wa country. They were described by the British as the "Wa states" proper, sometimes ambiguously as "statelets" or "circles." These are all deceptive terms, since there is no evidence here of states or "circles" in the Shan sense of communities arranged around a power center. The area was dominated instead by the same sort of autonomous communities that exist in a state of ordered anarchy, the same kind that would have surrounded Banhong's experiments with Buddhism and with Chinese titles.

Independent Wa mining, along with the corresponding sophistication in manipulating its geopolitics, clearly has a deep history. But with the scarcity of outside visitors who would record it, the evidence is necessarily fragmentary. Some can be resurrected: In 1778, only decades after the Burmese forces had reached the southern Wa frontier area (see note 15), the Chinese imperial official Li Shirao journeyed there, noting that the "Kawa"[46] had repelled a Burmese attempt to seize the "Mangleng mines beyond Menglian." The miners even fabricated rumors that Chinese forces would intervene in their favor:

> Your servant obtained information that the wild Kawa people beyond the Mian-Shun [Burma-Shunning district, Yunnan] border since former times possessed the mines of Mangleng. The man in charge of the mines is called the "Mangleng official" by the wild people. [I] heard that Burman bandits craved the profit from the mines, and went there armed, to claim their part of it. With the leadership of the chief of Mangleng, these Burman bandits were beaten and pursued into Mubang [Hsenwi], devastating the Burmese area of Lashio as they retreated. Since it was feared that they would come back to exact revenge, [Mangleng] spread the word that [they] had "heard the Celestial Dynasty was bringing in troops to attack the bandit bases, and said they themselves will join in the slaughter," and so forth. Comparing this with the accounts given by A-li, Lao-yan, and others captured at the time of the last two [incidents], all confirm that there have been battles between the Burmese and Mangleng . . .[47]

Later, in the nineteenth century, Chinese officials would write of their resentment of the independence of the Wa of this area:

> In the past Mangleng and thirteen of the border peoples [in the area] named themselves the States of Hulu [Hulu *guo*], and in the reign of Qianlong all affiliated themselves with the interior.[48] Later, because they were located in an area distant from the interior, and the officials feared the miasmas [*zhang*] of the area and seldom ventured there, they made use of the dangerous and precarious nature [of their land] to stubbornly bolster their ostentatiousness, [and claimed] not to belong either to China or to Burma, gathering their clans and kindred [*zu lei*] to live in between, on the frontier between the two states . . .[49]

In reality, then, the Mangleng mine was an independent Wa-controlled operation, located at Kat Maw, six miles from its "capital" Ta Küt, with silver mines that by the late nineteenth century had also come to be reduced to "fairly rich" lead pits, which were "only worked when there [was] a demand for lead, that is to say, when peace in the hills [was] disturbed."[50]

In 1824, armed Mangleng Wa also tried to take over the Munai silver mines to their east, which at the time were exploited by the Menglian Shan prince. However, they were repelled by Menglian forces. The Wa may have sought to expand their lead bullet manufacturing,[51] and also to usurp profits, but without intending to style themselves as Shan kings or adopt Buddhism.

In support of this interpretation, I have uncovered highly suggestive evidence of individual Wa who were stopped by their peers when attempting to develop a Shan-style mining chieftainship. A certain Ta Awng had attempted to set himself up as a chief based on silver and gold mining, but he was rejected and isolated by the traditional chiefs of the Mangleng area. He lingered on, supported militarily by the Shan polity of Hsenwi in exchange for an alliance with it, but he died in 1822. His son held on to the dream, submitting tribute to Hsenwi and deploying Shan paraphernalia. In 1849, Burma attempted to reclaim control; local struggles left a weak "West Mangleng" lorded over by the British, while an "East Mangleng" affiliated with the independent Wa continued to escape British rule.[52] Mangleng thus recalls the Banhong-Banlao pattern, including in the manner in which the China card was played locally (Banhong tried that too, but less successfully). But aspirations to Shan-styled kingship, whatever their motives, were rejected here, and in contrast to Banhong, Mangleng also managed to avoid becoming entangled in Chinese officialdom (even though here, too, the Chinese tried to issue titles, seals, and so forth[53]).

In the late nineteenth century, the mines exhausted, Mangleng's former glory was largely forgotten and its past seldom mentioned again. The exception was the lingering but vain hope of the British to find in the failed Shan-styled polity of Mangleng a true *sawbwa* who could help them, as elsewhere in the Shan states, to control the area. Even the lingering West Mangleng chief was but a shadow, turning instead to become subservient to the "Wild Wa."[54] The British thus faced a weakened Mangleng, divided on the predominantly Shan and mixed area of "West Manglün," which was ruled by a weak, British-friendly Wa chief attempting the style of a Shan *sawbwa*,[55] and "East Manglün," which was predominantly Wa.[56]

The autonomous Wa were also in a controlling position at nearby Ox Ag, in Chinese named Xinchang (new mines) because the area attracted Chinese miners later than at Laochang (old mines) at Munai. The latter had been exploited by the Menglian Shan prince possibly as early as the fifteenth century; it was then briefly occupied by Burma around 1760 before attracting Chinese adventurers, and then it closed for the same reasons that Maolong did. Xinchang is near the rumored "gold tract," in present-day Ximeng Autonomous Wa County; the mines there were reopened in the 1980s as Chinese tin mines, with local Wa workers.

In Wa, they are still known as *a rang me* Ox Ag, the "silver rocks at Crossbow Bamboo."⁵⁷ These mines too may have been started by local Wa, perhaps in tenuous collaboration with Shan neighbors. Here, too, the Wa, much like the earliest Banhong chiefs, engaged in competitive Wa-Shan alliances, even receiving Shan princesses as wives in some cases.

By 1882, considerable numbers of Chinese miners worked the Xinchang "new" mines, paying obligatory fees. However, a conflict arose, and the Menglian prince joined the Wa in massacring a "great many" such miners.⁵⁸ Even so, by 1891, Xinchang—still deep inside Wa country—was again worked by Chinese miners; they had a shaky relationship with their "Kawa" hosts, who killed two Chinese officials on a separate scouting mission:

> At a distance from Munai of more than a hundred *li* is Xinchang, located within the Kawa area. The barbarians here do not know the methods, and all the extraction and management is done by Han people. When the Kawa come, they are treated with liquor and food, for fear of otherwise provoking their anger and stirring up trouble. In 1891 [Guangxu 17], Wang Cheng and general Yuchi were surveying the area; arriving at this spot the Kawa and others in the area suspected that they might be planning to take over their profits. Thus they were slain.⁵⁹

One more line of evidence exists for Mangleng's independent, profitable status, and that is the fact that, like other self-ruling Wa areas, it exported large quantities of opium. Opium here as elsewhere was cultivated and traded as an instrument of independent wealth creation, and in this area it was traded to the outside mainly from Mangleng's eastern parts, not from the Shan-like tributary state of western Mangleng populated mainly by Shan peasants.⁶⁰ Elsewhere, a middleman function was occupied by Shan settlements that paid tribute to independent Wa polities in exchange for their position,⁶¹ much like outsiders paid tribute to mine-owning Wa who used such assets to assert their independence.

Wa Metalworking and Mine Slaves

In addition to concession fees, another reason the Wa sought to exploit mines like these is that they had a long history of maintaining and repairing imported guns, which also explains the drive for manufacturing bullets from lead. Another aspect of Wa mining was the need for iron. Wa smiths long used recycled iron to make tools like dibbling stick points, machete-like swords for clearing swiddens and waging war, and other weapons such as spear points. Early Shan immigrants noted that the Wa already possessed these tools (*Simao Yuxi Honghe Daizu shehui lishi diaocha*: 21), and there were even sites for mining and processing more iron

(Li Genpan and Lu Xun 1985: 366) than could be imported for these purposes. Imported iron was paid for in opium or other currencies, or was obtained by the self-ruling Wa from Wa peripheries as tribute in exchange for exemption from raiding.

Wa mining is rarely mentioned in the literature, even when these proud metalworking traditions are touched upon. Neither Chinese nor British authors could imagine that "primitive" Wa could possibly run mining operations for their own benefit, administering entrepreneur concession fees. Nor could they fathom that the Wa would capture and deploy mine slaves, which some did before the 1950s.

Interestingly, the Wa did not use slaves for any other activity, not even labor-intensive opium production, which was increasingly important over the twentieth century. Thus foreign mine slaves, by no means common, are unique compared to other Wa slave-like figures, and in their social universe they constitute the only category of acknowledged slaves. They were the only kind of "war captives" who were neither sacrificed in the context of Wa headhunting nor adopted as full social beings, as some child "slaves" were (see chapter 5). Since mine slaves were adult foreigners, it was difficult either to adopt them as full members of society or to place them in a separate stratum of nonperson mine slaves, which would be contradictory in this society so permeated by ideals of autonomy and egalitarianism.

In a case recorded from 1932, a group of able-bodied Chinese miners at Munai was captured by a group of sixty Wa, who divided the miners between themselves so that each Wa kept only one or two slaves. One was held for ten years at a mine "two days north of" Möng Hka (Ximeng), where he excavated silver ores sold to China until he started going blind—he was then set free. He was well fed and received rations of opium (Barton 1933: 41–42, 95, 111; the opium was perhaps used to prevent illness, as it can calm stomach irregularities). The Mangleng mines may also once have been run with such slaves. Reports from the 1890s mention captured Chinese being "drugged and sold" to the Wa by neighboring Lahu, probably as a tribute (Harvey 1932: 9).

Why should the Wa capture mine slaves for themselves when there is no evidence that they ever used slaves in equally labor-intensive opium or farm labor? First, capturing skilled miners helped to alleviate the scarcity of such skills among the Wa. Second, the Wa are generally reluctant to dig into the soil and disturb waterways. Excessive tampering with waterways is, in the Wa imagination and sacrificial ideology, bound to be punished by the *a yong*, a major deity that dwells underground and is disturbed by excavations obstructing the natural flow of water (though it does not arbitrarily harm people without having been victimized by such disturbance, as do some other Wa deities—see chapter 8).

In the vicinity of Xinchang, where I did extensive fieldwork, there are memories of freewheeling Chinese mining entrepreneurs who paid advance cash for small mining concessions nearby, dealing directly with local Wa much as opium buyers would. But once, the *a yong* caused the mountain to cave in, "devouring" an entire Chinese party of forty men and their transport mules. In another locally famous case told in stories by Wa in the Xinchang area, some Chinese miner-entrepreneurs were caught cheating the Wa concession-givers on the portion of silver they were owed, as they attempted to smuggle silver in a coffin supposedly holding a dead miner. Discovering the ruse, the Wa killed all the Chinese miners on the spot.

Slave exploitation may have originated with the expropriation of such smaller Chinese-initiated enterprises on account of offenses against Wa morality or honor. Slaves would face the wrath of the *a yong* while the Wa reaped the profits. Yet such a displacement of Wa sin onto immoral, profit-seeking Chinese appears morally ambivalent, and evokes the other moral struggles over the commodification of people, opium, and other things, that was becoming more pronounced in this period (see chapter 5). Though mine slaves represented only a minor component in the tribute and trade relations operating between the central Wa country and its surroundings, they constitute evidence that people in the egalitarian Wa area continued to seize on subterranean assets to enrich themselves and defend their autonomy; furthermore, they did this while consciously seeking to solidify existing nonhierarchical social structures and to prevent the emergence of new hierarchies or the building of a Wa state. This includes the striking example presented here, of how the egalitarian-minded Wa halted a nineteenth-century attempt to create a Shan-style mine-based Wa kingdom near Mangleng. As for the tentative emergence of a slave substratum, I propose that it suggests Wa society was being pulled in the direction of an internally stratified society on the empire's margin, as had once been true for the Yelang or, more recently, the Yi in southwest China, who held numerous foreign slaves (again, see chapter 5).

A Political Anthropology of the Wa Rejection of Hierarchy

Several key points emerge from this critical review of mining and the nondevelopment of Wa political hierarchy before the mid-twentieth century. We leave aside the Wa already living under the control of other powers, in a "peripheral situation" of exploitation and despair, who obviously could not develop autonomous political institutions like those of the central Wa.

As for the fledgling, aborted kingship of the Banhong chief, whose territory also lies on the edge of the central Wa country, it was developed in the shadow of mutually competitive Shan polities and belongs with a range of upland chieftainships developing out of "leadership in organizing trade" (Chit Hlaing 2007: xxvii), while also struggling to avoid becoming another "periphery." Here the trade was in mining ore or collecting concessions for its extraction, and in selling opium to Chinese and other global markets. But the Banhong chiefs actually seem never to have built themselves up as kings: setting themselves apart from their own people to command service and extract taxes to accumulate further wealth. We unfortunately do not know how mine wealth was shared in Wa communities beyond Banhong, but I strongly suspect that it was dispersed by sharing, by means of the collective feasting that sustained society. The wealth does not seem to have been gathered at Banhong to finance royal pursuits of state formation. In adopting kingship in name (and spectacle) only, Banhong may have served as a conditional representative for the nearby, broader communities of egalitarian Wa. Also, the shifts seen in the custody of the mines among Wa polities may be the expression of a rotating arrangement, designed to keep the peace and prevent individual enrichment.

But all these moves were derailed by the Chinese interventions, which overwhelmed Banhong's original autonomy at the same pace as Chinese titles rained down upon it. In sum, in my interpretation, Banhong at first creatively tried to adopt the trappings of competitive Shan kingship, but it remained a temporary spectacle that would have been closed down by egalitarian Wa if it had come to involve true royal ambitions. This is what happened to the Mangleng contender whose attempts to emerge as a Shan-style prince were cut short by egalitarian-minded brethren seeking to prevent both such hubris and the monopolization of mining wealth that might sustain it into the future. This also recalls the contempt of many Kachin, further north in Burma, for their fellow Kachin who tried to model themselves on Shan kings, recasting followers as hereditary subjects and rejecting traditional Kachin chieftainship procedures. Some such pretentious chiefs were even assassinated—a move that also expresses the agency that I have identified here.[62]

In fact, the shared enjoyment of fixed natural resources under a strong, shared egalitarian ethos is not unknown in upland Southeast Asia. The egalitarian Angami Nagas and their famous salt wells is one example.[63] Such wells did not exist in Wa country (Fiskesjö 2000: 179), but the challenge they present as fixed, high-yield sources of items desirable to outsiders is similar to that of the Wa mines: How will the exploitation of a highly profitable income source affect—or be permitted to affect—the existing internal political organization in these upland societies? Should these riches be allowed to form the basis of new kinds of rulership, with a royal dynasty set apart, as in the Shan-Buddhist model?

In kingship, royalty is mystified as somehow deserving wealth and obedience (tribute, corvée, and the like), simply because of dynastic inheritance of a position mediating the supernatural for the benefit of all, one that transcends kin ties. This ruse is a key element that distinguishes kingship from indigenous forms of upland chieftainship based in agricultural accumulation. In his powerful critique of Leach, titled *System, Structure and Contradiction in the Evolution of "Asiatic" Social Formations* (1998 [1979]) Friedman theorizes how such chieftainship might eventually develop into kingship and states, just as they first did in East Asia or Mesopotamia several millennia ago, when the primary states first emerged. Initially, there is an inflationary movement from competitive prestige accumulation to surplus; then occurs the mystification of the chief as performing mediation with gods that enables all production. If the moment is right, such a chief can then up the ante by declaring himself the son not of humans but of the gods, and as the representative of the gods to what now has become "his people." The people can now be compelled to worship him as if he were a god, and he also deserves corvée and tribute. This is the way emergent dynasties replace kinship with kingship as the organizing principle and begin to rule through bureaucracies, turning "their" farmers into subordinate peasants, by force if necessary.

This recalls Clastres's (1987 [1974]) understanding of the state as a violent break, which, however, does not provide an explanation for how this may have happened in the first place. Friedman's alternative, complementary model indicates just how processes of exchange, and resource accumulation and monopolization, could lead to state formation. He suggests that Burma, China, and other states originated in this way, and he cites Manipur as a recent example.[64]

Even more relevant are Friedman's answers as to why such evolution should fail on the margins of empire. The violence of state making is easier to perpetrate on lowland farmers, and highlands offer an escape. But the dynamics of state–margin relations may be even more crucial. Insisting on the global context as directly consequential to the internal dynamic of these upland Southeast Asian polities, Friedman points to how preexisting states may block the expansion that otherwise could fuel local aggrandizement. Environmental degradation, likewise inseparable from the regional context, may also preclude the mobilization of surpluses driving competitive spirals. Secondary states may emerge anyway, built on the control of trade routes or other resources, and evolve into large-scale "predatory" states based on conquest and subjugation just like primary states, albeit often reliant on trade rather than on agriculture.

But there is also another possibility: political "devolution," or the inhibition and reversal of political hierarchy. Friedman singled out the Naga and the Wa, where circumscribed space for agricultural migration and the resulting intensification of agriculture and degradation of the productive environment seemed to have blocked the development of hierarchy. Contrary to earlier and more simplistic evolutionary theory, the high population density developing among the Naga and the Wa did not—indeed could not—lead to state formation. Populations grew denser, says Friedman, when dispersal and expansion were prevented. With dwindling returns from agriculture—the basis of indigenous political institutions—these societies' inherent trend toward hierarchy, which did originally exist, collapsed because they were unsustainable. Chiefly, authority was rendered impotent, and society "permanently" egalitarian (Friedman, 1998 [1979]: 13–15, 268–73), as a result of a dynamic process involving both society and environment—as well as neighbors.

When Friedman's structuralist-Marxist book was reissued in 1998, the author insisted on his thesis but confessed in a new preface that he had overlooked the problem of the historical agency of the actual people involved. He sought to remedy this in part by adding a discussion[65] on the growth of export-market opium cultivation in the nineteenth century, in Wa, Kachin, and other areas. Opium, as yet another new source of wealth with potential political consequences, was different in that it could be grown as a cash crop anywhere by anyone, unlike Naga salt, Kachin gems, or Wa iron, which could only be produced in fixed locations, and unlike trade goods, whose imperial-regional routes of commerce fell prey to raids from the mountain peoples. Existing chiefs might try to exploit opium in the manner that they exploited other sources of wealth, but with social devolution already in process, opium would instead reinforce egalitarian tendencies. (Similarly, we may recall, Wa slavers each took a few slaves for themselves).

Indeed, areas most closely associated with opium also show the strongest tendency toward political egalitarianism.[66] The circumscription of the Wa lands by other states and the ensuing agricultural intensification and population density, together with the opportunities of opium, very probably had a role in further encouraging egalitarianism and individual commercial entrepreneurism.

These factors also reduced the importance of the hereditary *o lang*, who may indeed have been a more commanding figure in the past, even if he was no king but rather a Wa solution to the fundamental problem of how to constrain the authority that a community delegates to a chief (cf. also Clastres's American account). In the process outlined by Friedman, such an *o lang* became an illustration of chieftainship *manqué*, as Lehman (1989: 99) described Kachin *gumlao* chiefs. Friedman's theory—helpfully explicated in Lehman's (1989) account of the inflationary processes involved in Kachin chieftainship—is surely far more productive than Leach's weak attempt to suggest that the availability of Indian and Chinese models of kingship made them take them up, without any real explanation of the steps by which people like the Kachin would feel any attraction to such models.[67]

Friedman's discovery of the built-in processes of Kachin and Wa societies is a striking achievement, not least since it had been staring previous scholars in the face. In 1954, Edmund Leach, arguing for his own understanding of Kachin society as an "equilibrium system," noted that "simply as a model scheme [Kachin] social organization can be represented as an equilibrium system . . . yet as Lévi-Strauss has perceived, the structure . . . contains elements which are 'in contradiction with the system and thus should lead to its ruin.'" He was referring to how Claude Lévi-Strauss, in his monumental reconsideration of kinship systems (*Elementary Structures of Kinship,* 1969 [1949]) had noted how the competitive contests of bridewealth inevitably led to inflation. Kinship systems aren't static, but where does this trajectory lead? It was left to Friedman to seize on such insights and develop a far better comprehensive theory of how such inflationary processes play a part in larger structural transformations.[68]

At the same time, I also think Friedman focused too much on the highlanders' situation as the predictable consequence and outcome of processes seen as inevitable, as if in a controlled laboratory. He described the Wa situation as the "end of the road" of circumscription-induced impoverishment, and opium as "a cash crop of last resort of impoverished and declining polities" (Friedman 1987: 353). He also wrote that all Wa were hopelessly indebted to outsiders—but this ignores the wealth of the central Wa country and confuses indebted peripheries with the central lands, ones not yet reduced to periphery status. Neglecting Wa agency and wealth, he also disconnected headhunting warfare from the history of conflicts over land and honor, and even saw it as an "unconscious" means of population control (Friedman 1998 [1979]: 267). He mistook the tribute-receiving Wa around Maolong for evidence of "a more developed political organization with paramount chiefs" (Friedman 1998 [1979]: 271) in a distant Wa past—even though, as we have seen, "paramount" Banhong was not mainly an evolution of ancient Wa forms but a precarious innovation based on Shan models, and might itself have been terminated by Wa warriors if it had not first been overwhelmed by Chinese state incorporation.

In their precarious situation, the central Wa took charge of the egalitarian politics into which circumstances were driving them. Headhunting, developed from earlier indigenous models and redeployed as strategic deterrence, may be the prime example (see chapters 6 and 7). Opium is another: it too was seized upon as a new source of wealth, but also not permitted to become the fuel of individual aggrandizement leading to social hierarchy. As a profitable but illicit crop, it could be grown with impunity only in these mountains, well away from the interference of states.

The way I see it, the central Wa relied on their armed autonomy to trade opium and mining wealth for cattle, arms, and other necessities used to continue to fuel their own socioeconomic life in traditional forms, especially through large-scale communal sacrifice and shared feasting. Some outsiders saw these phenomena as indications of the "primitive" Wa, but from my perspective, they might have said "conservative." The Wa placed curbs on internal competitive trends, calibrating the rotation of duties in ritual community feasting, thus restricting the aggrandizement of individuals[69] who might otherwise, if permitted to rise in political stature, become vulnerable targets of cooption by threatening external powers (as happened in Banhong).

Overall, Friedman's scheme applies, except that the Wa did not walk blindfolded into a "devolution" compelled by inevitable circumstances. Their exercise of historical agency is the true explanation for why the Mangleng Wa so decisively rejected the attempt of one of their own to set himself up as a Shan-styled mine chief. From their own observations of Shan princes and Chinese mining entrepreneurs, they would have recognized mining as a formidable challenge to the egalitarian order they preferred. In the absence of writing, such lessons were perhaps unsystematically dispersed and haphazardly applied, but understanding the strange kind of egalitarian-based anti-state polity that the Wa (and the Nagas, etc.) developed demands a redevelopment of Friedman's model to involve historical agency—and in a way different from Scott's (2009) work on "Zomia" as a refuge for those fleeing the state.

Scott rightly emphasized the intentionality and agency in play among Zomia populations. But theirs is not merely the story of being pushed aside as victims of state expansion, and their conscious escape.[70] Like Friedman's powerful model, this interpretation is very fertile, including for addressing issues such as swiddening as escapist agriculture, the "friction of terrain," and such unexpected aspects as how it is that writing has been rejected by many upland peoples. The escapist argument actually does apply for some Wa, as some of them clearly once lived further north in China but either migrated south or became subjugated and assimilated in place.

However, even though this emphasis on historical agency resonates with the thrust of my own argument here, the notion of refuge is insufficient for the autochthonous central Wa who cannot be described as fugitive or marooned communities.[71] The central Wa lands cannot be termed a refuge, except for outsider runaways and bandits entering to settle there, on Wa terms. Their social space was certainly non-state (Scott 2009: 13ff.), but not because they "resisted the projects of nation-building and state-making of the states to which [they] belonged" (Scott 2009: 19, citing van Schendel 2002). They actually weren't part of any state. There was resistance to others' state making and expansion, to be sure, but the differences between the Wa, entrenched in ancestral lands, and refugees resisting by escaping is significant. Perhaps "resistance" must be reserved for refugees, since it seems so inadequate for the Wa. Scott's observation that the Wa have "both relatively hierarchical and relatively decentralized, egalitarian subgroups," of which some can develop a parasitic relation with their host empires (Scott 2009: 22, 216, 326–27), omits the whole discussion of how such strangely non-state, egalitarian, and predatory periphery formations are made.

Our challenge remains to explain the dialectic of fate and agency. I have acknowledged the reality of the Wa geopolitical situation, which to some extent predetermined and limited the possibilities of what could happen. But the Wa made a successful stand for their autonomy, fiercely embracing their egalitarian ethos as a way of conserving this autonomy—while also, it must be admitted, engaging in some of the worst sins of the states that surrounded them: war, slavery, the forced extraction of tribute or taxes, and so forth.

Arguably, even Wa headhunting belongs here: its main inspiration may have been Chinese state practices. As we shall see, they also mobilized the deterrent effect that such "wild" practices potentially could provide for them in their efforts to fend off the surrounding state projects and their expansion, which they had to face as the biggest threat to their autonomy (chapters 6 and 8).

Notes

* This chapter draws in part on my 2010 article, "Mining, History, and the Anti-State Wa: The Politics of Autonomy between Burma and China," *Journal of Global History* 5(2): 241–64.
1. Macquoid 1896: 24; Friedman 1998: 269ff.; and elsewhere.
2. As with many other peoples in the region, Wa men and women often did not wear clothing on the upper body.
3. Bronze drums have a classic position as objects of wealth, prestige, and communication across the entire region. See the brief discussion (with further references) in the introduction. Also see p. 93, and Figure 4.1.
4. See chapter 1; note that recent genetics research also appears to support the deep antiquity of Austro-Asiatic ethnolinguistic formations ancestral to the Wa. For older discussions, see Heine-Geldern 1976 [1914]: 32; Ehlers 1901: 96; Bastian 1866; Scott and Hardiman 1983 [1900], I:495–96, Scott 1906: 134; Ling Shun-sheng 1953: 2; Tian Jizhou 1983a: 3, "Wazu jianjie"; Wei 1995; You Zhong 1980; see also below regarding the Wa as well as the Lawa of northern Thailand. The power of the notion that the Wa country is the center of the world may also be reflected in how the imagined lake "Chiamay," as the source of rivers like the Brahmaputra, the Irrawaddy, the Menam, and the Salween, was equaled with the fabled lake of the central Wa country, Nawng Hkeo, on many Western maps of Asia from the sixteenth and seventeenth centuries (Scott and Hardiman 1983 [1901]: II.2:660).
5. See Wade 2009, who argues that the name "China" may derive from an Indian version of "Yelang." If so, it is a curious last laugh indeed for the long-dead ghost of Yelang's king. On Yelang's region, in today's Guizhou Province, see also Wang Ningsheng 1996; Herman 2007, and pp. 94–96, above.
6. Cotton as a trade commodity was historically important in similar ways, in the sense that it was key to the imperial economic system, and the trade was preyed upon by the Wa in the eighteenth century—for an account "Raw" Wa plundering Chinese cotton caravans returning to Yunnan from Burma, see Fiskesjö 1999a: 146n38 (citing Fang 1984a: 2:683–84). The mid-nineteenth century Panthay rebellion in Yunnan disrupted this trade and cotton lost its significance since it was predominantly shipped by sea instead. For more discussion of cotton in Wa history, including how the Wa grew cotton and wove cloth themselves, see Fiskesjö 2000: 177 ff., esp.184–88; also Michaud 2006.
7. A good overview on the Mediterranean region is Parkinson and Galaty 2007. See also Feinman and Marcus 1998, although like many similar works, it leaves out China. On China, see Friedman 1998 [1979]: esp. 273–95; Turchin 2009; and others. On Southwest China see also Wang Ningsheng 1996.

8. Leach 1970 (originally published in 1954); also Leach 1960. Leach reportedly tried to prevent the publication of Friedman's critique (1998), which first appeared in 1979—but then in "peripheral" Copenhagen. Strangely, much of the literature engaging Leach (even Robinne and Sadan 2007, which is a review of Leach's work) ignores Friedman's powerful critique of Leach's work (cf. Fiskesjö 2014).
9. Evans-Pritchard 1940; for an inspired use of Evans-Pritchard's concept, see Baumann and Gingrich 2004.
10. Scott 1893 (see also Fiskesjö 2000: 19–24).
11. The term comes from Pierre Clastres (1987). On Clastres's Amazonian anti-chiefs and the problem of how chiefs originated, see also Friedman 2011 (his review of Scott 2009).
12. For an extensive discussion of these matters, see Fiskesjö 2000: 237–42 (debating Friedman 1998: 268–71).
13. This "people" was not of course "the people" under their king, their emperor, or the elite but rather a sovereign people, such as those described by Evans-Pritchard.
14. In Friedman's scheme, the Wa State in Burma (Special Region 2) might be read either as a client state or, perhaps, as a modern-day "predatory polity," despite its heavy dependence on China and despite its formal recognition that it is Burmese territory. On the Wa State, see the introduction, and chapter 8.
15. Scott 1893; Scott and Hardiman 1983 [1901], II.1:305. If historical, this probably occurred when Burmese armies entered the area in the 1760s to the 1770s.
16. Zhang Chengyu 1941 [1891], in Li Genyuan 1941, *jizai* 23, Qing 12: 6a–12b; cf. also Couchman 1897, and other British documents.
17. Lee 1982, 1984, 2012. On Yunnan mining and on Maolong, see also McGrath 2002, esp. 130–58; Fiskesjö 2000: 146–47nn10–11; 148n14; Giersch 2006; Ma Jianxiong 2011.
18. Barton 1933: 61–62. One American expert, Draper, estimated that Maolong had three times the silver of Bawdwin (according to Xiao Zisheng et al. 1986).
19. Such payments of fees to legitimate owners is a practice also known to occur at Kachin jade mines further north, where Burmese royal authorities explicitly recognized Kachin chiefs as entitled, as owners of the land, to charge such fees (Sadan 2013: 94).
20. On these Wa and Shan place names, see also Barton 1933: 1–2, 69ff., 113ff.
21. Pasquet 1989; Duan and Zhao 1991: 90–93.
22. Banhong took control from Banlao in the early twentieth century. See Xiao Zisheng et al. 1986: 11; Fang Guoyu 1943c, fos. 1–50; and Tian Jizhou 1983b.
23. Chit Hlaing 2009: 18; 26n2; Liu 2009; Scott 2009: 81–82, 114–15. On trade and the evolution of Shan kingship, see O'Connor 1989; Izikowitz 1962, and others.
24. Harvey 1932: 57 ("Wild Wa" = autonomous Wa). Fang Guoyu (1943a) writes that those wary soldiers were provided by the Mengding *tusi*. See also Li Jingsen 1933.
25. On Wa agrohistory, with excellent critiques of the Chinese orthodox denigration of swiddening as primitive, see Yin Shaoting 2001, 2009.
26. Fang Guoyu 1943b, 1984b: 1273–76; Pasquet 1989; see also Ma Jianxiong 2011.
27. As noted earlier, "Kawa" is originally a Shan/Tai term used to group the "Ka" (*Khaa*; Tai "barbarian") Wa with other non-Buddhist upland people.
28. Gengma was derivative of Mengding, the seat of another Shan prince. On the *tusi* generally, see chapter 2.
29. A fascinating early example is the account in Yang Shen's *Nanzhao yeshi* (ca. 1550, repr. 1969: 2:31a–b), cited in Fiskesjö 1999a. See also the introduction.

30. Governor-General Zhang Yunsui's 1746 memorandum, cited from Pasquet 1989: 43.
31. This is the British version of the Shan term "prince," *cao fa*. For lesser Shan rulers, *cao meng* is also used (Chit Hlaing 2009).
32. On the Munai mines, see further below.
33. From the translation in Barton 1933: 117; 124.
34. Rocher 1880: 2:29ff.; also see Atwill 2005.
35. Dai Yingcong 2004; also see Bello 2005.
36. Barton 1933: 118, citing a 1905 Chinese memorandum.
37. Fang Guoyu 1943a, see too 1943b and 1943c. On the Chinese naming of their appointed *tusi* "native-chiefs," see chapter 2.
38. Barton 1933: 1–2, 59; Forbes 1988.
39. The Chinese name for (North) Hsenwi, an important Shan polity (Fiskesjö 2000: chap. II.2).
40. *Report on the Administration of the Shan and Karenni States for the Year 1920*: 3; Yuan Jianqi et al. 1940: 51.
41. Huang Qielin (1934) and many other Chinese writers contributed to creating this as a Chinese patriotic struggle. See also Fiskesjö 2000:157 ff.; because the Banhong incident occurred immediately *after* the preparation of the most extensive British sources on the Wa (Barton 1933; Harvey 1932), it is *not* covered there (and seldom discussed in later British sources).
42. *Report on the Administration of Burma for the Year 1934*: 7–8.
43. Yun Yao-tsung 1973; Luo Shipu 1974.
44. Yun Yao-tsung 1973: 131. Playing up his "taming" of the Wa, Li even claimed that one of their "wildest" members "gave him his son to raise."
45. Cf. note 37.
46. See above (note 27), and the introduction.
47. Li Shirao 1778. See also Fang Guoyu 1984a: 2:534–35. Fang Guoyu here noted that in his own earlier essay (1943b) on the much more famous Maolong (or Lufang) mines, he mistakenly equated Li Shirao's "Mangleng" (on the "Burmese" or westward side of the Wa lands) with "Maolong" (on the northern outskirts of the Wa lands).
48. The expression *neidi* ("interior lands") is a revealing Chinese formulation that means both "China proper" and something like "closer to the power center of the empire."
49. Fang Guoyu 1984a: 2:535, cited from a late-nineteenth-century revision of the Yunnan gazetteer (*Xu Yunnan tongzhi gao*).
50. Scott and Hardiman 1983 [1901]: II.2:176.
51. *Simao Yuxi Honghe Daizu shehui lishi diaocha* 1985: 9. Lead-bullet production is confirmed from 1888 (*Lancang Lahuzu zizhixian zhi* 1996: 5).
52. Scott and Hardiman 1983 [1901]: II.2:173 (citing Daly 1891).
53. Scott and Hardiman 1983 [1901]: II.1:172.
54. For more on Mangleng and its complex dealings with the British, see Scott 1893, and more sources in Fiskesjö 2000: 169n56, incl. Chen Can n.d. [ca. 1908]: 3.41b–44b.
55. *Wa Notes A* (1936) includes a Manglun (Mangleng) origin story (104a–107b), which unsurprisingly mixes Shan-style palaces with a perceived destiny to become "the rulers of the Wa people."
56. The frustrated Scott (1893: 22) said it was inhabited by "so-called Tame Wa."
57. A place name that must mean "the bamboo groves suitable for crossbow-making." Crossbows, *ag*, are still used for small game hunting, and in the past, large ones were used as weapons of war, alongside firearms and machetes.
58. Fang Guoyu 1943e (citing documents from 1911).

59. Chen Can n.d. [ca. 1908]: 3.14b–15a. Note how the writer, an enlightened administrator dispatched to Yunnan from his native Guizhou, repeats the commonplace denial of Wa capabilities.
60. Scott and Hardiman 1983 [1901]: II.1:414. The Shan-ruled Buddhist Tai Loi there (= upland Wa subservient to the Shan) did not grow opium in the late nineteenth century (Scott and Hardiman 1983 [1901]: II.1:168, 170, 421).
61. Scott and Hardiman 1983 [1901]: II.2:585 ("Na Fan").
62. Scott 2009: 214–17. On Kachin politics, which, as Friedman suggested, was badly misunderstood by Leach, see Friedman 1998 [1979]; Lehman 1989, and Chit Hlaing (= F.K. Lehman) 2007.
63. Chit Hlaing 2007: xl–xli; Fiskesjö 2000: 183; Hutton 1969 [1921].
64. Friedman 1998 [1979]: 277–79; also 15–17, and 17n4. For a theory of how Chinese states first arose from salt and metals monopolies, see Liu and Chen 2001: 5–47.
65. Friedman 1987; also included as an appendix in Friedman 1998.
66. Friedman 1998 [1979]: 352–53; see also Jónsson 1996.
67. Leach 1954, 1960; cf. Scott 2009: 115n51.
68. Leach 1954: 9; citing Lévi-Strauss 1949: 325 (orig. French ed.); corresponds to Lévi-Strauss 1969: 233.
69. As evident in the novel forms of core headhunting rituals (Fiskesjö 2000: 287–354; chapter 6).
70. Scott 2009: 126ff., 172–75, and elsewhere.
71. Scott 2009: ix (and 23, on how the Wa aren't mainly refugees).

5

SLAVERY AS A THREAT
TO THE IDEOLOGY OF KINSHIP

In the 1950s, Chinese scholars dispatched by their government to investigate the Wa identified Wa "slaves," whom they then helped "liberate."* For the Chinese, the "discovery" of these "slaves" served as proof of their own theory that the supposedly primitive and predominantly egalitarian Wa society was "teetering on the threshold between Ur-Communism and ancient slavery."

This awkward conclusion was based on shaky nineteenth-century evolutionist theories formulated by Lewis Henry Morgan and Friedrich Engels, which posited developmental stages supposedly necessary to human society. These were later read in translation by Soviet and Chinese Communists, who followed Stalin in embracing this severely misguided interpretation of human history and defining it as a new orthodoxy (Tong Enzheng 1989; also Wang Ningsheng 1985/87)—which I will discuss further below.

My own field research in the Wa lands revealed a very different picture of slavery there, and a dynamics of commodification, that also sheds light on slavery more generally, in addition to showing how the Chinese Communist theory is hopelessly wrong—in interesting ways. In this chapter, I discuss the historical and cultural context of slavery in the Wa lands and in China, including the adoption of child war captives and the related ideological rejection of slavery under Wa kinship ideology, as well as once again entertaining the anomalous Chinese mine slaves held in the Wa lands, who were briefly discussed in the previous chapter. I also discuss the trade in people that emerged with the opium export economy of the late nineteenth and early twentieth centuries, which helped sustain, yet also threatened, autonomous Wa society. I argue that the past Wa "slave" trade was spurred by the same processes of commodification that historically drove the

---

Endnotes for this chapter begin on page 140.

Chinese trade in people and in recent decades have produced large-scale human trafficking across Asia, often similarly hiding slavery under the cover of kinship.

People as Commodities in China, Southeast Asia, and in the Wa Lands

Trafficking in people reduced to commodities is on the rise all over the world. In the wake of globalization, it may have become the world's largest illegal business, eclipsing narcotics, arms, and looted antiquities. UN officials have labeled the increase in human trafficking among waves of labor migration across Asia as "the largest slave trade in history," claiming that among the estimated thirty million people sold to sweatshops or brothels over the past several decades, many have been kidnapped and imprisoned in ways "more cruel and devious . . . than in the original slave trade."[1] These are staggering figures even if, as some suggest, some prostitution is consensual and could be legalized, and victims of outright slavery are but a minor part of this human wave.

Human trafficking is a product of the same processes that drive labor migration, and outright slavery (people being forced to work without pay or freedom to leave) is a risk many labor migrants face. In the region of Southeast Asia's uplands, between China and the Southeast Asian nation-states, powerful economic forces that are now incorporating these hinterlands-to-be into wider spheres of accumulation are driving these human waves of migration and trafficking. China is increasingly becoming the main magnet, as not only the mountainous hinterlands but also Southeast Asian nation-states themselves are being integrated into its wealth-extraction sphere. Many previously self-governing or semi-autonomous non-state areas are being transformed into variations of the classic "peripheral situation,"[2] where the exploitation of local resources (e.g., rubber, sugar cane, tea, coffee, mining, forestry) mainly benefits outsiders. In the process, local people, like commodities, are also integrated into regional and global labor markets. Like labor migrants elsewhere, including impoverished Chinese, they become vulnerable to abduction into outright slavery or have their children kidnapped for sale. Also striking is the exodus of young women from ethnic minority peripheries either willingly traded or abducted to marry Chinese men in areas where female infanticide and female out-migration is creating a demand for wives—or pregnancy surrogates.[3]

Within China, despite the semi-autonomous formal status and preferential treatment granted to ethnic minority areas, labor migrants from these regions are at a distinct disadvantage even when compared to impoverished domestic Chinese migrants.[4] Minority migrants often become "illegals" similar to Central American migrants in the United States (De Genova 2005). These often also come from indigenous communities dominated by powerful outsiders, and they become ambiguously incorporated into modern nation-states, in which indigenous people even in "normal" circumstances can only be second-class citizens. Naw Seng's tale (2004) of a Burmese woman "sold" into marriage in Eastern China and then "opting for" prostitution back on the border reflects the fraught experiences of many such upland migrants.[5]

Of course, all such ethnic minority migrant laborers strive as far as possible to preserve their personal dignity, autonomy, and interest. This includes people in the ethnic Wa areas in the China-Burma border area, who are aware of the dangers and injustices facing migrants—not least today, when people have cell phones and can update each other across large distances.

Figure 5.1. Wa girls posing on a *ngrah* veranda, in their best clothes in local style, to celebrate the New Year in Yong Ou. Photo by the author, 1997.

The deep-seated Wa ethos of respect for personal autonomy means that no woman will be prohibited from leaving as a migrant, or even to be a Chinese farmer's wife. Many young Wa women are persuaded by itinerant Chinese "wife-recruiters" that such a life would be better—even if they will be isolated in a place where no one speaks their language. I once met such a woman on her first return visit to her natal Wa village after seven years, and she seemed to have fared well enough in material terms. However, to ensure their women's safety, male relatives are often dispatched to accompany such brides to their destination, to ascertain that their dignity will be respected and that they are not being sold to brothels or enslaved.

Things were very different in the past. Before the mid-twentieth century, the core Wa area was nobody's hinterland; obviously, people would not be drained away, like so many other "natural" resources are today. Yet I argue that the very same processes of commodification that enabled a vast people trade in China in the past[6] (and which is itself once again on the rise), were already infiltrating the autonomous Wa country and stirring the beginnings of a people trade there. It was this phenomenon that the Chinese Marxists mistook for the beginnings of a "primitive" Wa slavery.

Independent Wa Wealth and the Elusive Wa "Slaves"

In the past, the Wa lands were a center in their own right, generating and controlling their own wealth in the dynamic relations with outside trading partners and foreign powers, using it to reproduce their own society without outside interference. This social reproduction was achieved through the framework of kinship, which also organized economic activities, warfare, and politics.

As Friedman (1998 [1979]) argued, the egalitarianism of the kinship-based "ordered anarchy" of the Wa that we know from the late nineteenth and first half of the twentieth century is in part the outcome of circumscription by external forces blocking the potential for social stratification inherent in these mountain societies. But the Wa use of traditional kinship structures, to discourage social stratification that otherwise might endanger and destroy their autonomy, also reflects a Wa agency deployed to manipulate their difficult yet also advantageous geopolitical situation (cf. chapter 4). This has included attracting outsiders such as miners, opium buyers, and others who were prepared to deal with the Wa on their terms, so that the trade would support, and not undermine, their autonomy.

Wa history is unusual in how, in its special configuration as a "predatory periphery," the Wa country was part of a special class of powerful and independent "barbarian" polities that turned the tables on the empires surrounding them, and even preyed on them, as the independent Yi (Nuosu, or "Lolo"), further north inside China,[7] and other such "predatory" polities also did. Like the Yi, the Wa captured slaves from the Chinese and other neighbors, though not on the same scale. No slaves were deployed in Wa agricultural work (even in labor-intensive opium production)—only in mining, and then only rarely. As discussed in chapter 4, most Wa-controlled mining was done through concessions to Chinese entrepreneurs, and slaves only appeared in those few places where the Wa themselves ran the mines but wanted to avoid either the dangers involved or the taboo against excavations.

Most important was that unlike the Yi, the Wa lacked social stratification. This mitigated against the creation of a permanently subjugated slave class. Under Yi aristocratic sociologics, as in other already stratified societies that "kidnapped" outsiders and detained them as a permanent, inferior social stratum, no such thing emerged in the Wa area. The Wa also differed from the Karen and other peripheral polities that kidnapped and sold slaves to Tai states as a source of wealth and internal social stratification (but not of labor).[8]

The Wa-held foreign mine slaves that I already discussed in chapter 4 were an exception proving a general rule. Their situation met the basic definitions of slavery as the most extreme form of social inequality apart from death: the reduction of people to permanent exploitation as things, and the complete exclusion from membership in society and full personhood, making them "socially dead," as the ultimate "anti-kin" (Patterson 1982; Meillassoux 1991). Such mine slaves were not allowed to join or start families or clans, or create the genealogies that anchor Wa personhood. Some were manumitted and expelled from the area after they had become useless, which further underlines the point. It also distinguishes these "true" slaves, forgotten even by Chinese scholars, from the rather different "trade" in Wa children as adoptees looking like slaves—and who were the main targets of Chinese "liberation."

The Flawed Chinese View of Wa Slavery

As we have seen, the reason the Wa mine slaves are little known is primarily because of the lack of Wa written historiography and the strong bias in Chinese records to portray mining as an outsider's gift to the primitive Wa. Thus, the mine slaves are also absent in the literature that was generated with the new Chinese Communist government's annexation of the east-central Wa country in the 1950s. Chinese state ethnographers, who compiled reports that remain indispensable reading, facilitated these efforts of cleaning up Wa history.[9] The Wa as a people (*minzu*, a state-defined ethnicity; Fiskesjö 2006) were singled out, alongside the Yi, as an especially troublesome non-Chinese people to be surveyed and pinpointed according to the evolutionary scheme that had been adopted as the new Chinese state orthodoxy. These assessments would help in promoting Wa society's "socialist" transformation and in consolidating Chinese control and the long-term incorporation of the Wa into the new state.[10]

It was taken for granted in China (and still largely is) that societies like the Wa were ancient relics—they had, unlike "advanced" Chinese society, failed to progress. Their present stage of social evolution was to be pinpointed on a scale ranging from *yuanshi shehui*, "primitive communism" (classless society or Ur-Communism in Engelsian terms), to "slavery," the original class society, "feudalism," and so on.[11] In China, such "Marxist" theory was and remains closely aligned with earlier imperial ideology of Chinese tutelage for primitive barbarians (Fiskesjö 1999a; 2006). There was no attempt to undertake a Marxist analysis of seemingly primitive social forms as relationally produced within a dynamic global context.[12]

Instead, the Chinese government–sponsored scholars noted the strong "egalitarian" spirit and absence of social hierarchy among the Wa and concluded that the Wa society was still at the stage of primitive Ur-Communism. But the small number of "purchased slaves," and the apparent divisions of rich and poor related to this "slave" trade, made them add the qualification that the Wa were at a late stage of primitive society, on the threshold of class society. There was some disagreement over this, but because of the general state-sanctioned premises, it became orthodoxy as well.[13]

Thus, an official report defined the "pristine" Ximeng Wa area as a "patriarchal slavery" society characterized by incipient class divisions.[14] This, supposedly, could be observed from the existence of a small number of slaves in an economy otherwise dominated by free people, and by how the "slaves" appeared no different from ordinary Wa kinsmen in legal or social status. Still, it was claimed that these people were slaves, except that "the relation between slave-owner and slave has not yet developed into one of naked exploitation, but instead occurs *under the cover of kinship*" (*Wazu shehui lishi diaocha* 1983b [1957]: 57; my emphasis).

In accounts like these, the special significance of the kidnapped mine slaves is not mentioned; instead, the analysis has focused on the different sort of war captive/adoptee that the Wa call *qong*. These have some similarity to slaves (as they were obliged to do menial labor), but because they did not represent the outright negation of kinship, as in the enslavement of forced laborers in the mines, they were in an ambiguous state of potential kin—which is what the Wa term *qong* really implies.

The Story of the "Captured One"

One unusual but illustrative case was explained to me from a Wa point of view during my fieldwork by several elders in the old Wa center of Yong Ou, in what is now the Ximeng Wa Autonomous County, in China, in 1997. It is important in this instance to reiterate the following: The village Yong Ou, now partially in ruins and but a shadow of its former glory, is an ancestral center from which about thirty settlements had branched off in the past, forming what the Wa used to call a *jaig' qee*, a "realm," or in British parlance, a "circle" of related villages (in Chinese: *buluo*, tribe). These settlements were held to the moral duty of showing solidarity to each other because of their kinship through mutually intermarrying patriclans (see chapter 2, on naming; also Fiskesjö 2000).

The case concerns the true story of one young Wa man known in Yong Ou as Pun, who was first a prisoner of war, then a *qong* (a "slave") and an adoptee; who was groomed to become a full member of society under the terms of Wa kinship; and who then met with an unexpected new turn of history as the Chinese government declared him a liberated slave and returned him to his original village.

Pun's story happened long ago, back in the late 1940s and early 1950s (the dates are unclear, but the Chinese interventions on behalf of "slaves" began after the Peoples' Liberation Army first advanced into the autonomous Wa lands in 1952). Still, the case is remembered more clearly than others because it turns on a particularly memorable incident in the history of Yong Ou that relates to the fundamental tenets of Wa kinship ideology. Pun's story begins with a gaur, a large-bodied wild forest bison that used to be found in these hills where, since long ago, the Wa have practiced swidden agriculture. This gaur got away, but not before being wounded by Yong Ou warrior-hunters forced to give up their prospect of a gaur feast. The gaur's horn was important, because it belonged as paraphernalia in one of the foremost of all central Wa rituals, in which the remains of the previous year's headhunting warfare victims were transferred to their final resting place, the so-called skull avenue (also known as a *lah*, or public space), outside the Wa village-fortresses (discussed in detail in chapter 6). The right gaur horn was used when consecrating the house of the main sacrifiers (hosts), and was a highly prized possession properly held only at founder-villages (*yong dax*).

The escaped gaur ran toward another village, whose inhabitants killed it and feasted on its meat. This occurred within the same Wa "circle," but in an off-shoot or "child" village (*yong guan*) founded only several generations before. The "children" (of the offshoot village) then made a capital mistake in handling the gaur carcass. As required by custom, they sent one of the horns back to the founder-village—but they sent the left horn and retained the right. The right horn carried special significance as an instrument used by the main *ba pi*, or ritualist, in the ancestral village.

The ancestral descendants thus took this as an unforgivable usurpation that had to be punished, even though the offenders were kin. The next year, after the pretense of a long pause, a warrior force descended on the offending village and exacted revenge in the form of classical Wa warfare: a headhunting raid (*ning nyiex*, "war at home," i.e., an attack on the opponents' settlement, as opposed to the *ning grax*, "road war," or ambush often used in slower-running conflicts with other "circles," or non-Wa). The warriors killed many of the settlement's adults but took customary pity on the children, who were not honorable adversaries because they were not yet fully autonomous persons. One little boy taken alive was renamed Pun, which means the "catch," or the "captured one" because he was such a *ba pun* ("one that we were able to get," here using a vocabulary coinciding with that of hunting). Pun grew up as the adoptive son of one of the warriors in the ancestor village. At first he was termed a *qong*, that is, a not-yet-person adopted captive and potential kinsman. At this stage a *qong* could still be killed at any time if he caused trouble—as an extension of the same act of war that had killed his parents. Pun not only survived, he later passed through several rituals of formal adoption and name change to become incorporated as a complete person in a lineage, fully in accordance with Wa propriety. At the same time, it became clear through my inquiries about this case that people of *qong* origin like Pun would still suffer a stigma of continuing ambiguity—not least because his history was perpetually advertised in his name.

At that point, the Chinese annexation of the Wa lands was taking place, and the new Chinese authorities found and redefined Pun as a "slave," who was declared "liberated." Pun, at the time already a young man, was then free to return to his natal home. This he did, according to my sources.

"Headhunting" and the Moral Order of the Wa Economy

Pun was only one of a number of people that the new Chinese authorities declared to be liberated "slaves" (*nuli*), their liberation advertised for propaganda purposes. The intervention was part of a little-studied but broad policy shift around 1957–58, reflected across other recently conquered or reconquered peripheral areas. For example, in Tibet, China's new government invaded in 1950–51 but promised to leave the social order alone; then, in the late 1950s, the Chinese government abandoned this policy and proceeded to supplant Tibet's existing government, enforce land reforms, while similarly making maximum use of the orchestrated "liberation" of monastery bondsmen in Tibet, for propaganda purposes.

In the Wa view, as I understood my informants, Pun was a classic child war captive, but in the official Chinese interpretation he was a harbinger of an emergent social class of slaves, and of a "slave society" where the wealthy would own permanent slaves. Most examples of liberated slaves highlighted by the Chinese were actually *not* war captives like Pun—whose story for the Wa illustrated proper morality—but children who had been "bought" into wealthier families and labored in their households, and whose moral status was more ambivalent. In the Chinese analysis, as you might guess, the "owners" of such "house slaves" were presented as "the rich," pointing to Wa terms such as *ba mi* or *jo mi*, as if these terms represented something of a stable class in the making. In the Wa understanding, however, they simply mean "temporarily wealthy," and simultaneously more eminent, in terms of social prestige—something that could be lost at any time (such as to disease or death). Indeed, there was a trade of sorts, in children who were not war captives but "sold" by poor Wa. These children had also come to be called *qong*, and they were talked about in terms of buying and selling.

Before discussing them further, I must mention the occasional reports of Wa purchases of children to be killed for their heads. Wa headhunting rituals were organized to harness the threatening force of powerful enemies in two ways (chapter 6; Fiskesjö 2000). First, the biomass contents of freshly captured enemy heads seeped into the ground near a village center drum shrine as an intentional and formidable antidote to the forces of decay which threaten one's own survival and prosperity. After a year, their now-empty skulls were removed and arranged as a permanent display of deterrence in the "skull avenues" leading up to the victor's settlements.

Outsiders' reports of children purchased as "headhunting" victims suggest that in times of pestilence or drought, these rituals may have taken on a special urgency, thus generating the idea of purchasing live victims such as poor children from other parts of Wa country or even beyond. But in the central Wa areas where I worked, the notion of buying "friendly" children and killing them was unheard of and, moreover, regarded as reprehensible and incompatible with the very ethos of fighting only honorable adversaries and sparing their children. Thus I believe that some reports are fabricated, much as the rare reports of Wa cannibalism (cf. chapter 7) are unsubstantiated, unheard of in Wa country, and also seem to be based in misunderstandings that parallel the frequently encountered notion that the Wa headhunting rituals were agricultural sacrifices to fertility deities.

If indeed reports of children bought to be beheaded are true, they might refer to Wa areas on the outskirts of the autonomous centers, where warrior norms may have fallen in disarray as Wa social structures broke down. Such reports may also have arisen from outsiders' misunderstandings of cases where a disobedient or rebellious *qong* captive was really killed, as punishment, and in effect as the belated completion of a previous war that resulted in his capture. Perhaps this should result in his decapitation and then the regular installation of his skull in the usual "skull avenue" parade of defeated enemies—but we know of no such cases. Memories of these matters were already scarce and fragmented at the time of my main field research in the 1990s, but my understanding is that no child's skull could be so installed, only those of adult adversaries.

The whole issue of the *qong* is fraught with a strong ambiguity that is itself heavily significant. To get at it, let's consider another widely circulated story that I encountered during my fieldwork. Here, the classic Wa conception of the proper fate of young war captives (as diverging, either into social rebirth or death, as the enemy) is intriguingly brought into conversation with economic change, as well as with the origins of headhunting, and of the huge, hollow log drums (*kroug*) that before the 1950s were the ritual and communication centers of every village in independent Wa country. In this story, the primordial first human victim of decapitation is a *qong*. We are left ignorant of whether he was originally a war captive or a purchased adoptee. The story begins with a certain mythical Wa culture hero, the multitalented, trickster-like Glieh Neh, who in unspecified ancient times was away on a long journey (typically understood as engaging in some form of long-distance trade). When he comes home, his wife has seduced their adopted boy *qong*: the wife and the *qong* are making love, and it turns out that they are so firmly united in their illicit act that they cannot be physically separated, although the hero tries at first. He then somehow "realizes" that what he must do to overcome this situation is to fashion a Wa log drum (the first) and then cut off the *qong*'s head to inaugurate the drum.

Here Glieh Neh represents a traditional sexual morality, one in defense of monogamy. At other times, in other stories, he is a trickster guilty of related and even more appalling excesses, as when he impregnates every woman in a village after first deceiving all the men into temporarily leaving him alone with all the women. As punishment, Glieh Neh was supposed to be drowned in the river, but of course, he wasn't: instead, he begged to be placed in a coffin before being drowned. Then, using it as a boat, he began to play his various instruments from the inside, thereby enticing various other peoples along the shore into rescuing him. As a result, those people (Shan and others) learned writing and other great things from him, which were lost to the Wa, to the great annoyance of all the villagers who belatedly realized that they had made a mistake by getting rid of him.[15]

In any case, this story of Glieh Neh also competes with other, and probably older, stories about drums, but it is additionally interesting as a common version that serves, above all, to reaffirm the kinship order against the disruptions brought by the seductive wife, the *qong*, and the economic change that got everybody into this mess to begin with. I interpret the sanction against the illicit union as representative of a wishful evocation of the victory of traditional morality in the face of increasingly sharp contradictions between the ideals of Wa kinship and an emerging new economy, where people would leave to go on trading missions and would also trade in people, a trade itself propelled by the growing commodification of transactions within the Wa economy.

The original ideals of kinship must have formed earlier, when people pioneered agriculture in pristine forests (chapter 2). But by the mid- to late nineteenth century, growing Wa populations were increasingly supplementing subsistence agriculture with cash crops such as opium, which was grown on hill fields that were once forests. New settlement branches were established nearby rather than far away, adding to the population density of Wa country and exacerbating its environmental deterioration.

What is important here for our discussion of slavery is how the ethos of the forest farmers came to be deployed as a conservative ideology—as in the insistence on reserving the "archaic" right gaur horn for the founder-village. This ideological framework, built around patrilineal clan membership and kinship morality, helped protect Wa autonomy in the new and qualitatively different context of outside pressure and internal militarization. It helped the Wa to profit from exports while persisting as a fiercely egalitarian "ordered anarchy" or anti-state, in which the famous traditional feasts of merit—where locals competed to outhost one another in pursuit of social prestige (Lehman 1989)—took on the *new* function of dividing the dividends of the export trade so that social hierarchy could be prevented.

Jonathan Friedman suggested that the Kachin in the same region treated the outside as a source of human labor to be drawn upon by capture whenever possible, just like other similarly expansionist "Asiatic" social formations in history. Conversely, he saw societies like the Naga and the Wa as located on a slippery slope of social devolution, prompted by external circumscription, environmental deterioration, and higher population densities. Consequently, they would try to keep outsiders away, sometimes even killing them (as in headhunting) to transform them into "a spiritual force, to provide a badly needed increase in crop yield. . . . The notion of providing slaves in the next world is similarly a negation of keeping slaves in this world" (Friedman 1998 [1979]: 267ff.).

But this, at best, fits only partly with the Wa realities I was confronted with in the field. To begin with, it wasn't that anything beneficial would come from the force of the killed adversaries; rather, their remains were used as a sort of vaccine against the evil of the world (see chapter 6). And "slaves" were generally not recognized as such either in this world or the next; the children of adversaries were offered the chance of adoption into a new social existence as accepted members of society; after death they would then join the collective multitude of the ancestor spirits and not exist separately. Thus it is probably wrong to suggest, as Friedman did in this line of argument, that Wa headhunting rituals replaced and substituted for Kachin-style feasts of merit as part of a process of forced decline and devolution that transformed what would otherwise potentially have grown into a slave-gathering "Asiatic social formation" into an egalitarian society.[16]

The Wa feasts of merit actually continued, and flourished, alongside the development of the new headhunting rites; it was not that one replaced the other. Friedman did not do field research in the region, and Edmund Leach, whose 1954 book was the main target of Friedman's powerful criticism, on this ground tried to dismiss Friedman's work as a mere abstraction. But I do believe Friedman's approach is fundamentally superior to Leach's, and the insights generated are generally worthwhile. For example, the point that the Wa and other densely populated egalitarian societies on the margins of empire would largely forgo outside slaves is obviously sound—excepting the Wa mine slaves, who were really the exception that proved the rule that no inferior social stratum could be accepted.

But we should move to try to understand this renunciation on a deeper level. I think it is better understood as part of an ongoing Wa struggle to negotiate the threats against the traditional order, which the central Wa sought to uphold as the framework of their continued autonomy under new circumstances. This can better explain how in almost all cases children were taken on as adoptees instead of adults; because they lacked history and thus were not yet fully autonomous as social beings, children were much more likely to conform to and successfully join in—and help sustain—that very social order. Also, only Wa children were taken as far as I know, and no foreigners. Again, foreigners (such as the mine slaves) would present a much more difficult challenge for assimilation and recruitment into the defense of the conservative patriclan ideals.

The *qong* children were temporarily like slaves, but in the Wa view they figured in a very temporary "slave-to-kin continuum," where their potential kin status as fellow Wa was emphasized for ideological reasons: outright and permanent slavery was not acceptable for fellow Wa. If reduced to slaves, they would no longer be Wa. This dovetails with Meillassoux's (1991) thesis that slavery negates kinship and that the "slave" is "anti-kin," or alien par excellence. The point ties into Meillassoux's discussion of how, in exogamy generally, a lonely new wife can resemble a slave—very much so—but only *temporarily* before she is fully integrated as a "wife," enjoying corresponding rights not ever granted any slave (who is by definition permanently reduced to a thing). It also illuminates why occasional foreigners who willingly settled in Wa lands would be accepted, on condition that they assimilated into clan membership and Wa ways.[17]

For their part, despite their professed Marxism, the Chinese government ethnographers largely overlooked the edge-of-empire socioeconomic-environmental dialectics transforming Wa society in recent centuries. Their assumption that Wa society of the 1950s represented the survival of an isolated pocket of an ancient past was plain wrong. Far from being a primitive remnant, the 1950s Wa society was a transformed state of its previous existence. This we've learned from Friedman's insights.

The rapid commodification and monetization of social life that accompanied the transformation of the "primitive" Wa economy of subsistence agriculture into an export economy presented a serious threat to the Wa social order, prompting the mobilization of kinship ideology in new ways. This is the context of the incipient trade in Wa children, not some mysterious inevitable transition between evolutionary stages (as in the wrongheaded Chinese state orthodoxy) or any transformation between this-worldly and next-worldly slavery (as in Friedman's abstraction).

Commodification and the Buying and Selling of Wa Children

Export-market opium cultivation and trade was taken up in Wa country in the nineteenth century. It was not the first such cash crop (on cotton, Fiskesjö 2000; also compare mining, chapter 4), but it became crucial from the nineteenth century on (Friedman 1987). Opium was for export, mostly to China, and not for local consumption, and the expanding trade drove a process of commodification where the opium itself often served as the currency of all transactions. Chinese reports from the 1950s estimated that cash income from opium sold to middlemen accounted for one-third of all income in central Wa country households (Luo Zhiji 1995: 125ff.; *Wazu shehui lishi diaocha* 1983a [1957]: 11).

Opium could be grown by anyone; in fact, one might expect that it would have fueled social stratification, especially in the light of how illicit drug wealth today is often controlled by armed drug lords exploiting peasant growers. But instead, it solidified already present egalitarian tendencies, with autonomous farmers each growing their own opium.[18] Under the armed autonomy of old Wa society, no authority existed to enforce the enrichment of some over others.[19]

While some people growing and selling opium became richer than others did, distributive feasts and rituals continued to reinforce the existing framework of warrior-farmer patrilineages and helped to prevent the rise of a class commanding labor to enrich themselves, as we have seen with the measures controlling mining wealth. This is why the famed feasts of merit continued, to redistribute the new wealth. Similarly, the traditional *o lang* "chiefs"[20] continued to be revered and to officiate at the most exalted rituals and feasts, which were actually bolstered by opium income used to purchase more buffalo and cattle from outside,[21] though feasts were originally and ideally supposed to be based on traditional agricultural foods. The Wa also did not hoard slaves to do the increasingly important hard work of opium weeding and processing—as they might have had they already been organized along class lines. Instead, as former opium farmers explained to me, they organized this work as they did traditional farming, by recruiting family members and requesting mutual aid from kinsmen, who reciprocally invited their hosts to collaborate in planting, harvesting, and so on.

When, despite these arrangements of redistribution, some Wa fell into relative poverty and others fortuitously became richer (due to illness and deaths in the family, capricious weather, etc.), the poor would indeed "sell" children to the rich under the aegis of the new transactional model provided by the opium business (under which people would sell their harvested opium to dealers and use the money to buy food, buffalo, guns, and more).

The "sales" of children were said to be for adoption (as in the idealized war captive prototype), not for slavery. When asked about the pre-1950s era, my local informants insisted that such children were preferably and predominantly "sold" only a short distance away, and only within central Wa country. The sales, which might also be understood as fee-based adoptions, were generally mediated by well-traveled "brokers," who also were not foreigners but farmer-warriors like everyone else. As documented by Chinese state investigators in the 1950s, some transactions did involve children sold to pay debts (e.g., incurred for marriages); further variations on the infectious theme of "selling people" include fantasies of children planning to sell aging parents to get easy cash for food.[22] This, to me, represents the opium economy's widening erosion of the hold on people, of kinship ideology.

The compilers of the 1950s Chinese documents struggle to define two kinds of transacted children: *qong joug* (bought "slaves") and *guan joug* (bought children), but they admit that Wa people used one term to explain and define the other (*Wazu shehui lishi diaocha* 1983b [1957]: 88). The mistake of these Chinese scholars was to see society as a set of perduring categories—not a dynamic process with changing categories—that are both organized *and obscured* by ideology. Many of the circumstances noted by the 1950s ethnographers are better explained if we view Wa kinship not as an enduring custom but as an ideology, itself deployed to negotiate ongoing, unavoidable changes. Even the Chinese could see that well-behaved children Wa people had purchased were not called *qong*, but *guan* (child, e.g., by kinship), and were included into full personhood when their names later were read into Wa genealogies and included in addresses to the spirits during sacrifices (*Wazu shehui lishi diaocha* 1983b [1957]: 89f.; also chapter 2).

The term *qong* would also be used as a pejorative for misbehaving people, not just children—anyone upsetting this ideal order. Indeed, because the Wa kinship system and its ideology still partly survive many years after the loss of Wa autonomy and the abolishment of "slavery," this practice continues today in joke form; I myself heard the term used by parents who half-jokingly threaten to "sell" (*quh*) their naughty children.[23] They'd say, if you go on like this, "I'll go sell you some place or other" (*quh meix ndah tei*), conjuring up an image of the world out there, where people really are bought and sold just like that. It makes sense precisely because so many things all around us really are for sale, which makes it easy to fantasize out loud about selling your children.

In these examples, the deployment of both "child" (*guan*) and "slave" (*qong*) in various ways should be understood as mutually reinforcing aspects of an ideological insistence on a traditional Wa morality. In the praise for the traditional forms of kinship firmly anchoring the social order, and in the mocking play on the *qong* status that stands in dangerous contrast to those principles, there is an ideological insistence on using tradition to try to block the threats against it arising from socioeconomic changes—mainly the commodification of the economy and, by extension, even of Wa social relations. The expanding trade of Wa children and others observed in the twentieth century was likely due to this spreading infection of the commodification of goods and of social relations that became increasingly widespread in the economy.[24]

The Chinese Trade in People: Comparative Perspectives

Integration into China's economy greatly provoked these Wa developments, and it preceded the destruction of Wa autonomy in the 1950s. If we compare kinship and economy in China, where so many Wa brides and workers are headed today, we find equally strict kinship logics at work at the local level (Sangren 2017. This logic is harnessed within the Chinese state's control of much larger-scale market and social systems, within which household slavery historically has often been permitted (or more precisely, ignored by the law) only to the extent that it could be hidden under the guise of those same kinship structures that serve as one of the foundations of state power.

Under such conditions, household slavery has flourished in China "under the cover of kinship"—exactly as the Chinese ethnographers once surmised for Wa society of the pre-1950s era. Before 1949, China "had one of the largest and most comprehensive markets for the exchange of people in the world" (Watson 1980: 223), and traders dealt not so much in adults but in young girls (and some boys) as house slaves, often under the ambivalent guise of kinship procedures, as (fee-based) adoption, and with the prospect of being married away in adulthood. In the past, like today, kinship was recognized by state authorities as a key governance tool, but it was only superficially controlled. After the end of the Maoist era (from ca. 1949 to 1980, when marital and family relations were monitored more intrusively), the same tendencies toward purchasing or even abducting women and children and hiding them in patriarchal kin structures remained in play.[25]

Now, as in the past, state authorities openly admit the problem and present themselves as the main enemy of slavery while at the same time ignoring slavery under the cover of kinship. Market capitalism and government corruption create opportunities for profiteering Chinese entrepreneurs to hold laborers as slaves; officially this remains illegal and Chinese state authorities will perform a public clamp-down whenever such practices come to light (e.g., BBC 2009). Today, as in imperial times, the state's authority and legitimacy hinges on its role as protector of the regular citizenry against kidnapping into slavery, while it retains the monopoly on penal slavery (labor camps for disobedient subjects). Yet in the past, too, forced labor officially existed only as penal slavery controlled by state authorities and "private" slave trade and the enslavement of "good people," that is, law-abiding regular subjects (Fiskesjö 1999a; Jenner 1998) was forbidden. But meanwhile, today as in the past, powerful market forces and the ideological commodification of everything infect the practices of kinship, and in the absence of open, legalized, mass slavery,[26] kinship in fact becomes the only convenient cover for a "trade in people," such as house slaves or wives held against their will. And officials look away, as before.

Ideology aside, it is also much harder for the authorities to prevent the usurpation of kinship for the purpose of house slavery, than to crack down on hidden slave factories. Thus the pre-Communist trade in people that delivered purchased wives and children into slavery-like conditions[27] is reemerging once again under the "traditional" guise of legitimate kinship, as resurrected after the Maoist-socialist era. Though distant from the Wa situation, the conundrum for government officials in China and elsewhere similarly remains the contradiction between promoting the exchange of goods and preventing their subjects (in the Wa case, brothers and sisters) from ending up as commercial goods. (The other side of the coin is that people may try to make the most of the relative freedom they can fashion from the decline of patriarchy; see Yan Yunxiang 2006—and recent critics arguing that patriarchal values actually continue to hold sway).

State-sanctioned slaving is circumscribed in China by the inherited ideology of state benevolence, by whatever remains of the pretense of socialist solidarity with the world's oppressed (who otherwise, given the rising labor shortages in China, may quickly become prime targets of new slavery), and by commitments to the logic and shared rules of the global marketplace in which labor is exploited as a commodity. Thus, both the kidnapping and resale of children and the manipulation of for-profit exploitation of free laborers such as migrant workers for the most part stops short of outright slavery, which remains forbidden yet continues under cover—and is likely to disproportionally affect ethnic minorities.

In autonomous Wa society, power was invested in the people through their kin units, the patriclan system that was lauded and defended in their ideological framework, while in China hierarchical state power encompassed kinship, partly reducing it to a tool of indirect governance by the state. Although the commodification of people and incipient slavery in Wa society before the Chinese "liberation" in the 1950s was an indirect effect of how Wa society was drawn into a Chinese economic sphere well before the loss of Wa autonomy, the Wa struggled to contain this influence because it eroded their kinship-based order, and with it their independence. In the Wa case, kinship ideology was at least initially mobilized to defend against slavery, not to cover it up as the Chinese ethnographers would have it.

The Wa term *qong* can be compared to the similarly ambivalent Kachin term *mayam*, for "slave" or serf, which "is not a simple derivative of the kinship system, but the result of internal contradictions in the economy" (Friedman 1998

[1979]: 143). I suggest a twofold expansion here. The Wa "slavery"/adoption/ trade in children identified as incipient slavery by the Chinese government of the 1950s was indeed a result of the disruptions caused by commerce—though not just within the Wa country (producing "internal contradictions") but also in Wa relations with the external, opium-buying powers.

The crux for the Wa was how to preserve their autonomy in relation to those outside powers; the de facto disruptions taking place were actively resisted by attempts to uphold the normality of kinship. Kin status was extended to many of the adoptees or *guan joug*, who were simultaneously generated and afflicted by the novel and threateningly ambiguous developments of people commodification. This move defended against the radical ambiguity and threatening growth of the trade in people by resolving it into the security and intelligibility of the language and ideology of Wa kinship, in which the term *qong* came to serve as the contemptuous figure of disruption. Meanwhile, some *qong* may well have looked more and more like Chinese house slaves.

Meillassoux (1991) theorized that the emergence of slavery arose from conquest ("iron") and trade ("gold") and argued for the incompatibility of kinship-based "original domestic society" with slavery, which could not possibly be generated from within. The Wa case agrees, but we must note that Wa conservatism was not simply to ensure the continuity of tradition, to defend kinship for kinship's sake, or to defend the unity of the Wa as an ethnicity or nation. If the values of kinship are "dominant forms . . . considered transcendent from reality" (Graeber 2006: 81), the Wa deployed these transcendent forms not so much as identity markers as the social foundation of living autonomously and with dignity (the *Vornehmheit* of Georg Simmel). This is similar to how the modern notion of citizenship grants freedom from slavery but remains fraught by the limitation of this protection to one's own (national) community.[28] The commodification of people threatens to rob what were ideally and originally autonomous persons (potentially so, in children) of the capacity of making autonomous decisions—and hence was anathema to many Wa.

The Wa warriors insisted on the gaur's right horn as a symbol of what the social order based on kinship would provide. But this held true only in the autonomous, self-governing Wa society, in what was in many ways an extraordinary historical moment. Today, Wa people and the China-bound migrants from Wa country still, where possible, rely on what remains of their traditions for mutual support, but having lost their autonomy the people cannot be remotely as powerful as in the past. They must also develop a new awareness of the threats of slavery lurking within the larger economy, which they now unavoidably form a part of and which they must negotiate as best they can.

Notes

* This chapter draws in part on my 2011 article, "Slavery as the Commodification of People: Wa 'Slaves' and Their Chinese 'Sisters,'" *Focaal: Journal of Global and Historical Anthropology* 59: 3–18.

1. UN Wire (2003). The "original slave trade" refers to the transatlantic trade from Africa to the Americas, neglecting, of course, that the trade in slaves is much older than that.
2. Nugent 1988; Turner 1986; on the Southeast Asian uplands, see also Fiskesjö 2010b; Scott 2009; Sturgeon 2005.
3. The literature on ethnic minority labor migration from Southwest China toward the Chinese economic centers in the East includes Zhang Jijiao 2003; He Zhixiong 2003; Weng Naiqun 2006; on migration into Thailand, see Feingold 2000, 2002. On gender inequality issues in Chinese and inter-Asian labor migration, see Gates 1996; Davin 1999; Gaetano and Jacka 2004; Jacka 2005; Gaetano 2008; also Bezlova 2007 and Samarasinghe 2008; on the dangers of abduction and slavery facing women and children, see also Lorenz 2007, 2010; also Kneebone and Debeljak 2012; on the trade in forced brides and pregnancy surrogacies, see also, for example, Radio Free Asia 2018; Beech 2019.
4. On the politics of "ethnic minorities," or "minority nationalities," in China, see Fiskesjö 2006.
5. See also Kachin Women's Association Thailand 2008; also the references in note 3.
6. Watson 1980; Gates 1989, 1996; etc.
7. Hill 2001; Hu Qingjun 1986, 2004; Lu Hui 1998; Winnington 1959.
8. On comparative practices of slavery in the neighboring region, see Lehman 1984; Reid 1982; Turton 1998, 2004 (on Karen slaving); Scott 2009: 152–53; and Warren 1982 on Sulu slaving. These Southeast Asian slavers on the periphery of larger trading systems also deserve comparison with the West African states founded on slave raiding for resale, analyzed by Meillassoux (1991).
9. Cf. *Wazu shehui lishi diaocha* 1983–87 (originally compiled in 1956–57, but delayed until the 1980s, and abbreviated, for political reasons). See also Winnington (1959), the British Communist journalist stranded in China after the Korean War, who was taken on a tour of newly annexed Wa and Yi areas to report on their "ancient social conditions" and the "progress" made under Chinese tutelage.
10. This is not fundamentally different from the abolition of "primitive" slavery by other empires (cf. Chatterjee 2006 on the British in India; Means 2000 on Burma; Pedersen 2001 on the British condemnation of Chinese house slavery).
11. See, for example, McKhann 1995; Guo Moruo 1973; and Fiskesjö 1999a on this scheme and on Guo's key role in adapting it for the Chinese Communist Party (drawing on Dirlik 1978).
12. As notably attempted by Friedman 1998 [1979]. However, starting in the 1980s, brilliant Chinese scholars such as Wang Ningsheng (1985–87) and Tong Enzheng (1989) broke through the orthodoxy and gave voice to sophisticated criticism.
13. As reflected in the official summary of the Wa situation (*Wazu jianshi* 1986; see pages 37ff. for an example of how the central Wa are thus defined and distinguished from the Wa peripheries). See also chapter 4 above, and Luo Zhiji 1995: 251ff.; Luo and Tian 1980; *Wazu shehui lishi diaocha* 1983.
14. Most Chinese discussions of primitive Wa society refer to the Ximeng area, today a county within China and the main area of my own fieldwork. It was formerly part of the central Wa country, but it was largely annexed as Chinese territory in the 1950s.
15. Field notes XXX:102–16; another version of this story recorded by Chinese scholars

in 1957 is found in *Wazu diaocha cailiao* 1962 [1980]: 7:58–59. Glieh Neh is also sometimes called the Wa "Confucius," meaning a wise man.
16. See Friedman 1998 [1979]: 143ff.; also Leach 1981 [1954]: 160ff., on Kachin capturing Assamese slaves; and Scott 2009: 66ff. on such slave-raiding across the region; also note 8 above. Scott mostly mentions menacing lowland states raiding hill peoples, and notes the reverse situation only in passing (p. 266) on the incorporation of captive slaves into the masters' lineage—in which case, the master is no longer a master and the slave is not a slave, as in the Wa refusal to allow social hierarchy to develop.
17. I was told that a trickle of such people of Chinese and other origins did arrive in the past, some on the run from Chinese law. On the highlands as a refuge, see also Wang Ningsheng 2010a; and Scott 2009.
18. As mentioned before, areas most closely associated with opium were also characterized by political egalitarianism (Friedman 1987, 1998 [1979]: 348, 1–2; Jónsson 1996).
19. It is not easy to imagine how purchased *qong* or the mine slaves were controlled. One source says Wa slaveholders typically took only a few slaves each (Barton 1933). They must have taken turns to supervise them or put them in chains. The *qong* could, and sometimes did, run away.
20. Friedman (1998 [1979]) suggests that with "devolution," traditional chiefs became shadows of powerful former selves, reduced to presiding over the resulting "egalitarian" society (and mistaken for weak "primitive" nascent chiefs by Chinese and other scholars). It is difficult to judge whether the *o lang* were really more powerful and materially wealthy in the past or were originally designed to be symbolic chiefs concerned with communal rather than individual or family prosperity. However, what is clear is that even though they lacked wealth and coercive power, they were revered and had prominent positions in egalitarian, opium-rich Wa society.
21. Friedman (1998 [1979]: 353) also errs in claiming that the independent (central, head-hunting) Wa were widely indebted to outside middlemen; this should refer to Wa in the zone located between the independent Wa and the Shan or Chinese authorities. On the purchase of sacrificial buffalo from the outside world, see also Sprenger's astute observations (2005) on the Rmeet of Laos.
22. See the story "Ai and Nyi," in Yamada 2007: 81ff. In this story, after they give up the idea and their father eventually dies at home, the brothers split up. The elder brother remains as a farmer and marries a monkey of the forest; the younger brother goes out and engages in trading, eventually bringing them both new wives from outside. In chapter 8, I discuss evil disease spirits that are imagined to grab and then "sell" (for tree-leaf pretend money) people's souls to the spirits of the dead, a cruel joke that in practice means that the afflicted person dies (= joins the ancestor spirits).
23. Also compare Launay 1977.
24. On the legacy of such captures and "adoptions" in today's Wa State in Burma, see Hans Steinmüller 2019.
25. See note 3.
26. As in Athens, Rome, the United States, and only a few other "slave societies" in history (Finley 1979).
27. As dramatically described by Janet Lim, herself a former *mui tsai* ("little sister") house slave (Lim 1985 [1958]; Miers 1994); see also Gates 1989, 1996, on marriages as labor contracts.
28. That is, through the "rule of law," the limits of which have recently been probed by the Italian political philosopher Agamben, which should provoke similar reconsiderations of kinship (an identity-based system) as governing ideology.

6

War, Headhunting, and the Erasure of Wa History

The Wa have long been known for "headhunting," and, indeed, cutting off the heads of enemies really was part of Wa warfare up until the 1950s and 1960s. But when I spoke to Wa people in the former headhunting country who know about these things, they always emphasized that this cutting of heads, *kieb ndoung* or *a maog*, was part of war, *ning*, which was the more important thing. When the Wa decided to go to war, it was done in one of two ways: either as *ning grax*, "war of the road," where enemies were confronted in the open, or *ning nyiex*, "war of the house," where they were attacked inside their own settlement—and yes, in both cases enemy heads would be captured as trophies, and they were also used in complex war rituals. But contrary to all the reports in the literature about the Wa obtaining heads as a fertility-propagating, religiously motivated necessity, heads were *not* "hunted" for the sake of obtaining props for such rites. As one informant once pointedly insisted to me, "We did not cut peoples' heads off for no reason."

Without conflict, there would be no war; without war, no head cutting. I should confess that I too originally came to the Wa lands imagining that both humans and buffalo had been used as offerings to deities. My Wa informants laughed me out of the misconception: the buffalo was largely this-worldly, a social affair, and the enemy warrior remains were never revered or offered to a god but mocked as defeated enemies. There was no deity lodged in the Wa drum houses that figured prominently in the headhunting rituals: the pantheon of spirits resided elsewhere (see chapter 8) and had no direct part in the arrangements of the enemy heads and skulls. If so, the past Wa warfare practices cannot be framed as "custom." Instead, we must try to understand them within their dynamic historical context.

Endnotes for this chapter begin on page 171.

Figure 6.1. "After the battle, the Wa descend to the camp for a conference." From Prestre 1938; this may be the only photo of Wa warriors on the warpath. Note the crossbow (*ox ag*).

The following example offers a glimpse of how this worked in a very local setting. Lahu immigrants and the aboriginal Wa mostly enjoyed a peaceful if tenuous coexistence (which I will discuss further in chapter 9). But the Lahu, too, would also sometimes fall victim to Wa attacks. In a well-known story related to me by members of the Wa communities at Yong Ou, one such attack on the Lahu illustrates the consequences of what I describe as the circumscription of land and resources over time:

> About the Gui [the Lahu]: A long time ago, when the Gui had moved into Wa country and tended a field next to the Wa [the A Vex, as the Wa of this area call themselves]. The Wa field was on one side, and the Lahu field on the other. A Wa farmer was growing a pumpkin (*a gie*) in his field, and the Wa pumpkin was growing and went on to bear its fruit (*bliex*) on the Gui side of the field, crossing the border (*teang me*). Then the Gui picked it and ate it. This is taboo (*tueh*) for us Wa, we would never eat such a fruit, not since ancient times. It's since that time that they began to [kill them and] display (*daig'*) the heads of the Gui. They went ahead and picked the fruit and ate it all over the place, and that's why we cut the heads of the Gui,

in the old days. That was a long time ago, in the era of the pumpkin that crossed the border [*a gie teang me*]; today, we are as one people.[1]

This is a glimpse of historical enmities engendered in a situation where the independent-minded but ever more densely populated Wa country was confronted with new immigrant populations such as the Lahu, or the Shan princely statelets, and the neighboring states China and Burma, or the British empire, whose soldiers were also victims of Wa headhunting. And internecine warfare also occurred, even between closely related Wa communities (as described in chapter 5; see how kinsmen were killed over their lack of respect for the traditional supremacy of a founder-village).

I will return later on to the historiographical aspects of Wa uses of trophy heads; here I want to reiterate again that such tactics, tools, and weapons of war are its outward forms. The motivations for war, from what I heard in my interviews with knowledgeable Wa people, never involved the maintenance of a "custom" set apart from history; instead, they always arose within conflicts of interest over land and resources and because of disputes over the order of things in the Wa lands—including internecine warfare. Importantly, all such conflicts played out inside a Wa history, complete with actors and events, which unfolded over time on the ground in and around Wa country—and not outside of history as a "custom" endlessly repeated for its own sake.

In my view, foreigners' theories of Wa headhunting as a "custom" is founded on the *erasure* and overwriting of that Wa history. The most powerful foreigners have refused to recognize this history, instead choosing to replace it with a narrative of primitive headhunting, as if it were about a compulsive repetition of a "customary" phenomenon, unrelated to history and outside of history. That's how Wa warfare figures in the historical master narratives produced by outside powers like the Chinese, the British, and others, which also set aside and "overwrite" the various Wa genres of historical composition-without-writing, to which I will return later on.

There are at least four kinds of such master narratives produced about the Wa by others: those of the Chinese, British, Burmese, and Shan. Given the temporal correlation between the buildup of these state projects and such historiographic compositions—written mostly for the consumption of their own people—it seems clear that they emerged as corollaries to the state projects, bolstering their expansion and control of these lands by framing the Wa as primitive, hopelessly static, stuck in a motionless past, and in need of rescue.

The Chinese sources on the Wa, which go back a thousand years to Song dynasty times or earlier, are highly revealing. Before late imperial Qing dynasty times (eighteenth and nineteenth centuries), headhunting wasn't seen as anything remarkable, because the Chinese themselves had practiced such trophy taking for millennia and were still practicing it. (I believe that the Chinese practices were actually the direct source of the invention of Wa headhunting—more on this below.) Thus, while Chinese historical documents had long depicted the Wa as uncivilized, wild, raw, dangerous, and primitive, as people left behind in a timeless past, a nightmare of primitive violence to be pacified by civilizing influence, we only begin to see the label "headhunting" in this context following the confrontation with the British colonial empire in the late nineteenth century. This view of the Wa, with the new identification of headhunting as un-modern, was one revised under Western influence. It emerged in late imperial times and later solidified as the official modern Chinese interpretation of the Wa as stranded in antiquity, in need of tutelage for the sake of progress, and ready to be rescued from their own dreadful customs—now with headhunting as a paradigmatic example. This, I believe, is the reason why the idea of Wa headhunting as something carried out for the sake of *ji gu* (sacrifice to the crops), for agricultural fertility, came to be mobilized in Chinese writings as the main explanation for *lie tou* (headhunting)—itself a term coined only in the twentieth century by Japanese and Chinese scholars taking their cue from Western colonialist discourse and grafting it onto their earlier imperial parlance.[2]

Formulated in the 1950s, when about half of the Wa lands became part of China, the current official Chinese interpretation was built on accounts that largely omit references to Wa history per se. The scant reconstructions of local history that actually were painstakingly assembled by some of the government-dispatched Chinese anthropologists in the 1950s (who were often very sincere and dedicated) are further excised in official retellings. The result is a portrait of the Wa as historyless, and this is the foundation of the conviction often expressed by government officials (privately, or even publicly) that the main obstacle blocking Wa progress is Wa culture itself. They believe that, ultimately, progress for the Wa will begin only when they cease to be Wa, when they learn to speak Chinese, when they abandon an ancient but stagnant and primitive culture, especially their ruefully misguided compulsive headhunting. Existing cultural traditions, some of which are actually highly sophisticated, are always described as "simple" or rustic (*pushi*), as the reflection of simple and repetitive passions maintained by slaves of a set of customs, in which there is little or no place for conscious *agency*, acting on, and in, the world.

The officials' views also trickle down to the ordinary population. Once, I disembarked a bus at a county town from which I was to proceed, again, to field sites in nearby rural Wa areas. A local Chinese woman suddenly approached me and mustered considerable courage to ask me a pressing question: "Are you the foreigner who said he came here to study *the history of the Wa*?"

"Yes," I replied. Indeed, I had sometimes put it this way to many interlocutors along the way as I traveled "down" to the Wa, much to their puzzlement, and the word had spread that this was how I had framed my work in Chinese. The bewildered woman protested, "But they don't have any history [*lishi*]! How can you study it?" She had been taught that Wa history really began when Chinese administrators arrived to write a new one for them. Indeed, this contrastive historylessness of China's Wa others serves an important function in the production of Chinese identity. Here we may recall Stevan Harrell's (1996) ingenious paper titled "Being Poor, Peripheral, Outnumbered, and Han," which documented the migration of poor Han Chinese farmers, starved of agricultural land in home provinces like Hunan, to the Yi country in Sichuan, but on unsuitable land—all that was left. Their only solace came from their proud membership in Chinese civilization, exemplified by their ability to write—a skill that natives lack. This suggests that natives lack history, a characteristic that can only be attained by civilized people. Ergo, the Wa can't possibly have history (*lishi*).

The British records on colonial Burma closely mirror the Chinese records in relegating the "Wild" Wa to historylessness, notably by way of defining headhunting as primitive custom. In one of the most blatant examples, the famed British colonial administrator James George Scott proposed to "wean" the Wa off what he saw as their compulsive, repetitive and ahistorical rituals by temporarily substituting plastic human skulls. These would be mass-produced for this purpose, in the factories of Birmingham. Perhaps later on, he thought, after the Wa became part of history, they'd learn to consume other British industrial commodities.

Records of Headhunting as Part of Wa History

Scott himself actually recorded historical aspects of Wa culture. Indeed, it stared him in the face—though he was unable to see it as such. Scott took precious photographs of sacrificial prestige poles erected in a Wa village center.[3] To him, these were signs of primitive irrationality. In fact, they record important local events, and these records are historical in nature. In a society without writing, such poles, placed next to drum houses owned by particular clans, commemorated their hosts' successful mounting of important feasts; they served as a memory reference for those living there.

Such markers commemorating events were also deployed in relation to war. Another British officer, Macquoid, made drawings (1896) of the *njouh* bamboo skull containers holding fresh enemy heads, which were likewise planted adjacent to the village drum shrines.

War, Headhunting, and the Erasure of Wa History | 147

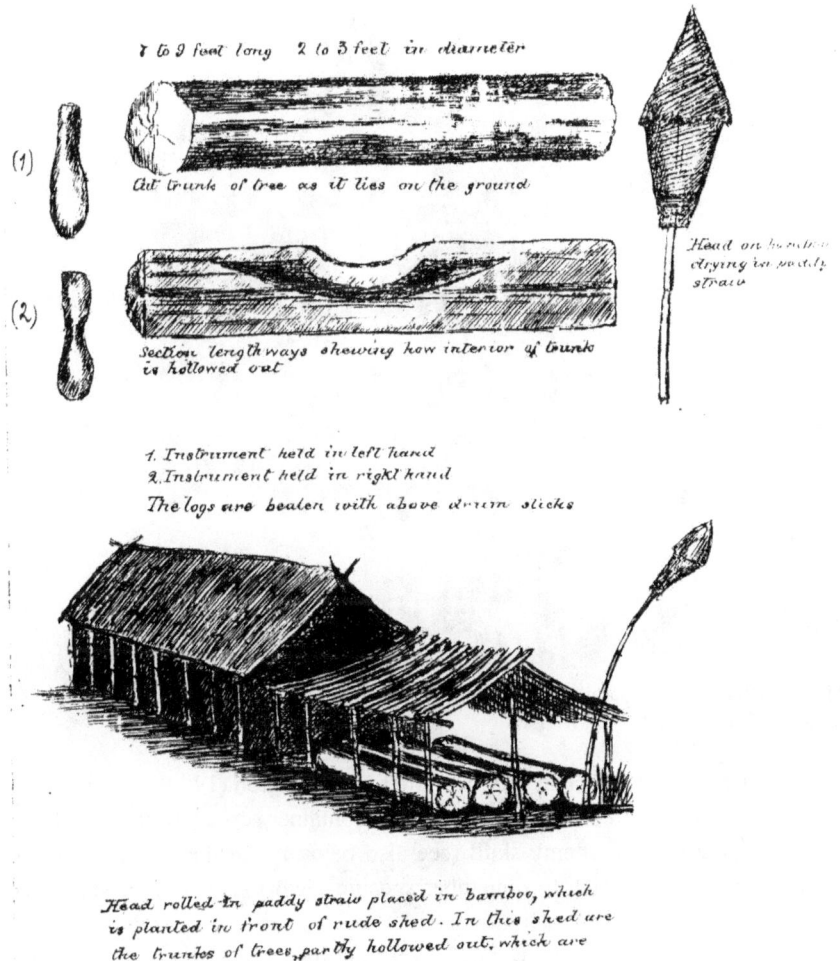

Figure 6.2. A drum shrine with four drums and one bamboo head post (*njouh*), from the village of Matet in central Wa country. "Sketched by Lt. C. E. Macquoid, 1st Lancers, Hyderabad Contingent" (Macquoid 1896)

Figure 6.3. Bamboo head posts (*njouh*) at a village in Yong Ou circle, in the winter of 1957–58 (Winnington 1959).

We see the same device in a 1958 photo by Winnington (1959).

These markers lasted but a year, while the container served its practical function of drying out the enemy skull (see also below). But they, too, were also reference points by which to remember specific victorious acts and when they occurred.

After they dried out, enemy skulls were permanently installed in so-called "skull avenues" that lined village approach roads. This telegraphed to would-be foes the fate of past enemies now permanently installed as a parade of dry, whitened skulls, each placed inside *a nog*, a "skull post" which formed the skull avenues that were photographed in 1935 by the Chinese ethnologist Ling Shun-sheng (Figure 6.4).[4] This roadside display served as a key Wa weapon of deterrence, legible as such by alien soldier-observers like the British and the Chinese.

What these observers did not know, and what I myself did not realize until my second year of trying to relocate and investigate the already overgrown and decaying skull avenues of the past, was that this parade in fact also embodies a built historical memory. It is, in effect, one of the curious and now almost completely erased genres of unwritten historical records that the Wa engaged in. Other such Wa genres include the *groung kod* (stories of the elders) that elders would recite, such as when they retold the origin myths; see Winnington (1959) for photos of

Figure 6.4. Skull avenue at a village near Mengtung. Ling Shun-sheng, 1935–36 (Academia Sinica collection, Wa-071; courtesy of the Institute of History and Philology, Academia Sinica, Taipei).

one of the last *o lang*, or high priests, of Yong Ou reciting the latest iteration of the Wa origin myths for Chinese ethnographers.

The "skull avenues" themselves served as a scene of ritual. Once installed, they also became the record of warrior achievements, ordered by individual feat. They are also notably grouped in the order of *ntoung*, the multiple intermarrying patrilines that make up the key building blocks of Wa social life, and which owned the drum houses — where enemy heads were first curated, prior to being permanently transferred to the *a nog* avenues.

Wa farmers on the way to their fields walk these roads almost daily, and while accompanying farmers for participant observation in the fields, I myself passed by these avenues many times without noticing. They are hidden in foliage, difficult to spot, and ignored or forgotten by many, especially by younger people. But in the past, when they were active as a weapon of deterrence toward outsiders, they were visible to all passersby. They preserved the historical memory of victories, when these victories occurred, who accomplished them, and which patriclan received the glory for them. At the same time this glory was shared by the community as a whole, which finds and recognizes itself in this mirror-lineup of its enemies. This history was enshrined here not through a library of written records but by constant oral transmission enabled by and relying on that visual embodiment of the skull avenue. So it was explained to me. Nowadays, the memory of which warrior accomplished what feat is being lost as the skull avenues themselves have reverted back into the forest from which they were once carved out.

In one place, a rival skull avenue was once established by lineage members as part of a "fissioning" initiative, to break off from the parent village and establish a new community. It was explained to me that such new villages would establish their own skull avenues as a matter of course—to affirm and celebrate their new existence, as the master of their own martial agency.

Ling Shun-sheng's record of a fresh, short row of *a nog* posts (Ling Shun-sheng 1960) may well represent such a new branch. This procedure indicates the role of the skull avenues as one of the key ways that Wa people engaged in "historiography without writing"—an interpretation that can also be extended to the built environment, including especially the impressive defense works, fortifications, and named gates.[5] These also carried immense weight for the Wa as tools for organizing an independent community's memory and sense of itself, by way of declaring and embodying the history in which the community made itself. All these things about the Wa past and its historical memory are typically absent from the narratives composed by outside powers framing the Wa as historyless primitives. They illustrate the (Marxian) dictum that people make their own history, even if it is not under the circumstances of their choosing.

Defeating Death: Ritualized War

In the Wa past, each war (*ning*), including every instance of raids organized for the sake of revenge or punishment, was carried out within a ritualized framework. Conceptually, it would include several identifiable steps:

1. Its motivation, which involved a dialectic of provocation and precedent.
2. Its preparation and completion: killing enemies either in an ambush ("war of the road" *ning grax*) or an attack on enemy settlements (*ning nie'x*). The latter was generally seen as more glorious and was carried out either as a sneak attack or with an overwhelming force that could overcome a large number of enemies.

3. Its celebration of success, on the way home and in the village, with the temporary installation of the rotting enemy heads at the relevant clan's drum shrine.
4. Finally, the year after, the dry skulls would be transferred to the permanent repository at the so-called "skull avenue." This step was accompanied by the "cutting of the calf's tail," which concludes the entire sequence and which was regarded as the most important element of communal ritual life—with the possible exception of the other "village sacrifices" (*si niee yong*), such as the rebuilding of the "big house" of the *o lang* and the making and pulling home of log drums owned by different patriclans.

My account here is based on interviews I carried out in the Wa language while visiting and living in former headhunters' villages. Their areas were "pacified" by the new Pax Sinica in the 1950s, after which headhunting was forbidden. It probably did not occur anywhere in China after 1958, when there was a small war over the Chinese confiscation of firearms of the independent Wa. Several decades have thus passed since anyone in this area last practiced headhunting, made and used the tools attributed to it, or performed the rituals associated with it.[6] I rarely had the chance to speak to any former headhunter, and most of the information is therefore from local people who participated as witnesses and bystanders rather than as direct participants. Memories have been further fragmented by the traumatic events of the 1950s on, so that the bygone days have receded into the sphere to of the former generations (*nqu ga*). This also, however, means that it is indeed possible to speak of these matters in a detached way, even if it is still a sensitive subject. My interlocutors were willing to share some of their memories of the former times of headhunting (*lai a maog nqu ga nu*, "in those former generations when [people] cut [heads]," in Yong Ou dialect). My account builds on both eyewitness and bystander memories, but additionally also includes reports by earlier travelers and other writers, both Chinese and Western.

While the reasons for particular wars can still linger in memory (as seen, for example, in chapter 5 with the gaur horn incident, or in the conflict with the Lahu, in chapter 9), few interlocutors remembered details of the concrete preparations for a raid. The Chinese ethnologist Ling Shun-sheng produced a detailed account (1953: 2–5) emphasizing how elders and young warriors would meet to plan a raid and use the classic Wa chicken-bone oracles to ascertain the likelihood of success—similar to what people would do today before setting out on important journeys. Planning a war raid would also include the *ba pi*, "the one who *pi*" or chants the headhunting ritual prayers (which are more intricate than the everyday *nqai*, ordinary "prayers").

The war party would then go out with machetes ready for the kill. Ling's is the only account I know that says the successful headhunter was expected to drink of the blood of his victim at the site of the killing. Wa people I have talked to deny this, and say there was never any consumption of blood or any other body parts. The only body part used was the head; the corpses of the victims were left unburied at the roadside. The spirit of the victim (his *ge meang*) is supposed to have remained at the site of the killing, forever lingering there—very much unlike those of the ordinary dead, who are ideally buried within their home village, in the vegetable garden of their own house.

The cut-off heads would then be carried back to the village in rather simple makeshift bags or baskets.[7] The warriors would fire guns along the way and chant a peculiar victory tune that was audible from a great distance, described by Harold Young, the local-born Baptist missionary who also wrote on the proceedings of Wa headhunting (n.d. [ca. 1946]; 2015), as chilling. This chanting and shooting was also meant to alert the villagers at home, who would be ready for the installation ceremony. To ensure that they were, the warriors were often made to wait with the heads outside the village at named waiting places that are still recognized today.

The warriors were also made to wait because the enemy heads were thought to carry a highly potent *si aob*, a power associated with death, putrefaction, and destruction. As such, the heads represent danger, and warriors must treat them correctly if this force is to be both contained and harnessed properly. The waiting spots were usually at a certain distance from the village, but within sight of one of the gates on either side of it—often at prominent trees left to grow in a spot visible from afar, alongside the path homeward, where they also would serve as rest stops for tired farmers before the last stretch home. The warriors, too, would rest under the trees, sending messengers to report their results. They would even be forced to wait for up to a day or so, while their bags with severed heads hung in the tree.

When the time came, the warriors would bring the heads to the village gate, where they would place them on the ground outside of it. The women of the village, led by the wives of the warriors, would come out of to greet their successful men, bringing food (cooked rice, meat, and greens) for them—along with raw eggs for the heads. The women would crack the eggs in mocking fashion on the teeth of the heads while these still rested on the ground. This practice recalls the treatment of newly cut log drums, on which eggs were also cracked during a mandatory three-day waiting period just outside the gate before they were ready to be brought inside.

I cannot be sure of the precise significance of this, but the intention seems to be for the women to "test" both human remains and drums to make sure they are fit for their role. The teeth are seen as a key indicator of health and strength in people, and in the case of enemy heads, their significance is highlighted by the fact that they were the only part exposed in the *a nog* skull posts—the eyes were typically blocked from view when the skulls were installed.

After this final stop outside a gate, the heads would then be carried through the gate into the village by the warriors themselves. Again the women, beginning with the warriors' wives, would dance alongside them in celebration. Then they would join the men and proceed into the village together. This is how the Chinese ethnographer Ling Shun-sheng described it:

> The men in front, singing; the women behind, wailing loudly, crying as follows: "Everyone knows how to walk, [yet] why did you, [owner of] this head, have to take the wrong way and lose your life? Your father and mother raised you, how would they know today is the day of your death?" Along the way, the sounds of songs, wailing, and firearms continue. . . . When they arrive in the village, the village drum is beaten without pause, and all villagers . . . come out to welcome the brave men. . . . The head is carried to the center of the village. The shaman takes it and places it on the wooden drum. He beats the drum, takes a cooked egg divided in four parts, with wine, meat, and rice, and offers these in front of the head. Most households in the village bring rice and wine and offers some at the head, putting some grains of rice and pouring some wine into its mouth. Everyone also weeps for it, mourning the person . . . who sacrificed his life for them and now cannot return home or see his parents. After the sacrifice of the head, parts of its lips, ears and so forth are cut off, and put in a small basket.[8] Then, cattle, pigs, chicken and dogs are sacrificed to the ancestors, who are informed that a head has now been offered to them in this year, and they should now protect the peace of the people of the village, secure a rich harvest and growth of the six domestic animals, as well as drive away any evil spirits. After the sacrifices are over, men and women mingle and shout with loud voices, playing flutes and beating drums, dancing madly in joy, drinking wine and making merry. The sacrifice lasts three days, and people get completely drunk every day, and sleep all around the drum-shrine. . . . the head is sacrificed on top of the drum for three days. . . . (Ling Shun-sheng 1960).

Ling's account includes his own interpretation, but its practical details are basically valid—although in the area I worked I was told that nothing was "fed" to the heads other than the raw eggs.

Before being placed at the drum shrine, a captured head would first be brought inside the successful warrior's own house. There it would briefly be suspended, still in its container, in the farthest corner opposite the lower right (*blag liog blag seih*) corner of the altar of the household deity (*si yiex*)—a family altar that today has been thoroughly abolished, perhaps due to this historical use.[9] Once the head was hung, the warrior would give the *si yiex* and the ancestors (*ge meang*) a brief report about his deed.

Then, at villages that had a resident *o lang*, the heads would be taken to the designated *o lang* drum shrine; in smaller descendant villages (*yong guan*), they would be taken to any of the drum shrines available (there was always at least one per patriclan, so at a minimum, at least one per village). In some cases where the achievement of the warriors was directly related to avenging a killing of someone from their own village, the heads might be taken to the drum shrine of the particular patriclan most involved in the matter instead of to the *o lang*'s drum shrine. In either case, the presentation was also accompanied by a feast of sacrificed buffalo, ideally accompanied by large amounts of rice beer and rice provided by the sponsors, who could not be the headhunters themselves but who had to come from another patriclan, an arrangement permitting the simultaneous celebration of warriors' individual deeds and their absorption into the glory of the community as a whole (more on this key issue below).

One of the few non-Wa ever to have attended such celebrations was the Swiss diplomat Willy-A Prestre, who served under Colonel Iselin, the Swiss chairman of the League of Nations–supervised Sino-British boundary commission working in the area 1935–37.[10] Having "punished" one Wa village (attacking and burning it for refusing passage), the boundary commission unwittingly earned the friendship of Awng Kai, another local village chief who was the long-standing enemy of the defeated village.[11] Prestre says he witnessed the return of warriors, covered in blood, to Awng Kai's village, carrying the heads of people from the enemy ("pirate") village. Everyone took great joy in their victory, and in the meat and "rice alcohol" brought to the scene. The joy was even stronger when the "tribe cantor" ("le chantre de la tribu," meaning the *ba pi*) commenced his incantations to the heads, and pushed cooked rice, roasted pork, and rice alcohol into the mouths of the captured heads. The joy intensified in the course of the evening, becoming a madness that "hurled couples into the jungle and brought them back again" (Prestre 1946: 81).

In the area where I conducted interviews, during the feast the heads would have been kept either on top of the drums or suspended inside the drum shrine under its roof (some such differences may have been geographical), but not sacrificed "to the drum," or to a *muid'* (as a supreme deity) or a god of crop fertility. All these frequently suggested theories are mistaken, according to my informants. There was no such deity, and no such sacrifices, only celebration, and mockery of the dead.[12]

After the celebration ended, the heads would be taken out of the drum shrine and placed on top of specially made bamboo head poles (*njouh*; or *njouh ndoung*, in the Yong Ou dialect) until they dried out completely—this could take up to a year. Only then could they be transferred out of the village. *Njouh*, which could be up to seven meters tall, would be planted on the side of the drum shrine. They were made by splitting the end of a fairly thick (about the width of an arm) bamboo pole so that the entire end is divided into strips, still connected to the trunk, and then forced open to form a container. The shape of the container is then fixed by weaving softened bamboo strips around it, giving the end of the pole the appearance of a basket (Figure 6.2; 6.3).

This kind of container is easy to make, and the concept is also applied to making cages for small wild birds, among other things. It can also be used as an impromptu chicken cage, simply by cutting the ready-spliced "cage" off of the bamboo pole and turning it upside down on the ground over the bird.[13] When used as a *njouh* for human heads, right side up, the open top was generally covered with a simple lid also woven from sliced bamboo.

Once the heads were enclosed, each *njouh* would then be planted by the side of the drum shrine, serving as temporary depositories for heads not yet transferred to their final location in the skull grove outside of the village. Each *njouh* also had a small window (like the *a nog* of the skull grove described below) through which one could glimpse the head, wrapped in straw, while the liquid putrefying material (known as *si aob*) from the head flowed down into the ground at the base of the drum shrine. Some say that in nearby Wa areas, a pile of ash or soil would be used as a receptacle for the fluids, and every household would receive some of this ash to spread onto newly burned swidden fields that were about to be planted: "Each household mixes the blood soil with some more soil, and spreads it onto the dry-rice swiddens, and it is said that as soon as this soil is spread onto the land, the rice plants at once flourish even more" (Ling Shun-sheng 1953: 3; see also *Sixiang zhanxian* editorial dept. 1981, among others). Harold Young (n.d.: 8) says it was not just soil but rice seeds that were soaked in this manner.

This version of the widespread theory that Wa headhunting was about fertility could perhaps make sense in the context of the traditional burning of the Wa swiddens, where the temporary clearing and burning of a stretch of forest is carried out in order to produce cleared fields for hill rice, which are covered in the fertilizing ash from the burned wood and debris of the forest. The connection between the ritual and the fertility of the fields would then be directly evoked in a practical and positive deployment of the remains of the decapitated enemy, seemingly conceived in the manner of the fertilizing soul-force seen in headhunting traditions elsewhere in Southeast Asia (Hoskins 1996).

However, in the areas I myself have visited, no one mentioned or recognized such a practice, or even the idea of one. Instead, my interlocutors held that the ground around the *njouh* could not be touched on account that it was poisoned, and if anyone inadvertently touched it or, worse, ate vegetables that had grown in soil contaminated by the *si aob* of the dead enemy, their own teeth would rot and fall out. Given this, it would seem strange if the contaminated soil would be spread on the fields in the manner reported by some scholars.

It could be that the area I worked in was special, but I don't think so. My understanding is that the heads were actually never gifted to any gods or fertility spirits and the ash was not used in such a way. I believe my interlocutors were expounding on a more widely embraced idea centering on the use of the *si aob* to harness the dangerous, deadly power of the putrefying enemy by using it as a vaccination of the community. The *si aob* is the dangerous, destructive poison of death, embodied in the dying and rotting enemy victim, a horribly repulsive, abject presence (Kristeva 1982 [1980]). Bringing it inside the wall-enclosed community and letting its rot invade the ground is an attempt to overcome it by inoculating oneself with it.

This is separate from the use of the dried-out enemy skulls as a spectacle to deter the next enemy. The rotting head still embodies the living human enemy that could have been us, yet the use of the dry skull was also preemptive, since it is directed at the next incoming enemy. The same dual effect is found in the more ancient Wa tradition of the tiger display, which I will explain in more detail later. It served as one model and source of inspiration for the Wa borrowing of the new spectacle of human enemy heads, from what was originally an imperial Chinese military practice.

The Transfer of the Enemy Skulls

After the heads were all dried out (which might take as long as a year), the *njouh* poles would be taken down and discarded—new poles would be made for the next round. Then the heads would be transferred out of the village, a ceremony regarded by Wa people as the most important of the entire sequence of war rituals. Its high point was a cathartic orgy of violence, a sacrificial ritual known as the "cutting of the calf's tail" (*maog si dah mui* in the Yong Ou dialect), which concluded the entire procedure of the enemy heads. In the scholarly literature, the "cutting of the calf's tail" is often discussed separately from headhunting, but it was really deeply intertwined and part of the same sequence of war rituals. I want to argue that it was about moving past war, death, and *si aob* and toward the regeneration of the community. More on this below.

The skull grove or avenue to which the completely dried-out skulls were transferred is known in Wa as a *lah*—which means a public space. It is the same word as the word for "market," perhaps a later derivation. It suggests a correspondence between the strange exchange that took place in the grove, and the human markets where people went to obtain salt, weapons, and other items from strangers bringing them to trade. The *lah* of the skull avenue was a patch of forest near the village, usually with a radius of several hundred meters and with a road or path running through or alongside it. In many cases, the location was outside the view of the village itself but alongside a road constituting one prominent approach toward it. The *lah* was without exception located in the direction of the setting sun, in the west,[14] the direction associated with death and decay.[15]

Every village had such a *lah*[16] with *a nog*, the skull posts to which the dried-out crania were transferred. The *a nog* posts were usually fashioned from extremely hard wood—some of these were still standing, forty years after the demise of headhunting. Drum shrines, log drums, and *njouh* are long gone, destroyed by the Chinese during their annexation and reformation of the Wa lands, and cannot be seen except in a few museums.[17] I did, however, see original *a nog* still standing in several places in 1996–98. No skulls are left, but the hard wood remains. The *a nog* would be arranged in a long row, with two or three meters separating each post, thus prompting the British name "skull avenue."[18]

The *a nog* were invariably arranged in a single long row; one that I studied had a total of sixty posts. This may have been a medium-sized skull avenue: early British sources mention villages with several hundred skulls.[19] Weaker villages, such as those established more recently, might only have a few skulls in their long-term skull depository, their *lah*. I too saw more recently established skull avenues at branched-off villages with as few as ten skull posts.

The row of head posts was always to be visible from the road approaching the village, and the skulls placed inside the hollowed-out *a nog* always faced the road.[20] Ling Shun-sheng (1953: 4) explained it well: "These head-post rows are located along the main thoroughfare of the village, which travelers must pass, so that travelers in the land of the Wild Kawa are made to be nervous and frightened already as they approach the village. When they arrive at the head-post rows, and see these strange views that they have never seen before, there is not one among them who is not completely terrified."

In times of war, the site itself would occasionally be used as a dramatic live display of the powers of the village: British military forces making their way through Wa country noted the "ostentatious manner" in which groups of Wa warriors confronted their expeditions in front of their *lah* (Pitchford 1937: 231). This was because the skull grove was by far the most "charged" of all places in the landscape surrounding the village. All this very much aligns with the information I discussed already, about how villagers built the skull avenues as historical records of their martial achievements.

There was some variation in the shape of the *a nog*: in some places, observed by Prestre, the head posts themselves had been given the shape of carved human figures, which held the skull in their belly.[21] Scott's observation (1896: 142) that the simplest head post designs could be found in the central lands while more elaborate forms (effigy style) appeared on the fringes is probably correct. Thus, in the Ximeng area (formerly part of the central Wa lands), the *a nog* were never carved but consisted only as plain wooden posts standing about sixty to eighty centimeters tall and twenty to thirty centimeters thick. They were hollowed out from above, with an opening at "belly" level midway up the pole, so that the teeth of the victim's skull would be visible after the skull was inserted. The exposure of the teeth seems to have been a very widespread design requirement.[22]

The skull would be inserted either from the front or down through the hollowed-out top of the post, which would then be covered with a flat rock (the latter head posts could also be made entirely with flat stones cut into slabs for the purpose). At the skull avenues that I observed, the *a nog* were all made of wood, but each was accompanied by a stone marker placed immediately behind it—flat stones of roughly the same dimensions as the *a nog* themselves. These stones were probably planted before the *a nog* head posts, and in some cases they were carved with human figures, possibly clan insignia, but they have faded so far (including in local memory) that this can no longer be confirmed. None of the original creators of these skull avenues survive, and people are nowadays often genuinely fearful of the forest spot where their remains linger—which means that very few local people have actually seen the *a nog* head posts in their village's *lah*, if they actually survive. Even so, people still know the general purpose of the procedures.

In the past, the transfer of the skulls into these posts was the last stage in the war rituals, and was primarily known by the accompanying ritual, the "cutting of the calf's tail" (*maog si dah mui*). It is almost as if the transfer of the skulls was a less important corollary of this ritual. As mentioned, the skull transfer ideally would take place in the year after a successful war raid, in late spring. It was associated with a ritual known as the "cutting of the calf's tail," which involved the highly formalized but very violent slaughter of a single young bull (cattle, *mui*; not a water buffalo, *grag*)—to get its tail, or any other piece. This was accompanied by feasting on water buffalo that were killed by spearing (*suad*), as was common in the past for many different social occasions, including weddings, funerals, and so on.[23] The "cutting of the calf's tail" was not carried out every year. It depended on whether there were skulls waiting, and also on the availability of sacrificers (beneficiaries and hosts) who could afford to mount the accompanying sacrificial rituals and feasts (here I use the terms of Hubert and Mauss 1964 [1898]: *sacrificers* are those actually carrying out the ritual, and *sacrifiers* are those hosting it and benefiting from it. See too Valeri 1994, and below).

The whole process—the transfer of the dry skull from its *njouh* inside the village, and out to the *lah*—would take up to ten days and required a large amount of supplies of sacrificial victims: cattle and buffalo as well as smaller animals like pigs and chickens (for divination purposes), and large quantities of rice beer and food. If there were more willing and able sacrifiers than waiting skulls, a skull already transferred might even be taken back from the skull grove for a second round of sacrifices in the village, and the second sacrifier would then escort the skull out for its final rest (see Luo Zhiji 1995: 328).

The transfer of the skull and the ritual of the cutting of the calf's tail would take place on the same day. When a transfer had been decided upon (by consensus?), officiating ritualists and sacrifiers (hosts providing cattle and buffalo) selected, various victims prepared and sacrificers selected, the ritual could be performed. First, in the morning, a preselected team of five or so young male and female virgins (*si nou si nga*; "clean young people," that is people who had not yet had sexual relations) would go to the skull grove by themselves. Their mission was to tidy up (*bih*) the grove in anticipation of the arrival of the village elders and warriors, who went in the early afternoon. The team of virgins would clear grass and fallen branches from the row of skull posts and the seating area in front and then return home.

Meanwhile, village elders would take down the *njouh* and put the dried-out skulls in cloth bags or bamboo containers. Then they would carry them to the skull grove accompanied by the same team of virgins, followed by all the men, women, and children of the village—this was the only time the general populace of the village visited the skull grove. Skull posts would be planted into the ground in the row, and each skull extracted from its carrying container and inserted into the niche with its teeth showing. The skull would then be humiliated and mocked—no offerings would be made to it, nor would it be established as a god in any way.

The elders and all others present would then share a meal of sacrificial rice and meat cooked back in the village, at the main sacrifier's house, where the bull calf whose tail would soon be cut was also being prepared. The food would be brought along by representatives of that household to an area with rock stools arranged in a half-moon shape, on which the elders of the village would sit. The food was served to the elders by the virgins, who would be the special *gon si mang* (waiters) of this occasion.

One of these virgins, an old woman who died in 1998, told me in an interview that she was fearful during the whole event and dared not look at anything, but she lightened up when one of the elders joked with her in typical Wa fashion, "complaining" that she was handing him too little rice from the basket she was distributing food to the elders from. This light moment was her most precious memory of her two trips to the skull grove (field notes, XXIV:116ff.). People would never otherwise visit the skull grove, and never on their own, because they were too scared; this is also why many people nowadays have never once been there. No-one told them, even though they may have walked by it a thousand times on their way to working the fields.

The "Cutting of the Calf's Tail"

The completion of the meal and the return to the village would mark the beginning of the end of the entire headhunting cycle. The dramatic finale would follow: the killing of a young bull calf, a special victim that had to be perfect in terms of the regularity of its color, horn shape, and the health of its hair and its skin. Great attention was devoted to finding one with "good hair and good *kuan*," the *kuan* referring to the swirl of the hair found on the forehead on cattle (*hmom haig hmom kuan*) as well as high atop the head of humans (a "cowlick"; humans sometimes have two *kuan*). The preferred color would vary, but pitch-black young bulls were often used.

The victim would be tied to a pole planted near the house of the sponsoring sacrifier, and a village elder would present a verbal dedication. The pole was a special straight piece of hard wood, unlike the forked posts regularly marking the sacrifice of cattle and buffalo on other occasions. After the dedication was finished, the elder would untie the young bull and walk it around the house three times. Then he would tie the animal to its pole again, cut off the tail in a dramatic movement, and throw it high over the top of the house of the sacrifier, after which the village children would fight over it as a souvenir. At the moment the tail was cut clear, all the able, willing, and married men of the village threw themselves at the living beast with sharpened knives, competing with each other in cutting it into pieces. In effect, all the men became sacrificers, and the entire community the sacrifier host, alongside the individual person serving as such.

Under the watch of the entire village, a frenzy would erupt, which might be very dangerous;[24] many men suffered cuts, and some would even be killed. It is noteworthy that knives were used for sacrificial killing instead of the more common wooden spear (*plih*), which is identical to the wooden dibbling sticks traditionally used when planting hill swiddens and spearing (*suad*) cattle and buffalo. The only time that knives were used instead of spears was during the "cutting of the calf's tail."[25] Even pieces of the calf that had already been claimed were not safe; these could be fought over until they had been brought within the confines of the house of a contestant sacrificer, where they would later be cooked, distributed, and eaten. The sacrifier and his family members, for their part, would struggle to drag the carcass and the head into their house, where it would be safe. Should they fail to save the head and body trunk, or at the very least the spine, from the crowd, it was seen an inauspicious sign for the family, as was any damage to the calf's ears during the action.

When the cutting frenzy ended, the hosts would spear and kill as many as thirty to forty water buffalo, which were cooked and consumed by the villagers, allies, and relatives invited from friendly villages. This, too, would then become a grand feast of merit, with the strange addition of the greatest prestige prize: the violent, competitive massacre of a single bull. The whole war ritual ended here, with the rapid carving and consumption of the last victim, alongside the added buffalo meat. The whole affair was occasioned by the transfer of the skull, yet the "cutting of the bull's tail" clearly shifted the focus of the community's attention away from their enemies and their dry, whitened skulls installed in the now-quiet *lah* outside the village.

The violently competitive catharsis of this "cutting of the bull's tail" ceremony came with a number of curious constraints, all of which point to harnessing the violence for the sake of the community, away from the individual warriors who had vanquished the enemy. For example, while many were willing to take on the prestigious sponsorship of all sacrifices, especially the cutting of the bull calf's tail, communally agreed limitations ensured that no single household could monopolize such events. Thus, potential sacrificers had to be approved by consensus among the elders of the village, and by tradition they would not approve the sponsorship of these important communal events by anyone whose position was already too strong in the village community, either in terms of wealth, prestige accrued from earlier sacrificial sponsorships (positions as sacrificers), or accomplishments as a head-cutting warrior. Instead, they would favor and even invite less prominent men, going so far at times as to give cattle and buffalo to the most reluctant sacrificer. These points were all stressed by my own interlocutors in the Yong Ou circle as highly significant ones.

War Ritual as Sacrifice

These arrangements indicate how the crescendo of the Wa war ritual paradoxically is set up both to acknowledge and celebrate the warrior's feat, to harness the competitive violent outbursts of other individual men, and pair these objectives with sacrificial feasts carefully shared with everyone. In my view, this was all for the sake of reaffirming and regenerating the community.

The entire war ritual complex, including the final outbursts of violent and apparently selfish grabbing and consumption of its last victim (every man trying to secure the prized tail of the calf, and its other body parts, for himself), is simultaneously an exhilarating sportive competition and a deadly serious sacrifice.

The sacrifice actually closely mirrors the four-part structure of sacrifices worldwide (Valeri 1994:106–8). First, the induction of the victim (often analogous to a hunt, such as the trap set in Wa headhunting war raids[26]). Second, the taking of the victim's life (which follows quickly in war raids). Third, renunciation (in the case of the war victims, the corpse is renounced while the head is kept as a token; in a sense, renunciation is also at work in the transfer of skulls out of the village, as well as in the throwing away of the tail of the last victim); and fourth, consumption—in the case of human victims, supplementary animal victims are consumed instead. Their meat accompany both the initial presentation of the fresh head at the drum, and the grand finale, after the journey of the remains come to an end. This also unfolds at a symbolic level, both through the use of the victim's *si aob* as a symbolic inoculation mechanism, and also through the long-term use of the victim's dried-out and symbolically blinded skull, which is lined up as a visual deterrent to enemies, to protect the community. The war rituals as a whole can be understood as one single sacrifice, which isn't directed to any deity but rather highlights the elements of renunciation central to sacrifice, even as it also unites the community by harnessing the various forces at work in the ritual to further its survival.

Even if the villagers report the capture of the heads and the offering of each and every one of the speared buffalo, as well as the final victim destroyed by all (save the tail), to the separate household deities (the *si yiex*) and the ancestor spirits (the *ge meang*) of each participant sacrifier, none of these things are actually offered to any deity per se. In this the Wa headhunting sacrifice is not unique, as Valeri also noted, in his seminal discussions of sacrifice.[27] By no means do all sacrifices have recipients as if they were gifts; the crucial point is the gesture of abstention, the *giving up* of something, and the social use of this gesture, as well as of the tokens of the ritual occasion, which may be appropriated in new forms by the very people who gave it up (as sacrifiers). In the case of Wa human sacrifice, the victims are renounced, and while their heads are appropriated, it is without a designated addressee. The sacrifice is also not one of first fruits, where forsaking one victim enables sacrifiers to consume and digest other members of the class to which it belongs (as with edible first-fruit victims in genocentric sacrifices such as the first salmon, or the American Thanksgiving turkey, on which I have written separately [2003]).

The sacrifices that figure in these rituals are instead organized to promote the community itself. They present an exceedingly complex picture, with multiple scenes where a number of different objectives are accomplished within different segments of the sequence. Thus the revenge action against the community's enemies also forms an occasion for the display of personal bravery on the part of individual headhunters, in their role of restoring the honor of the community as a whole, and for asserting the glory of their own lineage (every *a nog* head post becomes a permanent record of all three: the individual warrior, whose contributed act also invites patriclan glory while also adding to the communal village framework of the skull avenue as a whole). Similarly, the sponsorship competition and the meat-cutting frenzy in the village provide opportunities for vigorous status competitions that are still contained within the framework of the community as a whole.

The last grand sacrifice of the perfect young bull also addresses collective concerns, and is illustrative of the community-constituting role of such rituals.[28] But at the same time, it is also a vehicle of internal competition and status differentiation: young men staked their reputation in the cutting up of the sacrificial cattle (perhaps even more than in the war raids), and individual bravery and competition can appear as the overriding concerns in these risky rituals. Yet even here, "leveling" rules were in place. Participation was restricted to married men, tempering the potentially irresponsible bravery of immature unmarried young men; the sponsorship role was displaced from the prestigious, the rich, and the famous and granted to the poor, the quiet, and the unnoticed; also, the sacrifier was deprived of giving out meat whose killing he had sponsored and instead opened its distribution to a sanctioned, yet contained orgy. As such, it is reminiscent of sports competitions in other societies that provide a violent spectacle but are at the same time strictly policed and contained—configured as a celebration of the community holding it.

In this way, the final sacrifice of the young bull, while enabling the transfer of the captured skull, was actually created as a way for the entire community to also be made, provided for, fed, and protected. Yet this curious and complex set of community self-management devices would later unravel along with the rest of the institutions of the old Wa society: beginning in the 1950s, these rituals were forbidden, and the ritualists curtailed. Much of the physical setup for and paraphernalia of headhunting was thoroughly destroyed, along with the social institutions that sustained independent Wa society. Drum houses were torn down, along with any *njouh* head poles planted near them; the log drums were thrown out or burned, and only a few survive in faraway museums, such as those displayed at the museum of the Yunnan Nationalities University in Kunming, the provincial capital. The roadside *a nog* were destroyed or abandoned; the fortifications protecting villages were broken up and demolished. The major rituals of the past were forsaken. Chief ritualists and other leaders were deposed, marginalized, and persecuted.

Many older Wa people that I spoke to regarded 1958 as a key watershed (called *wu-ba-nian*, or, simply, "fifty-eight"), since that year marked a shift in the Chinese occupation activity from reconciliation to the dismantling of Wa institutions. These people often engage in self-blame, speculating that the once mighty Wa must have brought this calamity upon themselves by failing to properly service the mighty gods of their lands. In the words of one Wa farmer summing up recent history with a ready-made metaphor: *Grag quid' long* ("the buffalo's trampled down the fence," for which the fence-builder bears more responsibility than the grazing buffalo). Some elders reckoned that because they now live in a "Chinese era" (the *nqu Houx*), no one should dream of reviving these rituals, on pain of further punishment from the gods (see, however, chapter 10).

Headhunting Copied from China

The most revealing insight we glean from the Chinese sources on the Wa is that headhunting is not singled out as characteristic of the Wa before the late nineteenth century—the exact same time that Western-derived notions of primitive headhunting were gathering influence in China. In earlier times, headhunting was simply not seen as distinctive. The reason is, as we shall see, that the Chinese state was the bigger "headhunter."

Before the nineteenth century, the Chinese deployed classical or imperial terminology to the Wa, referring to them as uncivilized and wild "barbarians," divided on the "raw"/"cooked" dichotomy: barbarians remaining outside of imperial control were said to be "raw" (*sheng*); if they still belonged to the same ethnolinguistic formation and retained some of their language and customs, but had partly come under state control (taxation, corvée, drafted as soldiers, etc.), they were called "cooked" (*shu*) (Fiskesjö 1999a). Some older accounts, such as the mid-sixteenth-century *Nanzhao yeshi* by Yang Shen (2: 31a–b), note that warriors of the "Raw" Wa will cut off enemy heads. But this is only mentioned occasionally, and never elevated to a theory of headhunting as a sign of primitivity. The Chinese concept of "headhunting" (*lietou*) does not appear until late Qing times, becoming more common in the early twentieth century.

Like the people of many other premodern militarized states, the Chinese themselves practiced "headhunting." Since "headhunting" is a nineteenth-century, Western-derived evolutionist concept, it could be more accurate to say that the Chinese regularly cut off enemy heads as trophies—first and foremost those of enemy or rebel battlefield soldiers, and especially their captured leaders, whose heads were typically put on display after the accused were ceremonially branded offenders against the state. Beginning in pre-imperial times, the first millennium BCE, enemy heads were brought home by Chinese war chiefs and "presented" at ancestral temples as a victory report to the ancestors.[29] Later, in imperial times, such war-triumph rituals were transformed but never went away, and were sometimes resurrected in archaizing fashion, with barbarian opponents marched back to the capital for victory parades and decapitations. For example, the noted Sinologist Edward Schafer (1967) describes such ceremonies put on during the great revival of the Tang dynasty (sixth to ninth century CE).[30] And in fact, Chinese spectacles of decapitating and displaying vanquished enemies continued all the way into modern times, most recently during the 1940s civil war.[31] Interestingly, even in nineteenth-century late-imperial Chinese accounts, the classical Chinese vocabulary is prominently used, as if to continue to emphasize an ideological continuity with ancient China: they speak of battlefield "capture" (*qin*) of such enemy "bandits," and it was in vogue at the time to take "head trophies" (*guo*) from such offenders and display them in marketplaces and other public places for the maximum deterrent effect.

The southern fringes of the Chinese empire were, of course, no exception. Today's Southwest China was conquered by way of centuries of bloody wars, destroying a number of kingdoms and other polities in the region[32]—most famously the rich Bronze Age kingdom of Dian (its Chinese name) in today's

Yunnan, not far from the Wa lands, which was incorporated into the empire as a dependent state in the first century CE. Actually the Dian kingdom itself deployed similar methods of "state headhunting," as is richly illustrated on its figurative bronze vessels (Yao 2016). The Shan kingdoms of this region are also known for decapitating defeated enemies and displaying the trophy heads.

But none of these secondary state formations could match the scale of imperial Chinese warfare, and spectacular head cutting was an integral part of it from very early on. The practice is documented in central China a full millennium before the advent of the Dian kingdom; and in the southwestern conquests, explicit Chinese accounts from the second century CE tell of as many as thirty thousand heads cut on the battlefields in what is now Yunnan Province, when an alliance of thirty-six "barbarian tribes" resisting annexation were subdued by the Chinese empire (Ni Tui 1992 [1737]: 39–40).

These numbers need not be exaggerations. Yang Shen's sixteenth-century *Nanzhao yeshi* chronicle, apparently the first that speaks of Wa head cutting, also tells of incidents where Chinese armies decapitated numerous defeated Yunnan barbarians, whose leaders were marched to the capital, Beijing, and ritually killed there. The conclusion is unavoidable: cutting off the heads of one's enemies as part of a triumphant spectacle was likely introduced into Southwest China by the Chinese empire. This may have been as early as the first century CE, when Chinese soldiers penetrated the region to attack the Dian.

The Wa area escaped outright conquest until much later, but I believe they picked up the idea of cutting off enemy heads and displaying them as a weapon of deterrence from the Chinese military. A wealth of sources detailing such Chinese military practices in the immediate vicinity of the Wa exists, all the way up to the late nineteenth and early twentieth centuries. For example, one Chinese imperial official at Zhenbian noted in a report published in 1908 (probably written in the 1890s) that "[we] killed Zhadie the bandit [a Lahu rebel leader]; another, Zhatuo, was captured alive . . . his head [was] later put on display for the masses [to see]" (Chen Can, n.d. [ca. 1908]: *juan* 4.23a–b). Zhenbian, a Chinese military outpost, was established in 1887 to assist pursuit of ethnic Lahu rebels (see chapter 9), right on the doorstep of the Wa.

We should consider that before the Chinese state and other forces pressed into this region during last few centuries (notably to obtain the riches of the land, as discussed in chapter 4), war must have been uncommon in the Wa lands. There could not have been many reasons for it. Given what we know about Wa history, we must imagine a region with plenty of land where the Wa and other forest farmers could move freely, so there would be no reason for the Wa to take up war until neighboring, menacing states began to circumscribe the Wa area. This engendered frictions and confrontations with outside forces, from whom the Wa defended their autonomy, and also initiated internecine Wa warfare. And yet, for a long time, the Wa successfully navigated and handled this difficult geopolitical situation, intensifying their agricultural yield and cultivating cash crops for export, among other things, bringing about considerable wealth—and a population so dense that it surprised and confounded the British colonial agents that arrived on the scene (cf. chapter 8).

My contention is that it was in this context the Wa took up trophy taking as part of their own warfare, as a new weapon of terror and deterrence directly copied from longstanding Chinese practices. Recall that for many centuries, Chinese head-taking practices were widely and clearly noted in Chinese documents, not hidden as if they were inappropriate. It is only in the nineteenth century, under Western influence, that this "headhunting" weapon is recast and branded as "primitive," rendering it officially off limits for modern states, including China.[33] All in all, the view of the Wa as "primitive headhunters" is seriously flawed.

Mythical Chinese Origins of Headhunting

There are actually curious echoes of how the Chinese and their military inspired Wa headhunting in a series of Chinese fantasy stories about how Wa headhunting started. These stories originated in the borderlands between the Wa and the Chinese- or Shan-dominated areas, where they circulate. None of these stories are reflected in accounts of the origin of headhunting that circulate in the central Wa areas, where I worked; in the Wa versions, headhunting is explained either directly in terms of conflicts with neighboring peoples (as in the story about the gourd that bore fruit across the new border between the Wa and the newly immigrated Lahu) or indirectly in terms of internal social change and the related moral issues (as in self-blame stories that deflect the blame onto Wa women, who either collude with ethnic enemies or commit sexual transgressions in the absence of their men that supposedly could only be alleviated by killing).[34]

However, the Chinese stories—which probably don't predate the late nineteenth century, when the empire was pressing into the immediate vicinity of the Wa—will often involve Zhuge Liang (181–234 CE), who is very widely mythologized around Southwest China. He is also a historical figure, who in 225 CE invaded and conquered Yunnan. Partly because of his glorification in the historical novel *San guo yanyi*, he has become a Chinese hero of near-archetypal dimensions. He probably never actually came any further than Kunming, the present-day provincial capital (Jiang Yingliang 1939), but multiple temples and monuments all around Yunnan glorify Zhuge Liang and hail his accomplishments—in areas he never went to. They were originally built by local elites in dependent polities affiliated with the empire, who were interested in obtaining the credentials of a Chinese identity.

Thus, it is logical that while Zhuge Liang is nearly unknown in independent Wa country, he is famous in the Chinese borderlands. The Chinese headhunting stories, where Zhuge Liang directly initiates Wa headhunting, likely originated in the late nineteenth century, when the Wa area came into focus for the Chinese.[35] Tin Yee (2004: 35–36) recounts closely comparable Shan [Tai] stories about how they conquered Kengtung (see the Introduction) by duping its Wa rulers into losing their defensive powers.

In the Chinese stories, Zhuge Liang ponders how to subdue the Wa, and conceives of a scheme to make them fight each other rather than the empire. He gives them rice to grow—this is something of a giveaway regarding the conceit of these stories, since the Wa are ancient agriculturalists and their land abounds in indigenous stories of agricultural inventions.[36] Yet the cunning Zhuge Liang gives the credulous, dim-witted Wa some rice that has already been cooked. Nothing happens when they plant it. Then he informs them that in order for the rice to grow, they need to start cutting each other's heads off—that is, to engage in internecine warfare. This they do, and so they are neutralized. Zhuge Liang then gives them alive seeds, and this time they grow to satisfaction of the duped Wa—but they are doomed to repeat their "headhunting" as a custom to ensure the fertility of their "new" crop. (Curiously, the Burmese scholar Tin Yee [2004: 83–85] omits Zhuge Liang but repeats the exact same story, and ruse.)

This is exactly the flawed theory I argue against. It is true that different branches of the Wa were indeed often each other's enemies, but like other societies that have put "ordered anarchy" into practice (famously, the Nuer discussed by Evans-Pritchard — see the Introduction, and chapter 4), they were also capable of temporarily uniting in the face of outside enemies. Thus, the story is really an illustration of the willful neutralization of Wa history as part of a conflict over land and resources. It casts the Wa in the role of blindfolded automatons, who at most can receive instruction from more advanced neighbors—a frequently recurring theme in Chinese stories about the Wa, including those of mining entrepreneurs teaching them technology and industry, and present-day tales of Chinese tutelage in how to be modern (Fiskesjö 2010b: 249–50). As if still taking a cue from the Zhuge Liang stories, current New China chroniclers[37] depict Wa headhunting as an entirely internal affair, as primitive feuding, that caused unwarranted tremendous pain and fear in the Wa people and was brought to an end only by Chinese intervention. No mention is ever made of the terror that the Wa warriors, according to numerous accounts, instilled in outsiders like the Chinese, and there is of course no mention of the role this creative power of deterrence had in preserving the independence of the Wa lands.

The Zhuge Liang-style stories still circulate among local Chinese (and in Burma), but they are actually not endorsed by Chinese officialdom or generally allowed in print in China. They do not fit the current tenets of ethnic harmony within a nation-state format, and mentioning them even as mythic quasi-history can be troublesome. Past conflicts between the central state and peripheral peoples instead (during the "socialist" period, 1949–79) have been cast as a joint struggle against oppression, in which the people on the peripheries consciously or unconsciously took part in a revolutionary struggle within a China for which the ethnic makeup and political borders were taken for granted and could not be questioned. In return, the minorities receive "development." Today, as the older Maoist class-struggle framework is being abandoned, the fallback position of the Chinese civilizing project is increasingly celebrated, and the Zhuge Liang ruse may be resurrected yet again.

Envoi: The Native Sources of Wa Headhunting Ritual

Before moving on from the topic of headhunting, I must once more return to the Wa perspective. Unlike the Chinese stories, which make the Wa look stupid (in killing each other left and right), we saw earlier that in reality the Wa creatively adapted the Chinese methods of war. But—why were the specific forms of Wa headhunting given the shape that they received? Why did the Wa not simply borrow the Chinese way of hanging the heads of rebel and bandit leaders from tall poles in town marketplaces for all to see? There is one unexpected source that sheds light on why the Wa instead devised their own weapon of deterrence: the spectacular roadside "skull avenues." This source lies in the Wa traditions for dealing with tigers, and in particular the roadside tiger display—which I interpret as the direct precursor to the skull avenue.

The big cats of the forest, tigers and leopards, used to be quite common in Wa country and often took their share of the free-ranging herds of cattle and buffalo in the forests surrounding villages, sometimes even pigs inside villages. However, after the wars of the mid-twentieth century, and with the spread of modern firearms, they have now become scarce (as have all other big game animals of the area, such as gaur, elephant, boar, and the various forms of deer; only smaller forest cats and squirrels are seen). In a way, humans replaced tigers as the most dangerous adversary of the land.

In the past, tigers and leopards (both are *a vi* in Yong Ou; *si vai* in Yong Soi dialect) were either caught in traps using pitfalls or rigged guns or killed through direct confrontation using a special kind of long spear. In the event of a successful kill, the body of the cat was carried back to the village in a procession that included both the hunters and others, and was met and greeted by everyone on hand. The body was dressed and consumed in a shared feast, much like other forest animals hunted by the Wa.

But the tiger—as the supreme adversary of the land—was also used in a sacrificial ritual that has many parallels to the later treatment of human headhunting victims, though also significantly different in several ways. To begin with, the entire body of the tiger, not just the head, would be carried home.[38] The meat of tigers would be eaten, unlike that of human victims, which seem never to have been consumed in any form. The blood of the tiger would be smeared onto the drum at the drum shrine; the ancestors were told of what had transpired, and the meat was eaten in celebration. Tiger meat was regarded as redder and bloodier than all other meat; it was also seen as "foul" (*si oi*), because tigers, like humans, eat the meat of other living beings, including humans.[39] Tigers too have an especially powerful *si aob*, that strongly negative and dangerous force of any putrefying dead corpse, which had to be handled carefully.

After the sacrificial meal, the tiger's skin would be put to use with the head still attached to it, along with the complete paws and tail. The tiger's complete skin, carefully kept and prepared for this purpose, would be stuffed with straw and set up on a bamboo frame. This creation would then be carried back outside the village to a location just beyond the village walls, known as the *ndaig' a vi* (the "tiger display," "mounting stage," or "stretch"). The verb *daig'* means to stretch over and fasten upon, to mount, like a hide on a frame or a head on a head post, *a nog*, for which the same verb is also used; the noun *ndaig'* formed from this verb means the place where such mounted creations are put up, for display.

Here the tiger would be mounted in lifelike manner, head facing forward, but with a stone in its mouth (a reenactment of the origin myth mentioned in chapter 2). The location was chosen so that it would be visible from one of the paths approaching the village, and facing outward. There was often only one tiger, and such stuffed tigers do not seem to have been arranged in any rows or particular order beyond these basic requirements. They would be left in place to decay and eventually disappear (*hram*) on the spot.

That spot was always in the same general direction as the location of the "skull avenues" discussed above, the West, the direction of death. Sometimes the spot was referred to simply as the *si aob*—because it was a place where *si aob* was highly concentrated. But if the human and tiger sites were located near each other, they would be separated by a small distance (on separate sides of the road, or by some other arrangement) so that they did not overlap.

Eyewitnesses say the *ndaig' a vi*, the tiger display, would be a frightening sight while still freshly installed. We can see that tigers, although they were non-human animals and as such treated differently in some ways, tigers too were overcome, incapacitated, prepared, and then installed much like human victims. They were put to use in a similar way, forced by humans to symbolically protect and defend the living village by preempting new incursions—very much like what happened

Figure 6.5. A tiger rack, *ndaig' a vi*—here with a leopard. Line drawing by Jidapa Janpathompong, based on Xu Zhiyuan (2009: 54); the only known photo of this display.

to human enemies (and in the way they highlight the martial prowess of the owner village, very much anticipating the later human victim displays).

We should consider that long ago, when land was plentiful and the forests deep and dangerous, human competition wasn't primarily with fellow humans but with wild beasts, like the main predators of the forest. It was out of those forests that fields had to be cut out, burned, and planted. Tigers thus posed a very real threat to people, especially as populations grew over the last few centuries and all the way up to very recent times (until the mid-twentieth century). Before humans turned on each other, the only challenge to their presence was the tiger and the leopard.

For a while, of course, the danger of both would overlap. One of my first teachers of Wa described to me how her father used to admonish her as she was growing up as a little girl in the early 1950s. Her father had no sons, and he wanted her to go out and find the buffalo in the mountains—a perpetual task in Wa country, where farm animals like cattle and buffalo are set free to graze in the hills when they are not about to be used for food and/or sacrificed. When needed, someone must go out and fetch them. But my teacher was always afraid to go out in the hills, and mainly for two reasons: headhunter warriors who might kill you by mistake, by accident, or on purpose; and tigers.

Tigers and warriors converge both in practice and conceptually: It seems highly likely that the defeated tiger served as inspiration for how to create the "skull avenue" program, after the idea of cutting off people's heads and use them to display your power, had been copied from the Chinese. Both illustrate how the Wa people wielded "the power to neutralize and subjugate what counters or resists life-furthering projects" (Valeri 1994: 114).

Notes

1. Translation from sound recording with elderly woman in Yong Ou circle, Ximeng County, April 1998; tape 35, field notes XXX:19–22.
2. See Fiskesjö 1999a. Also note that foreign missionaries, beholden to their own version of an agenda to save the Wa, also believed the Wa hunted heads for use in fertility rites: "[The Wa] believed that to sprinkle blood from a human head on the soil before planting would ensure a good harvest. The Wa in Yunnan had a definite priority in the heads they sought: first, the head of a Chinese; second, that of a Tai; third, that of a white man. All of his research was of practical use to him for he knew that the danger was prevalent only during the rice planting season. Also, the white man was least vulnerable. Knowing these facts he planned his journeys accordingly. Eventually the British almost completely stamped out headhunting in Burma, and later most of the Wa tribe were evangelized and became Christians" (*sic!*—also not the truth) (Fife 1981: 125-26, citing Buker).
3. See the photos of sacrificial poles and drum shrines in Scott 1906.
4. More photographs were taken by Prestre (1938, 1946). Cf. also Ling Shun-sheng 1953, 1960. Ling presented one of the most extensive interpretations of Wa headhunting rituals, but although he visited real sites, his interpretation derives mostly from Chinese sources.
5. Such as drum shrines, water aqueducts, and other significant installations. Photos are found in Ling's Chinese expedition in the 1930s (Wang Ming-ke 2008), now a web database of ethnographic photography at the Institute for History and Philology of the Academia Sinica in Taipei, organized by Wang Ming-ke and his colleagues (Institute of History and Philology, n.d.).
6. In Burma, headhunting reportedly did not end until the 1970s (see Lintner 1990). Vail (1990: 10), citing personal communication with G. Diffloth, who discussed the matter with a "reformed" Wa elder, says that headhunting continued there into the 1980s. (It could of course also reappear, either in China, in the Wa country, or elsewhere).
7. Such bags or "baskets" are not nearly as elaborate as those of other headhunters worldwide, such as in the examples from Naga peoples of Northeast India and Upper Burma (Jacobs 1990; Ho 1953a; etc.).
8. This may seem strange at first, but it accords with contemporary sacrificial practice among the Wa (and in many other societies as well): letting a part stand for the whole. For example, when chickens are used in divination, one sprinkles the blood and adds parts of the beak, claws, and crest, as well as some feathers, to the leaves left for the spirits, while the rest of the bird is consumed by the sacrificers (the term introduced by Hubert and Mauss, 1898: 10; on this element of renunciation in sacrifices where the larger part of the victims are actually consumed by its performers, see Valeri 1994: 107). In the Wa human sacrifice, the body is, of course, renounced, but so are these parts, before the head (a part that stands, powerfully so, for the whole) is made to serve the human community in the final resting place of the skull grove.
9. This house altar has not been revived, even in the relative freedom since the 1980s when many other practices have been revived—though often only those that are impermanent and leave few traces (chapter 8).

10. In a somewhat sensationalist article written after his experiences in Wa country for the Parisian photo-news magazine *Illustration* (Prestre 1938), he indicates that this was in early 1936, in the villages of Oua Leng (Prestre 1946: 114–16) and Oua Pah (1946: 181–5), both in Wa country and now part of Burma, south of Mengdong (Cangyuan). Prestre mentioned that the Wa village chief Awng Kai spoke to him at length regarding the Wa origin myths on the seventh day of the third month—lunar, one would assume—which must refer to early 1936, since the border commission's work had begun in December the year before (Prestre 1938: 81).
11. On this fighting, a result of the boundary commission's attempts to survey the local topography, see Angwin 1936; Glanville 1936; Ogden 1936; Pitchford 1936; Zhou Guangzhuo 1935; Hua Qiyun 1937; etc. (see more extensive references on this history in Fiskesjö 2000).
12. On this issue of the addressees of the sacrifices, see too Luo Zhiji 1996: 337–38.
13. Illustration 110-2, in Its 1965, shows a drum shrine with one *njouh*; one photograph by Winnington (1959: facing p. 176) in 1957/58 shows the upper part of four newly made *njouh* at a village in the Yong Ou circle.
14. There is some confusion in the literature about spatial organization, perhaps for lack of easy translation of the four cardinal Wa terms of spatial orientation: *lieh / riog* (horizontally along the hillside toward the left / right direction *when facing uphill*), and *seih / long* (downward / upward on the hillside). These terms are commonly used ("That knife to the *seih* of you," etc.), more so than north / south, which in many areas don't exist at all, or than east / west, which are rendered by "where the sun rises / sets,' or, indeed, "left / right" (*daom / a veix*) which are only used rarely (for the paired chicken bones in divination, etc.). The skull grove was located *ga gleib si ngai* ("in the direction of where the sun sets"). (All in Yong Ou dialect).
15. In at least one location, the general surrounding of the skull grove was also the site of a leprous villager's dwelling. Leprosy was uncommon but did occur before the 1950s, and this particular person was banished from his village to live in a house built for him slightly closer to the village than the skull avenue. He would grow his own vegetables and would be given grain from time to time by his relatives, and would use the water from a particular stream running through the skull grove.
16. "Wherever there is a site of a village there is a *lah*," *dang guoi pean yong, lah guoi nung* (field notes, XV:80). There could be a number of forests of the *muid'* deity (*nong muid'*) and other such sites, but only one *lah* per village. Establishment of a new village would also entail selecting a site and installing a new *lah*. There was still only one high ritual specialist, *ba pi*, and this man had to be invited each time there was a transfer of skulls and a cutting of the calf's tail.
17. This includes two locations in Kunming (the Yunnan Nationalities Museum and the museum of the Yunnan Institute of Nationalities) at Cangyuan county's cultural center, and at the outdoor museum (which is no longer functioning) in Ximeng County once created by the former Wa county chief, Sui Ga.
18. The use of this term goes back to the 1890s. For example, Macquoid (1896: after p. 24) used the term on his excellent drawings of the skull avenue at the village of Matet.
19. Enriquez (1924: 30) and other British observers said the two villages most famous for their wealth of preserved skulls were Sung Ramang and Hsan Tung, immediately to the west of the Ximeng area that I investigated. Harvey (1957: 127) stated the largest number of skulls held at any one village was five hundred, in that same area; Ling Shun-sheng cited three hundred at the village of Aicheng, also in the same area.
20. Many misunderstandings have arisen about these matters. Winnington, who visited the village of Yong Ou where I also worked, wrote that the captured skulls were buried

in the ground (Winnington 1959: 161), a mistake that probably arose during his very brief visit (he saw only the *njouh*, inside the village, and not the *a nog* skull avenue sites located outside the walls of the village). Fang Guoyu and his associate He Diansheng seems to have mistakenly believed that the *njouh* and the *a nog* were variants of the same thing (Fang Guoyu 1943d: 18–19; note that Fang says his Wa interlocutors in 1936–37 refused to talk about headhunting-related matters. Ling Shun-sheng does not reveal his sources at all).

21. See the different photographs by Ling Shun-sheng (1953: facing p. 4); and Prestre (1938: 81; 1946: facing p. 145, p. 160). Ling describes another form, a ten- to twenty-centimeter-thick hardwood post, from which the head was still suspended in a basket and which was sometimes painted in red and white at the top. He also shows one photo of an *a nog* made by slabs of stone, probably a rare variant.
22. Note that this recalls the practice among the Sema Naga of accomplished warriors wearing *aghühu* (enemies' teeth) ornaments made with cowries and red hair (Hutton 1968 [1921]: 16, illustration facing p. 37, 48). The same teeth pattern is also present on Naga megaliths and forked sacrificial posts similar to those of the Wa, which are called *genna* among the Naga and are carved with *mithan* horns and very prominent *aghühu*-style teeth (Hutton 1968 [1921]: 48n1, illustration facing p. 69), also seen on house post carvings (1968 [1921]: illustration facing p. 101; reproduced in Jacobs 1990).
23. As mentioned, this no longer happens, mainly because of poverty. On traditional buffalo spearing, see Luo Zhiji 1995 and others; specifically on its demise and "reform" also Qu Ming'an 1985.
24. The "cutting" ritual too has been discontinued since the 1950s, because of its connection with the headhunting complex. The Chinese authorities also cited, as an excuse, the dangers and high risk of injury and even death for those involved.
25. Luo Zhiji (1995: 330) notes that one village used their bare hands only, not knives; others have used wooden or bamboo knives instead of metal ones (the bamboo knives especially can also be very sharp and efficient), which are used to kill sacrificial victims like pigs.
26. On the way sacrifices closely model hunting (and vice versa), see Valeri 1994, 2000, and also the contributions in Howell 1996; on the Mon-Khmer-speaking Kammu people of Laos, see also Lindell and Damrong Tayanin 1978; Damrong Tayanin and Lindell 1991; and Fiskesjö 2012.
27. Cf. Valeri 1994: 107n19–21, etc.; also the corollary rejection of any dualistic typology of sacrifice and supposedly nonsacrificial "ritual killing" (1994: 105n7, etc.).
28. Compare the Durkheimian notion of religious ritual as the society's worship of itself and see, for example, Madeleine Biardeau's discussion (1984) of how, in rigidly stratified caste societies in India, buffalo sacrifices served to manifest the unity of kingdoms and brought together whole village communities "from the Brahman to the untouchable."
29. Fiskesjö 1992, 1999a; Gao Zhiqun 1992; etc.; for more references and discussion of ancient Chinese headhunting, see also Milburn 2018.
30. It is unclear if the Tang Empire decapitated them all or only the leaders, during these ceremonies.
31. Birns (2003: 60–61) shows images of such displays in the suburbs of Shanghai.
32. Including the Yelang, mentioned earlier, and others in today's provinces of Yunnan and Guizhou. See Wade 2009; Herman 2007; Yang Bin 2009b: 72; etc.
33. Head cutting and head trophy display as part of terror warfare, and in judicial killings (which may be the original source), is of course not just a Chinese feature but has a

long and global history, which is fundamentally due to the prominent potential of the human head to serve as a token of both the body and of the enemy collective from which it is taken (see, for example, Kristeva 2012). However, with the development of modern laws of conduct in war, such head taking or "headhunting" came to be discouraged in modern warfare. This is the background for why head trophies were prohibited among, for example, US soldiers in the Pacific during World War II, even as they continued to be popular among soldiers on the battlefield, and enemy heads are still being discovered in the attics of private homes in the United States (Harrison 2012). The rebranding of head trophies as a primitive custom characterizing rogue barbarians had made it impossible for modern states to openly engage in such conduct (except when modern powers manipulated such barbarians to serve as their proxies, as described by Ricardo Roque [2010] from Dutch Timor).

34. Fiskesjö 2000; also see above, chapter 5, on one such story.
35. One indication is that at the very end of the nineteenth century, when the Chinese and British empires engaged in border negotiations, the Chinese side named a mountain in the Wa area, which previously does not seem to have had a Chinese name, as Kongming Shan (Zhuge Liang Mountain; Kong Ming being one of his alternative names).
36. Even in the 1980s, the Ximeng area still had more than a hundred indigenous hill rice variants under cultivation (Li Genpan and Lu Xun 1987). This number may be diminishing now that the government increasingly issues seeds for planting, although many such seeds cannot grow on mountain slopes; cf. Yin Shaoting 2001.
37. Such as in the official *Wazu jianshi* (Brief history of the Wa people) (1986).
38. All sources unanimously insist that human victims' bodies were always, and mostly unceremoniously, left by the road at the site of the killing.
39. As in the common saying that points to the similarity of tigers and Wa people: "The food of the Wa, [is like] the feed of the tiger" (*som A Vex, prex a vi*), both in terms of "table manners" (eating with one's hands, without utensils, unlike some non-Wa people who use utensils and more elaborate table manners) and in that they both are predators killing *others* for food.

7

BARBARIAN RUSE

Playing with the Fears of the Civilized

Outsiders have long seized upon the idea of the Wa as a dangerous people, off-limits, yet at the same time alluring and attractive.* In the last chapters of this book, I will discuss foreign missionaries' attraction to the Wa lands as a supposedly godforsaken place; also, I will discuss how the fantastic, exotic qualities of the Wa people today are converted into a commodified attraction in today's strange Chinese ethno-theme parks. This chapter, however, is concerned with foreign visitors' fear and allure of the Wa, and how these played out in times past, especially in the nineteenth and early twentieth centuries. I also mention how the Wa intentionally played on these fears, beyond the use of "skull avenues" and headhunting deterrent devices discussed in the previous chapter.

The main trade route arteries between the Chinese empire and Southeast Asia all largely bypass Wa lands. These ancient thoroughfares of the Southwest China–Burma region run through the market towns of Ruili and Mengmao to the north of the Wa country and the tea-trade center at Sipsong Panna to the south. These trade routes largely bypassed the Wa lands, and this is one major reason these borderlands remained among the least-traveled during the last few centuries—and it is also one reason why they gained a reputation among outsiders as the most mysterious. Rumors generated of hidden danger, which made the Wa lands one of the foremost "good-to-think" (Tambiah 1969) fantasy lands of beyond-the-limit violence and "primitive" perils in the minds of people in the neighboring self-declared civilizations of China, Burma, and even Britain.

During the last few centuries, many outsiders regarded the Wa areas as so dangerous that they were deemed impenetrable for travelers unless assisted by

---

Endnotes for this chapter begin on page 190.

a full-fledged army, its gunpowder dry and its guns loaded. The more pragmatic opium buyers (whom I will discuss further) comprised one exception. But we read about Chinese soldiers serving on the 1930s border commission who were so much in the grip of fear of the Wa that "the whole escort was in a state of nerves, men sleeping in their boots, for terror of the Panghung [Banhong] Wa (& these are not wild Wa, but comparatively tame)."[1]

The deterring effect of the violent posture of the Wa was one major factor in this fear. It ran so deep that the British colonial observer Godfrey Harvey could write that their "hills were No Man's Land even for the Chinese, and the Wa massif was especially *terra incognita*. Nobody ever went there, and even the approaches were dreaded, the Salween and Mekong valleys being malaria-ridden—Chinese officers regarded the whole area as a penal station" (Harvey 1957: 129). Aside from the curiosity of Harvey's formulation that "nobody ever went" (even though opium traders and others did go), the "No Man's Land" phrase in itself is rather offensive since it implies that the autochthonous Wa themselves were no "men."

Regardless of these rumors and fears, in the late nineteenth century the numbers of Chinese and other visitors continued to increase. This was prompted not least by the British conquest, occupation, and colonization of Burma next door but also by the increasing opium trade; the famous "Yunnan mud" opium sold in China's opium dens was often sourced from the Wa mountains. Thus, both British and Chinese officialdom became preoccupied with how to split these the mountains, and while the first attempt of delineating a Burma-China border in 1887–1900 failed, a second joint British-Chinese survey was launched and almost completed in the late 1930s. World War II interrupted, but this led, eventually, to the demarcation of a new international border in the early 1960s.

These activities, from the late nineteenth century onward, also prompted a flurry of patriotic-scholarly efforts in China, with newly nationalist scholars rising up to claim these borderlands for the new, modern Chinese state.[2] Many traveled to the borderlands, either for real or while remaining seated in their armchairs, displaying a new nationalist concern with "every last inch" of territory. This was new to China, where intellectuals traditionally dreaded what they imagined to be the sorry badlands of the margins of empire. The new nationalism derived, of course, from the spread to China of the European model of the territorial nation-state (Fiskesjö 2006). It was also during this time that the Wa, sporadically mentioned as "Wa" in Chinese writings since about the 1770s, began to be referred to by the pejorative Shan term "Kawa," which was adopted into Chinese and then used until the 1950s. The new visitors came with Shan middlemen, who placed the pejorative *Khaa* before every hill tribe's name (see chapter 2).

In this chapter, I explore the conflicting views of various kinds of travelers to the Wa country, and also the Wa views of them. I am especially interested in Chinese judgments of the Wa, both those made by nationalistic and scientist travelers and writers of the 1930s and earlier, as well as by the Chinese teams of state-supported ethnologists and soldiers dispatched there in the 1950s and 1960s. I will also discuss British travelers, such as the inimitable Alan Winnington, the famous British correspondent for the Communist newspaper *Morning Star*, and his Wa writings, which actually concerned the very same areas near the Chinese trading town of Ximeng where I pursued my own field research.

The "First" Chinese Traveler, and the Rumors of Wa Cannibalism

The geopolitical realities of the Wa lands explain why historical references to the Wa seldom contain much detail, and what detail appears is often based on hearsay—this is also why such references often occupy the farthest corners of customary notes on regional barbarians found in the Chinese historical gazetteers and other such literature.[3] There, one finds colonialist-style enumerations of people and resources associated with each part of the empire and the world at large, compiled for the purposes of identifying and classifying important characteristics of known peoples—but with the Wa typically placed at the end of such listings, if found there at all.

These gazetteer accounts were often copied in subsequent editions or into other books, but the facts cited were seldom checked or updated: the main concern was not with these facts but with finding a suitable place for the barbarians and their lands within an imagined "civilized" world, one centered on the original cosmology of the empire as originally formulated in ancient north China. Chinese officials authoring these books, especially in newly conquered lands, struggled to make their gazetteers comply with this imaginary.[4]

In this imperial Chinese perspective (that of the central state, in the literal translation of "China," *Zhong guo*), the Wa lands could not possibly be a center by themselves, as the Wa would have it. Most Chinese observers may never even have heard about such claims. Instead, Wa country was always a far-flung periphery, ideologically determined to be attracted by, drawn near to, and incorporated into some indefinite future like so many other barbarians have been in the course of Chinese imperial expansion, for the uplifting benefit of the barbarians. This ideology, of course, is often contradicted by the actual reality of such ingestion: typically, when a periphery is drawn into the orbit of a central power, it sinks into a "peripheral situation" characterized by economic dependency, extraction, and inequality, which produces glaring discrepancies between the imperial ideology and reality. But the civilized power will typically shift the responsibility: as in China today, the poverty of the barbarian margins will be blamed on the stupidity, nastiness, and brutishness of the backward barbarians themselves, their lack of business acumen, or even the devil's influence.[5] In the current modern era, this disdain for the ungrateful barbarian is renewed as a new form in the Chinese frustrations with "developing" the Wa—as discussed earlier.

This lasting ideological bias has shaped the literature not least by mostly excluding the observations of the many different Chinese adventurer-entrepreneurs that ventured either directly into Wa country or traveled on its outskirts, often interacting and building alliances with local Wa power holders.[6] They obviously would know quite a lot about the country: the opium-traders of later days, preceded by Chinese buyers and traders of cotton and salt, not to mention the miners, and others, from stragglers of the big Burma-China wars of the eighteenth century to private Han Chinese who sought to settle in the Wa lands (Wang Ningsheng 2010a). Unfortunately, few such people, even if they had long been venturing into the Wa lands, ever put anything down in writing themselves. Their observations or knowledge were seldom recorded and only brought into the gazetteers after they had been duly edited and made to conform to the imperial view of things.

In the late nineteenth and early twentieth centuries, new scientific and new nationalist attitudes were added to the mix (Glover et al. 2011), which prompted the production of new, "modern" kinds of records. In Yunnan Province, a large compilation (Li Genyuan 1941) was made in this new spirit, containing all previous writings deemed useful as reference materials for a modern approach to the new question of China's borders facing British-dominated Burma.[7] The compilers discovered a text by a certain Zhang Chengyu, whom they said was the first Chinese ever to venture into the Wa heartland. He had traveled there in the winter of 1890–91 as an intelligence officer, a spy of sorts, who attached himself to a British military exploratory expedition into the area—one of the first, after the British annexation of Upper Burma in the 1880s. Zhang's story is highly interesting, even though the assertion that he was "the first Chinese traveler" is clearly an exaggeration (unless they meant the first *modern* Chinese traveler).

Zhang Chengyu, as an "official" traveling spy with a mission, kept a diary while training his eye on the British.[8] It was published after his death of malaria at Bhamo, in northern Burma, right at the end of his Wa journey. Zhang's fate is itself an indication of how difficult traveling in these mountainous and sometimes malarial lands could be for newcomers. He moved rather hastily but managed to take notes on both the route of the British soldiers and what they saw along the way, also making some notes on the local Wa, which set the tone on certain issues. He established that the Wa were indeed headhunters, mentioning the classic "skull avenues" (the British term), with enemy skulls installed in wooden posts, lining the approaches to Wa settlements (chapter 6). He then also, in the same breath but based on no evidence, went on to relay the rumors of Wa cannibalism. These included the unsubstantiated charge that the Wa ate overaged parents no longer able to work,[9] a rumor circulating among many Chinese, and quite plausibly conjured up out of a fertile wish to paint the barbarian Wa as out of bounds and in violation of Chinese norms on filial piety.[10]

Cannibalism is a charge sometimes levied against the Wa by outsiders, but it's untrue. Many knowledgeable Wa people that I interviewed often related rich memories of headhunting, but every time I asked about cannibalism, they categorically denied that there had ever been such a thing. It seems the cannibalism charge is pure invention, added by outsiders to a list indicting the Wa for lacking in civilization—as in other cases of colonialism and imperialism, in other parts of the world.[11]

In the Wa case, the cannibalism charge has been repeated at least since the suspected mention of the Wa in the late sixteenth-century Portuguese heroic travel epic *Os Lusiadas* by Luis Vaz de Camões (perhaps a Caribbean projection).[12] The charges continued, intermittently. In Scott and Hardiman's important *Gazetteer of Upper Burma and the Shan States* (1900–1901: 1:498), they referred to secondhand Burmese Shan beliefs that the "Wild" Wa let their old people fall from a tree as "ripe," and then ate them. They had already framed the autonomous Wa as "wild," so it made sense to include the unsubstantiated cannibalism hearsay.

The idea of Wa cannibalism was dismissed by the modern, scientifically oriented, and independent-minded historian and ethnographer Fang Guoyu. After his own travels in 1936–37 (see below), he wrote that the rumored practice of Wa cannibalism could not be confirmed (Fang Guoyu 1943b: 12). He himself belonged to one of the indigenous peoples of Yunnan (the Naxi, in the northern part of the province), and this provided him with a certain awareness of the reality that not all Chinese (or other) rumors about the indigenous peoples were true.

The outsiders' fanciful accusations of cannibalism did not go unnoticed by the native Wa. During my own fieldwork in Wa areas in 1996–98, local people sometimes joked about certain Han Chinese bent on interpreting the ever-present bloodlike stains on mountain paths as proof of Wa cannibalism. The locals would say, "Those Chinese saw the betel spit on the trail and think we killed someone and ate them right here!" In reality, of course, the stains come from the betel juices, which everyone spits on their way to working the fields or some other commonplace business. Betel chewing is a common and important part of Wa social life in most places, and it is also practiced by Shan and Burmese people—but very rarely by Han Chinese immigrants or their descendants, so they would not necessarily know what the red spit on the road could be. Such circumstances provide a fertile opening for Chinese minds to make imaginary associations with blood spilled in violence, the eating of one's parents, and other such cannibalistic horrors—rumors that help people relegate the Wa to a barbarian station in a Chinese account of the world. Wa people are aware of this and put their own spin on such Chinese fantasies, discussing them and cracking jokes about them. Concocting such mutual imaginaries has most likely been going on for a long time.[13]

Chinese travelers imagined that the "primitive" Wa were cannibals as well as headhunters, but there is no evidence that Chinese settlers themselves cannibalized the aboriginal Wa, as they did with aboriginal Taiwanese in conquered Taiwan.[14] On the other hand, one can argue that the imperial Chinese project did envision a cannibalistic ingestion of barbarians like the Wa, if only metaphorically. In the imperial Chinese imaginary, "raw" barbarians served as the counterfoil of civilization, as a zone of still-to-be-conquered dangerous people waiting to become "cooked" (those who had been conquered and integrated into the state system, drafted as soldiers, made to pay taxes, and so on, yet still showing cultural distinction). These barbarians, in turn, were on their way to complete and total—and "cannibalistic," as it were—cultural ingestion into the body of the imperial state (Fiskesjö 1999a).

From the Early British Forays to Winnington's Visit

While the Wa lands—alongside many other "barbarian" frontiers—continued to serve as a primitive counterpart for China (and for Burmese civilization, too), the British occupation of Burma, as well as the increasing opium trade in the last part of the nineteenth century, prompted further increases in the numbers of occasional Chinese travelers—traders, officials, soldiers, and others—and also a corresponding response from the British. The British in Burma hoped to complete their conquering mission and include even the "ambiguous" borderlands of earlier Burmese regimes that had either ruled themselves, like the Wa, or practiced indirect rule while engaged, as far as was possible, in the constantly shifting premodern "galactic" tributary systems of princely statelets subservient to either Burma, China, or both.

However, in the end, just like the world empires of Burma and China before them, the British ended up stopping short of incorporating the Wa country under their direct rule. The first failed attempt at delineating a new, fixed, and complete border between the empires of Britain and China took place in 1898–1900. During that time, two British soldiers lost their heads, in an incident that may quite possibly have been engineered by Chinese patriots loosely attached to the border demarcation parties and then blamed on the terrible Wa.[15] The British tried again in the late 1920s, now attempting to revive the exploitation of centuries-old silver mines in the northern part of Wa country. The silver had been exhausted long before, but there were enormous amounts of lead-rich slag that could be drained of their content, and these now became a new focus of interest. This attempt also failed, due to local fighting that has since become known in Chinese history writing as the Banhong incident (see chapter 4).

The British imperialistic efforts caused an outcry in China, now a republic with a host of intellectuals awakened to modern nationalist concerns. In the wake of the outcry, a second official joint British-Chinese survey and delineation was launched, now carried out under the supervision of the League of Nations. It was almost completed in the late 1930s, and a treaty nearly came to be (as it was first signed in Chongqing in 1941), but as is well known, many events intervened to prevent the work from coming to completion things (World War II, the Japanese occupation of Burma, the civil war in China, and the preparations for Burma's independence in 1948). In the end it was up to Communist-ruled China and independent Burma to finish this job, in 1960–62.

The events of the 1920s and 1930s, and especially the so-called Banhong incident, had caused a flurry of "patriotic" and scholarly efforts to claim these borderlands for the new Chinese state, now recast as a modern state in possession of absolute territorial sovereignty, including about half of the ancient Wa lands. It was against this nationalistic background that, in the early 1950s, the new Communist Chinese government dispatched the Peoples' Liberation Army to establish control and begin the incorporation of the Wa lands into the body of the Chinese state. They also sponsored investigative teams of ethnologists in the 1950s and 1960s to work alongside the soldiers (chapter 2).

As part of an effort to propagandize these efforts, to lift up the primitive and backward people now in their charge, they invited Alan Winnington, correspondent of the British Communist newspaper *Morning Star* (formerly the *Daily Worker*) to visit the Wa lands in 1957–58. Winnington's Wa journey in a sense represented an inversion of the Zhang Chengyu perspective of the 1890s, even though Zhang's travels weren't supervised by the British government. As a Communist correspondent reporting from the "wrong" side of the Korean War, Winnington had seen his passport revoked by the British government because of official anger at his war writings.[16] Stranded in China, this lone British traveler-writer and reporter was hired instead by the official New China (Xinhua) News Agency in Beijing, which sent him to see the Chinese work teams sent out to transform and integrate the Wa lands. Winnington was very sympathetic to his hosts and bought into their developmentalist framing of what was really a neo-colonial takeover of the ancient Wa lands. Winnington's journey, in fact, illustrates the historical shift of geopolitical weights tilting heavily back in the direction of "China" as an encompassing structure of influence, within which the Wa lands would now fall.

As mentioned in chapter 1, I was once myself unsuspectingly compared to Winnington. I was told, "You are just like Mr. Su-siu, only your camera has no legs. His camera had three legs. Otherwise he was just like you, carrying a little book everywhere and scribbling in it all the time, just like you do." This was put to me quite suddenly one day during my fieldwork in 1997.

"Just like who?" I responded in surprise to my Wa interlocutor. His explanation conveyed the weight of much of the recent, late-twentieth-century history in these same Wa mountains. I was told that Mr. "Su-siu" had come to these very same places several decades ago; his designation suggested to me that he had been a Russian—"Soviet-Revisionist" (*Su xiu*) was the Chinese derogatory shorthand for Soviet Russians after the Sino-Soviet rift in 1960, after which all Soviet experts supporting the construction of the new socialist state in China were withdrawn. The usage continued for decades, until the fall of the Soviet Union.

More than twenty years hence, the shorthand, misused for the unusual British character, echoed from beyond the time of regimentation in the Wa country under the heyday of Mao's political campaigns in the 1960s and 1970s, when the Burma-China borderlands and cross-border contacts were very tense (Schoenhals 2004). At that time, the People's Commune system of work brigades and work points earned to obtain shares of a communal granary was sometimes pursued with even greater fervor in these borderlands than it was in the interior. During this long darkness, the appellation "Mr. Su-siu" would have been a Chinese shorthand for a suspected traitor, renegade, or saboteur, of any ilk or origin.[17]

I tried to find out which previous traveler this could possibly be. Had I not already, I wondered, gone through all the possible library materials and almost every archival source, every Chinese *fangzhi* local gazetteer from recent centuries, and every once-secret British military report from Upper Burma, all the journals from the 1930s League of Nations boundary commission, war diaries, and nostalgic novels from a paradise lost in the Shan States, so I would know beforehand the identities of the Westerners who had come before me to these lands and who had ever put a pen to a paper to write about them, not to mention taken pictures? I had even scanned all the Russian-language publications concerning the ethnography of northern Mon-Khmer-speaking peoples. But perhaps I was not as thorough as I had thought. I entered into a correspondence with Russian colleagues, venturing that it might have been Chesnov or another Soviet ethnologist active in the Sino-Soviet friendship era of the 1950s who had traveled to the Wa lands, despite leaving no traces of such trips in his publications (such as Chesnov 1968). But I was told that no Soviet scholars made it to the Wa lands—and that this had to be a reference to Alan Winnington.[18]

Some Wa locals must have been told—or must have concluded retroactively (in Chinese terms, rather than in Wa terms)—that Winnington was Soviet. This is possible, since Britain as a specific country was quite far off the mental maps at the time, despite the quite recent colonial history in other parts of Burma. Winnington may have been too much of a singular occurrence to be remembered as British, even though in the 1990s he was classified by some elders under the more general term Grax.[19]

This term Grax figures among those used in Wa for the kinds of foreigners or non-Wa that exist in the world, which are the Siam (e.g., the Shan), the Gui (the Lahu, mostly nineteenth-century immigrants), the Houx (the Chinese, flying different flags), the Man (Burmese), and sometimes also the Kang (Kachin, who are known as Kang in the northern parts of Wa country that are close to Kachin areas—but often unknown in the central areas where I have mostly worked). There are yet other categories, such as the Grax, which can be translated as "Indian" or "Westerner." Indians may have shown up from early on, as traders coming through Burma from the Indian subcontinent, and the word may have been borrowed into Wa from Burmese—the Burmese also used it for the English.[20] The British military columns of the past also were often placed in this category, perfectly logical from the Wa perspective, especially since they would have included many Indian soldiers alongside their whiter European counterparts. Yet even though the British and their colonial military may loom large in history, their apparitions were singularities, not permanent presences, to the Wa. Memories of the British are fragile and fading, even though in some places, it is true, a path they once walked will still carry their name, or a rock will mark the precise spot where they once camped. At the time of my visits, while the category of Grax still survived forty years after Winnington the Su-siu and over fifty years after the last British military journey during World War II, typically only elderly Wa people remembered the actual British "Grax"[21]—sometimes known as the Trouser People, due to their strange clothing (Marshall 2002).

At the time of Winnington's brief visit, Chinese work teams were investigating the local society with the goal of reforming and reshaping it in accordance with the neodevelopmentalist and nationalist ideology that had been adopted to follow on from the very similar but less vigorously pursued and poorly coordinated policies of the pre-1949 Chinese Republic.[22] A large-scale ethnography project was first launched by the central Chinese government in 1956–58, in the wake of the military project of securing and taking over the Yunnan border areas. Scores of data gatherers (ethnologists and others) were sent out to investigate economic and social relations among a series of peoples in sensitive border areas, including the Wa, the Jingpo (Kachin), the Yi (Nuosu), and others, many of whom were located along the China-Burma frontier. And it was on this wave of renewed interest and investment that Winnington rode into Wa country.

Winnington's famous 1959 travelogue, *Slaves of the Cool Mountains*, describes his trip undertaken after the massive launch of this new Chinese border initiative (and just before the disastrous Great Leap Forward), and the subtitle of his book aptly describes what he believed he was invited to witness: the *Ancient Social Conditions and Changes Now in Progress on the Remote South-Western Borders of China*. The journey took Winnington to three major peripheral hotspots, all identified both to him and by him as in dire need of this same kind of Chinese assistance, a "lifting up" from a lagging backwardness: the Wa, known as former headhunters; the Jingpo (Kachin), further north along the Burma border; and the Nuosu (or Yi, or formerly the Lolo) of Liangshan in Sichuan Province (who of course had famously held the slaves of the Cool Mountains). Winnington's coming was part and parcel of this project.

For all his biting criticism of the Whitehalls and White Houses of the powers that be, and his unswerving directness in later criticism of the bureaucratism and rigidity of Mao, even castigating his own Beijing minders after they made him another "non-person" (Winnington 1986),[23] Winnington adheres all along to the same basic view of the "primitives" as the Chinese hosts who brought him to Wa country. Traveler and travel agent were, of course, of the same ideological stock, and therefore people in the Wa country were "anthropological rarities" (Winnington 1986: 178) who remained in a time lag from which they must be pulled out, and up. Note that the Wa are defined as "remote" (from us), which is why they have not been updated on progress but can only be "ancient," according to Winnington's Communist evolutionist parlance.

It must be noted that this evolutionist stance is also directly comparable to the basic attitude of the missionaries, in the Wa case mainly Baptists, who had attempted to work the area. It is also comparable to that of the industrial-age British colonial officials, who labeled Wa headhunting a "custom" and consequently hatched the idea of placating the Wa's urge to kill by replacing human victims' heads with synthetic crania made in Birmingham.[24] The cut-off heads were imagined by the Chinese, the British colonialists, and Winnington the Communist alike as necessary to the Wa *because* "*customary*." Such custom, construed purely as something internally generated while really an integral part of Wa warfare and regional history, was then dismissed as outdated on the temporal scale of evolution, and any attempt at an explanation achieved through sustained analysis was conveniently evaded. Needless to say, no one drew any parallels with the massive scale of head cutting in "traditional" Chinese warfare or in judiciary killings (see chapter 6). Here, the differences are less interesting than the basic similarities of the various evolutionist explications of Wa affairs, and Winnington fits squarely into this larger pattern of outsiders seizing upon the Wa lands as the favorite vehicle of their thought, especially, then, the civilizationist and evolutionist strands that have typically accompanied industrialism and colonialism everywhere, the Wa lands being no exception and the remedies offered only slightly different.[25]

Unofficial Perspectives

Winnington's texts and photos are invaluable, not least because they spotlight people who are still identifiable. Indeed, it was partly because these former Wa strongholds had been visited before and had been so thoroughly penetrated by Chinese reform efforts from the late 1950s onward that I myself decided to go there. I had come to the Wa highlands, deep in the interior of the Asian continent, on very roundabout roads. I was a born-again anthropologist who had found enlightenment in flatland, foreign Chicago, and who had set out on an anthropological quest from there, yearning to find my own answers to the big questions about the meaning of life as some people know it, in terms of sacrifice. And so, yes, sacrifice also is a vehicle of my own thought, if in another way. In the Wa country, sacrifice is hugely important and a basic element of everyday thought and action (chapters 1, 8, etc.), and the Wa people are by their own admission the sacrifiers par excellence (in the Hubertian-Maussian terminology): sacrifiers, as well as sacrificers, on behalf of all of humankind. Since humankind at the beginning had emerged out of the earth right at the heart of Wa country, guardianship of the gods of the lands of that marvelous beginning has fallen to the Wa. They were the ones who stayed in place to care for this land and for these gods on behalf of all of us humans who came out later, and hence went further afield. From the Wa point of view, it will seem, no matter how far we others have strayed from that point of origin since the time we emerged out of the ground after our elder brothers the Wa, we are still in their debt. This is not because they claim some heroic status by having fought their way out in a struggle (which they don't[26]) but because they have not strayed, and still care for these ancestral lands and original gods whose wrath and capriciousness might otherwise destroy us all. We see examples of this when the gods of humanity's Ground Zero throw out flares of disaster our way, in the shape of floods, storms, and so on, supposedly in every part of the world. As an anthropologist, I choose to take such theories seriously, even as I am forced, not least for the sake of intelligibility, to attempt to translate them into a different language, and to make sense of them by subsuming and drawing them into my own theorizing, which also necessarily must strive to encompass the larger spatio-temporal realm in which I may roam but most Wa cannot—for now.[27]

But the anthropologist is not the only one to have put no money in the stock of any of the various competing businesses launching civilizing projects or flying evolutionist flags. Perhaps we may make the generalization that the only exceptions to the rule and domination of the civilizing projects of the various brands are, on the one hand, the anthropologist's uniquely interpretive perspective, bearing the burden of the grand aim of dissecting the discrepancies between the real and the believed and the force of the belief upon the real, and on the other hand, the perspective of the Little Man with some distance to the formulation of the grand projects. I am thinking here of the local Chinese traders and others who historically dealt with matters closer at hand than did the emperor's officials or, later in time, a work team dispatched from afar to implement a scheme conceived out of context. I believe this is what is in evidence when the Chinese traders and other local, for-profit travelers *alone* among all those writing and speaking about the dangerous Wa areas have historically used terms like the Big Wa (Da Wa, Da Kawa) for the autonomous Wa, and Small (Xiao) Wa for those who had been transformed and placed in a Shan, Burmese, or Chinese peripheral situation (Fei Xiaotong 1955: 104–5).

Note that these traders are not generally people exploiting anybody in a zero-sum game but simply merchants making a living off their exchange business (salt, opium, etc.). Their designations of the Wa also, like official discourse, run completely outside of or, better, *alongside* the variety of different Wa autonyms and auto-distinctions. But they, too (and this is what is interesting), like the Wa designations and distinctions, run directly counter to the whole family of civilizationist degrees of uplift (really the extent of the power of attraction of the civilizing outside force, whichever it may be), no matter if it is the British colonial rulers or missionaries on the Burma side or the Chinese distinguishing between "Tame Wa" and "Wild Wa," "Cooked Wa" and "Raw Wa," and so on. The distinctions made by the traders and local Chinese smugglers, existing in the Chinese language alongside and parallel to the official civilizationist discourse in the same language, indicates that it was never lost on these local Chinese that the autonomous (or "Big") Wa were indeed *really* wealthier and more powerful than the impoverished Cooked Wa nearer to civilization (who might have been expected to be better off, in the Chinese theory, at least, than the so-called "primitive" central Wa). Here we see the way in which the civilized person and "his" barbarian opposite number, locked in interaction, conceive of their world quite differently. And, the glaring discrepancy between "official" Chinese constructions and the actual situation created by processes that are not acknowledged by the dominant Chinese or other civilizationist terms but *masked* by them becomes very clear for all to see.

Nationalist and Scientist Travelers

My analysis of travelers' intentions, so far, does not help to explain the flurry of nationalistic-scientific Chinese intellectuals' discourse regarding the southwest and the Wa hills in the 1920s and 1930s. The civilizing element is also really but one in the continued efforts to integrate these same borderlands in new, post-1949 China. All of these efforts must also be linked to the emergent "Sun Yatsenian" nationalist project of producing a new unified Chinese nation-state out of the remains of the old empire (Fitzgerald 1992, Fiskesjö 2006)—and notably to the ways in which this project in turn was guided by other ideological weapons appropriated from the West, including Science with capital S (Glover et al 2011). This whole process in itself has been much discussed, and it can barely be appropriately summarized here. Basically, it concerns the hope among Chinese intellectuals of copying Japan and recreate "China" as a unified nation-state on the model of the European states that had come to shape the new international system, in which "China" the empire now reluctantly found itself. Science served as one of the tools used both to measure one's actual strength and to preserve and in effect also reengineer the new nation through a variety of scientific means and practices, like statistics, eugenics, and so on.

The difficult context and tortured history of these partly successful attempts to recreate "China" are the underlying factors that shaped the responses to British activities in the Burma-China borderlands by Chinese intellectuals and also administrator-officials living in the southwest or concerned with the southwest, from the late nineteenth century onward. The nation-construction project involved a whole reconceptualization of the borders, famously pertaining to the meaning of the borderline and territorial sovereignty but also to the integration of the border areas.

Thus we have the grandiose border colonization schemes of the early 1930s compiled by the ultra-civilizationist Li Shengzhuang who, much like his contemporary British opponents, indulged in labeling the problematic Wa (whom he called the "Raw Kawa") as subhuman and uncivilized.[28] There were also others, including all sorts of mixed calls to arms from angry patriots based in Kunming, the provincial capital of Yunnan, China's southwesternmost province, or issued from various smaller cities in the province where the exact demarcation of the border took on a new dimension of significance—under the influence and inspiration of nationalistic literature and thought emanating out of metropolitan China, which seemed to lend legitimacy and significance to a whole new kind of local patriotic grandstanding.

Most of these local patriots simply wielded their writing brushes from home, directing indignation toward the British from the comfort of their own desk and circulating journals and newspapers among themselves. We can believe that some of these armchair writers have seen at least some of the areas they discuss—especially those living more closely to the scene, such as the patriotic Shuangjiang professor Peng Gui'e.[29] But even such scholars generally seldom had the means to bring their notebooks into the field and travel in truly risky areas. Thus, even these armchair patriots must be imagined as rereading their *Xu Xiake youji*, the famous seventeenth-century travelogue; or the more ancient stories of Zhuang Qiao, the Chu general who fought his way to Yunnan; or those of Zhuge Liang, another famous Yunnan conqueror who stars in the bestselling novel *Romance of the Three Kingdoms*. These are, to this day, still the local patriot's traveling and conquering heroes.

It was really the League of Nations border commission in the mid-1930s that first provided armed escorts, in the form of joint Chinese Republican and British columns of soldiers, and created the first real opportunity for the penetration and closer study of the Wa areas by Chinese ethnologists, most famously for scholars such as Ling Shun-sheng and Fang Guoyu.

The 1935–37 border demarcation work was carried out under the auspices of a joint commission chaired by a Swiss representative (Colonel Iselin), appointed by the League of Nations, and with two members each from Britain and China. The commission worked in the field in the dry seasons from December 1935 to April 1937.[30] It was under the aegis of this expedition, in 1935–36, that Fang Guoyu of the university in Kunming and Ling Shun-sheng of the Academia Sinica traveled to Wa areas (Wang Ming-ke 2008). Substantive parts of their respective journeys took place under direct military protection. Fang Guoyu (1903–83), nestor of the discipline of nationalities' history (Chinese-style ethnohistory, *minzu shi*) in Yunnan, even witnessed at least one of the instances of bloody suppression of Wa resistance to the joint movement of British and Chinese troops through their lands—every Wa village or cluster of villages formerly insisted on absolute sovereignty and the acceptance of Wa diplomatic practice, and if neglected, there would be a standoff that the Wa could hardly win.

Apart from seeing villages from afar, and stepping inside them only insofar as was possible in the vicinity of the camps of the military columns protecting the border commission, Fang also visited certain small towns along the way, writing about the geography and folklore of the area together with his collaborators. He visited Mengding, Banhong (near the old Maolong silver mines), Mengdong, and the Wa and Lahu areas near Xuelin, and the even older silver mine of Munai, and focused much of his energies on finding out the history of the exploitation of these mines.[31] In Fang Guoyu's writings we note, alongside his patriotism, a certain sympathy for the locals, which probably relates to the fact that Fang was born among the Naxi, one of the minorities of Northern Yunnan, and thus was well equipped to notice the possibility of distinct and even competing perspectives.

What overshadows both the underlying sympathy and the overt patriotism or nationalism, however, is Science capital S. This striving for the acquisition of scientific evidence, historical and ethnological, was demanded by the forms of contemporary Western science, which in itself inspired a kind of separate loyalty, not unlike that of a distinct faith and certainly not fundamentally different from the function of Science in many Western minds. In China, of course, given the foreign origin of this new cult, loyalty to Science takes on the added element of adopting a foreign creed in the belief that it may help China's problems, and this belief always seems to have been very important in the minds of all the scholars engaging in "border studies" (and to argue otherwise would certainly not have been politically correct at the time).

However, the same loyalty to the general project of Science apparently also fueled the work of Ling Shun-sheng, the ethnologist, one of the main emissaries from the new Academia Sinica (established in 1928, in Shanghai and in the capital city of Nanking) to the Wa lands on the occasion of the League of Nations–supervised expedition. Ling also visited the same area at this time (1936/37), taking a number of photos of headhunting-related paraphernalia and sites in the area (which have recently been rediscovered in Taipei). Perhaps sadly, Ling's main writings based on the trip are silent on the conditions of the journey. While he describes the full shape and form of the central headhunting rituals (chapter 6), he does not explicitly claim to have witnessed any such rituals in person and also does not explicate how he would know these details in the absence of interviews—or how such interviews were conducted (Ling Shun-sheng 1953).

Fang Guoyu, for his part, offers more of a description of the general circumstances of his work: for example, he admits in a preface that he was not able to stay long in any single place of the Wa interior but was forced to move with the troops. He also gives such details as the offering of salt and tea as presents in order to obtain passage for himself and the Iselin border commission in northern Wa country, presents that were reciprocated with the classical Wa gifts signifying peace and friendship: sweet plantains and sugar cane.[32] These suggest a true ethnographer, keen on seeing what is important to the other side of the situation.

But it is still as if both Ling and Fang aimed to disregard the conditions under which they wrote. I would argue that this is conscious, and guided by a certain version of scientific thought. It is as if they were eager to establish the way things *really were* in the general scientific sense, unadulterated by the sometimes very dirty or even bloody business of border demarcation and other goings-on of the day. This focus on a perduring reality behind the vicissitudes of temporary phenomena betrays a loyalty that goes to Science, one that is not necessarily limited to their country—even though in these agitated circumstances, their country (with its army, officials, and so on) obviously is a necessary prerequisite for any writing, whether travel writing or scientific documentation. It is also not limited to any outright moral concerns or sympathy toward the people they meet who instantiate their true object of study—the Wa or other ethnic groups; nor is it loyalty to the nation, as with the new modern nationalists defending the border. Instead, theirs is a loyalty above all to Science as a project.

The Possible Merits of the Project of Science

It is true that many of the scientistic observations and attempts at analysis of the Wa lands that were produced in the name of Science by twentieth-century scholars were almost as tailored to suit the theories and practices of evolutionism and civilizing on unequal terms as were many of the other dominating discourses pertaining to these peripheral places. These include the grand projects of the 1950s as well as, dare I say, the current all-out developmentalism under scientific flags that dismisses and eradicates indigenous knowledge, not least in the area of agriculture (which I have not made much space for here, but see Fiskesjö 2000). Arguably, today's developmentalism follows quite closely from a genealogy that builds on the ideology of earlier civilizing projects. Yet there is also in these fledgling efforts not only a certain unmistakable detachment from the conditions of study but also a certain independence from those dominant discourses themselves—or at least such a striving.

There is, I would argue, an aim of establishing some truth independent of those discourses, and an openness for an analysis that would be simultaneously both emphatically engaged and consciously detached from the distractions that will always threaten to engulf it (including the scholar's petty self-aggrandizing, and other common flaws, of course). But, and perhaps paradoxically, apart from the breathing space provided in the gap between the nondegree and for-profit small travelers and the officially sanctioned discourse-producers, such a project of capital-S Science and its practitioners (for all their faults) may well constitute nearly the only other path toward an understanding of why things have come to be the way they are, so as to offer renewed hope of mutual recognition and a coming community (Agamben 1993) that will erase the pernicious old imaginary boundaries between the "civilized" and the "barbarian."

The hope of such a coming community is, I would argue, the most important signpost on the road to Wa country. Any traveler would do well to beware of the heavy responsibilities that it indicates, and to travel slowly, and with great care, among fellow human beings.Remember, those red patches is betel juice, not blood!

Notes

* This chapter draws in part on my 2002 article, "The Barbarian Borderland and the Chinese Imagination: Travellers in Wa Country," *Inner Asia* 4(1): 81–99.
1. British eyewitness account cited in Harvey 1932: 57; also see chapter 5.
2. In the twentieth century, such efforts were also taken up in Burma, to some extent; see chapter 1.
3. One of the best compilations of such local history sources in Chinese is Byon 1979.
4. For a brilliant discussion of these issues, see Lin Kai-shyh 1999. This ideologically governed editorial style continues even in today's gazetteers.
5. I am thinking here of the classical Chinese notion of the barbarians having a lower or animal-like mental capacity as one reason why this civilizing process takes so long (see Fiskesjö 1999a; 2011b). The idea has its parallels in the corresponding and modern capitalist story that the poor are poor because they are innately stupid, and in the frustrated missionary's concept of the devil as the fallback explanation of why backward people should fail to embrace the creed he is trying to impose and continue to stick to their "idols" even when the new creed has been clearly explained to them again and again in their own language (see chapter 9).
6. See chapter 4; also, for example, Fang Guoyu 1943b.
7. Li Genyuan's editorial comment (preface) in his *Yongchangfu wenzheng* (1941; and Zhang Chengyu's own diary, 1891; on this work, see also Fang Guoyu 1984a: 2:666–67). It's possible it was modeled on Harvey's 1933 compilation.
8. The British were unaware of his double identity, so their reports make no mention of him (for example, Warry 1891).
9. Zhang 1891 (entry for the thirtieth day of the second month).

10. On the Chinese obsession with such taboos, see Chong 1990 as well as Lu 2008, and Knapp 2014 on Chinese "filial cannibalism" (children offering their own body to feed starving parents), etc.
11. Civilized Westerners have long hurled accusations of cannibalism at various "primitives," ever since the European encounter with the Caribbean natives and even before. To be sure, at the same time, cannibalism did exist in some places. For an overview of the Western literature, see Lindenbaum 2004.
12. Camões 1973 [ca. 1572]: canto x, 86.
13. This can also involve what Sprenger (2008) discussed as the "ability to process information" from the surrounding social environment as a necessary aspect of the self-reproduction of any society. That is, the revamping of myths can involve the integration of anti-myths and footnotes to them—such as in this example about betel-spitting and rumored cannibalism.
14. Chinese settlers in Taiwan actually killed aborigines and cooked them to make health supplement extracts, which they sold as they would animal extracts in Chinese medicine. See Li Jiaxin 1988; Dakung Wadan 2000.
15. Barton 1933: 97, 101, 124; Harvey 1957: 130.
16. Winnington was banned until 1968 from returning to Britain; he settled in East Berlin where he died in 1983 (see the biographical note in Winnington 1986).
17. It was against this background that local people also naturally suspected me as a possible "spy" (see chapter 2).
18. I thank Professor A. M. Reshetov of the St. Petersburg Kunstkammer Museum of Anthropology and Ethnography, for helping me confirm this.
19. In Wa orthography, "x" at the end of a word is deployed for an abrupt glottal stop, thus *grax* is pronounced like "gra!" There is also a common homonym in Wa for *grax*, meaning "road," but it is a different word from this one, which itself likely is a direct borrowing of the Burmese *kala*.
20. As in, for example, one of the last Burmese royal proclamations, dated 7 November 1885, ordering resistance to the English: "Those heretics, the English *kala* barbarians" (translated in Scott and Hardiman 1900–1901: I:110, "Thibaw's Proclamation Royal Arms of Ava").
21. Apart from British soldiers, an elder's knowledge might be limited to once having seen, as a boy, an occasional itinerant Indian trader showing up at a Wa market as a guest from the Burmese lowlands. It may also be that few such elders tell anyone. Elders often guard a body of knowledge that is not available to all, and this may explain why few younger people have even heard of instances of Grax columns passing through and are thus unfamiliar with the conceptual framework or vocabulary required to know and speak of the Grax (cf. Valeri 2001).
22. See, for example, Chen Yuke 1933 (esp. Xiong Guangqi's chapter).
23. Winnington, as mentioned, had been stranded in the new People's Republic of China by his own government—it had canceled his British passport after he reported for the *Morning Star* newspaper on the Korean War from the North Korea side, in terms unfavorable to the British and the United States. Winnington tells that whole story and many more in his *Breakfast with Mao: Memoirs of a Foreign Correspondent* (1986). This is in itself clearly one of the most unjustly forgotten gems of a Westerner's travelogues from China. Perhaps strangely to us who live now, there is not a trace of political correctness there.
24. As suggested by Scott 1896: 139.
25. There is one completely different type of discourse that breaks rather dramatically with this pattern. This is the strange genealogical tracing and pursuit in the Wa lands

to find the true roots of the ancient Japanese (also known as "Wa," but written with a different Chinese character): See Torigoe 1983.
26. In certain origin myths, which carry a strong flavor of Wa sacrificial ideology, the first people to emerge onto the surface of the earth were saved by the grace of certain helpers such as sparrows, rats, and spiders, without whom the original threat posed by natural forces (e.g. the tiger and the tree) could not have been overcome. See chapter 8.
27. Because of lack of means to travel around the globe, widespread illiteracy, and the like. (Compare the earlier discussion of whether the sun and the moon circle the earth, or the other way around.)
28. Li Shengzhuang 1933: 129ff. Note that the title pages of this collection are graced with the personal calligraphy of the Yunnan governor, Long Yun, himself of non-Han ancestry.
29. Peng Gui'e 1926, etc. On the Peng family's history in the Shuangjiang area, see also Ma Jianxiong 2012b.
30. On the Iselin Commission's work, see Harvey 1957 (*op. cit.*), as well as the accounts by Willy-A. Prestre, one of Iselin's assistants (Prestre 1938, 1946; see also chapter 7).
31. Fang Guoyu 1943a. See also Wang Jianmin 1997: 182–83, 379.
32. Prestre (1938) also noticed them and published photographs.

8

DISEASE AND DEATH IN THE PERIPHERAL SITUATION

Because of their assumptions about the poverty of the periphery, British colonial administrators in Burma were surprised to discover that Wa people seemed "sturdy," strong, and vigorous.* Moreover, they were surprised by how the central Wa country had larger, denser, and much wealthier populations than in the surrounding areas, quite unlike the poverty seen elsewhere in many of the sparsely populated peripheries of Burma and China.[1] For outsiders even today, this can seem hard to grasp or accept, especially after decades of characterizations of the Wa as hopelessly backward and in need of Chinese development, and after the overall impoverishment that has followed the marginalization of the Wa lands, and their transformation into, more or less, another periphery.

The material wealth of the past was mentioned earlier (in chapter 4). It was not far away in memory: older photographs show women with silver and gold ornaments, and when I asked, people still remembered such jewelry. They also remember how they lost it in the 1950s, either having sold it for cash or relinquishing it in the process of the forced demise of the indigenous institutions of Wa society or in the turmoil of refugee escapes. The wealth of the past, of course, had to do with the Wa forming a center on its own, as discussed in several chapters.

The health and "sturdiness" of the people, by the same token, was quite possibly a result of a rich diet with lots of buffalo, cattle, and other meat, consumed within the format of ubiquitous sacrificial feasts, but sometimes purchased with income from the export cash crops. Indeed, the concept of the sacrificial feast providing for a rich diet is still here today, if only on a much smaller scale than in times past, as everyone in Wa country would note. They still celebrate special occasions where they consume richer foods, especially meat, but even the simplest meals or drinks are actually always sacrificial rituals in themselves, both

---

Endnotes for this chapter begin on page 219.

Figure 8.1. Consuming the sacrifice. Photo by the author in Yong Ou, 2006.

ideologically and in practice. Before partaking of the nourishment, everyone must first pause and call on the ancestor spirits, with at least a short prayer, and then pour some scraps or liquid drops on the ground for their benefit.[2]

The continuing Wa egalitarian ethos also ensures that all food is widely distributed: everyone gets a share. At the more elaborate sacrifices—like those warding off evil spirits, which I will discuss more below—special attention is given to people with special needs, because they especially are threatened by those spirits. I remember vividly how this insight came to me while watching two small Wa girls engaged in a small, rather private feast at their own house, devouring some of the best meat from a chicken just sacrificed there: one of them was sick, and a village oracle had judged she was being afflicted by evil spirits, and thus the sacrifice.

Wa Concepts of Disease

Small sacrifices of this private kind, often undertaken to ward off disease, were condemned and forbidden by Chinese authorities as wasteful superstition during the 1960s and 1970s, after the Wa lands came under Chinese rule. In recent years, family rituals (comparable to the "small sacrifices" discussed by Schiller [1997]) are once again permitted, or at least not interfered with, so they have been widely revived. The current configuration of ritual life notably lacks the public or communitywide ritual aspects, which have largely been discontinued, especially the great war rituals described in chapter 6. This is partly because of the general Chinese demolition of the structures of Wa independence: the political offices, such as that of the revered *o lang*; the drum shrines; and the major communal rituals. The less political Wa New Year celebration is the only feast still allowed, probably because it parallels the Chinese New Year.

Chinese influence extended across the Wa lands, even in those parts that formally became part of Burma. The areas where I have done most of my field research (figures 0.1, 1.2, and 4.2; see also chapter 1) lie right on the international border, which now cuts right through the traditional and once powerful Yong Ou "realm" (*jaig' qee*) of thirty or so settlements. The realm's original founder-village Yong Ou, where I worked for extended periods, is within China's new borders today, under the Ximeng Wa Autonomous County, which is Chinese land. It is near the territory that became part of Burma and now makes up the Wa State of Burma. Despite the border, it is all the same cultural area, and the same dialect is spoken throughout it.

The Chinese army penetrated well into today's Burmese territory in the early 1950s, but after negotiations with independent Burma, it withdrew from some of the western areas. In 1958, a local armed confrontation sent many Yong Ou Wa people into Burma as refugees. Afterward, the new Chinese authorities imposed changes to curb the power of the traditional leaders, the patriclans, and the ritual system, which until then had served as the basis of Wa autonomy.

Much the same happened in the Wa areas in Burma. In the late 1960s, this territory was taken over by the Chinese-supported Burmese Communist Party, which, inspired by China, pursued campaigns that were equally harsh against Wa "superstitions": prohibiting rituals, burning log drums, and the like. Elements of such rituals are only revived today as choreographed, truncated, and staged events as part of festivals linked to commercial tourism, in theme parks, etc. (chapter 10). While the Chinese couched their campaigns in a language of progress, in reality they targeted Wa practices for destruction because they involved indigenous forms of authority.

During this period, the Chinese government and its Burmese agents also sought to eradicate Wa sacrificial practices and replace them with modern medicine, and they did make some investments in basic healthcare. In some Chinese-controlled areas, they sent out health workers to seek out sick people and distribute medicine for free, or for very low fees. Many Wa people welcomed this, since they did not in principle see any contradiction between seeking modern medical help and pursuing ritual remedy in their own way.

But the care provided was never more than basic, and in the 1980s to the 2010s, a period of relative relaxation of Chinese state activism, the benefits were withdrawn across the board and replaced with a fee-based system. Apart from inoculation schemes for children, which still seem to be maintained (not least since it is related to the state attempts to control population and mete out fines to those who have begat more than the permitted number of children), medical services and hospitals are now for profit. Importantly here, these services are basically limited to the Chinese county towns, and to the mixed population of Chinese officials and entrepreneurs and Chinese-trained Wa cadres who live there, many of whom enjoy state insurance.[3] One consequence of this is that some traditional forms of Wa religious practices, including the sacrifices (which I shall discuss further below), have been openly revived (as in the example of the private ritual cited above). This trend is seen in both rural areas and in the new, mixed Chinese-Wa towns (whether on the Burmese or the Chinese side of the border).

At the same time, in some rural areas, villagers who once received basic medical training during the socialist era have attempted to carry on with their practice, turning themselves into local for-profit pharmacist-salesmen of medicine, keeping small supplies that they resell locally. Such dealers in "Western-scientific" medicine[4] have some success, not least with injections, mostly of antibiotics, which can sometimes be effective in the short term but which are also widely misused, often falling short of the required cycle length and thus fueling resistance to disease organisms. Injecting medicines such as antibiotics is a hugely overused method in China, even in hospitals, and is widespread in rural medical practice despite the risk of secondary infection. The main issue in this hybrid form of healthcare is the faulty diagnosis of disease. It also obviously competes on unfavorable terms with the indigenous understanding of the origins of disease. More on this below.

Today, in theory, Western medicine is still available to people in rural areas. They can travel to a county hospital, and some even cross over from the Burmese side—if they can pay. Still, both the slightly better off and the poor may run out of options—for example, in June 2006 I met a rural Wa man with an eye disease who used up his savings at several nearby hospitals, but still did not find a cure. Doctors' examinations and procedures, medicine, and hospital care are all fee based, and sometimes overcharged. It's the same as elsewhere in China today, despite some progress on public health insurance for rural denizens (though state employees and others in county seats, etc., already have it). Thus, villagers are generally hesitant to seek medical aid from Chinese hospitals, and generally do not.

Death and Its Causes

The Wa are reluctant to go to hospitals for reasons beyond the high fees. They also often have to travel long distances. People are fearful of dying away from their ancestral home as well, either in a hospital (as has indeed happened) or, even worse, dying "on the road" (*yum nung grax*). Worst of all from the Wa perspective is dying accidentally and being deprived of the traditional, elaborate funeral that everyone hopes to have.[5] Wa people are often preoccupied with how death happens. Most hope for it to occur peacefully at home.

I have attended quite a few funerals during my fieldwork, by far the most painful event for an anthropologist. In many cases I came to know those who died, old or young, and I was saddened by their passing, but at the same time I had to treat each funeral as ethnography. Moreover, I was often helpless when faced with diseases, including intestinal parasites and other such problems, when people asked me for help and I could provide little more than first aid.[6]

Funerals are social occasions of great importance for the living. They usually include a tremendous outpouring of affection among the survivors, who show respect for the dead and commemorate the deceased. In so doing, some of the most hauntingly beautiful songs in all of the Wa repertoire are performed. They only perform these beside the corpse, during the quiet hours in the dead of night at the all-night wake held for the dead person.

All of this is also food for the imagination of the living, especially as they reach old age and begin to be seen by those who still belong with "the strong ones" (the *ba nbrah*) as "living ancestor spirits" (*ge meang eim*) who soon will merge with the *ge meang*—that collectivity of ancestor spirits for whom one pours some of every drink or drops a few food morsels from every meal onto the ground. The *ge meang* ancestor spirits are an anonymous plurality, one including one's own recently deceased relatives but also those of other people. The living must attend to them always, because (like other spirits) if they are displeasured, they can bring about misfortune and disease (known as *saix*, which is also the word for "pain"). As the spirits of people who once lived among those still living, the *ge meang* specialize in disrupting eating and digestion, and can bring about indigestion, loss of appetite, difficulty swallowing, and other such ailments. Strangely, they are said to lack any sort of compassion for the living. They never help the living but only harass them, and also, as if jealous, seek to pull the living over to the other side.

This is why living elders who will soon cross over to death are treated with a mixture of respect, love, embarrassment, disdain, and fear. The elders themselves are aware of this, and they fear the resentment. At times they use a set phrase to admonish the young not to resent the old: *po s'reng' nah kod* ("do not show contempt for the old," the verb *s'reng'* meaning "to look down on, to feel contempt for," especially the old and hapless). Old and frail, the elderly illustrate for those still living the approaching crossroads of life and death—opposing forces locked in a never-ending struggle. This in itself is not unique, and parallels can be found across highland Southeast Asia and elsewhere[7] to this

Wa conception of the ancestor spirits as part of a broader "animist" pantheon of spirits.

The Wa recognize numerous other spirit forces alongside the *ge meang* ancestor spirits: those that bring disease and death. The list of evil entities that are believed to harm people in various manners, both specific and general, is rather long. There is no collective Wa term for these spirits; rather, each is distinct and independent as its own kind. Only the *ge meang* and the *qong taox* are linked. At the same time, they all share the distinction of being invisible, though some are capable of appearing as a ruse. The general term "spirits" is imposed by me on all of them as a shorthand for nonhuman forces of disease and death.

I prefer "spirits" to "demons," which might suggest they are full of ill intent against humans. As I understand it, in the Wa conception, other than the *ge meang*, most are actually indifferent to humans, even if all spirits are potentially harmful. They exist alongside us and are only sometimes harmful when directly encountered, whether accidentally or due to our neglect (as with the *ge meang*). In a way, this conception of disease is rather close to modern medicine's understanding of bacteria and viruses. In what follows, I leave out a number of spirits and the expressions of disease linked to them, and instead discuss the most prominent: the ancestor spirits, their evil recruits the *qong taox*, and a few additional significant types.

Diagnoses of spirit-caused disease are often nonspecific, in that only a minority correlate with particular, recognizable diseases. Thus, the specific variety of spirit and the intent of the offending spirit must be correctly identified in each case, so that it can be dealt with properly through proper sacrifices in the proper place. But the kind of spirit is not mainly identified through a diagnosis of the bodily symptoms of the patient, which are believed to be only broadly indicative. Instead, an oracle or medium can perform more accurate diagnostics, known as the *si boug* of the oracle (more on this below).

The de-emphasis on symptoms can perhaps explain the frequent failure to take preventive measures, or countermeasures, for an injury or illness. I was always bewildered by this as an outsider. Wounds from work injuries, for example, are hardly cared for at all until they become infected. Wounds are hardly ever washed; this may seem incredible to those in other parts of the world where the germ theory of disease is by now taken for granted. Sometimes I dressed the wounds of people coming to me for care, such as after they received a cut to their leg on an underwater rock in a rice paddy, and then waited until a painful infection arose. Nobody had been taught that wounds should be cleaned immediately.

In contrast to many other mountain-dwelling peoples, the Wa use very few herbal or other natural remedies derived from the surrounding forests. It's hard to explain why. Although some, such as herbal pastes, are in use, they are mostly to treat skin ailments. Even so, the general absence of traditional herbal medicines in Wa country is quite striking.⁸ In the areas I know better, medical knowledge may have been disrupted by the violent transformation of Wa society after the disastrous watershed year of 1958, when many Wa became refugees in Burma and ritual life was interrupted or even entirely discontinued. The post-1958 period has certainly also meant the accelerated depletion of the region's once-rich forests.

But elderly informants have assured me that herbal medical practices never really flourished, not even before the 1950s. Paradoxically, the reason may be due to the heightened emphasis on human agency as opposed to the analysis of nature's whims. In any case, the sacrificial regime was *de rigeur* in dealing with disease in the central Wa country, not herbal medicine or indeed other forms of medicine.

A large percentage of sacrifices are made to one particular kind of evil force, which no discussion of Wa disease concepts leaves out. This is the ubiquitous *qong taox* (in some areas pronounced as *tung tu*). This type of spirit is conceived as an important ally to the ancestor spirits, who recruit *qong taox* to attack people. The *qong taox* often dwell in large trees or isolated forest patches. From there, they sneak up on people on their daily journey to and from the fields or on other ventures and lash out at them. The unseen *qong taox* then lead people astray, tearing at their soul (*ge pae*), which they seek to entice out of the person's body. Many human disease symptoms are seen as expressions of the imbalance or fragmentation of the individual human being that results from such *qong taox* efforts. Death itself is the permanent departure of the *ge pae* soul from the person they have attacked. The *qong taox* do not care about the life or death of humans, but they can indeed kill humans, which is known as "to have you join the *ge meang*." They do this by seizing one's soul and "selling" (*quh*) it to the *ge meang*—who apparently always are eager to buy, ready to see the living join them through such commercial transactions.

The *ge meang* as well as the *qong taox*, in their mean-spirited alliance, and other similar spirits as well, certainly fit the picture painted by Scott and Hardiman in their *Gazetteer of Upper Burma and the Shan States* over a hundred years ago: "None of the spirits are beneficent.... The fairy tales are all grim; the goblins are none of them goodnatured."⁹ These are starkly categorical words. But they do ring true to me. As I understand it, there don't seem to be any beneficial spirits. This is a difficult conception to fathom for those of us brought up where many believe in benevolent gods who can be prayed to and who can hear their supplicants. Not so here.

Other examples of capricious, merciless, and harmful spirits include the *a yong*,¹⁰ "dragon" in Chinese translation, a being that dwells in water and uses the rainbow as its drinking straw. When particularly angry, such as when there is human interference with the waterways, it can bring about landslides. It is rarely encountered directly, in person, but it can also cause intestinal problems of a different kind from those brought by *ge meang* ancestor spirits—which make you suffer from indigestion or cause you to choke on your food as punishment for your violation of proper social relations with ancestor spirits. In contrast, the "natural" *a yong* infests you with parasites and other diseases of the kind that may lurk in standing pools. Such water is therefore generally avoided. Instead, the Wa traditionally use bamboo aqueducts (pipelines) to feed moving water from safe mountain sources into their villages. We might say, paraphrasing Tambiah (1969) on how people think about their social world through its animals, that parasites, like other animals, are also "good to think," although in the Wa context they are thought of as spirits that are "good to prohibit," or avoid.

I don't see the Wa conceptions of spirits as constituting an "animism," if we mean the assignment of human-like attributes to natural phenomena.[11] The Wa ideas also don't imply that the human world is extended to "nature" by "socializing" it, imagining it in human terms or in terms of human social relations, or that the "intentionality" or "agency" that may be perceived on the part of nonhuman things must be conceived on human models. Instead, it seems that the animist-like conceptions serve as an extension of the human work to classify the world of living things and everything in the world, so that the world can be safely navigated. This creative labor is extended to unseen and invisible aspects of our world, such as, in effect, even the unseen microscopic parasites in contaminated water. The main interest is to defend the human community against such dangers, and the work of the classifications and the navigation is specifically concerned with those beings that harm humans. The Wa conceptions of the "spirits" accomplish this without theorizing a nature-culture divide.[12] I will discuss this further below.

One other spirit that supports these points in dramatic fashion is the *hlox*, which is an extremely lethal, capricious, and invisible being that roams the landscape. It also has no link to human society, and absolutely no placating sacrifices or respectful conduct will help against it. If you encounter the *hlox* on the road, you drop dead instantly for no apparent reason, as if "shot down" (*bun*) by an invisible evil force. It is a harmful force, which strikes more violently and suddenly than any other spirit, and thus it is eerily similar to heart attacks, strokes, and other such afflictions. Other spirits will still "do" (*yuh*) you (in), but more slowly: that is, they will harm you and ultimately kill you, and in some cases they target you more purposefully because they originate in or near to human social relations, as with the *ge meang* and their *qong taox* intermediaries. It is possible, therefore, to detect, divine, placate, or ward off these other kinds of spirits. It is not possible to prevent *hlox* attacks.

The spirit called *muid'* is sometimes portrayed in the scholarly literature on the Wa as a sort of supreme deity, a concept that might sound benign. It is, however, also often referred to in everyday Wa diagnostics as just another potential source of illness (comparable to the *qong taox* and others), and in this respect it is not fundamentally different from other spirits. It too is a multiplicity, a collective of beings, which may be instantiated and appear in different localities. It is thus not like a singular supreme god, which makes it different from what Christians, and some missionaries, have believed.

The *muid'* don't bring good fortune or any sort of protection. It is true that *muid'* are special in one respect: they do mysteriously endow certain people with special powers or talents, including, above all, the capability of "seeing," as oracles, who are then able to diagnose spirit attacks. This is the closest any Wa spirit comes to benevolence. But this power is offered mysteriously and capriciously, not as a benefit. There is no quid pro quo, and no *muid'* will offer any further help. Otherwise, they exist rather like other spirits; that is, one can at most hope to keep them from sending misfortune. *Muid'*, too, must be placated by way of sacrifices that attempt to ward them off with the help of prayers that inform these spirits that they are being recognized, respected, and cared for in the sacrifices duly performed for them.

There is one other curious exception to the general rule that humans will get no help from non-human forces, and may even be harmed by them. This is the *nbring* bird, whose call warns of impending danger. If one hears it when setting out on a journey, that person must turn back. This wild bird thus "helps" humans. In addition, chickens and other sacrificial animals similarly yield clues or warnings about the future, as happens in chicken bone divination and other forms of divination using parts of animal corpses.[13] Yet all these warning signs, strictly speaking, are legible only to those who respect the menacing world of spirits and other such forces. They are not intentional messages sent by a benevolent *nbring* but instead are traces of the future that humans must know how to read and decode. Again, it is human action that counts.

The Helpers of Ground Zero

The only true exception to the absence of human helpers is found in origin myths, of which there are many versions and elaborations. In some of them we meet Sparrow, Spider, and Rat, who are not everyday spirits but special, associated with an origin myth. Each assisted humanity in surviving the first grim, vulnerable moments of existence on earth, as humans first emerged from the ground (as explained in chapter 1).

In the versions I heard, these Wa origin myths recount how the first humans (who were also the ancestors of the Wa) were attacked as they emerged from the *Sigang lih* (the aperture in the ground that yielded all of humanity). First, Sparrow (*ruig'*)—said by some to labor under the guidance of a *muid'* deity—picked at the slab of stone that blocked the hole in the ground from which humanity (*gon pui*, people, humans) was about to emerge. The humans were waiting beneath it, peeking through cracks, noticing that many different beings already had tried and failed to open up the hole. Only Sparrow (which is, as everyone knows, very skilled at picking for seeds) managed to open the path for them.

Then, as humans climbed out, Tree (*kox*) was about to fall on them and crush them—in unspoken anticipation of how, in the future, humans would cut the trees. But at this crucial moment, Spider (*nbai nbreeh*) jumped out and spun a thread that tripped Tree, making him fall in the wrong direction. Thus, we humans were saved. And so it is that trees are cut by people instead of the other way around.[14]

But then, Tiger (*a vi*) lurked, and was about to lunge at the humans and bite them (in anticipation of the deadly competition that Tiger would later present against humans in the forest). Rat (*keang*), however, jumped onto a rock, fooling Tiger to bite off his teeth on it, while saving himself by hiding quickly from Tiger's assault. The humans emerged unscathed, and thus, whenever a tiger is caught and mounted at the tiger display (the *ndaig' a vi*; see chapter 6), a stone is mockingly thrust into its mouth, denying it the prize of blocking humans from entering the world to appropriate the fruits of the forests and the forest fields for growing crops.

In true mythic[15] fashion, these unique, primordial acts of Sparrow, Spider, and Rat set the stage for humanity's survival and existence, but they no longer actively influence it today. They do, however, quietly demand eternal tolerance from humans: not as spirits, not as humanlike beings, but now as sparrows, spiders, and rats.

The Wa Theory of Evil, and How to Cope

The general absence of beneficent deities or spirits is striking, and also unusual around the world. In my view, the Wa conception of a grim landscape devoid of help and benefit from any spirits or deities whatsoever must be derived from the tenuous and challenging historical situation of the Wa, which placed a prime on the creative capability of the living to take forceful measures to further their interests and fend for themselves in this world—which is the world that matters, to humans.

In my understanding, the Wa have come to see the world as inhabited by both humans and a range of nonhumans, the latter constituted by a variety of forces at various distances from humans. Some of these have little to do with humans, and some are mysterious and unknowable. It follows that the threat of disease and death is capricious and omnipresent, and can only be managed or warded off to a limited extent.

The self-reliance of the Wa and their abstention from conjuring up divine intervention on their own behalf is also directly related to their fiercely egalitarian ethos (chapter 4). I believe it may well be that beliefs in benevolent gods are mainly generated in situations of social hierarchy, where the downtrodden are promised salvation in another dimension, after death. Not so with the egalitarian Wa, whose this-worldly thinking acknowledges both death and life, but more as they really are, in our world.

What is a resourceful person to do in the face of the menacing forces that lurk everywhere (capricious disease, accidents, and so on)? I will describe here some of the remedies available, starting with how to guide your soul back from having lost its way (as it already does when it wanders during night; that is, when you dream) and moving to how to retrieve a stolen soul from *qong taox*, which is more serious.

If your soul has temporarily lost its way and you get sick, it can be fetched back by a soul-calling ritual, a search-and-rescue operation akin to those mounted in many other societies in the region.[16] The Wa call this ritual *om pae*, the "hugging" of the soul, which is enticed back home by a team of close adult relatives who are led by one of the experienced ritualist-performers of the village (distinct from the village oracles, who only diagnose and take no other action). The team goes out into the mountains together and call on (*gog*) the soul, throwing out rice grains to entice it back and smacking fondly with their lips, as one does when trying to get the attention of a human baby. Arriving back in the home of the sick, one must close the door to any outsider. Then, a piglet and a chicken must be sacrificially slaughtered in order to divine messages regarding the diseased person's future from the chicken leg bones and the pig intestines. Finally, a closed basket filled with rice is elaborately prepared, in which a human hair will mysteriously appear if the ritual has successfully caused the soul to return.

This *om pae* ritual was once explained to me[17] by comparing it to a Chinese "birthday party," pointedly understood as the sort of ritual where one family member is surrounded by the warmth and concern of his or her living kinfolk and friends. The element of shared concern is actually present in all of the many sacrifices made to ward off disease and death. They all gather allies in this life among their fellow humans, who are mobilized to confront and guard against harm, or evil, with which they temporarily come to terms. The sources of evil (and misfortunes like soul loss) are many, and it is not possible for ordinary people to distinguish them all or determine the precise nature and severity of a situation. Each time someone is afflicted with disease, his or her parents, spouses, siblings, other relatives, or friends must instead seek out an oracle (*ba dox si boug*, literally "the one that gives *si boug*").

Oracles are fellow villagers, most often elderly women, endowed with a special gift for knowing the origins of disease. People say that the oracles do not study or apprentice, but instead simply and suddenly realize they are endowed with their powers and intuitively know how to use them. They perform ("give," *dox*) the *si boug*, which means "diagnostics," the performance of a search for the origins of the disease at hand. They obtain, and then explain to the family members, oracular instructions on the identity and geographical origin of the disease, and consequently on where sacrifices must be made and in what manner. The oracle is thought to "hear" (*hngiad'*) the necessarily precise answers to the questions asked (what color the sacrificial chicken should be, etc.). She listens to and "hears" them inside of her body (in her "tendons, and bones," *si neag, si ang*, as one of them told me). The oracle thus uses her own complete, healthy yet aged and wiser body as a medium, and as an embodied instrument (attuned, as it were, by the *muid'*) for catching and collecting the necessary sensitive information about the source of a fellow villager's disease. She then translates and transmits this in plain language to the afflicted, for a modest fee.[18]

The most common finding is that the cause of an affliction is a particular *qong taox*, located in a particular place outside the village. Common remedies include the sacrifice of a chicken of particular color at a specific *banlieue* (suburban) location with *si miux m'pai* cooking stones used for such rituals. These three-stone sacrificial cooking sites are usually built in the surrounding hills or on some road leading out from the village in the direction where this evil resides. The sacrifices are commonly known as *hlax doh*, as they are laid out on the ground using plantain leaves (*hlax*).

Chickens often comprise these small sacrifices, not only because of their availability and relative ease of replacement but also because their twin upper leg bones (the femora), when extracted and cleaned, are additionally utilized to determine the chance of success for the just-performed ritual, as well as the chance for the victim's recovery.[19] This divination is done by inserting fine bamboo splinters into the tiny holes found on the side of the bones—technically, these are nutrient foramina, usually two on each femur. There may be more on any individual chicken, and they appear in slightly different places and emerge from different angles on each bird. The experienced observer can then "read" the unique butterfly-spread pattern of these pointing sticks.

Importantly and interestingly, in my understanding, after the *banlieue* sacrifice is completed, the emphasis already seems to shift away from the *qong taox*, which are regarded as already placated by the opportunity offered them to feed on the burning feathers and morsels of meat from the chicken that are thrown at them, and also by hearing the many prayers urging them to go back to their usual abode—emphasizing that they have been duly paid respect and have had their fill.

Note that this "feeding" is not supposed to be taken literally: while attending suburban sacrifices in the mountains, I pressed this point, in the light of the anthropological debates over the nature of sacrifice and how it may be distinct from gifts. This was another moment when I was heartily laughed at, and it was one of many *Aha!* moments of my fieldwork. It was explained to me, the anthropologist, that the spirit's acceptance was symbolic, not literal (almost as if I was

Disease and Death in the Peripheral Situation | 205

Figure 8.2. The *hlax doh* sacrifice. Photo by the author in Yong Ou, 2006.

a naive novice, which of course I would indeed seem to be, and in a sense also really was).

In Wa terms, the spirit accepts the *reang* (literally "light," here in the transferred meaning of "appearance") of the offering, and not the material offering itself—the sacrifiers and sacrificers cook and consume the meat of the sacrificial animal as a matter of course, while the spirits make do with the smoke of the feathers as they are burned off in the open sacrificial fire. This isn't seen as stingy, because what counts is the performance of a symbolic renunciation of the victim, and by extension of any mistaken presumption that humans might be ignoring the spirits and the unpredictability and capriciousness they stand for.

The concern with the chicken bone oracle clearly returns us to social interactions among the living. The ingenious conception of the chicken's femur is that one side of it represents the Self (ourselves, *eix*), and the opposite side stands for the Other (*nbioung*)—that is, a divide between kinfolk and those with whom one is not related, and who are thus not bound by kinship, on the other. This illuminates the social dimension of health and reflects how other humans, by extension even including ethnic others of the Wa, are regarded as having a part in disease etiology and suffering. This means that they are liable for both missteps and malevolent moves, which may increase the risk of such events as *qong taox* attacks; in effect, others may help send evil your way, either with explicit intention to do so (see below) or unintentionally. (The latter actually appears to be much more common.)

This unintentional harassment can be compared to what in Western societies might be called psychological abuse. The causal connection here is often left unexplained (it's complicated and difficult to detect), but one explicit interpretation is that unspoken malignant feelings between people, lurking beneath the surface of social interaction, create rifts in the social fabric that then literally become windows of opportunity for the *qong taox*—which likewise cannot be seen by the ordinary naked eye but comprise the unseen destabilizing factor in a vocabulary

Figure 8.3. Interpreting the chicken bone oracle. Village of Yong Ou. Photo by the author, 1997.

of health and hurt. These unintended but potentially harmful rifts in the social fabric arise because of the conundrum of self and other, which was at the heart of Lévi-Strauss's (1969 [1949]) project on kinship and has been much discussed in psychological anthropology.

The particular Wa sacrificial-religious idiom expresses what is probably a more general truth increasingly acknowledged by medical science: that a healthy social context able to overcome its own fractious tendencies toward jealousy and suspicion can in itself help prevent and even alleviate psychosomatic and physical illness in its individual members—concretely so by avoiding feuding, by holding "birthday parties" to care for people by way of "embracing" them, by performing suburban rites on behalf of others, and so on.

Ruptures in the social fabric can also be brought about in another manner. If your unrelated neighbor (*nbioung*) thoughtlessly lets himself be seized by uncontrolled envy, and praises your belongings or resources (such as the strength of your buffalo or the good prospects for your upcoming harvest), then a certain, different kind of malignant spirit, the *qog juah* (which mainly harm crops and farm animals, not people), are enticed out of their dwelling places. This is both curious and telling, and was quite difficult for me to understand at first since I had not thought of envy as something that ought to be suppressed. These *qog juah* seem to feed on it, especially when the envy is expressed in terms of praise, and then they can cause a harvest to be eaten by rats, a buffalo to have a miscarriage, and so on.

When malicious *qog juah* activity is detected, it must be warded off by a special kind of sacrifice. Here, offerings are affixed to a bamboo pole at the gate of one's house, in a spot very visible to passersby—as if to remind them to be careful about what they say and do. For me, these curious *qog juah* aren't to be envisioned as goblins perched on a tree branch, as the demons of Christianity can be; instead, they are conceptions of the frictions generated in everyday social relations, theorized and put in concrete form by naming them so as to render them more comprehensible than the invisible and esoteric processes that unfold, or which appear in nightmares. The countermeasures take the concrete shape of the special bamboo stake with a scarecrow-like hanging pendulum. On the surface it's an arrangement that will ward off the *qog juah*, but it also signals to neighbors, "We need to cool it, or we all lose more."[20]

People may also intentionally cause illness in others, using a sort of "remote control" curse, a voodoo-like witchcraft-by-"prayer." This type of curse is similar to those that ward off spirits, and both are, indeed somewhat curiously, called *nqai*. Evil "prayers" or incantations are not common in the Wa country these days, under Pax Sinica; in the past, they were perhaps more frequent, arising as a result of feuds over farmland or boundaries. They are regarded as one of the weapons in the same arsenal that also includes real, open warfare.

We may recall in this regard that there is no word for "pain" separate from that of "disease" (*saix*), and the vocabulary of being "hit" or "done" by the forces that bring disease is akin to that used in war in the human realm: the straightforward lexical term for "to kill," *blaix*, is used alongside the broader term for attacking and annihilating, expressed with the verb *yuh*, to "do," which normally means simply "do" or "make" (as in the everyday phrase "What are you doing?" [*Yuh meix poh?*]) but which here stands for "do" in the sense of "seeking out in order to destroy," just like the imagined *qong taox*, which are out to "do" humans. They harm them and kill them by "selling them" to the *ge meang* (and to "join the *ge meang*" effectively means to die). Clearly, people here are extending their vocabulary of explanation and remedy to account for the invisible world of spirits, human-affiliated or not. The important thing is that humans provide a language that enables a program of action for themselves to deflect as far as possible and to handle the consequences of the potential harm that inevitably lurks in the landscape they inhabit—whether it is contagion and disease, accidents and disasters, or harm emanating from fellow humans, whether unintentional or intentional.

Indeed, evil "prayers" are known to cross ethnic boundaries. In the region I am most familiar with, they are mentioned most frequently in relation to the Tibeto-Burman speaking Lahu people, who, fleeing tensions further north in China, migrated into the Ximeng area during the nineteenth century, causing more friction over local land and resources. However, curiously, none of the more powerful neighbors—the Shan, Burmese, or Chinese—are mentioned frequently, if at all, as capable of such evil speech (at least not today). This is despite their obvious, historically proven, and amply exemplified capability to harm Wa interests in very consequential ways, much more so than anything caused by Lahu people. The Lahu are a much weaker people, fractured and scattered by protracted confrontations with the Chinese imperial state (Ma Jianxiong 2012a).

I suggest that the absence of the Chinese and others in these discussions is not because of their historical distance from the Wa but because, as state societies backed up by military force, they represent powers among the human that are so much more formidable and so much more like suprahuman forces of nature than the Lahu, a neighboring fellow mountain people whose conditions of existence and limited capabilities are more similar, and therefore more readily confronted.[21]

This understanding is supported by the Wa "anti-myths" that (laced with a certain amount of mockery) account for the role of this-worldly but much more powerful fellow humans—as opposed to other nonhuman otherworldly forces that typically are given credit in origin myths for creating and arranging the most fundamental conditions of existence in the world—including such aspects that people cut down trees and kill tigers, not vice versa; and that people eat cattle, not vice versa.[22] In any case, disease and death are always just around the corner—whether they originate with human enemies or are provoked by them, or whether they arise from the invisible capricious spirits who may always remain potential adversaries of humans in their own right (as nonhumans, they don't share our goals or hopes—as in the case of viruses and bacteria). The pantheon of spirits, combined with the array of capricious fellow members of humankind, indicates the height of tensions that continue to govern life in Wa country. And even without raising the old specters of foreign wars or serious internal strife, which have largely been eliminated in the current "Chinese era" (*nqu Houx*, as the Wa themselves say; or as I put it, Pax Sinica), it remains clear to everyone (Wa, Westerner, or Chinese) that disease and death are frequent, unavoidable, and unpredictable. Nobody can say why it is that some will prosper while somebody else's pigs will die, their harvests fail, or their family members perish in freak accidents or from heart attacks.

Even those temporarily enjoying bliss—such as seeing buffalo and chickens proliferate or the accumulation of long rows of cylinder grain containers after a good harvest—know very well that they might lose everything at any time. This insight is a key reason why the standard refrains on topics related to health and wealth always sounds like the "complaints" so often uttered to guests: "Oh, we never seem to have anything to eat . . ." (*ang eix yiux tei eih poh tei*); "Not that our family will ever be successful at raising chickens . . ." (*ang eix yiux tei ei 'ia*)—suggesting that in effect, "Everything always dies and withers for us." Everyone works very hard to ensure there is food in their stores, but they also know it is wise to cherish the moment. Like the impromptu Wa host often says, while offering food for guests, "We die easily" (*yie yum yix*)—an ultimate statement that seems to imply that we should try to get along, while still on this earth, and live as best we can.[23]

Despite every effort and all the help from oracles and ritualists, the circumstances of life and death are still unfathomably random. This insight has its parallels everywhere on earth (as in how cancer and other afflictions seem to strike at will and whose origins and detailed etiology are difficult to understand; for a solution, see the profound discussion of realist philosophy and the limits of human understanding in Madagascar and beyond, in Graeber 2015).

In Wa country, decades or even centuries of hostility and war in the human realm have nurtured a general theory of evil in which human enmity is also understood as something to be recruited by the nonhuman aspects of nature, which menace us at every turn. This risk was always there, but it was intensified in the past by the tensions stemming from the circumscription of the Wa country, which was driving up the price of its autonomy.

In the face of this, the only way to remain a step ahead at the "private" level is to consult a good oracle at the right time and follow the instructions for sacrifices or other measures. It might be the best one can do at the level of family and household (in Wa, the *si niee nyiex*, "house sacrifice"). As mentioned in chapter 6, people once had house altars, but these have long been prohibited by the Chinese. Thus, the *si niee nyiex* genre of today consists mainly in rites that leave no trace.

If Western medicine is available, such as injections of antibiotics and other medicines, these may be applied as well. The sick would like nothing better than to get rid of their pain and discomfort, and taking Western medicine is not in conflict with the underlying belief system regarding the origins and nature of disease—which itself seems to remain intact, even if evolving under new circumstances.

Health and the Community

Earlier, I mentioned that at the "public" level of clan, village, and wider community, the *si niee yong* "village sacrifices" of old sustained Wa autonomy and power. But these too have been discontinued since the 1950s, when such public rituals were attacked by Chinese and Burmese Communists alike as superstitious, primitive wastefulness. Aside from the obvious fact that this assault on the old, autonomous Wa social order has signified the transformation of the Wa lands into something more like the usual, exploited peripheral situation, what does it mean for the health of the Wa communities to interrupt those rituals, the organized expressions of collective concerns for each community as a whole?[24]

The answer is complex. In some places, especially where the 1950s assault on local autonomous structures turned particularly violent, one finds people engaging in profound self-blaming, placing the responsibility for the collapse of traditional Wa social order on their own perceived failure to properly service the gods of old. The obvious follow-up question (which I sometimes tried to ask), "Who will care for the lingering gods of old?" becomes impossibly contradictory, and it seems to be best avoided, not confronted. Indeed, for a long time, such unanswerable questions have been consequently set aside, and are not often raised.

All this appeared in a new light from the 1980s onward, as Chinese state agencies began to relax their rigid prohibitions on "religious" practices. They have even, in the early years of the twenty-first century, actually started to seize on and appropriate some of the seemingly exotic elements of the very same rituals they prohibited in the 1950s (chapter 10). This is a selective revival, which is carried out both as part of a profit-making tourist commerce sometimes bordering on the disrespectful and as an element in the government-sanctioned celebrations of "sanitized" ethnic culture, in which Chinese-trained Wa cadres play an important part.

The general population is mostly assigned a role of passive spectatorship. Often it is no unwilling spectatorship: Chinese-produced VCDs and DVDs with old-style song, dance, and drum beating remixed with Chinese disco tunes have gained a wide circulation in recent years. But they are a world apart from people's actual belief in the spirits, which is still allowed only as decontextualized "exotic customs" or in hidden, small sacrifices. In the 1980s and 1990s, when traditional rituals were sometimes staged for the sake of documentation or as a domestic-tourist Chinese enterprise, or both, many Wa would shy away from such events for fear of offending the gods further and be afflicted with disease as a consequence.

For example, I met one woman who developed epilepsy after having her first baby, and her illness was widely ascribed to her participation several years before in such a staged and filmed fake ritual. She had appeared in a Chinese-directed film about the pulling of the log drum (chosen because it is indeed a grand ritual, yet seemingly apolitical). Her attacks would come during the night, and she sometimes rolled into the fireplace on the sleeping floor, where she'd be burned by still-glowing embers. Eventually, her husband divorced her. However, such drastic reactions are uncommon, and with the passing of time, there is also a possibility that new generations of Wa communities will begin to reappropriate and revive some forms of communal ritual for their own perceived intrinsic efficacy. I explore some of these issues in chapter 10.

Separated from the Spirits: The Wa State Forced Relocations

This chapter ends on a more ominous note: the recent mass relocations disrupting the heavily localized diagnostic-sacrificial and remedial regime described above. Here I address the situation specific to the Wa State as a new state-like formation in Burma, especially the recent relocations of its own rural populations. These policies have severely impeded traditional-sacrificial medical practices, as the people have been removed from their spirit world, something that has caused many unnecessary deaths. Discussing these devastating developments helps to further reveal how the Wa sacrificial ideology of an imagined world of spirits is fashioned by people to help navigate their world.

Most of my previous discussion of Wa disease management and health practice in the Chinese-controlled parts of the Wa lands also holds true for the Wa State in Burma. I have not traveled very widely there, but the absence of Chinese-style population control policies is one notable difference. On Chinese territory, people are given fines for exceeding birth quotas;[25] on the Burma side, such restrictions have not been introduced, and it is not uncommon to see large families, as was common in the shared Wa past (see chapter 2, on naming). Many people in the Wa State in Burma submit to the campaigns for vaccinations that are prominently fronted by the top Wa State leaders, and, as with much else on the Burma side, with Chinese support (cf. Lintner 2021).

Just as many consumer goods are, Western-style medicines made in China are also sold on the Burma side,[26] but access to Western-style medical care is even more limited than in China. Officials and others from the Wa State who have the

Figure 8.4. Portraits of Wa State leaders, posing while administering vaccinations. Photo by the author in Wa State, 2006.

means will seek care in China when needed. Other beliefs and sacrificial practices in managing death and disease are largely similar to those of Chinese-controlled areas. The devastations of modern times have unfolded similarly on both sides of the Burma border.

But history is also divergent, in that the Wa State is now its own state formation and acts as a sort of proxy and ally for China in Burma, and which enjoys considerable real autonomy under arms. The Wa "autonomous counties" in China, despite the name, are wholly under Chinese administration. Bertil Lintner (1990, 2021, etc.) and others have documented how the Chinese-supported Burmese Communist Party (BCP), equipped with modern weaponry, moved from central Burma into Wa country in the late 1960s. They turned what had been autonomous Wa lands into their main base area. In the process, they annihilated the longstanding Wa autonomy, or, more precisely, what remained of Wa autonomy after World War II, when parts of the Wa lands became the battleground of Chinese Kuomintang forces on the run from the lost cause of their civil war in China, which was won by the Communists, and also after the Chinese annexation of the eastern-central Wa country in the 1950s.[27]

The broad assault on Wa cultural and political traditions under the BCP in some ways was even more drastic than what occurred in Chinese-annexed Wa territory. After the BCP's demise in 1989, the driving motivations of the shared Chinese-Burmese Communist ideology were now moot; but the Wa State of the United Wa State Party and United Wa State Army (UWSA) is still deeply marked by its Chinese affiliations in a number of ways, including the dual party-state structure; the widespread use of Chinese language and writing, in particular by Wa officials; the ubiquity of Chinese businessmen, entrepreneurs, and consumer goods; the dominance (in Burma) of Chinese currency, which allows purchase of cheap Burmese commercial products like cigarettes; the proliferation and distribution of medicines; the cracking down on Christians (Lintner 2018); and so on—above all, in the way the Wa State sees things like a state.[28]

Wa State authorities carried out forced mass relocations on Burmese territory in 1999–2006 (and which still continue, but at a lesser scale). They deserve an important spot in Wa history as a whole, but the detailed account has yet to be written. A few ethnic minority news and web services, as well as some international news media, did mention what happened, but the relocations were never documented in detail by independent observers and have rarely been discussed by scholars.[29] The sources are limited, and bias is everywhere, including in media affiliated with other groups inside and outside of Burma, as well as the international media. Unlike many aspects of the traditional medical practices that I discussed above, I also have not directly observed any of these relocations. Thus, I write this largely based on secondary sources, extrapolating from my knowledge of the Wa situation in China, where state agencies have often force-relocated villagers in the name of progress and modernity, often to new roadside settlements where they can be more easily monitored.

The massive Wa State relocations took place in several stages, starting in 1999 and continuing in several waves, until the process was largely completed in early 2006.[30] Whether we accept the higher numbers suggested in news reports (approximately a hundred thousand people, with some sources claiming even more) or the lower numbers confirmed by the Wa State authorities (about fifty thousand),[31] it is clear that these coercive relocations affected a vast part of the Wa population, which amounts to about one million people. The motives for the forced moves remain complex. On one level, they were linked with the commitment that current Wa State authorities made to international organizations, under pressure from countries like the United States, to stop large-scale opium growing in Wa State.[32] While opium production here goes back at least to the nineteenth century (see chapter 5), it was largely halted on Chinese territory in the early 1960s, yet it continued on Burmese soil into the early twenty-first century.[33] There, too, it was discontinued after the year 2000 in many areas, but it has seen some resurgence in recent years.[34] In June 2005, Wa State leaders declared their area "drug free," seemingly hoping for international recognition and assistance to alleviate the expected suffering among the ordinary population.

As pointed out by Pierre-Arnaud Chouvy, Tom Kramer, and other observers, it is clear that such a drastic reduction of opium production and sales carried major risks for the general farmer population for whom it long represented a source of livelihood.[35] Indeed, on the surface, the relocations mainly involved moving people away from the formerly opium-producing northern parts of Wa State, an area often described as poor and dependent on opium cultivation because of the lack of terrain suitable for wet rice farming.[36] The Wa farmers were relocated mainly to southern areas, including those near Thailand that came under the domination of the UWSA only in the early 2000s (as a result of a deal they made with Burma's military government after the UWSA prevailed over competing, out-of-favor forces[37]).

But the success of any replacement crops was never guaranteed—items such as sugar cane, rubber, tea, coffee, etc., are already widely grown in China, the presumed outlet for many substitute cash crops. Even the head of the United Nations Office on Drugs and Crime in Rangoon, Jean-Luc Lemahieu, noted that "the crucial question is whether the ban can be sustained through tackling the underlying problems of poverty, and effectively dealing with the other important issue—the production of methamphetamines."[38] The international drug trade clearly carries huge weight here, and the wealth of the Wa State, at least that of its elite, is derived in part from such trade—but drugs are by no means the only issue in play and cannot be the only explanation.

As mentioned, forcible displacement of populations has been carried out numerous times in both China and Burma. Both states have provided models for the Wa leaders to follow. In Burma, the military government's actions and policies created a series of precedents of population displacement, mainly as a tool of war.[39] There are many such examples from across Southeast Asia,[40] and also from China: while the imposition of Pax Sinica since the 1950s has prevented large-scale warfare there comparable to the multiple-front civil war in Burma, the forced relocation of villages and populations as a tool of government policy has also been deployed in China, including in Wa and other ethnic minority areas there.

In China in particular, the involuntary removal of rural minority settlements has been a consistent feature of government policies since the 1950s.[41] China's main aim has been relocation for ease of monitoring and control. Often they have targeted mountain peoples accustomed to a higher degree of autonomy, forcing them to relocate down to the valley floors. This basic policy continues, even though some villages have actually moved back by their own initiative following the overall selective downgrading of activist state interference since the 1980s, or they keep dual residences at different elevations and with different styles of construction: Chinese concrete or mud brick houses versus structures of indigenous wood and bamboo, often raised on poles.

There are several reasons for this, but some relate to health. The preference for hillside climate is often based on traditional concerns about the hot weather and stagnant waters of valley floors, which naturally generate many more mosquitos and therefore feared diseases like malaria (known in Wa as *saix houig'*). Also, raised-pole houses are not prone to earthquakes, and they provide better air circulation.

The resettlement policies pursued by the Wa State authorities were probably most directly inspired by China, if also indirectly influenced by Burma (which used resettlement as a state weapon). Indeed, one consistent component of Wa State policy in recent years, separate from the massive long-distance relocations, has been to force the consolidation of villages and to concentrate or move them within the reach of roads—a policy obviously copied from the long-term Chinese policies. In the case of short-distance local moves, people may not need to uproot very far, so they still have the option of visiting and maintaining sites of ritual importance, which may even remain within walking distance. This explains why sometimes people may even have dual residences, old and new.

The recent long-distance mass relocations of villagers in Wa State were more drastic, and they far exceeded such measures. They clearly succeeded in disconnecting large numbers of people from their traditional local spirits, sacred groves, and the familiar landscape, along with their locally anchored historical memory. Basso's classic work (1996) on this global phenomenon from the perspective of the Apache summed it up as "Wisdom sits in places." We have seen how this is also the case in Wa country. Given the Wa conceptions of disease etiology and management, rooted in the knowledge of native places, it is no surprise that there are reports of awful deaths on the road among the populations that were brutally relocated, cut off from their knowledge of the land.

In one instance, the village farmers targeted for relocation were given half an hour's packing time and told that they could take only a few personal belongings. Apparently, in most cases, villagers were not allowed to take their livestock either, and so they would have to start over from scratch in unfamiliar situations. Then they were trucked out or marched off on short notice to their new destinations. (For illustrations, see Fiskesjö 2017a).

And so, it is no surprise that we find ubiquitous reports of disease, even on an epidemic scale, among those removed from their homes. Several reports suggest an insufficient supply of modern medicines:

> Upon arrival in the south, the Wa are allocated one small bamboo hut per family and given one small milk tin of rice per day. Oil and salt are rarely available, and meat and vegetables less so ... disease is rampant. Between 1999–2000, over 7,500 died of malaria, typhoid and anthrax. The closed border makes delivery of medicine difficult and medical vaccination almost impossible.[42]

Another report elaborates the same theme:

> Unused to warmer climate along the Thai border, many Wa re-settlers began falling ill, of malaria and other diseases shortly after their arrival, according to *Unsettling Moves*, a report published last year. Estimates put the death toll at 4,000 for the year 1999 and 1,000 for 2001. However, one news report by AFP in September 2000 quoted a Thai military source as saying as many as 10,000 Wa had died during the rains of 2000 . . ."[43]

The report cited here, *Unsettling Moves*, has a whole section, titled "Sickness and Death" on disease among the relocated people. It quotes from translated eye-witness interviews that appear authentic, and would be deeply disturbing even if only partly true:

> Soon after the Wa arrived, they started to get ill with malaria and dying. They were dying one after another. Sometimes ten people in one day. I've never seen anything like it in my life. There were some Wa medics, but they couldn't save the people. They ordered large trucks of medicine, both Chinese and Thai medicine, but it didn't seem to work. They buried the bodies outside the village. No sooner had they buried one person, then another person died. Men, women, children, whole families were dying. Some people tried to run away when their family members started dying, but if they were caught they were arrested and beaten. Some men were even killed for trying to run away. (LNDO Interview #5 [Lahu National Development Organisation 2002])

Stricken with fear, the newcomers tried to save themselves using their local remedies, but to no avail:

> They tried to cure themselves with magic and traditional medicines. They used chicken, pigs, dogs and more than 10 buffalo to offer to the spirits, but they did not get better. 3–4 people died each day. Because of all the wailing and crying, I sometimes thought I had come to a living hell. . . . My older daughter fell sick and we gave her opium as medicine. Her body was hot, like fire. She had bad diarrhoea at night. In spite of the opium, she died early in the morning. After two days, her mother too had bad diarrhoea and died. I was grief-stricken and felt so helpless. . . . At that time, our new neighbours also died. All five members of the family next door died. Altogether 50 people died within two weeks. In our native place, we used to cure ourselves with the spirit-doctor when we were sick. . . . The spirit medium said the gods in the south were different from the north. (LNDO Interview #1)[44]

We are told here that "magic and traditional medicines" were also attempted. But, in an unfamiliar setting, and with the disruption of social and kin ties, there would be no way for these Wa to confidently assert the origin of the problems and deal with them in the traditional ways that I outlined earlier. This is certain to have immensely worsened the situation. Beyond the issue of "new" encounters with lowland malaria and so on, the desperation that arose from the confrontation with unfamiliar terrain and unfamiliar disease etiology seems to have been equally horrific.

Many of the reports suggest the relocations were ordered from the top down, without consulting either with the villages from which people were going to be removed, even depopulated in their entirety, or the destination areas already inhabited by Shan, Lahu, Akha, or other people. People were instead simply torn from their familiar places and thrust into unfamiliar terrain. Their oracles and ritualists surely would struggle to cope and perform their role; if they died, their loss would further exacerbate the despair of their own communities. Also, without adequate supplies of modern medicine, which might have helped remedy some of the suffering, the deaths among the relocated Wa commoners surely rose even more.

Future histories may well label this massive relocation a twenty-first-century death march in the name of modernization, a man-made refugee crisis of internal displacement, for which the "international community" certainly also bears some responsibility. I am thinking of the lopsided, simplistic attitudes toward the narcotics trade, treated as if it could be dealt with apart from the larger context of war and ethnopolitics in Burma. The result has been a failure to embrace comprehensive approaches promoting the well-being of local communities, or at least not undercutting their own ability to manage themselves (see below, and note 35).

But why this top-down approach of the Wa State, which caused so much suffering among their own people? The approach may have several origins, but the example of the Communist-style centralized command and party leadership practiced in China, as well as by the Communist Party of Burma (1968–89), clearly played a key role. There is also the model of the brutal Burmese military. But just emulating the militarized regimentation of the population under other regimes does not seem too convincing by itself as motivation for these draconian measures. Other explanations also seem to fall short, such as the need to quickly forge ahead with the recently adopted opium eradication policy under pressure from China, the United States, and Thailand in order to win international assistance through the UN system—which could replace long-standing opium revenues. Or the need to consolidate control over newly conquered areas in the south, close to Thailand, using the general populace as pawns in a strategic geopolitical game arranged in consultation with Burma's government. Or, indeed, the accommodation of Chinese requests to vacate former opium-growing areas to make room for Chinese-owned or -controlled agroforestry industries.

All of these possibilities hold some truth; in particular, the design of for-profit rapid-growth forestry or rubber plantations requires the displacement of farmers and appropriation of their land. Indeed, some reports mention direct Chinese involvement in both the relocation and the aftermath of the emptied-out areas, and it will be no surprise if the ancient land of the evicted farmers is reforested with commercial timber to be shipped to China.[45] This would mimic the way in which such mountain farming lands, traditionally "owned" by Wa rural realms, have already in many places been transformed into commercial forest land, with assets and profits slipping away from the descendants of those Wa circles.

More research is needed, but a comprehensive hypothesis can be suggested. The complete, Chinese-style neglect—refusing to ask the people themselves about their needs and concerns—is a giveaway here. In fact, the Wa State shares in common with several governments that surround the area the use of force and violence against the people in the name of development and modernity. It seems the Wa State authorities, under Chinese influence, are aligning their policies with the notion of modernity that is dominant, even hegemonic, in China and Burma.[46] It places an abstract ideal of state modernization ahead of the fate of the people to be modernized. It could be said to resemble a version of "killing the people to save the people," as some Americans once claimed to do in Vietnam.

This is a dark interpretation, but if we accept it, it allows us to simultaneously acknowledge and account for the good intentions stated by the Wa State and other officials to provide for "the people"—including, as they claimed in justifying the relocation project, by removing them from supposedly hopeless opium badlands and resettling them on better agricultural land for the sake of "development." Publicly, at least, the ethnonationalistic leaders of the Wa State are not less committed to the well-being of their people than are the leaders of China, Burma, or other state governments.

This dark view also seems—strangely, by negative example—to not only confirm the indigenous Wa theories of the capricious nature of disease and death but also reaffirm the Wa theories of sacrifice and validate both their mythology and their anti-mythology, which imply that all viable health solutions must be grounded in the fabric of local society, even when aided by modern medicine. Tragedy and loss ensues when overwhelming external force prevents local society from seeking its own path and adapting to and incorporating new help from the outside, on its own terms.

The forced transformation reduces the population to a means or a tool, to be herded around "as necessary" in the service of state building (Agamben 2000; also Fiskesjö 2022). This in itself may be the truly important and lasting legacy of the model of China and other powers, in the Wa lands. If so, it is very much a repeat of what we have seen in other tragedies of modernity analyzed by James Scott as instances of "seeing like a [modern] state."[47] Moreover, it also provides a real-time view of the creation of "the people" as a separate concept, one that did not exist in egalitarian, autonomous Wa society. In the Romantic vision of "the People" entertained by Jules Michelet[48] as well as by other powers, both capitalist and socialist,[49] formerly autonomous people are redefined as the foot soldiers of the state. It is a momentous, consequential move that masks how, in reality, this new People is sacrificed on the altar of their State.

Notes

* This chapter draws in part on my 2014 article, "People First: The Wa World of Spirits and Other Enemies," *Anthropological Forum* 27(4): 340–64.
1. Macquoid 1896: 24; Harvey 1933: 91; Friedman 1998 [1979]: 269ff.
2. On the ubiquitous Wa rice beer, the foremost vehicle for these everyday rituals, see chapter 3.
3. For a broader view on the dismantling of Mao-era socialist medicine in China, see Duckett 2011.
4. Modern (Western scientific) medicine is actually mostly known among the Wa as "Chinese" medicine (*a dah Houx*), because it is brought mainly by Chinese agents. As for Chinese herbal medicine, which relies on daily or frequent preparation or administration, it does not have the same currency as it often does in majority-Chinese areas.
5. In the Ximeng County area, this is traditionally done with an unmarked burial in the garden of one's own house. This tradition may have developed historically in the Wa heartland as a means of countering thieves who would steal the head of the deceased. It also reflects the prevalent sense that dying at home offers comfort and solace.
6. I came only with training in basic emergency medicine learned as a onetime navy medical orderly during military service in my native Sweden, and I was mostly only able to help with dressing and maintaining flesh wounds and administering medicine for certain illnesses; the handbook *Where There Is No Doctor* aided me in such diagnostics (Werner et al. 1992; indispensable for any fieldworker). See further below; and Fiskesjö 2013b.
7. The classic discussion of spirits and "animism" in our region is Telford 1937; see also Hackett (1969), a rather anti-racist missionary in Burma who developed a certain sympathy to local cultures, realizing that local "animism" is not so different from that found in his own Bible (which he rereads to find Jacob in Genesis 28:10–22 dreaming of a stone where a spirit dwells; and in Joshua 24:27 a suggestion that another stone would be a witness to the events that had taken place in front of it).
8. See, though, the annotated compilation of traditional herbal medicines gathered, by Guo Dachang et al. (1990–92), mostly from the Wa peripheries in Lancang and Cangyuan, which suggests there may be a regional difference. An exception is how Wa women eat iron-rich clay (Reid 1992, Young 2011).
9. Scott and Hardiman 1983 [1900]: I.2:29.
10. Chinese scholars translate the Wa *a yong* as *long*, "dragon," but even though it dwells in water, it most likely does not correspond directly to Chinese ideas of the dragon.
11. Descola 1996: 87; cf. Tsintjilonis 2004; also Descola 2013. For a penetrating critique of the views of Descola and other poststructuralist scholars' views on animism, totemism, perspectivism, and so on, see Turner 2009.

12. Turner (2009) nicely explicates the lingering but misguided poststructuralist preservation of the idea of a nature-culture divide as something ubiquitous or universal.
13. On Wa chicken and other forms of divination, including the observation of cattle livers, pig intestines, and so on, see Li Daoyong 1996; Ling Shun-sheng 1953; and below.
14. Trees are also fashioned into drums, the Wa ritual paraphernalia par excellence. However, every time a tree is cut, a stone must be put on the remaining stump to calm its anger.
15. This is in distinction to anti-myths, which account for the emergence of human, not extrahuman, forces that are capable of changing the fundamental circumstances of life (according to Turner 1988; see chapter 1). The Burmese 1962 expedition noted mythic variations where the little birds or sparrows instead saved humans both from trees, and from tigers (Than Sein Thit 1962: 114–116).
16. See Telford 1937; Izikowitz 1985 [1941]; Walker 2003; Langford 2009; and others.
17. I was allowed several times to attend the part confined to the house, but I could never join a search team.
18. Early Communist Chinese analysis and propaganda portrayed the oracles as cheaters who stole from the common people. This tendentious, self-serving judgment misses the point. Also, in my experience, the fees charged are modest indeed: a small bottle of liquor, etc.
19. One can also take the preventive step of *ti'eib nkeang*, "setting up a threshold" on behalf of, for example, vulnerable children in one's family. This is a *hlax doh* type of sacrifice one can even undertake on a monthly basis—if chickens are available.
20. Visiting outsiders who do not know the dangers of praise and envy, and cannot read these messages, may of course still create havoc by lavishing praise on such things as nice fields full of promising crops.
21. The Shan, immigrants but also valley-dwelling state builders, present a more ambiguous case. Sources indicate that Shan immigrants often at first paid tribute to the Wa and lived side by side with them, by permission, but this arrangement later broke down. For example, the Wa of Gengma were defeated by such Shan immigrants and had to retreat into the hills of Sipaishan between Gengma and Shuangjiang (old Mengmeng). Still, the first chicken killed for the Shan *se meng* (place guardian deity sacrifice) at Gengma was traditionally brought to the Wa of Sipaishan (Zhu 1996: 248), *because they were still feared by the Shan for their threatening witchcraft capabilities* (see *Lincang diqu Daizu shehui lishi diaocha* 1986: 54). Note that Gengma's name, unlike many of the Shan *meng* (polities), is also still a Wa place name: it means *gaing mex*, "Mother's fields."
22. Anti-myths (Turner 1988) in Wa country and around the world address discrepancies and injustices such as the unequal possession of writing systems, modern machinery or weaponry, the loss of ancestral lands, etc., that are brought about by powerful alien people, not by animals, deities, or the like, as in mythic accounts, which explain how these beings originally set the stage for humanity's presence on earth. See also chapter 1.
23. Again, obviously, outside visitors should never respond to such claims by pointing to how the speaker does have some wealth or prosperity—as I might have done early on. This would be a foolish invitation to the *qog juah* to come out and ravage whatever was pointed out to them. Instead, the proper answer would be something like, "Alas, the same goes for me . . . look, I have not been able to bring you anything, really."
24. In the past, both villages and their inhabitants were autonomous. In the event that the community faced a major choice about something, a village meeting would be called,

at which everyone could speak and decisions could be made by consensus. After the 1950s, of course, such local autonomy has been limited to minor issues; for major issues, one mainly follows the top-down directives from the Chinese government.

25. In 2020, it seems unclear what the new population policies will be. The Chinese government has abolished restrictions on family size in the face of a rapidly aging population that may soon begin to shrink. There are now panicked encouragements to Chinese women to have more babies, but these are mainly directed at Han majority Chinese, and they are still coupled with a strident chauvinism that may seek to suppress births among the "useless" minorities (which may even be formally derecognized and more aggressively assimilated).
26. There is also some influx of Burmese medicine to marketplaces in China, but availability is fluctuating, and Burmese medicine is not used as frequently as Chinese-made Western-style medicine.
27. Lintner 1990, 2014; also Miller 2001; see also chapter 1.
28. On "seeing like a State," see Scott 1998; on these issues, see also chapters 1 and 3. For a new discussion of the moral economy of the Wa State and its army, see Steinmüller 2020.
29. But, see Renard 2013. Renard served as manager of the United Nations drug substitution project in the Wa area from 2006 to 2007, under the UNODC (the United Nations Office on Drugs and Crime; until 2003 known as the UNDCP, United Nations International Drug Control Program), and gathered information about the relocations. He also refers to some of the other sources cited in the following.
30. S.H.A.N. 2003, 2006a, 2006b; Lahu National Development Organization 2002 (*Unsettling Moves*, the most extensive report on the relocations); Internal Displacement Monitoring Centre 2004; Global IDP Database 2005: 36–38; also Renard 2013.
31. The Lahu National Development Organization, which published *Unsettling Moves*, cited 126,000 people just for 1999–2001; the figure given by the Wa authorities was only 50,000; yet others have cited 250,000 (cf. Global IDP Database 2005; 36–38).
32. In this context, the US government's blanket condemnations and indictments (US Department of State 2006; see also Lintner 2010; Kramer et al. 2014) identifying the Wa State authorities' leaders as criminals and drug dealers, delivered at about the time those same authorities were declaring their own war on opium and holding out for some amount of recognition, seem indifferent to the dimension of the *de facto* and also official position of the Wa State leaders as ethnonationalistic leaders and administrators of the area and people under their control.
33. On the place of opium and other cash crops and enterprises in Wa history and their role in enabling Wa autonomy, see Fiskesjö 2000, and chapter 3.
34. Kramer 2009a, 2009b; Kramer et al. 2014; Jensema et al. 2014; etc. Synthetic drug production is more important across the region today.
35. Chouvy 2004; Kramer 2005; also Jelsma and Kramer 2005 (especially p. 3; 13–20); on the UN efforts to help, see Renard 2013. This is quite apart from the Wa State's allegedly continued, even expanded, production of synthetic drugs, which need a different kind of lab-factory infrastructure and less labor input.
36. This is of course not a value-free judgment but one strongly influenced by the Chinese policies for the systematic replacement of dry-land shifting rice cultivation with irrigated, fixed-fields rice farming, which is regarded by the Chinese as intrinsically superior, regardless of local soil conditions or topographic conditions. See chapter 1, and Yin 2001, 2009.
37. On the involvement of the Rangoon government in co-planning the evacuations as part of a declared plan to depopulate opium areas, see BBC 2000.

38. Cited in Jagan 2005.
39. See the Global IDP Database (2005: report of 27 June 2005, 36–38) on how "displacement continues unabated in one of the world's worst IDP situations." (Calling the people in question IDP or "Internally Displaced Persons," presumes of course their citizenship in either Burma or China, which could be problematic when it comes to the Wa, who historically did not belong to either. This may be a moot point, since no one today, not even Wa State leaders, challenges the territorial ownership of these two states.)
40. For examples, see Evrard and Goudineau 2004; Baird and Shoemaker 2007; and High 2008, on Laos; Cholthira 2000 on Thailand (where strategic forced relocations also has a long history; cf. Grabowski 1999). British and American wartime forced resettlement of populations in Malaysia and Vietnam come to mind; and, in today's Vietnam, "development-induced" relocations continue (see, e.g., Doutriaux et al. 2008).
41. On modern Chinese ethnopolitics in comparative perspective, see Fiskesjö 2006; Leibold 2019a; etc.; on Burma (Myanmar), see, e.g., Lambrecht 2004; Gravers 2006; Walton 2013; Cheesman 2017.
42. See Internal Displacement Monitoring Centre 2004.
43. S.H.A.N. 2003 ("Sickness and Death Hit Wa—Again").
44. Lahu National Development Organisation 2002. Opium, in small doses, is recognized as an effective drug against diarrhea; unfortunately there is no more information here on other "traditional medicines" that might have been used, apart from the "magic" sacrifices apparently carried out in tragically blind desperation, absent the oracular information on the geographic sources of the diseases.
45. Woods 2011; Kramer and Woods 2012; also Lambrecht 2004.
46. One can of course also liken it to a modern Western model, since the nation-state model as such is copied in Burma and China and arguably in the Wa State. But one must note that while it is indeed in some ways Western-derived, it is also fused and combined with local histories of state violence, especially the deeply patronizing tendencies of historical Chinese imperialism and its attitudes toward the "barbarians."
47. Scott 1998.
48. Michelet 1973 (orig. 1846).
49. In Russia, the creation of the state and the Russian empire has been aptly, if paradoxically, characterized as "self-colonization" (see Etkind 2011): the transformation of autonomous people into subjects, specifically referring to their status as the means to an end—the state's end.

9

Hope against Hope

Border Prophets and Foreign Saviors

It is perhaps unsurprising, given its fraught history, that the Wa region has seen its share of charismatic prophets and savior cults. Such entities emerge from the despair of the peripheral situation, declaring themselves to possess special powers to save the people from the sufferings of war and oppression. These prophets and their movements resemble the millennial cults that arise in similar historical situations elsewhere, to promise deliverance from suffering.[1]

This is why it is also no surprise that these prophets and cults, historically, did not come from within the well-to-do central Wa country but only emerged among the suffering on its peripheries, which are also the peripheries of neighboring states. Similar to the Christian missionaries that occupy and exploit the same niche in history, these prophets and cults seldom if ever were able to even penetrate the central, autonomous Wa areas. Local messianic cults and foreign missionaries are basically features of the peripheral situation.[2]

Yet both prophets and cults have figured prominently on the Wa horizon and entered into complex relationships with the Wa of the interior. In the late nineteenth century, a Lahu cult and its followers migrated into the Ximeng area, bringing about far-reaching social and economic changes in the vicinity of the "headhunting country" where I undertook fieldwork. In this chapter, I first discuss this Lahu migration into the Ximeng area, and then proceed to discuss the foreign (American and European) Christians who have proselytized among both the Lahu and the Wa, exploiting the despair of the peripheral situation.

Endnotes for this chapter begin on page 241.

Lahu and Wa Buddhist-Inspired Prophet Cults

In the 1720s, the Chinese empire, seeking to expand its control, began to impose direct rule on southwestern imperial frontiers where "native chiefs" had ruled before.[3] In the eighteenth and nineteenth centuries, a series of protracted conflicts related to this imperial expansion took place between Chinese imperial forces and indigenous peoples of the region, including the Lahu people, a Tibeto-Burman-speaking people found to the north of the Wa area, in what is now China's Yunnan Province.[4] Many of the Lahu defeated in these conflicts moved south through Yunnan, into the Shan states and the Wa lands, and also into Burma and Thailand, forming part of the pattern of "hill tribes out of China" (Hanks 1984).

On a number of occasions, prophets emerged out of the ranks of Lahu migrants and defeated warriors, proclaiming themselves as new leaders, with some even becoming recognized, in millennial fashion, as "kings" who would deliver the followers from evil (Kataoka 2013). They were often articulate people who previously held more ordinary positions, and who then declared themselves the bearers of a new message. Walker (1974, 2003) observed that these Lahu "holy men" were like the Nuer prophets in Africa described by Evans-Pritchard, possessing a "revelational role deriving from spiritual inspiration."[5] They claimed to have special, superior powers, going beyond the priestly role of mediating contact with the divine. In Evans-Pritchard's words (1956: 303), in these prophets, "the possessed . . . is also the possessor."

The teachings of the Lahu prophets (or prophet-kings) were often inspired by Buddhism, and they also referenced the supreme Lahu deity, G'uisha.[6] Seeking a similar appeal of universal validity, their movements had a syncretistic quality, taking cues from various brands of Theravada Buddhism, from Shan practices, or from Mahayana Buddhism practiced by the Chinese to the north. A few prophets also took up Christianity (see below). Most borrowed heavily from Buddhist practices and paraphernalia, including building temples.[7] One early Buddhist connection is said to have been established by a monk traveling from the north, from Dali in Yunnan, and arriving in an area of "the Kawa and the Luohei" midway between the Shan princely states of Gengma and Menglian (but now part of Lancang County), where another, local leader later claimed to be the "Sixth Buddha" and held charge over several places renamed Gaixin (literally, "change of heart").[8]

These movements discouraged such debilitating vices as opium and liquor, which the people on broken, oppressed peripheries were particularly susceptible to. In both Lahu and Wa areas, opium was also widely produced for profitable export, but (peripheral-situation) Lahu areas with a "change of heart" (as in both Lahu and Wa Christianized areas) would forgo both the production and consumption of opium.[9] In contrast, in the central Wa country, which continued to produce exported large amounts of opium, its use was generally prohibited because of the known ill effects of addiction, and—in the absence of a government or police—this prohibition was enforced through the kinship system.[10] This was a balance that people in the peripheral situation were not able to strike.

The Lahu prophets sometimes sought allies among other highland peoples, including the Wa, with whom they came into contact after entering the region as refugees. The relationship was often tenuous, as we shall see. The larger aim of the Lahu movements was to escape and to resist the extension of Chinese rule, or Shan or British power. As a consequence, the Lahu also sometimes allied themselves with ethnically Han Chinese bandits and rebels that sought refuge in the region (repeating an age-old pattern; cf. Fiskesjö 1999a).

These prophets are remembered in local oral traditions, but few have left traces in the historical record (whether British or Chinese). We usually only find notes on "rebellions" that have risen and then faded.[11] One of the largest such Lahu uprisings took place in the Jinggu, Lancang, and Shuangjiang area around the turn of the eighteenth century, culminating in an attack on the important Chinese town of Mianning. The main fighting was in 1798–1802, after which the Lahu were suppressed by the Chinese imperial army. Zhang Fuguo, one of the leaders, was himself also a former Dali monk, known under his Buddhist name of Tong-jin (copper-gold). The rising lingered until 1813, when Zhang was killed in an effort by the imperial army, assisted by the forces of as many as three nearby Shan *tusi* (Mengmeng, Gengma, and Menglian), acting in their role as Chinese-appointed "native chiefs."[12]

One of Zhang's descendants, Zhang Bingquan, emerged to launch new uprisings in 1881 and 1887 against Chinese and local *tusi* allies in the Mengmeng (now Shuangjiang) area.[13] In 1903, Zhang Chaowen, another heir of this rebel dynasty, launched an uprising jointly with Bao Aimeng, a Wa leader from the important opium trading point of Aishuai (Yong Soi), reportedly gathering tens of thousands of fighters to attack the Mengmeng *tusi*, who fled northward to Mianning in March 1903. The local Chinese military strongman Peng Kun then crushed the rebels, killing Zhang. Bao Aimeng is said to have been struck dead by lightning.[14]

What were these struggles about? They were clearly over land, and autonomy—the power to avoid being controlled, taxed, drafted, and so on. The Baptist missionary Harold Young said the Lahu formerly "owned from Monglem to Mekong" (that is, they successfully settled there after fleeing from areas further north), but they were "dispossessed" as a result of these renewed wars, "displacing their rulers and driving the cultivators from their holdings wherever the climate suited Chinese settlement, and ousting them even where it did not, in favor of Shans, a race more pliable to Chinese ends. . . . Lahu social structure was crushed, and their monasteries (*fufang*) destroyed."[15]

In the late nineteenth century, a similar dynasty of Lahu spiritual-warrior leaders led by a Sanfozu ("three Buddha ancestor," or Zhu A-xia) took refuge at Ximeng, on the eastern side of what was then still the autonomous central Wa country. Sanfozu was originally a follower of the Lahu movement of a nineteenth-century Wang *foye* ("Buddha Wang," or "Nanshan *fozu*"), who was building Buddhist-Lahu temples in the Gengma area and fashioning a tributary system with Lahu villages, who owed annual rice payments to the leader. But this system later faded,[16] and around 1874 Sanfozu tried to negotiate with the Wa for his settlement in the Wa-dominated area of Ximeng. He established a Buddhist temple-residence near what is now the old town of Ximeng, where he revived the earlier tributary system, and remained there until his death in 1888, in effect founding a Lahu dynasty there.[17] I have visited the eerie ruins of these rather imposing brick buildings, which still attract annual Lahu New Year's celebrators.

In the 1950s, Chinese researchers investigated the "legends of Sanfozu" among Lahu and Lisu people in Ximeng,[18] finding people among both who claimed that their forefathers would gather in Ximeng at Sanfozu's request, although some had already arrived before and some after Sanfozu himself. One Lisu informant said that Sanfozu told his grandfather that he "must not be afraid of the Wa people; at Ximeng they would find the blessing of Buddha" (*Wazu diaocha cailiao* 1962 [1980]: 6:32).

Sanfozu settled at a spot where, as he had presaged, there was much beeswax (used for the all-important Lahu candles; also used in later Lahu-Wa cults). Although Sanfozu tried to negotiate safe passage with the Wa, his people still were attacked by Wa warriors from Masan three times after settling at Ximeng (Yong Ou, the "Meng Hsam" of Scott 1893). In return, he organized counterattacks on Yong Ou, Yuxi, and Mugu (a site between Yong Song and Yong Ou), as well as on Banyue and Yong Bulie (Yong Brie). He achieved a cease-fire with the Wa with the help of thirty-six Chinese mercenary gunmen hired from Lancang. Later, the Wa and Sanfozu made formal peace through the covenant-sacrifice of cattle, and by mutual gifts of meat (*Wazu diaocha cailiao* 1962 [1980]: 6:33).

Meanwhile, in the early 1890s, the Chinese increased pressure on the Lahu leaders to submit to Chinese rule, in part because of growing British interest in the area, after the British annexed Upper Burma in 1886. Chinese accounts maintain that in 1891, the Lahu chief at Ximeng submitted to the imperial Chinese authorities, which named the Lahu a god-king. In 1887–88, China had already established a new strategic military-administrative outpost, aptly named Zhenbian ("subjugation of the frontier"; renamed Lancang in 1914), just a few day's march to the southeast. Some suggest this was to ward off British influence, and this may have played a part, but the Yunnan Chinese governor's stated desire was to have this outpost approved so he could better suppress the Lahu.[19] Thus it is no surprise that when Sanfozu's successor received Scott at his temple in early 1893, in his capacity of "Ta Fu Yè or Great Buddha of Möng Hka" (Ximeng), he requested British protection as well.[20] However, this was not just to escape Chinese rule (the basic *raison d'être* of the whole movement) but also to ask for assurances for protection against the Wa.

The Lahu presence in this Wa area was extremely tenuous. Sanfozu as well as his predecessors had probably taken their cue for the organization of this polity from Chinese administrative practice, since he named leading Wa from a number of nearby villages as "officials" within his system—"officials" that in turn were recognized by the Wa only as contacts for the Lahu. The Sanfozu system, known as *kaxie*, is said in Chinese sources to have divided the Ximeng realm into four areas, or *jiaoma*: Lisu, Masan, Yuesong, and Yongguang. They also say that his influence at its height extended from Xinchang (south of Yongguang) in the north to Menglian in the south; from Munai and Heihe (Black) River in the east (in what is now Lancang County), and Shantong in the west (currently in Burmese territory). However, this division was not one imposed by the Lahu; instead, it corresponds to the spheres of the (already existing) different Wa realms (*jaig' qee*). As Scott already noted, Yuesong (Scott's Yaw Hsung; Yong Song in Wa) was allied with but also independent of Sung Ramang (Yong A Meang); Yong Ou (Chinese: Masan; Scott's Meng Hsam) was a realm of its own, and one where the Lahu presence and influence had recently emerged.

Much later, when the Chinese took over the area in the 1950s, the local Lahu said they had to pay tribute every year since coming to Wa country. If not, they had been told they would have to "go back where they came from" (Fei Xiaotong 1955: 107). Scott specified that the "Ta Fu Ye" (Sanfozu) had to submit (annually and on special occasions) "offerings of bullocks, pigs, opium, and liquor, which the Wa regard as tribute and the [Lahu] affect to consider friendly gifts" (Scott and Hardiman 1901: II.2:360). This contrasts with Lahu claims that they received annual tributes from the Wa in the form of a grain tax, which Sanfozu does seem to have been able to impose at times. It thus appears that the balance of power between the Lahu guests and the Wa hosts shifted back and forth: the authority of the immigrant-turned-resident Lahu overlapped with, and was continually contested by, their Wa neighbors, who were not ruled by them, but who recognized him as he recognized them. While each group would repeatedly claim the other had become a subordinate tributary (an echo of Chinese state practices), in reality each group avoided becoming the other's tributary.

The balance of power again shifted in favor of the Wa in the early twentieth century. Sometime in the 1930s or 1940s, the Wa of Yong Ou (Masan) established a marketplace under their own control not far from their village, away from Ximeng, which had been an important commerce center since the late nineteenth century. The site is now located under a reservoir, established in the 1950s, after the Wa-controlled market was closed down; instead, the Chinese promoted the trading outpost of Ximeng (Mengka), which gained preeminence as a marketplace under Chinese control.[21] Empire is about economics: I used to think about this when I walked by that reservoir, on my way between Yong Ou and the Ximeng market town.

On some occasions, the Lahu prophets also struggled with the British, as I will discuss in the next section on foreign missionaries. One such Lahu leader was Ma Heh G'uisha, active in the 1920s–30s, who led a group of believers to build a fort south of Kengtung, where he established himself on the model of Sanfozu at Ximeng. But the British conquered the fort and drove out this new competition.[22]

Lahu messianic cults arose both alongside and in opposition to the Christian missionaries, who saw them as competitors. One such Lahu prophet sent word that he would dispatch tigers that would maul the foreign missionaries.[23] Even so, the missionaries were partially successful in the region, and among the Lahu in particular, because they (unknowingly, perhaps, at least in the early years) picked up on what had become an unfulfilled Lahu response to the "peripheral situation," even seizing upon the Lahu lore of a "lost book" (cf. Kataoka 1998; and below). The foreigners were able to attract followers and even win over lesser local prophets in part by deploying superior powers expressed in evening *laterna magica* shows containing gramophones and other novel techno-wizardry.

Christian missionaries also unintentionally provided an arena for the regeneration of prophets within the ranks of the new Christians. In one such incident, a Lahu Christian adopted the language of the new foreign religion and rose within the ranks of new converts, but he also, in syncretistic fashion, claimed to be a Lahu-style holy man with magic powers. Later it was revealed that he had been using forbidden traditional Lahu beeswax offerings even under his new Christian cloak, and the missionary (Allyn Cooke) felt compelled to disassociate himself from this competition, and denounce him as a demonic incarnation of the devil himself (Walker 2003: 519–520, "Lahu Messiahs and the Search for Utopia," citing Cooke 1930).

Wa Prophets

Messianic movements also originated with the Wa of the peripheries, beyond the scope of the "refugee" Lahu. For example, in the first years of the 1900s, a new religious movement was started among the Wa by a Pu San Long, an elder said to have come back to life while he was being buried. According to Harvey, he then began to teach a Buddhist-inspired "law of loving kindness" and persuaded many to lay down headhunting warfare. However, after his death in 1906 at the hands of a Lahu "fanatic" (Young n.d.: 3), "there were several bad harvests and headhunting resumed in many places" (Harvey 1957: 131). There does not seem to be any notice of this prophet in Chinese records, and it is possible that he lived well beyond the Chinese sphere of influence and knowledge.

He may have found a successor in the widely respected and admired Wa-Lahu leader, famous under the name of Dax Jadie (the Elder Jadie), who propagated a similar Buddhist-inspired syncretistic teaching in the central Wa areas starting approximately in the 1950s and 1960s (or at least as seen in Chinese records). His message was very similar to that of earlier prophets. He urged his fellow Wa to end their own feuds, stand together, and abandon headhunting warfare and its paraphernalia, such as the village drums. I myself heard about this prophet, who was supposedly still alive in the 1990s, but the Chinese scholar Wang Ningsheng told me that similar stories circulated in the early 1960s when he worked in the same area: either Dax Jadie existed in several reincarnations—or he is immortal.

I often heard Wa people talking about this man in the 1990s, and I once asked how old he was. I was met by ridicule. People pointed out that it was common knowledge that Dax Jadie was ageless yet always looked young, so that if I met him, he would look younger than me (I was in my thirties). However, later, rumors had it that the prophet had been arrested (by the UWSA in the Wa State, perhaps on Chinese orders). According to one story, Dax Jadie is (or was) not born by any human mother but by a buffalo. He is said to have been found by the Lahu among a herd and then raised among the Lahu, even though he is also Wa. He is highly intelligent, multilingual, and reportedly invested with supernatural powers.[24]

While Dax Jadie's teachings primarily address the current Wa situation, there seems to be no question that the inspiration for his syncretistic teachings derive in large measure from the past mixture of Wa and Lahu millennialist traditions. They even include the beeswax candles that replaced the Wa sacrifices; I once chanced upon and visited briefly a converted village in about 1996, where everyone was busy lighting these candles. Thus, the candles and a version of the teachings they shone a light on had finally traveled all the way to the heart of Wa country. I understand this as a consequence of how the central heartland region by this time had also been thoroughly transformed into someone else's periphery (that of the Chinese state). It is one indication of the fact that, in a political sense, there is no longer any central Wa country.

Foreign Saviors

While their messages may have been different in many respects, the European and American Christian missionaries arriving in these lands toward the end of the nineteenth century were able to succeed, at least in some places, because they occupied a niche similar to that of earlier cults. Like them, they mobilized people by offering new "hope against hope," that their situation could be overcome despite the odds against it. The Wa were never really the main focus of any foreign missionary efforts, but American Baptist and British Protestant missionaries made contact with them as well as their Lahu neighbors in the last years of the nineteenth century. Because of the risks of travel and the vigilant suspicion of outsiders in the Wa country, missionaries rarely penetrated the central Wa areas, and there is little trace of any missionary activities at all in what is now Ximeng County, where I did my fieldwork. In the Yong Ou village where I stayed for extended periods, only one elderly man remembered having once visited, as a very young man, what he called a *"lah* Yesu," a Jesus "market" (or gathering).

The Wa who became the object of missionary activities were predominantly those who lived closer to Shan settlements or lived intermingled with Lahu people in what are now Menglian, Lancang, Cangyuan, Shuangjiang, or Gengma Counties (and I have not worked among them). The American Baptist and other missionaries who came there had first started out in Shan, Lahu, and Wa areas in and near Kengtung (in Burma), and in adjacent areas in China in what are now Menglian, Lancang, and Shuangjiang Counties. They worked in all these areas from the beginning of the twentieth century up until 1950, when they were forced to leave.[25] William M. Young (Yong Weili, active 1896–1933) pioneered the movement, and he was followed by his locally raised multilingual sons, Harold Young (Yong Hengluo) and Vincent Young (active ca. 1926–50).

Their efforts were an extension of the wide-ranging Baptist work in Burma. A missionary named Cushing who had worked among the Karen further to the south in Burma visited Kengtung in 1869–70 and noted that the Lahu people of the area seemed receptive to foreign missionaries, especially as Lahu traditions suggested theological conceptions akin to Christianity; he thought they might be influenced as readily as the Karen were (Young 1906: 212–13). Thus William Young's early work was among the Lahu (called Muhso, using the Shan term), Akü (Akha), Kaw (a branch of the Akü or Akha), Kwe (or Kwi, understood to be a branch of the Lahu, "Yellow Lahu" or Lahushi), Wa (including the so-called Wa Küt, the "remaining Wa," also known as Tai Loi or Tai of the hills in the Shan language), and the majority Shan in the Kengtung area, which had a total population of several hundred thousand.[26]

Young had arrived in Kengtung in 1901. The Buddhist Tai-speaking people of this powerful Shan state proved highly resistant to Christianity, as others elsewhere had been (see Keyes 1993). But already after a few years he saw some success in converting Lahu people (many of whom were recent immigrants from Chinese-controlled areas) and in training native Lahu preachers. He also successfully converted some Wa, which he regarded as a promising field, especially in Chinese-controlled areas to the north where populations appeared much larger. Young said he felt greatly drawn to them, impressed by the hearsay that they were "strict Monogamists, [and] did not use liquor and opium."[27] Reporting home for fundraising purposes, he held out the prospect that even some former headhunting Wa now seemed prepared to give up that practice and become Christians (Young

1906, seemingly preferring, in evolutionist fashion, to assume they had always been headhunters). These Wa of the peripheries appear to have been influenced first by the Lahu (many Lahu spoke Wa, and many Wa spoke Lahu):

> In several sections the Wa people had accepted the Muhso customs and traditions ... thousands of them were longing for the Foreigner to bring the Knowledge of the True God ... a Muhso teacher went among the Wild Wa people three years ago ... they received his teaching and ... are now waiting anxiously for us to bring them the Gospel.[28]

These successes among the Lahu, and by extension the Wa, had much to do with the way that many Lahu came to regard William Young as a successor to their own spiritual leaders. The historical connection is a direct one. After the anti-Qing uprisings in the nineteenth and early twentieth centuries, some Lahu fled into Kengtung, where they may have heard Young preach. They brought translated materials[29] back to Shuangjiang, spread the word that there was now a second Living Buddha (probably counting from Sanfozu), and that a white horse had led them to Young's station in Kengtung.[30] Thus, Young was able to draw upon the historical coincidence of his arrival in the aftermath of the Lahu uprisings, and fill the void left by their earlier spiritual leaders after the Lahu defeat.

Young noted early on that the Lahu spoke of a holy man or angel who had left them, ascending to heaven on his own, while promising that a "Foreigner" would return in his place and deliver his holy book.[31] The Lahu themselves (although illiterate) turned out to be carrying "papers covered with Hieroglyphic marks that they [did] not understand the meaning of themselves" and longed for "teachers to make clear the way."[32] They claimed that their language had once been written, and mentioned a lost book. In one case, they even brought a book, which turned out to be "a Chinese book on astrology and evil spirits worship."[33]

Clearly, the Lahu refugee movements were already permeated with stories of this kind, the primitive periphery's mimetic desire for writing as the powerful weapon of the civilized, otherwise out of reach except on condition of submission to the temporal authorities of the civilized (Shan, Chinese, and so on). The missionaries seemed to provide the answer to this quandary.[34] Note, here, the stark difference with the Wa—who located the origin of writing with themselves—not taking it to be the gift by human prophet-saviors from afar.[35]

The idea that the True God was coming soon was readily accepted—because such a god was already present, among the Lahu (or Muhso). Both sides could agree that the Lahu had retained knowledge of a true god forsaken by all other peoples, and therefore should welcome the new teachers from afar. The early Lahu pastors associating themselves with the Baptist missions insisted on opposing both (native) idolatry and "Buddhist priests"—a practice that would include shunning the Shan princes, the overlords of the Buddhist polities of the region, and their powerful written traditions preserved in Buddhist temples and temple schools.

Instead, as before, they created a new faith based on a prophecy that fit very closely with earlier Lahu attempts to seek redemption from the peripheral situation in which they found themselves. Young himself saw the prospects regarding the Wa as follows, in "Lahu" terms:

> The Chinese have horrible tales to tell about the Was and the Taoyin [a Chinese official] asked [the British] Consul General to try to dissuade me from making tour. The Wa country is called "unadministered territory," that is, the part that is under British rule has not been put under any direct administration and they are not willing to assume risk for private parties touring there.... The Chinese have made raids on them, and have lost some men. They have destroyed many Wa villages.... [The Chinese] would have to supply a large escort in administered districts while they could offer me no protection whatsoever in the Wa country. I consider the Wa country perfectly safe for us ... we can travel there as no-one else can. The Was and even the Wild Was have strongly urged that I come, and ... the religious leaders called Pu Sam are held in great esteem and respect by even the wild Was and there is no case where any Pu Sam has been illtreated by the Was, even the wild Was. I have made careful inquiry on this point. *We would be regarded as a Pu Sam, only a Pu Sam over all other Pu Sam.*[36]

Here is the key to the foreign missionary activities and their success among the depressed hill peoples, migrants, and refugees in the turbulent intermediary zones between the central Wa lands and the Shan and Chinese polities. With his access to formidable resources (in all respects, including armaments, since the missionaries carried technologically advanced personal weapons for hunting and self-defense) as well as to exotic remedies from afar ("from beyond the heavens," in the jealous wording of the staunchly anti-missionary Chinese resident of Mengmeng, Peng Gui'e 1926: 137), the missionary becomes a savior bigger than anyone known before—but in the same category as those saviors of old.

At the same time, the main field of proselytizing was clearly the intermediary zones, not the central Wa lands. The Wa reached by the missionaries were primarily those that already had a history of submitting to, and/or attempting to escape, Shan, Chinese, or other exploitation. The Wa had already been seeking "salvation" from their predicament, just as the Lahu did. In Young's words:

> Many thousands of Wa are full converts to the Lahu traditions and beliefs. They have the same earnest longing for the Foreigner to bring them the

knowledge of the True God. These Wa are known as Kaishin Wa, which means seekers after blessings or seekers after the good path.[37]

As I mentioned already, "Kaishin" here (Gaixin in *pinyin* spelling) is a Chinese term that simply means "change of heart," that is, it relates to abandoning one's traditions because they no longer seem useful in coping with the present situation.[38] Elsewhere, Young refers to a Lahu term (Bon Shin), for such "seekers of blessings, or of the true path."

Although many conflicts occurred between the original Wa inhabitants of this region and the recent refugee Lahu, warrior Wa in certain areas had pledged to never kill a Lahu; in other areas, Lahu prophets managed to persuade the Wa in the borderlands of the influence of local Shan rulers to renounce headhunting warfare altogether. In certain places where headhunting had once been practiced but had been abandoned, some were even persuaded to "throw away the skulls that they had placed by the paths leading to the village."[39] Only then did they qualify for the label Kaishin Wa, which become a prime new target for Christian missionizing.[40] Young believed that the Gaixin Wa represented a majority of the Wa, and in 1920, seeking perhaps also to abandon the stubbornly and strongly Buddhist Shan of Kengtung and concentrating on the much more promising field of the more receptive hill peoples, Young obtained permission from the Chinese governor of Yunnan Province to move there permanently. The move may also have been influenced by the competition from the Italian Catholic mission in Kengtung in Burma, which also had begun eyeing the hill peoples, including the fabled, ferocious Wa (the headhunters; *cacciatori di teste*).[41]

Young left Kengtung, traveled by way of Shanghai and Kunming (around half of Asia!) to Menglian, and settled there with additional Shan *tusi* permission. The missionaries then divided their efforts between two different fields in the Menglian-Lancang-Shuangjiang area: the Lahu, and the "Kawa" (Wa) hills nearby, the old rebel lands between Menglian and the central Wa areas.[42] They built a network of schools, teaching subjects such as Christian doctrine, English, and mathematics to local Lahu, Wa, and others. Initially they communicated in Shan, but Young's son Vincent later devised writing systems, translated Christian scriptures into both Lahu and Wa, and taught their recruits the writing systems. They received audiences for instruction and conversion at their residence and toured the area with their pastors, converting people on the spot and training evangelists to tour the lands farther afield.

By 1926, when two more Baptist missionaries arrived (the Buker brothers), about forty thousand conversions had been claimed, chiefly among the Lahu (Fife 1981: 100). By the early 1930s, according to one contemporary Chinese count, the Youngs had built ninety small churches (*fuyintang*, "Lucky Sound Halls") and more than ten schools in the peripheral Wa areas; in the Lahu hills, they were even more successful, with 136 new churches.[43] They were always less successful with the Shan, who remained strongly Buddhist and maintained their own temples and temple schools. In some Wa areas controlled by powerful local chiefs who had converted to Buddhism, such as at Banhong, people were prohibited from converting to Christianity (Xiao Zisheng et al. 1986: 8).

Among the Wa of the central autonomous areas, missionaries faced much greater difficulty in their activities. Just as the Shan Buddhist populations did, the missions faced powerfully entrenched polities with their own firm belief systems, ones less easily shaken than those of the Lahu or Wa of the broken peripheries. In addition, there were security concerns. The missionaries were warned from the start by sympathetic officials (both British and Chinese) that special caution was important with regard to the dangerous Wa ("Kawa").[44] Although the missionaries were never attacked by headhunters,[45] the relations with the central Wa seem to have been uneasy, with occasional hostilities.

In "Wild Wa" country, both Christian and Buddhist missionaries were occasionally attacked by "were-wolves" (*hpi hai* [in Shan] or *mao-pi* [in Chinese?]) (Barton 1933: 56, 102, 116). From the scanty accounts available, it appears these werewolves may have been local spirit mediums attempting to drive the missionaries away. The Baptist missionary Harold Young once fired a shot at a humanlike werewolf that broke into his dwelling at night, and a "shaman" is said to have died in a village not far away the day after, with a huge wound to his stomach (Barton 1933); in 1925, Allyn Cooke of the American CIM (China Inland Mission) was captured by a "Wa queen," but then liberated by Panthay Muslim opium traders, a deed seen as "the Lord stretching forth His hand" (Harvey 1933: 93–94).

The Youngs were also attacked by some Wa and Chinese (opium bandits?) who joined forces at the important Wa opium trading center of Aihsoi (Yong Soi).[46] However, on several occasions, Wa headhunting warrior parties refrained from attacking the missionaries even though they presented themselves as easy targets. Apparently, in each case, the headhunters first thought they had encountered Chinese and began attacking, but they stopped when they realized this was not so. The missionaries instead took these escapes from certain death as signs of providence, and also of "the reputation of the accuracy of the white man's aim with modern guns, and the influence of his pen on outside circles," among headhunter warriors, robbers, and local Chinese officials alike.[47]

The missionaries' explanations of why they were saved generally omit the important point that there was no history of conflict between the Wa and them, such as could have served to justify headhunting raids (see chapter 6). It was not strange that the Wa should refrain from killing the missionaries, who had (so far, at least) only come with gifts and sermons rather than demands for taxation and domination.

In 1927, the Baptist twin Buker brothers arrived to take up work in the northern part of Young's missionary field, at Mengmeng (today's Shuangjiang, a predominantly Dai/Shan valley town), where there were already fifty Lahu and Wa pastors and ten thousand each of Lahu and Wa Christians, all in Yunnan areas "adjacent to the head-hunting Wa area, southwest of Meng Meng" (i.e., today's Ximeng, southern Cangyuan, and northern Lancang Counties). Raymond Buker took some interest in ethnological observation, including of the Wa around Mengmeng, Aihsoi, and Mengtum.[48] Buker and some Christianized Wa set up a station and three chapels at the village Yawng Rok, at the northeastern end of the Wa country, only several hours from Meng Tum (Mengdong), currently the county seat of the Wa Autonomous County of Cangyuan. For the first time, he noted, he was living under Wa jurisdiction: "The central village, where our house is built, is the seat of the government for the Wa in this section. Independent of Chinese and Shan, the Wa have their own local rulers whose power is supreme in their particular district. Thus I might say that I am now residing with and under the protection of the Wa King. His domain extends over several thousand subjects. All ... are Christians; they have been baptized about four years."[49]

When funds began to run out because of the Great Depression after 1929, the missionaries were hard pressed to continue to pay the many pastors they had trained to proselytize, and some began to abandon the cause (Fife 1981: 108ff.). Raymond Buker, along with other more conservative Baptists, became critical of Young for placing too little emphasis on the converts' grasp of theological matters, arguing that the result was "superficial."[50] By simply abandoning their old "idols" and "[keeping] Sunday," the Lahu were baptized; but the recruited pastors (*sala*) didn't seem to care beyond that, having joined for the sake of "a financial career" more than anything. "To be a teacher in Lahu and in Wa work means to rank equal and above any local officials in prestige, food, transportation etc. It is not a sacrifice, it is a blessing to be a teacher here."[51] Buker observed that "teachers" set out on ponies with fine clothes and guns, which sent a louder message than their preaching did, namely the hope for a "new economic era" in which

> to study and work with the white man meant to be raised to a new and higher state in economic society. ... The people *are interpreting* the new custom we are introducing in terms of the economic prosperity of those who receive American money. ... Under the old wage system the preachers and their families had clothes way beyond the standard of their well-to-do villagers. They had guns, they had ponies. Ordinary villagers do not have these luxuries.[52]

Buker is also said to have accused veteran fellow Baptists of "mass-conversion à la St. Remi" (Barton 1933: 97) and to have suggested that the elder Young used brutal methods to punish offenses against preachers. In another letter, Buker considered in a more conciliatory tone that the difference in style had arisen in part because Young's sons Harold and Vincent were a new generation of local-born missionaries: "Mr. Young's theology is o.k. but he does not speak Lahu, and the boys do. The boys are more Lahu than Americans, they live and breathe Lahuism. Accordingly the simple gospel is considerably adulterated with Lahu traditions, I fear." (He also admits in pencil, in the margin, that these traditions are "to a certain extent, desirable.")

Here, we get another hint of just how these missions could thrive in the local context, better than their competitors to the north in Yunnan, the China Inland Mission (with whom some territorial disputes had developed): "The ABM has better buildings, pay their teachers more, give their pupils more, have better guns, can shoot better, and all have better ponies . . . than does the CIM. But we have never been accused of being more like Christ, feeding the soul better, etc., than the CIM . . ."[53] Elsewhere, Buker noted the dispersal of medicine, one of the most impressive aspects of the missionary work in this disease-ridden land (the tremendous demand for medicines sold or given out is often mentioned in the records).[54]

In 1930, the American Baptists reached a compromise with the CIM, and they also struck an accord within their own number. The salaries for pastors were limited as a result of Buker's criticism, but Buker was removed from most Wa work and then transferred to Kengtung in Burma, away from the veteran missionaries' Lahu and Wa fields. Chinese government requests for the withdrawal of the Young missionaries were only partly met,[55] and the missions were able to continue for the time being.

This type of controversy between following orthodox teachings to the letter and allowing local practices to prioritize practical gains over "true" conversion reminds us of the Jesuits at the Chinese capital centuries before. The same conflict has probably played out on many a missionary "field." I cite some of the arguments here to highlight the main point of anthropological interest: the missions had been partly successful not because there was a yearning to accept the Christian doctrines but because their work fit into the local economy of the peripheral situation, just like the preexisting native forms of millennialism. The Lahu and Wa who answered the missionary call heard something different from what the missionaries imagined.

On one level, the local pastors followed the missionaries as if they had been joining one of their own savior cults, if not to obtain positions of influence and wealth within it. The people at large followed, seeing the payments made to pastors as a horn of plenty sounding the way to deliverance. I heard an echo of this hopeful credulity when, on a recent return visit, an old acquaintance asked me whether it was true, as he had heard it said, that converting to Christianity would mean that anything one prayed for would literally rain from the sky. The villagers had again met American missionaries, backpacking through the country with Bibles and medicines. Negative, I answered; they probably do not mean that in any literal sense, only symbolically.

Back in the missionary days, ordinary folks in the "field" had to provide food and shelter during such tours—a most sensitive issue for the missionaries themselves: on the one hand, they were tasked by their home headquarters to support their own missions, but they also ran the risk of accusations from suspicious Chinese authorities that they were soliciting a form of taxation by accepting native gifts, which were given in hope against hope. These contributions could be substantial: at one church gathering in 1927, "the native Christians donated everything, twenty head of cattle, eleven hogs and eleven thousand pounds of rice, to give a few items."[56]

Among the few sources that offer details on church administration are Communist Chinese reports from the 1950s detailing the prevailing conditions in areas that China was assuming control over. These note that, for example, there were about three thousand Christian converts in the Mengmeng area where missionizing had started in the 1930s. The converts had to pray Wednesdays and Sundays or face fines; they paid regular tribute to the preachers in the shape of grain at harvest time, and meat from every slaughtered pig or head of cattle. Every Sunday, prayer was to be accompanied by cash contributions that also helped feed the preachers (*Wazu diaocha cailiao* 1962 [1980]: 5:66). Echoes here of Sanfozu's tribute system.

Local generosity sometimes overwhelmed the missionaries. "The Wa are generous people, and no matter how poor they seem to be, they simply are not happy until they have made us a present. . . ."[57] The Chinese sources, unsurprisingly, leave this unexplained, or regard it as forced exploitation—as taxation, better left to the Chinese state. To the missionaries, it seemingly confirmed that their message was welcome. But in my view, what we have here are echoes of the original philosophy of the Wa as hosts (chapter 1), as well as the new element of hope against hope. Both "Tame" Wa and Lahu, like so many other peripheral peoples of the region, saw Christianity as a foreign religion that might help to deliver them from the Chinese or Shan, both of which pointedly did *not* share this creed. This is why the Christian ritual of the Lord's Supper came to be "looked upon as a sort of a covenant whereby the folks are pledging their allegiance to Mr. Young."[58] To the "Foreign" preacher of preachers, people were prepared to give their allegiance in order to receive the much greater blessings of deliverance from the peripheral situation.

Again, the continuity with indigenous savior cults was most obvious in the case of the Lahu missionizing: the Lahu had been seeking spiritual support for their struggles against the Chinese imperial state in Buddhist-derived prophetic cults, and their traditions had ample precedence for such organizations, as in the savior movement of Sanfozu and other figures who had set themselves up as revenue-collecting god-kings of a new kind. The conditions for an uninterrupted growth of such savior cults persisted, and new saviors continued to come forward.[59] This whole aspect of adopting foreign creeds is missing from most missiological accounts, where deliverance from the burdens of the native's "old religion" as well as the "boredom" (*sic!*) of life before Christianity are cited self-assuredly as an explanation for their relative success (Covell 1995: 240, citing Li 1987).

It is notable how closely these views align with official Chinese views of the benefits of civilization and assimilation. In pointing this out, I do not mean to denigrate the actual efforts in providing medical help to and expressing unselfish concern for the welfare of the peoples of this region, or to depict them as smoke screens hiding ulterior motives. I believe that this distinction was also recognized both by local people and indeed even by many a Chinese observer, as I have noted.

As for the British, even if some of the British administrators of the Shan states were also Christians and wished the missionaries well, they usually were more worried about the political implications of the proselytizing. Sometimes they noted sarcastically that the Lahu and the Wa were the "special victims" of the American Baptists. Young was forced early on, by both Chinese and British prerogatives, to insist on the distinction between religious proselytizing and anything resembling political power or ambitions to influence anything other than the minds of the people involved. Perhaps this is also why there are so few actual descriptions of missionary economics—the complex network of gifts and counter-gifts that sustained the church-building efforts beyond the initial ABFMS financing, which then evolved into large-scale engagement with the local frontier economy.

In a letter to the ABFMS on 28 May 1906 (American Baptist Foreign Mission Society n.d., FM 213-2-2), W. Young argued against a British report on the Wa situation and the missionary work, complaining that the British could see no other aspects than the political and that they only had eyes for the essentially political division of the "wild" and the "tame." He himself already was tuned in to much finer cultural distinctions, with the Wa divided on "the Palaoungs, En, Son or Sawn, Sam Tou, and Sam Tun (Tai Loi)" and others in the Kengtung area, and he hoped that every one of these might embrace his message. Young even acknowledged a contemporary savior cult in the Wa areas that had made contact with him. It had "led a tribe to give up headhunting, to abandon polygamy, to give up the use of opium, to abstain from intoxicants, and all evil, so far as they know," and he saw this as a sign of progress toward the only true faith.

But the British were wary of a "strong political motive" (read: political coherence outside of British control, instead of the baffling and unpredictable disunity that otherwise characterized the Wa lands).[60] Such differences continued throughout the period of missionary work, and of British power in Burma. The general British attitude toward indigenous savior movements as such was much less sympathetic and more like that of the agents of the Chinese state on the other side of the frontier. At one point, "the British in Kengtung" are said to have hanged a Lahu religious "fanatic," for claiming to have received gifts from the king of England and saying that said king would soon arrive to worship him.[61]

During the 1935–37 Sino-British boundary demarcations, the British received delegations from Christian Was urging Britain to assume control over the entire Wa country. The eventual boundaries, however, left many Wa Christians in China, where they were often harassed by local officials (for money reasons), even though higher Chinese authorities were not necessarily averse to missionizing.[62] This was the beginning of the end for missionary work on the China side, as Chinese assertiveness and anti-missionary activism increased dramatically. Chinese residents in the predominantly Shan town of Mengmeng mobilized to drive the missionaries away; in Lancang more charges were pressed against them, and the persecution of converts and others increased.[63] During the 1935–37 Boundary Commission work, Christian villages came under organized Chinese attack, and a great many churches or chapels were destroyed or converted into Chinese schools.[64] With deteriorating security, many hill people continued to migrate into Burma, especially those of the intermediary lands between the central "Wild" Wa country and the expanding effective range of Chinese administration, which increasingly diminished the powers of the Shan *tusi*.[65]

The missionary activities on the Burma side had come to seem more feasible, and Harold Young even sent his Wa pastors and interpreters into the "unadministered" Wa country from his new base at Pang Yang in Manglun, the old Shan-style Wa state at the southern end of the Wa country, just north of Kengtung, which had caused so much trouble for the British in the 1890s.[66] However, the missionary work was interrupted by the war and by the Japanese invasion of Burma in 1942, which finally derailed all British attempts to establish administration over the Wa areas—on which the missionary work ultimately depended.

Some of the missionaries still returned after World War II ended in 1945. The British, who had evacuated their Burma government to India while Japan occupied all of Burma, had returned and again attempted to achieve control over all of the Wa areas while clearing out soldiers-turned-bandits and the new opium warlords that had emerged in many places. Some missionaries offered support, hoping for a new and more powerful position from which to proselytize.[67] But in the end, all foreign missionaries were forced to leave after Burma achieved independence in 1948 and the Chinese Communist armies took over Yunnan in 1949–50. The missionaries left behind the converts and believers they had made, and in some areas (in the northern part of Lancang County, and in Cangyuan County) Christianity still survives among the Wa as well as the Lahu.[68] Since 1949, foreign missionaries in China have generally been depicted as evil agents of imperialism, and the Youngs have been similarly described as armed spies for British imperialism, only interested in using their religious work to dupe the people and deploy it as a cover for their real activity: providing intelligence for the British on mineral deposits and mining in the Chinese border areas (*Lahuzu jianshi* 1986: 40–42), which the British were rediscovering in the 1920s.

Some missionaries did hope that all of "Wild Wa" country would come under British administration so that headhunting could come to an end and that the Wa would "receive the Gospel." Thus, C. G. Gowman urged in 1928 for prayers "that God will speedily move upon the British authorities concerned to take over this 'no man's land,' and give it the blessing of good government, as elsewhere in Burma," for, as he believed, there were "very strong indications" that the Wa would end headhunting and become receptive to the Christian teaching if only they came under British rule. (As we have seen, this was a total misconception of what Wa warfare was about.)[69]

Actually, Western missionary efforts were not entirely unwelcome in China, at least not during the Republic (1912–49). Lu Guofan, one of a group of Yunnan intellectuals urging renewed efforts to civilize the borderland areas and strengthen Chinese control there (Chen Yuke et al. 1933), offered a brief contemporary account of the educational efforts of the Young missionaries and found much that was good about it ("I do not see it as cultural invasion," etc.). Nevertheless, he urged that Burmese should be replaced with Chinese as the main language of instruction and that Chinese should be promoted in general.[70] In his argument that this would be feasible (contrary to the belief of many), he pointed to the fact that the Youngs had in fact been able to turn Wild Wa into Christians ("impressing and transforming them by infiltrating them with their Jesuism"), here using traditional Chinese terms for activist civilization, *ganhua* (to impress, or render in awe, and transform). He concluded that they also ought to be able to learn Chinese (Lu Guofan 1933: 8), and he was, of course, correct in this regard.

British and Chinese imperialism are obviously kindred in spirit. Yet regardless of the distinction of Christianity as a vanguard of Western imperialism and colonialism, there is also a deep affinity between the Lahu and Wa prophet-saviors and the foreign Christians. These cults are necessarily syncretistic, in practice drawing on older, traditional value systems that not even the jealously intolerant Christianity could ever completely displace. This is a function and also a hallmark of the peripheral situation as such. When no alternatives seem to be in sight, faith in salvation and miraculous deliverance from this predicament is ever present as a hope against hope.

Notes

1. For discussions of millennial movements in mainland Southeast Asia and China, see for example Stern 1968, Chatthip Nartsupha 1984; Cheung 1995, Zeng 1995; globally, Christianity itself is an example—and is itself the very origin of the term "millennial."
2. Compare Cheung 1995; Tapp 1989, 2005.
3. On this process, see also chapter II.2 in my PhD dissertation (2000). The so-called *gaitu guiliu* policies involved the abolishment of "native chief" (*tusi*) offices (see the introduction) and their replacement with appointed officials. Ma Jianxiong assembles the evidence for Lahu "rebellions" against Chinese rule, found in Chinese historical compilations (1997: 36–46).
4. The Lahu are first identified in Chinese documents on the Nanzhao state (ca. eighth century), northern Yunnan, among the peoples on its peripheries, but they weren't known as Lahu (or Luohei) until the Yuan dynasty (Ma Jianxiong 1997: 25, citing *Lahuzu* 1985: I:1). Some Lahu people began to grow tea and involved themselves in the Shan regional tea trade (Hill 1989, citing Jiang 1983: 365–71, 373; Chen Hansheng 1949). On the Lahu more generally, see also Telford 1937; Bradley 1979; the *Lahuzu jianshi* 1986; the *Lancang Lahuzu zizhixian zhi* [Lancang gazetteer] 1996; and Fei Xiaotong 1955; as well as Walker 2003; Walker 1992, 2014, etc.; Kataoka 1998, 2013; etc.; Du Shanshan 2002; Ma 2012a, 2013b; etc.; also, Young 1991 (on the Lahu of Thailand).
5. Evans-Pritchard 1956: 308; on Nuer prophets also Johnson 1994.
6. On G'uisha as the supreme Lahu deity (but also a *primus inter pares*), see Telford 1937: 170ff., 223–30; and Walker 1974: 700, 706; also Kataoka 2013.
7. On Lahu borrowings from Shan Buddhism, see Telford 1937: 172; for borrowings from Chinese Buddhism, see Ma Jianxiong 1997: 42–46; Walker 2014.
8. *Yunnan tongzhi*, cited in Ma Jianxiong 1997: 42; also discussing a Chinese-Buddhist Lahu movement near Menglian, which competed with the Shan Theravada Buddhist temples there in the early nineteenth century (citing the *Pu'erh fu zhi gaoben* from 1900).
9. In the late nineteenth century, both the Lahu and the Wa were among the largest producers of opium in the region (Scott and Hardiman 1900: II.1:355). Similarly to areas under the influence of indigenous cults, Christian villages also generally refrained from producing or using either opium or liquor. See Fang Guoyu 1943e, on his journey across Lahu country, from Mengdong to Munai and Lancang, in 1935–36; and below.
10. I was told that during the era of Wa independence, if anyone was found to have taken up opium use, fellow clan members would show up on their doorstep as a group and strongly discourage them. This method was apparently quite effective.
11. The Burmese-Chinese wars in the frontier region during the 1760s weakened the Shan polities of the area and made it possible for some Lahu to break free from them (*Simao Yuxi Honghe Daizu shehui lishi diaocha* 1985: 2–3). On the Lahu messianic movements, see Walker 1974; etc.; Qian Ning 1997a, 1997b; Kataoka 2013.
12. Dang Meng 1905, "Wubei zhi," 16.31a,ff.; *Lancang Lahuzu zizhixian zhi* 1996: 5, *Shuangjiang Lahu zu Wa zu Bulangzu Daizu Zizhi xian zhi* [Shuangjiang gazetteer] 1995: 10; *Simao Yuxi Honghe Daizu shehui lishi diaocha* 1985: 8–9, etc.
13. This occurred as the Chinese state was reasserting itself in the region after the suppression of the great Panthay (Chinese Muslim) rebellion of 1855–73 (mentioned in chapter 4, on mining).
14. See Dang Meng 1905: "Wubei zhi," 17.35a (this uses a Shan name for the Wa leader: Dao Wenlin, a *yaoren*, or "witch"); see also the *Lancang Lahuzu zizhixian zhi* 1996:

6; *Shuangjiang Lahuzu Wazu Bulangzu Daizu Zizhi xian zhi* 1995: 621; on Peng Kun (1854–1928), see the biography in the same Shuangjiang gazetteer, 858–59.
15. H. Young, in Barton 1933: 112–13; on these Lahu struggles, see also Peng Gui'e 1926; Ruey 1948.
16. *Lancang Lahuzu zizhixian zhi* 1996: 5; see also 673ff. regarding several remaining Lahu Buddhist temples in other parts of Lancang County. On Sanfozu, see also *Ximeng Wazu zizhixian zhi* [Gazetteer of Ximeng] 1997: 29, 261, 395; Li 1987: 42ff.; Ma Jianxiong 1997: 45.
17. Sanfozu was succeeded by his son-in-law, Li Tongming (1861–1901), who had also arrived in Ximeng in 1874 (biography in the *Ximeng Wazu zizhixian zhi* 1997: 395–96).
18. *Wazu diaocha cailiao* 1962 [1980]: 6, 32–36. Like the Lahu, the Lisu are Tibeto-Burman speakers, who have also migrated into the area from the north.
19. *Lancang Lahuzu zizhixian zhi* 1996: 5, also the *Qing shi gao* (*zhi, juan* 74, 49, *dili* 21: "Zhenbian zhiliting"). Some of the Lahu of the area previously under Sanfozu had already been lost, not to Chinese rule but to the nominally autonomous *tusi* of Menglian, to the south of Ximeng, where they came to be ruled by Menglian-appointed Wa village headmen. Some also obtained assurances from the independent Wa in the Ximeng area that they would not be attacked by headhunters (Gong Peihua et al. 1982: 41).
20. This constant search for new allies and alliances was a feature of the universe of galactic polities (Tambiah 1976, 1985), which involved not only the Shan princes shifting between Burma and China but also other actors, like Sanfozu. The recent county gazetteer says Sanfozu was visited and courted by Scott in 1890 (*Ximeng Wazu zizhixian zhi* 1997: 261), which is incorrect—it happened in early 1893. Scott had never visited before then (Scott's handwritten diary, 1893).
21. On these markets, see too Fiskesjö 2000: chap. 2.2.
22. Telford 1937: 144; Walker 1974: 702ff. Walker also discusses yet another Lahu prophet active in the same area and in much the same manner, in the 1970s.
23. Walker 1974: 701, citing Young 1905b: 11.
24. He is almost like a modern-day Glieh Neh, cf. chapter 5; or, because of his semi-foreign origin, like a belated Wa version of the famous Stranger-King (cf. Sahlins 2008; Liang Yongjia 2011).
25. On these missionary activities, see Barton 1933 (incl. the "Depositions" by W. M. Young and Harold Young; Peng Gui'e 1926: 75ff.; Lu Guofan 1933; *Wazu jianshi*; and the missiological account in Covell 1995: 222–41 [esp. chap. 10: "Cutting the Ancient Cords: The Lahu and Wa Are Liberated from Ancient Demons"], and Li 1987 (an M.A. thesis devoted to the Young family). Both Covell and Li cite unpublished materials in several American Baptist archives that may well hold many further materials of interest regarding the Wa. I have not been able to see all of these archival materials (such as those at the Ray Buker Archives at the Denver Conservative Baptist Seminary, Denver, Colorado), but some are available in the ABFMS microform records that the University of Chicago Library has purchased on my request (many thanks to our librarians, including Chris Winters, and to the librarians at the American Baptist Archives in Valley Forge, Pennsylvania).

In addition to the American Baptists, there were China Inland Mission (CIM) missionaries, mostly British but some American (Allyn Cooke and Carl Gowman, among others), based at Fuyinshan (Fuhinshan) near Mengding and working mainly among the Lisu but also on the outskirts of Wa country (Barton 1933: 36–37; Crossman 1982: 119; Covell 1995: 237; on Fraser's work among the Lisu farther to the west, see also Fife 1981). Furthermore, Swedish Pentecostal missionaries worked in nearby Gengma, chiefly among Lahu people. They "ceded" their converts to the American Baptists in 1926 in connection with territorial divisions between the Baptists and the CIM (Covell 1995: 236; R. Buker, letter from the Lahu and Wa Mission, 31 May 1927; ABFMS, FM 233-3-9; also W. Young, "A Brief Review of the Work on This Field for 1927," from Bana, Mong Lem, China, 21 January 1928, FM 264-5-2; Johannesson 1996).

26. W. Young, letters to T. S. Barbour dated 22 November 1904 and 4 April 1905; ABFMS, FM 213-1-5. (On the Wa Küt of Burma, see Fiskesjö 2000, chap. 2.2).
27. W. Young, letter to T. S. Barbour, 4 April 1905; ABFMS, FM 213-1-7, p. 8. He probably meant distilled liquor, rather than the native rice beer (cf. chap. 3).
28. W. Young; American Baptist Shan Mission Annual Report 1904, ABFMS, FM 213-1-5.
29. These were probably in the Shan script (the most widely used writing system in the region, along with Chinese), as Young the elder knew only Shan (Li 1987: 36, 71). As mentioned, Young's sons later learned both Wa and Lahu. Vincent Young devised writing systems for both Wa and Lahu (both of which are still in use, with modifications), and translated a number of Bible texts into Wa.
30. This story is still remembered in Shuangjiang (Li 1987: 42ff., citing a communication from Professor Wang Jingliu, Yunnan Institute of Nationalities, in Kunming).
31. Young 1906: 214; Young, letter to T. S. Barbour, 4 April 1905; ABFMS, FM 213-1-7, pp. 5ff.; also Covell 1995: 228–29; Kataoka 1998.
32. Young, letter to T.S. Barbour, 5 November 1904; ABFMS, FM 213-1-5, p. 2.
33. Young, letter to T. S. Barbour, 4 April 1905; ABFMS, FM 213-1-7, p. 5 ff.
34. William Young, too, mentions a widespread story originating with the Kaw people of Kengtung that the Kaw also once had writing inscribed on a buffalo skin, which they foolishly sold for food. For similar myths regarding the lack of writing, see Enwall 1994; Cheung 1995: 241; also, Oppitz 2008a; and Scott 2009—the most intriguing aspect of this remarkable book by Scott may be the insight that, regardless of the actual origin of writing, the recent historical lack of writing among many mountain peoples has been seized upon by them as a self-defining character, by which they create a potent contrast between themselves and the civilized, and indeed, as Scott suggests, become more difficult to trace for the states eyeing them.
35. In Wa country today, one also sometimes hears the story that the people simply ate the buffalo skin with writing on it, which they had, because they were hungry (e.g., Shang Zhonghao et al. 1989: 37–39); but I have more often heard writing described as originating from Glieh Neh, the Wa "Confucius" mentioned earlier (chapter 5); still, it was the people who lost it—once again engaging in self-blame over not being able to appreciate the value of what Glieh Neh was up to.
36. My emphasis. Young, letter of 2 October 1905, ABFMS FM 213-2-1, p. 3–4. I do not know the origin of the term Pu Sam, but if it indeed derives from the Wa language it might be a variant on the structure "ba . . .," which means "those who . . ." (there is, for example, a common Wa term, *ba jao*, which refers to "those who officiate [at ceremonies]; *sam* would then be a verb: "to preach"?).
37. Young, Annual Report, American Baptist Shan Mission at Kengtung, 2 February 1907; ABFMS FM 213-2-2, p. 2.
38. The so-called Kaishin Wa did not have a separate language and did not form a separate ethnic group. That is, at least not yet. The Kaishin Wa of the late nineteenth and early twentieth centuries are comparable to the Bulang, or Blang, who are Wa-turned-Buddhists.

39. Young, letter to T. S. Barbour, 26 September 1906; ABFMS, FM 213-2-3. On Wa headhunting and war, see chapter 6.
40. "They gave up headhunting long ago, and most of the grosser practices of the so called wild Wa people. . . . This matter of the Kaishin Wa is of [the utmost] importance. It makes it much easier to work them. We can first go to those people who have more recently given up the cruel practices of headhunting and other things in connection with evil spirit worship." (Young, letter to F. P. Haggard, ABMU Boston, 20 September 1906, ABFMS FM 213-2-3). See also letter to T. S. Barbour, 26 September 1906 (also in FM 213-2-3; with a special report on the Kaishin Wa field).
41. The Catholics were, however, denied access to the (Burmese) Wa country by the British, along with all other Europeans (Maganza 1975: 86).
42. Lu Guofan 1933; *Lahuzu jianshi* 1986: 41. In Chinese sources Nuofu (= Lofu) in Lancang is always given as the Youngs' main base on Chinese territory. The church there still stands, having been restored as a historical monument. One sometimes antimissionary Chinese account suggests that Young was first denied permission to settle at Menglian itself, then was able to obtain permission from the Yunnan government (sometimes known as a "warlord government"), and finally was allowed to "rent" the "deserted hill" of Nuofu by paying 1,000 Burmese dollars to the Menglian *xuanwusi* (*Lahuzu jianshi* 1986: 41). The village of Nuofu belonged to the Quanhai district of the Nine "Circles" (*quan*, or *ken*) ruled by Menglian (*Lahuzu jianshi* 1986: 53; on the shaky tributary relations between Nuofu area Lahu villages and the Shan ruler at Menglian, see pp. 52–56). After arriving at Menglian in 1920, the American Baptists established two permanent stations at two locations, to the south and east of Ximeng and the headhunting country respectively: Bana (e.g., = Nuofu, which mainly served areas of Lancang, including the Shang Gaixin or "Upper" Gaixin area), and Mongmong (= Mengmeng or Shuangjiang, built later, from which the Bukers extended the work into the Meng Tum (Mengdong) area and also came into contact with the China Inland Mission work in Gengma to the north) (W. M. Young, n.d. [1927]; also Li 1987: 60–61, citing this document under two different titles. Li seems to suggest [Li 1987: 47] that "Lofu" was but a field "missionary station" opened by the Youngs to supplement the more permanent station at "Mongmong" [Mengmeng, or Shuangjiang]).
43. Fifteen thousand or more Wa had been "taught" there, including thirty-five hundred classed as "noncivilized" Wa (those that were *sheng*, "raw," who had "not yet returned-to-the-fold" [*wei guihua*], e.g., who had previously been outside of Chinese administration altogether). They only "educated" about the same number of Lahu as Wa in these areas (Lu Guofan 1933: 7–8).
44. For example, the British Consul at Szemao (Simao) in Yunnan conveyed such warnings to Young in 1905: "The Chinese officials unite with myself in eulogizing the estimable motives which actuate you in engaging in this good [missionary] work. It is followed by their best wishes and mine. But in undertaking it they would suggest caution, circumspection, and care. They cannot assume responsibility for personal safety, especially where dealings with the Kawas (Was) are in question" (cited in Young, letter of 2 October 1905, ABFMS, FM 213-1-5, 3-4).
45. See also below on the preferences for victims of headhunting (chapter 5).
46. There appear to have been two such attempts: First, in late 1924 (W. Young, letter from Bana, 18 February 1925; ABFMS FM 264-4-11), and then in 1933 (V. Young, letter from the Wa and Lahu Mission at Bana, 14 August 1933, 2-3; ABFMS, FM 307-2-6). In the latter incident, they apparently escaped death by ambush because a gun failed to fire properly, something that was taken as a bad omen. Otherwise, unconfirmed rumor suggested, the killers would have received a prize from the Chinese officials (or

opium dealers?) who had instigated them. In any case, the missionaries turned around since there were reports of many more such ambushes waiting for them farther into Wa country. The missionaries still suspected that local Chinese officials had planned to use the Wa and then lay the blame on them also.

47. R. Buker, report from the Lahu and Wa Mission, 4 May 1927, 2; ABFMS, FM 233-3-9.
48. It seems Buker never published any of his findings. In 1933(?), while studying at the Andover-Newton Theological Seminary and at Harvard University for a master of theology degree (in a furlough year between two postings), he took anthropology courses and wrote a paper on "Headhunters of Southeast Asia." According to a somewhat whimsical biography based on interviews with Buker, he included observations of the Wa in this paper (Fife 1981: 125–26).
49. R. Buker, letter of 16 April 1928; ABFMS, FM 233-3-10. The mission suffered setbacks when this Christian Wa leader died several years later (H. Young, letter of 25 June 1934; ABFMS, FM 307-2-4), and the villages were burned by Chinese soldiers during the Boundary Commission work in 1935–36 (Circular Letter, from the Lahu and Wa Mission of 15 January 1937; ABFMS, FM 307-2-5). Fang Guoyu (1943d: 10) held that the circle was despised by other Wa for having "given in to the British."
50. Covell 1995: 231ff.; Fife 1981.
51. Emphasis in original. R. Buker, letter from the Lahu and Wa Mission, Yawng Rok, 16 April 1928; ABFMS, FM 233-3-10.
52. R. Buker, letter from the Lahu and Wa Mission, Meng Meng, 21 January 1930; ABFMS FM 279-5-2. Buker also noted the opposition among pastors to reducing the privileges they were accustomed to (letter to the ABFMS from Kengtung on 15 July 1930; ABFMS, FM 279-5-4). Note that "ordinary villages" here does not refer to the central Wa country but to the periphery on which the missionaries were active.
53. R. Buker, letter from the Lahu and Wa Mission, 31 May 1927; ABFMS, FM 233-3-9.
54. "Christianity has been preached as a way to get a free ticket to the Big Missionaries drug supply. Mr. Y[oung] has not so preached, but his teachers have" (R. Buker, in a letter from the Lahu and Wa Mission at Yawng Rok, 16 April 1928; ABFMS, FM 233-3-10).
55. These requests were made at the highest levels, building on charges of gun trading, failure to teach Chinese in missionary schools, etc. The accused missionaries hinted in their internal correspondence that such charges originated with petty local officials who saw them as a threat to opium or liquor revenues. In addition, they admitted that when the missionary work was extended into new non-Christian areas, this oftentimes led to persecution of new converts and incidents that came to the attention of higher Chinese officials (H. Young, letter of 8 February 1934; ABFMS, FM 307-2-4). William Young was in the United States on furlough and died there in 1936. His son Vincent returned, but the ABFMS acquiesced to a Chinese request that Harold Young not return to Chinese territory. Instead, he went to the Burma side (circular letter from the Lahu and Wa Mission, of 15 January 1937; ABFMS, FM 307-2-5, etc.). Years later, when Vincent Young also was forced to leave, and met with difficulties on his return, Raymond Buker praised him as a superb translator into Lahu (letter of 16 January 1958; ABFMS, FM 368-3-4).
56. W. Young, letter with copy of Chinese complaints forwarded by the US consul at Yunnanfu, 1 June 1922; ABFMS, FM 264-4-8. See also Fang Guoyu 1943e, citing the 1935 complaints against the missionaries by Tian Jun, a Chinese administrator posted at the Lahu township of Muga, just east of central Wa country, where Christian Lahus refused to drink or grow opium and avoided bringing internal legal disputes for judgment by Chinese authorities. Incidentally, these kinds of Chinese accusations

are basically the same as those levied against Wa religious specialists later, when they were attacked, and their authority dismantled in the 1950s and 1960s; they are of course also inseparable from the missionaries' own definition of native Wa religious life as "evil spirit worship" (see chapter 8).
57. Casto (1937: 152), of the China Inland Mission. On this local generosity see chapter 1. This-worldly investments of the native converts are also evident as the underlying element in the territorial disputes that arose between the different Baptist missionaries, regarding, for example, the prohibition against converts of one territory performing "public" missionary work (road repairs, church construction, etc.) in the other territory, and so on.
58. R. Buker, letter to W. E. Wiatt from Maymyo, Burma, 29 November 1930; ABFMS, FM 279-5-2.
59. For example, one such "Lahu fanatic who calls himself a god" told the people that they "need not pay attention to other rulers or laws," and solicited offerings from among his following west of the Bana station near Menglian (H. Young, letters from the Mong Lem Lahu Mission [at Bana] 22 February and 2 April 1932; ABFMS, FM 307-2-3). During the immediate postwar years, a similar savior arose in Manglun State in the southernmost part of the Wa country (Mangleng). He too claimed he was not born a mortal—he was invincible. He impressed people by playing the Lahu gourd pipe while dancing on branches of trees, and appeared to have called for a rebellion, which was suppressed with the aid of the missionaries (letter by Mrs. Ruth Young, 11 June 1947, ABFMS, Reel 332).
60. On this movement, see also Young, letter to F. P. Haggard, ABMU Boston, 20 September 1906, ABFMS, FM 213-2-3; also the letter to T. S. Barbour, ABMU Boston, 14 January 1907, where Young mentions that the charismatic Wa leader of this movement had been killed by a Lahu. The movement appears to have ended after this assassination, the circumstances of which are unclear (one might readily suspect either rivalries within and between the various cults in the frontier area or agents of the nearby states). In any case, some of the followers of this unnamed leader later became Young's pastors.
61. The younger missionary Harold Young (the son of W. M. Young) showed some sympathy for such new religious leaders, even implicitly criticizing the British. But one similar Lahu leader (the "fanatic" Chalei) who had taken refuge at Monghka/Ximeng in independent Wa country, was enticed out of there by the Chinese authorities and "jailed at Syenlawt (Chuanlo) and put to death in his cell" (H. Young, in Barton 1933: 112).
62. Buker, letter to the ABFMS on 5 April 1939; ABFMS, FM 279-5-2; H. Young, letter 25 June 1934, in 307-2-4; and Fiskesjö 2000, chap. 2.2.
63. Interestingly, several such reports mention that Chinese officials threatened the converted Lahu and Wa villages and requested that they give up the foreign religion. They went so far as to restore the traditional spirit altars in the houses of some village chiefs and to issue fines if they did not keep them (W. Young, letter from Bana Village, Mong Lem, 15 October 1923, p. 2; ABFMS, FM 264-4-9; V. Young, letter from the Wa and Lahu Mission at Bana, 14 August 1933, p. 2; ABFMS, FM 307-2-6).
64. Harold Young, letter from the Lahu and Wa Mission relocated to Lashio, Burma, 2 May 1936; ABFMS, FM 307-2-5.
65. See, for example, Harold Young's letter of 6 December 6, 1934; ABFMS, FM 307-2-4.
66. On Mangleng (Manglun, etc.), see above (chapter 4). The mission still held some attraction, especially so in these turbulent times when Chinese robber bands with several hundred members roamed the area with looted army weapons at their disposal.

For example, it was visited by eleven delegates from four chiefs of central Wa country in June 1948: "They brought gifts of Wa bags and skirts and silver ornaments and money, along with letters from the chiefs of four different Wa sections representing over 5000 people. They had ... decided that they wanted to be part of America ..." (Ruth Young's letter of 27 June 1948; ABFMS, Reel 352).

67. Including Harold Young, operating out of the mixed (Wa, Shan, Lahu) Manglun State in the southernmost part of the Wa country (also known in Chinese as Mangleng). See the reports submitted by Mrs. Ruth Young, ABFMS, Reel 332. At the time of the establishment of independent Burma, he initially remained, "invited by the Constituent Assembly to stay," along with only two other foreigners, both British citizens whose services were also needed (R. Young, 1 October 1947; ABFMS, Reel 332), but who eventually also had to leave Burma. Before leaving, he was involved in putting down another, much more widespread rebellion in the wild Wa states themselves (R. Young, 4 March 1948; ABFMS, Reel 332). Little is known about this rebellion, but official news reports in the English-language Rangoon newspaper *New Times of Burma* from 20 and 21 May 1948 indicate that the Wa had sought to obtain independence from Burma when the British withdrew: "Some of the wild Was, remote from authentic news, were led to believe ... that the British have withdrawn from Burma, that the Burmese Government who has succeeded it has no strength behind it and that the time has come for the Was to strike for independence. The Was ... had acquired modern weapons in the troubled days of the war. They staged a little rebellion. They soon found that the Union Government have plenty of armed troops and modern weapons." It is not clear how these events relate to the British-Burmese "Burma Frontier Areas Committee of Enquiry," which operated in 1947, and presented its final report in April that year: recommendations as to the administration of all the various frontier areas (non-Burman areas) of the new independent Union of Burma, in 1948 (see the introduction). Harold Young was still employed in "suppressing rebellions" (which also seems to have involved neutralizing Chinese bandit groups) in early 1949, but was forced to leave, later in the year (R. Young, letters of 13 January and 25 October 1949; ABFMS, Reel 352; Vincent Young, letter from Kengtung of 28 September 1953, ABFMS, Reel 396).

68. Vincent Young continued to work the Wa and Lahu field in China from Kengtung, in Burma. Many Christians in China fled to Burma, though "the reputation of the Wa people in general is of such a nature that the Chinese Communists have been very cautious in their dealings with them, so far" (letter from Kengtung of 28 September 1953, ABFMS, Reel 396). Some of the native pastors left behind in Lahu and Wa country were active up until 1958, when their churches were closed at the time of the Great Leap Forward, not to re-open until 1961; they were then closed again in 1966 and not permitted to reopen until after the Cultural Revolution (around 1980). (Li 1987: 91, citing Lei Hong'an 1984: 80, a work I have not been able to locate). Not just Christian converts but the general population fled back and forth to Burma throughout these difficult decades.

69. It did not even matter to the China Inland Mission (CIM) worker that the Wild Wa country in question, "an unadministered section of British Upper Burma," would "fall within the field allotted to the American Baptist Mission who now have stations at Bana and Meng Meng." Generally, on missionaries under European colonialism, see William Hackett in the *South East Asia Journal of Theology*: "The political realities of the late eighteenth, and early nineteenth centuries, when Western colonial powers were in the ascendancy, contributed to the thinking of missionary-minded churches and boards. Benefits of Western civilization and Christian dogma were inextricably

intertwined, so that in later days there was enough truth in the charge that Christian missions were hand in glove with imperialistic designs of colonial powers, to make the criticism hurt. The advanced, superior peoples of the west looked upon themselves as the saviors of the heathen, and motives of political domination, economic exploitation and religious conversion became so confused that we are still having a try to divorce them . . ." (1969: 64–65).
70. Already in 1927, the Chinese authorities requested the Youngs to use Chinese in education. This was difficult, as the Youngs had only studied Shan, Lahu, and Wa, but they later hired Christianized Chinese teachers who also taught the Chinese language.

10

THE POWER OF THE EXOTIC

Negotiating the Future

The Wa people have long occupied a special place in the state-directed political spectacle of minority nationalities, both in modern China and in Burma.* In China today, state policy promotes commercial entrepreneurs who mine the new Chinese nostalgia for "primitive-exotic" peoples like the Wa. This fascination also builds on older Chinese views of the Wa as dangerous barbarians, but it closely evokes other "primitivist" and Disneyesque spectacles from around the world today.

One of the strangest expressions of this new trend is how the "Wild" Wa headhunting paraphernalia prohibited by the Chinese in the 1950s now reappears as kitsch in new Chinese-built ethno-theme parks. This new repackaging of "primitive violence" as exotic material typically sets aside the Wa people's own understanding of their culture and ignores their own attempts to revive aspects of their cultural past as they look to the future. Paradoxically, what can seem like an all-encompassing domination of the Wa still offers some new possibilities for a Wa cultural revival. In this chapter, I first consider how this story plays out in a Wa theme park at Ximeng, in the old Wa country right near the border with Burma, and then at the much larger for-profit ethno-theme park in Shenzhen, the distant Chinese coastal megacity just outside Hong Kong.

The Wa Homeland as Theme Park

The recently built Wa festival ground in the county town of Ximeng, near China's modern border with Burma, also doubles as a theme park. In one spot, a large number of water buffalo skulls have been piled up in a cave-like hill site wrapped

---

Endnotes for this chapter begin on page 265.

in green forest foliage, and with a headhunter's head container (*njouh*) added for good measure. These adornments are meant to be tokens of a mysterious Wa culture, to entice Chinese and other tourists. Yet the whole site and its design is a brazenly inaccurate invention, purporting to represent Wa traditions drawn from war and from competitive feasting—both defunct since the annexation of the Wa lands by China in the 1950s—but gravely misrepresenting them.

In the old days, buffalo skulls would not be preserved in a mystery cave. They would instead be laid out at the home of the host of feasts that measured social prestige—an example of the "feast of merit" widely practiced across highland Southeast Asia (Lehman 1989; see also chapter 6). In this grotesque Ximeng grotto installation, however, Chinese domestic ethnotourist entrepreneurs have arranged the skulls in a semi-hidden place—obviously to evoke a Chinese feeling of mystery about the Wa as practitioners of ancient and mysterious blood sacrifices of buffalo and people.

The term *grotesque* is very much justified here, since it originally referred to the profane art hidden away in cave-like palace ruins in Rome (Dacos 1969; Summers 2003)—thus the word, from Italian *grottesco* and Latin *grotto*. Since then, grotesque has come to mean "outlandish" or "transgressive" (Connelly 2003; Diederich 2008); I use it here to evoke the Chinese view of something exotic-transgressive that has been tamed by design, for tourist viewing. Tourists are meant to understand that sacrificial victims' remains are stashed away here. But the display is off—it is very different from the intentionally public historical display of buffalo skulls as prestige tokens, which was common in Wa villages in the past. Then, no one would put away the remains of their feasts of merit in a hidden cave; they would put them up front outside their own house, to make the most of the meritorious deed (see illustrations from the 1950s in Li Jiarui and Li Yaoping 2011). The only reason this is not done today is simply because people can no longer afford it, and because communal sacrifices have largely been forbidden since the 1950s. On some occasions a Chinese official may still arrange a public killing of a buffalo, an appropriation of the ritual as an empty gesture toward "ancient custom." Yet in the invented narratives of the Wa as primitives that underpin today's theme park versions of Wa culture, these crucial aspects of the Wa past are generally either absent or heavily distorted.

Let's recall how British colonial officers in Burma, despite their tentative recognition that the Wa were really no ordinary primitives, also quite similarly reveled in interpreting them as primitives. As with today's Chinese tourist reappropriation of the buffalo skulls, the colonial administrator James George Scott chose to read the forked wooden posts he saw in Wa village centers, placed near the appropriate patriclan drum shrine, as signs of primitive folly (Scott 1896, 1906, etc.). But in reality, these posts, like the buffalo skull display signaling the grandeur of recently hosted feasts, were also intended to broadcast and boast about the number of feasts hosted by each household. Wa wealth was dispensed in "traditional" redistributive feasting, building temporary prestige with these markers, yet at the same time preventing the rise of social hierarchy and reconfirming the egalitarian Wa society (chapter 4). It's clear that the forked tree posts Scott tendentiously interpreted as a sign of sacrificial primitivity were actually a precursor to the grotesque cast of buffalo skulls we see today in the theme park cave at Ximeng.

During the first few decades of New China, Chinese authorities—and their Burmese Communist allies in what is now Wa State—were bent on wiping out traditional Wa culture. They especially targeted the crucial log drums, the symbolic backbone of Wa society and a focal point of Wa patriclans, and also rites such as the buffalo sacrifices, which also embodied Wa power. Many of the huge log drums were dragged away from their drum houses (or temples), and burned or discarded on both sides of the border.

Then, in the 1980s, as part of their overall shift away from a pure socialist economy, Chinese state authorities abolished the work point system of the Peoples' Communes and rescinded the socialist planned-economy micromanagement of local people's lives in other aspects as well. This is when the state authorities, as if by default, permitted a certain revival of some cherished local traditions—such as rice beer production, which was forbidden under Mao as "wasteful" (see chapter 3).

In the new era, while state control remains forceful—and in some areas is even being reasserted yet again, since the 2010s especially—private Chinese and other entrepreneurs, often themselves state employees, have been allowed almost a free hand in exploiting local natural resources (e.g., plantations of tea, sugar cane, mining, and agroforestry)—as long as they do not oppose the state.[1] The tourism entrepreneurships arose from this same money-making drive. These exploitations often play out on land that was traditionally collectively owned by the Wa "realms" (*jaig'qee*) but which now is free for the taking, in the name of development, even as profits go elsewhere. Wa farmers can join in as best they can (although they don't have investment capital for tree saplings, etc.), or they can become plantation workers, or, in many cases they can leave to become migrant laborers (chapter 5).

Somewhat surprisingly, there is still among the Wa in this "Chinese era" a lingering sense of a unique identity and even superiority. Given the simultaneous sense of a catastrophic, utter defeat of their old world in the 1950s, this is an almost schizophrenic, or at least profoundly ambivalent, sentiment. The sense of superiority is based in past Wa power, wealth, and glory, and also on the origin myths that give the Wa a unique role as pioneers in the original human settlement of this earth (chapter 2). Many still regard themselves as custodians of the ground zero of human history, and therefore they shoulder a special burden in caring for the potent gods of the region—even now, after the end of their autonomy and amid the drastic reduction of their region to, in effect, just one more exploited peasant economy on China's margins.

I also met many older Wa who blame their own people for the catastrophic demise of their autonomy in the 1950s, and they insist that the old communal rituals connected with the headhunting past should not be revived. They believe it was a failure of "nurturing" the gods, and any revival, including pretend reenactments, would constitute irreverence, which the spirits might punish. Theirs was an argument for letting go.

When the first reenactments of the cutting and installation of a new log drum were done by Chinese filmmakers and ethnographers in the mid-1980s, young people were warned by such elders not to take part. As mentioned in chapter 6, I met a woman whose husband divorced her and asked her to leave his household after she developed epilepsy and kept rolling into the fire during her nighttime attacks. It was all widely seen as retribution for her participation as an actress in one such staged video, where she dressed in traditional costume and accompanied the mock drum as it was dragged home by a large crowd.

As in the case of the theme park buffalo grotto, the people engaged in recording authentic Wa culture are mostly not rural locals but a mix of enterprising Chinese scholars and ethnic Wa officials, all inspired by the new, more permissive climate of the late 1980s and 1990s. Their Chinese education had taught all of them that Wa culture was a primitive mix of deplorable traits to be rectified and fascinating exoticism worthy of exploitation. In the case of the cadres, they had been prepared to serve at an intermediary level in administering the Wa lands for China within the post-1950s framework of "minority nationalities," mostly rectifying them but now also reveling in their dances, buffalo skull traditions, and so on. Taken together, they have crafted a striking example of "orientalism," a mix of condescension and reverence, as defined by Baumann and Gingrich (2004; more on this point below).

During the Mao era, Wa songs and dances and other "folkloristic" minority cultural phenomena could only be appropriated to show adulation for Mao and his regime. Now, "authentic" Wa culture can be actively appropriated and put on stage, in carefully choreographed performances that celebrate a sanitized Wa culture. Still, these performances must avoid any subject too closely related to taboo topics like past independence or warfare.

Before the theme parks started up in the 1990s, the huge log drums were only occasionally recreated, but these were not shaped properly and were made only for decorative purposes. Such drums are still safely kept in the lobbies of local government and Communist Party headquarters, as if to signal the true location of power in the "Chinese era." (It's like how, nowadays, the only buffalo-spearing ceremonies are held by local Chinese Communist Party dignitaries.)

An official socialist-era image had been created of the Wa. They now found themselves as members of the happy family of nationalities within the unified Chinese nation, in which a Soviet-style recognition of lingering but slowly vanishing minority peoples was the core idea (Fiskesjö 2006). Like other peoples, such as the Uyghurs in Western China, they have been mobilized since the 1950s as exotic dancers full of primitive energy, now safe, sanitized and harnessed under the Communist Party's command—a socialist-era version of Wa primitivity. County dance troupes typically performed on confined stages in political centers (county towns, and the like), in socialist-era purpose-built theater halls designed to separate seated audiences from the performers.

One stock element of these performances was a traditional Wa women's hair-shaking dance, which nowadays is seldom seen in rural Wa settings but after the 1950s takeover of the Wa lands were rearranged and performed by daughters of city cadres of Wa, Chinese, or mixed Wa-Chinese ancestry, who were often brought up without the Wa language. This dance became a classic if not indispensable element in such performances of Wa primitivity. The reason is much the same as why it is now always featured in the new theme park repertoires: it harnesses the appearance of traditional Wa culture as a way of indulging in the alluring sexuality of female dancers' bodies and movements—first, for the pleasure of the new class of town-based cadres in charge of administering the annexed territories, and then for profit, for the amusement of Chinese tourists.[2] The Wa tellingly use a borrowed Chinese word, *tiaowu* (dance) for all such Chinese-style staged dances. Their own indigenous word, *ngroh* (dance) is reserved for their own social dancing (such as the traditional, now revived, "dancing in" of a new house).

To the general Wa population, the spectacles staged since the beginning of the socialist era have seemed quite remote. Rural Wa would rarely even see such performances, since they were mainly staged for town-dwelling audiences, with Communist and government leaders sitting in the front row. In the Mao years, occasionally, this genre of "improved" Wa culture would be taken on the road in the form of a traveling *gewu tuan*, the official county-government song-and-dance troupe. But trips to rural areas were largely abandoned after the shift in Chinese politics after Mao.

In the 1980s, the Wa cadres and Chinese folklorists who started to initiate reenactments of traditional rituals were testing the limits of government policy. At the same time, the Wa among them were also beginning to seek to redefine themselves and their people, and as we shall see, they too had to recognize the potential of the exotic Wa culture in the new, emerging market sector of the economy. In this they were later joined by the new kind of for-profit Chinese entrepreneurs who were typically uninterested in the culture and cared only for its commercial potential.

In the "reform" era, China's elite set aside the hollowed-out socialist-Marxist ideology that had tabooed private enterprise, and instead embraced private capitalism insofar as it remained under party control and existed alongside key state-held industries that would not be relinquished. In this new world of state capitalism with Chinese characteristics, people are still obliged to adhere to socialism in name, and also to the reformulated post-1980s teleology of Chinese civilization that now emphasizes nationalism instead of class struggle (Fiskesjö 2010c). It is in this situation that a new landscape of commercial enterprise in tourism and culture has formed—one promoted by the state, whose agents often also profit.[3]

These developments have already undermined or shifted many earlier assumptions. Chinese officials may still see themselves as the banner carriers of Chinese civilization, believing in the manifest destiny of Chinese assimilation, but they may be more interested in making money. So it was with Wa cadres concerned with capturing and preserving a pure and authentic Wa culture, even if their motives were also different (mostly nostalgic). Even the opinions of "defeatist" Wa elders in rural areas were undermined by seeing young Wa joining Chinese spectacles and the theme park industry as performers pretending to be themselves. More on this below.

New technology also entered into the picture. Chinese entrepreneurs began to produce VCDs, DVDs, and other media of Wa cultural life, such as Wa girls (or Chinese girls dressed as Wa) performing their alluring hair-shaking dances, or young men beating drums, among others. Much is produced around Shenzhen, the sister city of Hong Kong, where one of the major ethno-theme parks in China was established in 1992. Large quantities of commercial videos are shipped back to marketplaces in the Wa lands.

New generations of the Wa people who grew up under Chinese rule and never saw the original events in their own villages are understandably fascinated with these recreations of Wa culture, even though they are produced by outsiders. People may often be aware of the issues of authenticity and appropriation (about which they can do nothing), yet they do not primarily concern themselves with these problems. They are also not troubled by how VCD spectacles are performed in Chinese, the language that dominates the marketplace, which for many young people is the only language they learn in school (if they go to school). This is often the case even in the Wa State on the Burma side of the border.

Instead, younger people are often appreciative of the depiction of the Wa conveyed in these Chinese renderings. It is a picture of the Wa as primitive, yes, but also as vigorous, energetic, and thus perhaps also proud and powerful. It may be that they appreciate this imagery all the more greatly because its qualities contrast with the daily realities not just of Wa life under subjugation, poverty, and dependence but also of the drug addiction and associated HIV/AIDS afflictions that have plagued the China-Burma borderlands in recent years (Liu Shao-hua 2010), not to speak of the economic despair among young Wa laborers who are forced to migrate for work in China, Burma, and beyond (chapter 5).

In the early 2000s, many people in rural areas bought TV monitors and VCD/DVD players and would regularly spend evenings watching these staged performances. This contrasts with what I observed during my initial fieldwork in the Wa lands in the mid- to late 1990s, when there was often no TV (no broadcast signal or monitors). Sometimes, there was just one television per village, often bought by a shop owner who would then charge a fee for village children (rarely adults) to watch kung fu movies bought or rented from Chinese marketplaces. At that time, the Wa VCDs did not yet exist, and at night many still engaged in the *a peak*, the time-honored Wa "evening conversation."

The Theme Parks of the New Market Economy Era

The explosion of choreographed spectacles of Wa vigor has reshaped the way young people see their own past and perceive their identity. The documentaries of the 1980s and their quest for authentic reconstructions have largely been abandoned; in their place we see the entrepreneurial reappropriation of everything Wa, including the symbols of the "headhunting" past, the log drums, the buffalo skulls, and so on. In several places, and most notably in the Chinese Wa counties of Ximeng and Cangyuan near the Burma border, local political elites have joined with opportunistic entrepreneurs to invest in fairgrounds and festivals that double as theme park–style attractions for tourists, even resurrecting previously forbidden paraphernalia for their attractions, as we have seen with the buffalo grotto and other installations at Ximeng. In the neighboring Lincang district, a curious new mud-slinging festival has been invented from scratch to attract tourists,[4] and in Cangyuan Autonomous Wa County an entire thatched-roof village near the county seat has been recreated and frozen in time as an explicitly primitivist-tourist destination.[5]

At Ximeng, the theme park there was created on a former sportsground (the classical Chinese socialist-era festival ground on which political parades were, and sometimes still are, performed). On the adjacent hillside, Wa houses were built to represent the different constituencies of the county, and rural citizens could stay in them when attending a parade or festival—but later, in 2014, part of the hillside was appropriated for a high-end jungle hotel project. Spectacles for new generations of locals are regularly staged here, often every other year since the early 2000s, outshining those previously staged indoors in the country theaters or in studios for DVD/VCDs recordings. These performances are also captured for video productions, which apparently also help to financially underwrite the recurring festival.

The fairground walkway is lined with *njouh*, which is outrageous. As mentioned in chapter 6 (on headhunting warfare), the *njouh* are bamboo poles with a basket-like container at the top, which is supposed to hold a freshly cut head. Such use of *njouh* as decoration outside of any real war would be a complete affront to the older Wa, who are opposed to such revivals. But then, elderly rural people rarely visit the festival ground, and they have no say in the design.

For anyone familiar with the Wa past, the festival ground would be an eerie experience. But that eerie quality does not register with younger Wa—especially not those raised in the mixed Chinese-Wa towns or the tourist-entrepreneur cadres. They all see the spectacle as unproblematically drawing on a primitive past, their attitude predicated on a disconnect from those societies that actually participated in such warfare. Yet a scholar like myself is also frustrated with these types of blatant appropriations and the multiple ways in which such installations distort the Wa past, here representing the *njouh* as a token attribute and not as an instrument integral to Wa warfare.

This display occurs only a few steps from the downtown area of the county seat, only just recently relocated from the much older opium transit town also known as Ximeng, which has become a smaller market center up in the mountains above. As usual in peripheral areas in China, street banners typically continue to urge faith in the ever-strengthening rule and continued victories of the Chinese Communist Party. At the same time, there is a new civilizational chic in this new Ximeng, which indulges in the type of imitation Greek architecture that would signify a desirable Western modernity to most urban Chinese elsewhere in the country—such styles are of course copied from Chinese cities. And so it is that today, in the cadre-town of Ximeng, the song-and-dance troupe officials and performers now live a Greek-imitation modernity, in direct, civilized contrast to the primitive and mysterious Wa culture presented at the suburban fairground just nearby.

At the fairground, the contrast is played up by grotesquely oversized reproductions of Wa drums, which tower over mass-produced normal-sized log drums of the same kind once placed in Wa drum houses that were burned in the 1950s and 1960s. In what is perhaps an unintended mockery, one house is billed the "O-lang fang," the "house of the O Lang [chieftain]," that is, the residence of the traditional Wa chieftain (see chapter 5). This position was one of the key indigenous institutions terminated by the Chinese after 1958, and while his residence used to be deeply symbolic, at the fairground it is now the site of a restaurant. This recycling of indigenous political institutions as exotic kitsch is also encountered both at primitivist tourist destinations (Liu 2013: 177–78) and at the ethno-theme parks in Chinese cities (see below). The remodeled Ximeng hillside also includes several more odd sideshows, such as full-scale copies of the ancient Wa rock paintings found in neighboring Cangyuan County. (Authentic rock art has never been found in the Ximeng area).

The Ximeng megadrum is not for beating but purely for display. It features a buffalo design that again has no direct basis in Wa tradition but suggests the fusion of the sacrificial buffalo with the drum as an imaginary Wa totem (indeed "primitive totem" is a favorite term of tourist brochure language). Its towering size truly implies the reduction of the Wa people. However, once again, we must note that the design is no affront to new generations of Wa people. It is better than nothing, and for them, the design happily recalls the angry bull logo of the popular Chinese-made knockoff Chicago Bulls caps, which are widely worn by Wa young men precisely to appropriate the Chicago Bulls' image of a powerful buffalo.

The festivals held here are visited by local Chinese and town-dwelling Wa cadres, and by a few people from rural areas. It is difficult to attract crowds of domestic Chinese tourists, who flock instead to more easily accessible locations in the province. But this would-be theme park, however detached from ordinary people on this peasant periphery, has taken on a strange significance: it is simultaneously a festival ground offering tourists a way to consume Wa exotics and, at least potentially, a celebratory space of the Wa as a vigorous people—albeit all within precise limits of political and economic control.

Dark Exotics as Ethno-Theme Park Commodities: The Wa in the City

The Wa areas are quite distant from Chinese population centers, so domestic tourist agencies struggle to attract profitable numbers of domestic Chinese visitors to the "pristinely primitive" Wengding Wa village in Cangyuan, to Ximeng, or to other sites. The obvious alternative is to bring the primitive Wa to the city for them to appear in theme parks that are more conveniently located. One of the first such for-profit theme parks was built next to the government-financed Yunnan Museum of Nationalities, in Kunming, the provincial capital of Yunnan, which prides itself on its ethnic mosaic as something attractive for tourists. Another such park is located outside Beijing, the national capital. The Chinese ethno-theme park package is a new industry, modeled on international precedents, but with distinct Chinese characteristics. It is currently being exported to places around Asia, such as Cambodia, and even to Africa.[6]

Shenzhen is a new megacity built next to Hong Kong in order to dwarf it. Since 1992, it has featured a huge ethno-theme park known under the combined name of its two sections: Splendid China—Folk Cultural Villages. The park is quite well known even among Wa people in the distant Wa lands, because many young Wa dancers have since worked there as performers, in both sections.[7] The park is a for-profit commercial venture, financed by mainland and Hong Kong Chinese investors.[8]

The "China Folk Cultural Villages" section is a vast area with houses and other settings that evoke most of the fifty-five official ethnic minorities in China. Some are quite limited, but about a dozen of them are fully staffed by ethnic minority guides. The guides lead tours and perform titillating dance dramas, which are attended by regular crowds of domestic tourists, Korean charter groups, and some other foreigners.

The "Splendid China" section highlights similar aspects of mainstream or Han China, including models of the Great Wall, Tiananmen Square, and other landmarks. There are also grand and lavish, if highly kitschy, dance presentations that laud Chinese culture. In these shows, Wa and other ethnic minority dancers also perform—not pretending to be themselves as they would in their own show across the park but playing part of an overall Chinese narrative of glorious national origins. Wa dancers can earn extra overtime money by participating in these events, which add to the meager salaries they are paid for performing at their Wa theme park "village."

Wa performances are actually among the most well attended. The Wa are famous as wild exotics, and according to numerous witnesses and participants, their dark Wa skin color also helps to attract crowds. To many visiting domestic tourists, the appearance of the Wa confirms their exotic otherness, contrasting with the visitors' own civilized selves. This is reinforced in the setting, which

Figure 10.1. Wa dancers at the Shenzhen theme park. Photo by the author, 2015.

prominently includes buffalo skulls, *njouh* head poles, and substantial "primitive" houses on raised poles. It is also an element of the dance choreography, which includes the Wa dancers waving spears and swords in front of the audience and beating log drums. It is also evident in the costumes that reveal as much naked skin as possible, particularly in that obligatory, mesmerizing women's hair-dance—a staple of each "wild" performance. All of it is designed and choreographed by the company, not the performers.

The relatively dark skin color of many Wa, like that of other Mon-Khmer-speaking peoples (such as the Khmer, of Cambodia), can be partly attributed to the fact that they descend from one of the oldest population strata immigrating into South and Southeast Asia. Even more importantly, they have lived continuously, over several millennia, at latitudes farther to the south than the lighter-skinned northern-derived populations that dominate China today—which largely descend from ancient East Asian agriculturalist populations that have greatly expanded southward over the last two millennia.[9] The biological reasons that explain the darkness of southerners like the Wa is the same as in Europe, Africa, and so on (Jablonski 2012). Some Wa actually have skin as dark as anyone in Africa, or elsewhere.

To the self-identified civilized Chinese, the dark-skinned Wa present a mix of allure and repulsion—which again is very similar to European attitudes, at least in bygone eras, toward dark-skinned Africans. Many Chinese people today still maintain an instinctive negativity toward people with dark skin while priding themselves on their whiteness, but they also find the allure of the dark-complexioned Wa fascinating. This makes the dark skin of the Wa itself a major selling point for the theme park show, and it also serves as a hiring criterion: light-complexioned Wa need not apply.

Down the road in Shenzhen is another theme park, called Windows on the World, where young Wa dancers also work—but they perform there as Africans, New Zealand Maori, and American Indians. The park also has white Eastern European ice-skating performers featured for their own exotic value, but the three main ethno-racial categories of African, Maori, and American Indians in this park are entirely performed by Wa dancers, often from the very same region of Southwestern China as those working just down the road at the "Folk Villages."

When I visited the air-conditioned "African hut" of the Wa performers in the Africa section, they emphasized to me that large portions of the Chinese tourists actually do think they *are* real Africans, etc. Chinese tourists often try to speak to them in their limited English, calling out a "Hello!"—they assume that "Africans" speak this international lingua franca, and *hello* is often the only foreign word they know. Ironically, most of the Wa performers don't speak any English at all. However—and this is the most amazing part of the ethno-theme park known as Windows on the World—this hasn't prevented them from interacting with the occasional genuine visitor from Africa. Some had provided the "fake" Wa "Africans" with real music videos, featuring contemporary African music, for reference, and one of the African numbers they performed during my visit was an excellent stage dance program of contemporary West African pop music, complete with lip-synched lyrics in Lingala, the main language of Zaire's fabled *soukous* tradition. The Wa singer from Cangyuan who led the show at times seemed to capture the high style of the great African singer-diva Mbilia Bel.

While the Wa performers are reported to have since been fired and replaced with real African dancers (in 2020), for a brief time these young Wa were clearly able to display a creative flair for global-transnational cultural exchange, even while they staff this Chinese-designed and tightly choreographed freak-show-like performance (other numbers they were made to perform included grossly inaccurate pieces such as "The African Man and His Four Wives.")

The performers I met certainly had a high degree of self-awareness, as well as deep knowledge of their own cultural traditions. One of the dancers among those employed "pretending to be themselves" at the "China Folk Cultural Villages," selling Wa exotics to thousands of Chinese tourists, explained to me in 2012 how the company-commissioned "Wa log drums" are actually poorly made imitations. They are not properly hollowed out, as a real Wa drum would be, so they don't yield the same astonishing far-reaching beats as the real drums. When I heard this I was deeply impressed—my interlocutor would have grown up without any such drums, since they were destroyed long ago, in his home village and beyond. But even a young Wa person far from home clearly can be very much aware of such matters.

This might serve to illustrate real as opposed to appropriated authenticity. It also exemplifies both sophistication and frustration, evident in the dancers' current situation, and their self-knowledge and awareness. They work at the theme park because they prefer the performer's contract to the assembly lines of nearby Chinese factories. But they also resent their situation, not least the minimal salary levels, similar to those of factory workers. Often their pay is low, less than 2,000 RMB per month (about 300 USD), which makes it difficult to save much due to the high cost of living in Shenzhen. Moreover, as for authenticity, ownership, and sovereignty, even as they sometimes host fellow villagers on their days off from the factories, who come and enjoy the fakery of their fellow countrymen, they still know that they are performing an imitation of something that could belong to them, and benefit them.

Performed Primitivity and Its Unexpected Potential

As mentioned, many Wa are actually not categorically opposed to the many inaccurate, even grotesque, for-profit Chinese appropriations of their culture. On the contrary, the new generations especially appreciate that it casts them in a role of a certain strength, whether "primitive" or not. They even know that the fake drums, buffalo skulls, and *njouh* head poles all lack in authenticity relative to actual practices terminated in the 1950s and 1960s. But this matters less: just like older people who witnessed the old society with their own eyes, those of the younger generation also know that these mystifications are unfaithful to their own culture and history.

The issue of authenticity is fuzzy. For one thing, it is compounded by the fact that almost every Wa locale had its own way of doing things, like variations on a shared theme. Even the number of days in the week was a different count in different places (yet synchronized around Shan market days, I should add). Moreover, the eyewitnesses to the past might not transmit exactly what the local tradition was. As in other places around the world (see, for example, Valeri 2001 [1994]), elders guarding such traditions often see their knowledge as their social leverage. It may be the only asset they can use to secure a position of power and respect in society, especially given that their bodily strength is fading and they cannot fend for themselves in food production, house construction, or other areas. I myself encountered elders who refused to tell me things, preferring to take it to their graves. In today's situation they may think that "all is lost." But even in the society of old, such elders would not take lightly the transmission of knowledge about the actual traditions of the past. Some today will simply let youngsters commit whatever foolish acts they want—in Wa society, people are free to do what they like. And the elders may not be believed, even if they did speak out. The combined effect of these circumstances and attitudes (especially the radically different relation to what others may call "heritage") can explain why there are no evening classes in local culture. There is only real-life transmission of knowledge, to eligible local apprentices only.

Younger generations today have grown up entirely under Chinese domination, or what they call the "Chinese era" (the Pax Sinica). Yet the memory, even if badly distorted, of amassed buffalo skulls, log drums, or human head posts (even if empty, fake, etc.) can still help suggest the prowess of their forebears. This is not a bad thing *in the present*.

The term "indigenous" is largely disallowed in China,[10] yet the younger Wa, as the indigenous and autochthonous inhabitants of this land, may tactically endorse their own exoticization and mystification. They may choose to do so, to present themselves as a culture be reckoned with. This is why, unlike older people, they can relish taking part in this "revival" even if it is really a reinvention, or even a fake.

For the Chinese, in contrast, the entire enterprise of "celebrating" and mocking the Wa serves to hide the violence of the Chinese conquest of the region, allowing the "barbarism" it provoked to be "consumed" in the feast of the theme park spectacle. It's a bit like how the Americans conquered the Native peoples there:

"They killed the Indians, then stole their culture." In Chinese terms, it is of course not presented as a history of conquest (cf. Fiskesjö 2017b). Instead, its main significance is meant to be how the Chinese are the saviors of the Wa. They "save" them by virtue of their supposedly superior capabilities and historically superior position, from which they deign to hand down the treasures of modernity and development to the primitive, backward Wa.

Even though this is never made fully explicit, the key concept of the theme parks is ultimately the celebration *of the identity of the Chinese themselves* as a conquering civilization. It celebrates both the past imperial Chinese efforts of civilizing-at-a-distance (the Wa being one of those distant people who didn't directly encounter the imperial state until the nineteenth century) and their project of direct intervention carried out in Wa areas since the 1950s.

A few years ago, Baumann and Gingrich (2004) put forward a highly interesting and provocative proposition, a theoretical scheme presented under the rubric of "grammars of identity/alterity." If we look at the Chinese "civilized" self-identity and their staging of the Wa as exotic primitives who play the role of contrasting confirmation, we may first conclude that it exemplifies their "grammar of *encompassment*": The Wa are cast as inferior, subsidiary, and voiceless (silenced), yet conceptualized at the same time as constituent parts of the Chinese body politic. They are cast as members of the elusive meta-entity known as *Zhonghua minzu* or "Chinese nation," which includes both the many different state-recognized ethnic minorities and the Han Chinese, linked together not just historically but also genetically-biologically, so as to join in what is not a historical but a natural body of the state, into which newly conquered Others are ingested, or incorporated (Fiskesjö 1999a; 2006). Yet at the same time, the "celebration" of the Wa as energetic, boisterous, dancing primitives (exemplified in the obsession with the loud drums, the hair-shaking dance, and even "headhunting" paraphernalia/kitsch), also suggests an *Orientalizing* fascination with the Wa as a tantalizing Other, whose irrational, primitive, violent traditions hold some fascination in themselves.

Somewhat strangely, this Chinese fascination seems tainted by reluctance, sadness, and melodrama. In private, Chinese Communist Party officials will often lament that the implication of the official evolutionist framework to which they adhere (something that is directly inherited from the imperial Chinese theory of civilization) is that Wa culture and other such recent conquests will soon inevitably be extinct, and their intriguing attractions will be extinct with them. This is the burden of the Chinese officials whose thinking really is a version of classic colonialism: for them, Wa culture, while fascinating in some regards, is mainly an impediment to progress and development, and as such, since it is a hopelessly primitive culture and not viable, it is destined to be annihilated through Chinese assimilation.

The Baumann and Gingrich typology of grammars does not address this temporal-developmental aspect of the evolutionist theory of civilization, in which the superior culture, by manifest destiny, encompasses and obliterates the primitives altogether, despite the exotic qualities that would seem appealing from an Orientalist point of view. Orientalism may thus be fit for those cases where the imperial metropolis is stalling, incapable of carrying out the encompassment that would go with colonization and assimilation. Instead, people may become locked in mutual admiration coupled with contempt.

Friedman (1994, 1998, etc.) and others have linked the production of identities to the political-economic constellations in which they figure—that is, within the larger cycles of socioeconomic processes that make and break the foundations of different kinds of identities. In this most fertile interpretation, self-identity as developed on *both* sides of the Wa-Chinese historical relation (in the course of their mutual relation *as primitive and civilized*) is to be understood as produced within those real historical processes in which these identity conceptions are formed. This here means the expansive structure of the imperial-Chinese encompassing stance, with its open-ended civilizing program, as well as the Wa, one of the targets of that civilizing machine. The Wa are relegated first to the role of a primitive periphery, and then lose their voice altogether. Even with the token spectacles and theme parks and the like, the silencing "encompassment" of empire is in effect erasing them, and reducing them to just another voiceless Chinese peasant periphery.

The Wa indeed seem to be under assault, a devastating, overwhelming assault that has also severely divided them internally. As mentioned, there is widespread resignation to their new status as a subjugated and impoverished minority on the margins of the states to which they de facto belong. This can be seen as a form of resignation to the terms of a Pax Sinica, in effect a Chinese-defined grammar of encompassment. Being slowly erased, they can only carve out whatever benefits and self-worth they can gain while they still have time.

To be sure, Chinese colonization and assimilation is still incomplete. The historical Wa sense of martial invincibility and unique superiority still survives, serving as a sort of alternate model of equals among peers and deploying what Baumann and Gingrich called the "segmentary" grammar (yes, borrowed from Evans-Pritchard) under which the Wa would have their own voice as the equals of the Chinese, the Burmese, and so on. (Incidentally, this is the grammar that underpins the idea of the United Nations, equal and without a king).

A key difference remains: in the past, autonomous Wa were able to regenerate their society and the ideologies and mythologies that sustained it; however, as they now find themselves in a subordinated situation, they become, over time, less able to formulate their relation to outside powers on their own terms. Recognizing that past Wa political independence coexisted with deep economic interdependences, Friedman (1998: 341) described the Wa as follows: "Unlike the usual peripheral zones of larger centers of civilization, predatory structures are independent *insofar as the maintenance of their internal organization does not depend on their integration in a larger reproductive process*" (my emphasis; see also Friedman 1998: 35).

The key part here is that they "maintain" themselves—nobody is taking down and burning their log drums, they build and keep their shrines as they please. The "predatory" part refers to how the Wa and others like them turned the tables on the menacing states that surrounded them, raiding and harassing them. While the Wa developed commercial ties to the wider region through mining, the opium trade, and more, the egalitarian Wa orchestrated formidable displays of seemingly "primitive" violence, deterring powerful outsiders by instilling fear through highly effective rumors about headhunting, as well as by their readiness for real war (Fiskesjö 2010a; cf. chapters 4 and 6). This is an indirect product of forces exerting themselves on the Wa in the past era of independence, but these forces were not yet able to destroy the self-reproduction of an independent Wa society—and its self-image or identity.

This also recalls Turner's comments on Brazilian anti-myths, where native "society is confronted with a 'natural,' anti-social force it cannot contain, co-opt or reproduce within its own structure." Thus, while myth, as in the basic myths of cultural origin, "explains the possibility and the essential nature of native society[,] anti-myth explains its limits and inferiority in relation to Brazilian society" (Turner 1988: 256; also Da Matta 1971). "The anti-myth . . . provides at once an appropriate ideological representation and *an apt program for this type of [limited and inferior] native society, inasmuch as it remains able to define the alien encompassing society in terms of its own internal social reproduction*" (Turner 1988: 258; my emphasis).

That ability is what was lost in the 1950s during the catastrophic end of Wa autonomy. Afterward, their society's internal organization has largely come to depend on the larger reproductive processes of the Chinese state—down to how many children you can have, and when, and including the economic incentives that have caused a massive drainage of both women and men away from the Wa lands (see chapter 5).

In this context, the Chinese exoticization of the Wa as they remain appears as another kind of "heritage abuse" (Haviser 2011). Yet we can see how the Wa themselves have not yet wholly lost their voice. In the course of their exoticization, as we have seen, they are regaining and refashioning certain instruments of their tradition and manipulating them for their own purposes. While they have to "play the primitive," they are using some of the tools they were previously barred from possessing according to Chinese government command as well as their own elders' resigned disapproval.

The combined theme park and festival ground at Ximeng was set up by a strange combination of agents of the state, including state-sanctioned Chinese adventurers looking for exotic profits, and town-dwelling Wa who have joined the Chinese-trained managerial class of middlemen. Yet, paradoxically, the creation of venues like this, and the reenactment of such sites in rural settlements, can offer a space where Wa pride in the long-devastated past of "wild" and "primitive" Wa self-governance can be expressed and articulated. It is a new kind of space that didn't exist in the Socialist era, yet now it does. We can't tell what will happen on this new stage. Will the drummers and dancers continue to reenact the fake traditions seen on their televisions after the tourist show is over, or will they invent something new? Perhaps they will. There have been examples (despite the lack of capital, among other things) of Wa entrepreneurs themselves selling their culture as performance while keeping charge of the choreography. This is certainly one small possible way the Wa can combine the fragments of their shattered past with inspiration from other colonized peoples' reinventions to eventually reproduce and recast themselves once more, in their own new voice.

Notes

* This chapter draws in part on my 2015 article, "Wa Grotesque: Headhunting Theme Parks and the Chinese Nostalgia for Primitive Contemporaries," in "Primitivist Tourism," special issue, *Ethnos* 80(4): 497–523.

1. Some call it "postsocialist," but this is not fully correct in China's state-led market economy, with state enterprises under government control and society under a party-state dictatorship. On reform-era China and its market economy, see Nonini 2008. Today, the Communist Party is reasserting itself with cells in every private company, as well as people's lives (see the epilogue).
2. Compare Mueggler 2002; also Notar 2007; Nyiri 2006.
3. See, for example, Broudehoux 2004; Ren 2007; Oakes 2013; also Zhang 2018.
4. This newly created festival, in which participants and tourists smear themselves with mud, implicitly yet unmistakably plays on the Chinese idea that the Wa are dirty. It contrasts uncomfortably with the widespread Tai (Dai) water-splashing festival, also massively exploited for tourist-entrepreneurial purposes today.
5. This village was long prevented from switching from the traditional houses on stilts and made from wood and bamboo, to the brick or concrete structures that the Chinese government is aggressively promoting everywhere else (despite the earthquake dangers). See Liu 2013; on primitivist tourism targeting the Wa in this area (Cangyuan) see also Coulouma 2019.
6. The Cambodian Cultural Village in Siem Reap, Cambodia (which I visited in 2012 and 2014), like many such international ventures, involves Chinese investors, as well as the same conceptual package for choreographing the ethnic primitives, often for Chinese tourists. In Siem Reap, this involves several ethnocultural cousins of the Wa, though for the lack of native manpower, these Cambodian minorities are impersonated by Khmer dancers. Here I omit a large corpus of literature on theme parks globally, but on Indonesia see Bruner 2005 (esp. 211–30, "Taman Mini: Self-Constructions in an Ethnic Theme Park in Indonesia").

7. Most performers come from my former fieldwork areas in the China-Burma border region. One young man recognized me from an encounter long ago, in 1996, back in his mountain village, when he was ten years old and I visited his village for the day.
8. For further discussions of this megapark see Tapp 1993; Campanella 1995; Anagnost 1997: chap. 7; Pun 2003; Ren 2005, 2007; Stanley and Chung 2005; also Yang 2011 on migrant workers' perspectives; and Tamara Gordon's 2005 film *Global Villages: The Globalization of Ethnic Display*. (Apart from Tapp and Gordon, these items mostly focus only on the "Splendid China" and not the ethnic portion of the park).
9. Fiskesjö and Hsing 2011. Incidentally, recent genetics research affirms, to a certain extent, the Wa view of themselves as an ancient people.
10. So that the tension between Chinese settlers and aboriginal peoples on the former imperial peripheries can be suppressed (see Sturgeon 2007).

Epilogue

Dark Clouds Gathering

In 2017, the Chinese government launched a massive forced assimilation campaign targeting the over twelve million indigenous Uyghurs, Kazakhs, and other ethnic minorities in the Xinjiang Uyghur Autonomous Region, in the westernmost part of China.

Since 2017, several million have gone through a force-conversion procedure, from their native ethnic identities into Han Chinese, carried out inside massive concentration camps (Leibold 2019a, 2019b; Roberts 2020; Fiskesjö 2020b, 2021). The gigantic campaign also includes mass sterilizations, forced family separations, the mass confiscation of hundreds of thousands of children who will be raised in Chinese only, and other forms of cultural erasure. Indigenous languages and cultures in Xinjiang (Chinese for the "New Frontier," of the last empire) are harshly discriminated against, and indigenous cultural heritage is systematically bulldozed—including Uyghur graveyards, mosques, saint's tombs, and other pilgrimage sites and memorials (Thum 2020; ASPI 2020).

These atrocities, including the vast concentration camps that apparently serve both as identity-conversion centers and as transit points for forced labor arrangements (ASPI 2020), are continuing unabated as I write this, showing no sign of being halted, despite considerable international protests (Buckley 2020). Taken together, the campaign can only be described as a new form of genocide.

Moreover, these policies are also being extended to the Tibetans and the Mongols within China's borders. Both these peoples, like the Uyghurs, were once part of major nations that formerly had their own states, before being subdued by the past empires. Now their identities are also being suppressed, and their culture supplanted with the majority Han identity, to the point of forbidding their languages and forcibly introducing alien Han Chinese customs as a litmus test of loyalty.

All this seems to herald a fundamental, ominous shift in Chinese ethnopolitics. It raises questions about the future of Chinese ethnic minorities as a whole. Will the "minority nationalities," of which the Wa is one, even be permitted to exist in the future, let alone flourish on their own terms?

The constitutional rights in the People's Republic of China, which supposedly guarantee the recognition of minority cultures and the uninterrupted use of ethnic languages, are clearly being brazenly set aside. It is true that the rights of indigenous peoples in China have actually long been hollowed out: the government has long pursued assimilation through its policies, albeit at a slower pace, as I discussed in chapter 2 on Wa names and naming. Government policies have long been "directed at destroying the possibility that non-Chinese national identity might have any political meaning, at destroying the minorities' capacity to think and engage in politics independently as sovereign ethnic groups" (Bulag 2010: 426).

However, today, with the recent rise of neo-nationalist ideology in China, and its political influence within the ruling Chinese Communist Party, the very question of the future of China's ethnic minorities as such, has arrived again (Leibold 2013). Today's Chinese neo-nationalists, who are also surfing a global wave of narrow-minded intolerance, are arguing for the rapid and forced homogenization of a unitary and modern Chinese nation that would stand as a glorious successor to the conquest empires of the past. Today's identity-conversion camps in Xinjiang suggest these ideologues have already brought about a dramatic policy shift in this direction—despite the immense suffering, and cost.

The modern national space of China, including the numerous distinct minority nations—with altogether about 120 million people today—that inhabit this space, is of course part of an unresolved legacy from the conquest empires of the past. In this perspective, the new policy shift toward cultural intolerance and the virtual extermination of distinct minority cultures is another chapter in the unresolved Chinese struggle over the meaning of this imperial legacy in the modern world (Fiskesjö 2017b).

Once, before the Chinese Communists came to power, they promised the nations conquered by the empires past (such as the Tibetans, the Miao, and so on) that they would allow them to retain their independence, and even to secede if they so preferred (Fiskesjö 2006). After 1949, this promise was withdrawn, and a Soviet-style system was enacted that has existed until recently, and still exists, on paper. It provided only for a hollow autonomy, yet it still afforded a certain level of recognition of these nations' right to exist, to have and use their own language, and so on. Now, while the current regime increasingly hail the past empires as ancestral predecessors of the modern state, the delegitimization and assimilation of minorities, rather than their continued recognition, seems to have become the new direction of the state.

What will this mean for people like the Wa, who lost their autonomy a half century ago, who number only a million people, and have been the target of assimilation policies ever since that time? I realize in hindsight that when I did research among the Wa in the 1990s and 2000s, I was witnessing a period of cultural revival and relative openness and tolerance. This followed on the brutal years of the "Cultural Revolution" under Mao, which devastated local societies and cultures—even rice beer was outlawed. The period of revival enabled the reconstruction and reinvention of Wa culture—similar to what was also happening in Xinjiang and other places, within that same period.

Wa culture, like those of all minorities and former nations within the Chinese state, has also been faced with a different, economic challenge: the forces of economic integration with China's economy have turned many locals into laborers on their own ancestral lands, and also relentlessly press many able young Wa and other ethnic minority people to become migrant laborers in Eastern China. They are forced to absent themselves for work, leaving few people back home to sustain new attempts to reformulate their culture in their original homeland. This has been a different, yet deeply serious kind of challenge; and now, it seems it will be combined with another new and even more dangerous assault: the ideologically motivated ultranationalist policies of intolerance, which seek to force-convert ethnic minorities to a majority Chinese identity and exterminate their distinct cultural potential. In many places, this also takes the form of "poverty alleviation schemes" designed to force-relocate and transform whole ethnic groups into Han Chinese, integrated as labor in the Chinese economy.

These challenges together may well exceed the destructive force of Mao's time, and they could wipe out the potential for the Wa (and other ethnic minority peoples) to hold charge of their own destiny—and even undo their existence as distinct peoples. In the prevailing frenzy of Chinese nationalism and chauvinism, we may indeed soon see the formal abolishment of the ethnic minorities as recognized since 1949 (though some tokens of otherness might remain in the zoo-like theme parks for Chinese tourists).

The situation of the Wa is somewhat special, in that half of their ancient lands ended up as part of Burma, forming today's Wa State. Although the military regime in Burma is also deeply distrusted among Burma's ethnic minorities, and Wa-language literacy, education, and cultural conscience has been systematically discouraged on both sides of the Wa border, it is also apparent that the very existence of the Wa State holds out a certain hope that the Wa may still survive into the future as a distinct people, similar to how Kazakh or Mongol identity is more difficult for the nationalist Chinese regime to erase, because there is a country of Kazakhstan and a country of Mongolia where these cultures can still flourish. (This does not pertain to the culture of the Uyghurs, whose population is based only inside China—and now, among exiles and refugees.)

Figure 11.1. The future of the Wa people. Schoolchildren in Wa State, Burma. Photo by the author, 2006.

The genocide now under way in the Uyghur region casts a dark shadow over the future. But no one should dismiss or underestimate the resourcefulness and creativity of Wa people when it comes to taking charge of themselves, sustaining and even reinventing themselves, even in a deeply dangerous and constantly shifting landscape.

REFERENCES

Note: Works without an identified author are listed by title, as are those compiled by institutes, committees, and other collective bodies. All other materials are arranged by the author's name. Chinese authors for publications in Chinese are listed in the Chinese order (surname and given name, without comma in between).

Also note: A good source for further materials on the Wa, as well as for Wa texts and transcriptions, is the website of the Wa Dictionary Project organized at SOAS, London (Watkins et al. 2006; also Watkins 2013b), with "A Bibliography of Materials in or about Wa Language and Culture." For more materials in all languages, see also my dissertation's bibliography (Fiskesjö 2000: 432–87); on older Chinese materials also Rong Ruoxi (1988), and for a recent Chinese-language review, Li Guo-ming and Yang Bao-kang (2006). Some Wa communities are also mounting a presence on the internet.

* * *

Achaya, K. T. 1994. *Indian Food: A Historical Companion*. Delhi: Oxford University Press.
Agamben, Giorgio. 1993. *The Coming Community*. Minneapolis: University of Minnesota Press.
———. 2000. *Means without End: Notes on Politics*. Minneapolis: University of Minnesota Press.
Ai San. 1992. "Daizu" [The Dai nationality]. In *Zhongguoren de xingming* [Surnames and names of China's peoples], edited by Zhang Lianfang, 317–24. Beijing: Shehui kexue.
Alleton, Viviane. 1993. *Les Chinois et la passion des noms*. Paris: Aubier.
American Baptist Foreign Mission Society (ABFMS, Valley Forge, Pennsylvania). N.d. *Records, 1817–1959*. Archive of missionaries William Young et al.; incl. microform reel FM-264.
American Ethnologist, 2006. Special issue: "IRBs, Bureaucratic Regulation, and Academic Freedom," 33(4): 477–548.

Anagnost, Ann. 1997. *National Past-Times: Narrative, Representation, and Power in Modern China.* Durham: Duke University Press, 1997.

Angwin, J.B.P. 1936. *Report of the Sino-Burmese Survey Party, For Season 1935-36 by Captain J.B.P. Angwin, R.E., Officer-in-Charge. (Confidential).* Rangoon: Superintendent, Government Printing and Stationary. British Library, Oriental & India Office Collections, Mss Eur E 252/32f.

Anker, Christien L. van den, and Jeroen Doomernik, eds. 2006. *Trafficking and Women's Rights.* Basingstoke: Palgrave Macmillan.

Ardeth Maung Thawnghmung. 2017. "Signs of Life in Myanmar's Nationwide Ceasefire Agreement? Finding a Way Forward." *Critical Asian Studies* 49(3): 379–95.

Aroonrut Wichienkeeo. 2002. "'Lua Leading Dogs, Toting Chaek, Carrying Chickens': Some Comments." In *Inter-ethnic Relations in the Making of Mainland Southeast Asia and Southwestern China*, edited by Hayashi Yukio and Aroonrut Wichienkeeo, 1–22. Chiang Rai: Center of Ethnic Studies.

Atwill, David. 2005. *The Chinese Sultanate: Islam, Ethnicity, and the Panthay Rebellion in Southwest China, 1856–1873.* Stanford, CA: Stanford University Press.

Aung-Thwin, Michael, and Maitrii Aung-Thwin. 2012. *A History of Myanmar since Ancient Times: Traditions and Transformations.* London: Reaktion Books.

Australian Strategic Policy Institute (ASPI). 2020. *The Xinjiang Data Project.* 23 September. Retrieved 27 September 2020 from https://xjdp.aspi.org.au.

Backus, Charles. 1981. *The Nan-Chao Kingdom and T'ang China's Southwestern Frontier.* Cambridge: Cambridge University Press.

Baird, I. G., and B. P. Shoemaker. 2007. "Unsettling Experiences: Internal Resettlement and International Aid Agencies in the Lao PDR." *Development and Change* 38(5): 865–88.

Barclay, Paul D. 2003. "'Gaining Confidence and Friendship' in Aborigine Country: Diplomacy, Drinking, and Debauchery on Japan's Southern Frontier." *Social Science Japan Journal* 6(1): 77–96.

Barton, G. E. 1933. *Barton's 1929 Wa Diary.* Rangoon: G.B.P.C.O.

Basso, Keith H. 1996. *Wisdom Sits in Places: Landscape and Language among the Western Apache.* Albuquerque: University of New Mexico Press.

Bastian, Adolf. 1866. *Die Völker des Östlichen Asien.* [Band I: *Die geschichte der Indochinesen*; Band II: *Reisen in Birma in den Jahren 1861-1862*]. Leipzig: O. Wigand [etc.].

Baumann, Gerd, and Andre Gingrich, eds. 2004. *Grammars of Identity/Alterity: A Structural Approach.* New York: Berghahn Books.

BBC. 2000. "Burma Drives Out Opium Farmers." 16 January. Retrieved 2 June 2014 from http://news.bbc.co.uk/2/hi/asia-pacific/605533.stm.

———. 2009. "Arrests in Chinese Slavery Case." 22 May. Retrieved 2 June 2014 from http://news.bbc.co.uk/2/hi/asia-pacific/8063038.stm.

Beech, Hannah. 2019. "Teenage Brides Trafficked to China Reveal Ordeal: 'Ma, I've Been Sold.'" *New York Times*, 17 August. Retrieved 20 January 2020 from https://www.nytimes.com/2019/08/17/world/asia/china-bride-trafficking.html.

Bello, David. 2005. "To Go Where No Han Could Go for Long: Malaria and the Qing Construction of Ethnic Administrative Space in Frontier Yunnan." *Modern China* 31(3): 283–317.

Bender, Mark. 2011. "Echoes from *Si gang lih*: Burao Yilu's 'Moon Mountain.'" *Asian Highlands Perspectives* 10: 99–128. Retrieved 20 January 2020 from https://www.academia.edu/8194487/AHP_10_Echoes_from_Si_gang_lih_Burao_Yilus_Moon_Mountain.

Bernet Kempers, A. J. 1988. *The Kettledrums of Southeast Asia: A Bronze Age World and Its Aftermath.* Brookfield, VT: A.A. Balkema.

Bernstein, Dennis, and Leslie Kean. 1996. "People of the Opiate: Burma's Ruling Junta Appears Willing to Addict an Entire Nation to Drugs." *The Nation* 263(20) (16 December): 11–17.

Bezlova, Antoaneta. 2007. "China: Feudal Custom of Getting 'Ghost Wives' Far from Dead." Inter Press Service News Agency, 27 June. Retrieved 20 January 2020 from http://www.ipsnews.net/text/news.asp?idnews=38333.

Biardeau, Madeleine. 1984. "The Sami Tree and the Sacrificial Buffalo." *Contributions to Indian Sociology* 18(1): 1–23.

Birns, Jack. 2003. *Assignment Shanghai: Photographs on the Eve of Revolution.* Edited by Carolyn Wakeman and Ken Light. Berkeley: University of California Press.

Blackmore, Michael. 1967. "The Ethnological Problems Connected with Nanchao." In *Symposium on Historical, Archaeological and Linguistic Studies on Southern China, Southeast Asia and the Hong Kong Region*, edited by F. S. Drake and W. Eberhard, 59–69. Hong Kong: Hong Kong University Press.

Bloch, Maurice E. F. 1998. *How We Think They Think: Anthropological Approaches to Cognition, Memory and Literacy.* Boulder, CO: Westview Press.

Blum, Susan D. 1997. "Naming Practices and the Power of Words in China." *Language in Society* 26(3): 357–79.

Bouan, Xavier. 2001. "Wa Alternative Development Project." In *Alternative Development: Sharing Good Practices, Facing Common Problems; Regional Seminar on Alternative Development for Illicit Crop Policies, Strategies and Actions, 16–19 July 2001, Taungyi, Myanmar*, 49–53. Bangkok: UNDCP Regional Centre for East Asia and the Pacific.

Brac de La Perrière, Bénédicte. 1999. "Le nom personel Birman." In *D'un nom a l'autre en Asie du Sud-Est: Approches ethnologiques*, edited by Josiane Massard-Vincent et Simonne Pauwels, 27–43. Paris: Karthala.

Bradley, David. 1979. *Lahu Dialects.* Oriental Monograph 23. Canberra: Australian National University, Faculty of Asian Studies.

Brandt Smith, C., Jr. 2012. *Look Out for the Headhunters.* Self-published. Retrieved 20 January 2020 from http://www.smashwords.com/books/view/216129.

Brassett, Philip R., and Cecilia Brassett. 2005. "Diachronic and Synchronic Overview of the Tujia Language of Central South China." *International Journal of the Sociology of Language* 173: 75–97.

Briggs, D. E., J. S. Hough, R. Stevens. 1981–82. *Malting and Brewing Science.* London: Chapman and Hall.

Broudehoux, Anne-Marie. 2004. *The Making and Selling of Post-Mao Beijing.* New York: Routledge.

Bruck, Gabriele vom, and Barbara Bodenhorn. 2006. "Entangled in Histories: An Introduction to the Anthropology of Names and Naming." In *The Anthropology of Names and Naming*, edited by Barbara Bodenhorn and Gabriele vom Bruck, 1–30. Cambridge: Cambridge University Press.

Bruner, Edward M., ed. 2005. *Culture on Tour: Ethnographies of Travel.* Chicago: University of Chicago Press.

Buckley, Chris. 2020. "Brushing Off Criticism, China's Xi Calls Policies in Xinjiang 'Totally Correct.'" *New York Times*, 26 September. Retrieved 27 September 2020 from https://www.nytimes.com/2020/09/26/world/asia/xi-jinping-china-xinjiang.html.

Bulag, Uradyn E. 2010. "Twentieth-Century China: Ethnic Assimilation and Intergroup Violence." In *Oxford Handbook of Genocide Studies*, edited by Donald Bloxham and A. Dirk Moses, 426–44. Oxford: Oxford University Press.

Burkill, I. H., W. Birtwistle, F. W. Foxworthy, J. B. Scrivenor, and J. G. Watson. 1935. *A Dictionary of the Economic Products of the Malay Peninsula*. London: Crown Agents for the Colonies.

Burling, Robbins. 1984. *Learning a Field Language*. Ann Arbor: University of Michigan Press.

Burma Frontier Areas Committee of Enquiry. 1947. *Report Presented to His Majesty's Government in the United Kingdom and the Government of Burma: Maymyo, 24th April 1947*. Vols. I–II. Rangoon: Superintendent, Government Printing and Stationery, Burma.

Busza, Joanna. 2004. "Sex Work and Migration: The Dangers of Oversimplification; A Case Study of Vietnamese Women in Cambodia." *Health and Human Rights* 7(2): 231–49.

Byon, Jae-hyon. 1979. *Local Gazetteers of Southwest China: A Handbook*. Parerga Occasional Papers on China 5. Seattle: University of Washington School of International Studies.

Cai Kui. 1984. "Jiefang qian Yunnan Ximeng Wazu de gaikuang—jianlun Longshan wenhua de yixie kanfa" [The circumstances of the Wa nationality of Ximeng, Yunnan, before liberation—with some views on Longshan culture]. *Shiqian yanjiu* 3: 95–99.

Cairns, Malcolm F., ed. 2007. *Voices from the Forest: Integrating Indigenous Knowledge into Sustainable Upland Farming*. Washington, DC: Resources for the Future.

———, ed. 2013. *Shifting Cultivation and Environmental Change: Indigenous People, Agriculture and Forest Conservation*. London: Routledge.

Caló, Ambra. 2013. *Trails of Bronze Drums across Early Southeast Asia: Exchange Routes and Connected Cultural Spheres*. Singapore: Institute of Southeast Asian Studies.

Camões, Luis Vaz de. 1973 [ca. 1572]. *Os Lusiadas*. Edited with an introduction and notes by Frank Pierce. Oxford: Clarendon Press.

Campanella, Thomas J. 1995. "China's Gardens of Time and Space." *Places* 10(3): 4–7. Retrieved 27 September 2020 from https://placesjournal.org/article/splendid-china/.

Casto, Mrs. J. H. 1937. "Bible Schools in Tribesland." *China's Millions* (North American ed., Toronto) 45(1): 6.

Chang, Wen-Chin. 2015. "Circulations via Tangyang, a Town in the Northern Shan State of Burma." In *Asia Inside Out: Connected Places*, edited by Eric Tagliacozzo, Helen F. Siu, and Peter C. Perdue, 243–70. Cambridge, MA: Harvard University Press.

Chao Tzang Yawnghwe (Eugene Thaike). 1987. *The Shan of Burma: Memoirs of a Shan Exile*. Singapore: Institute of Southeast Asian Studies.

Chatterjee, Indrani. 2006. "Slavery, Semantics, and the Sound of Silence." In *Slavery & South Asian History*, edited by Indrani Chatterjee and Richard M. Eaton, 287–315. Bloomington: Indiana University Press.

Chatthip Nartsupha. 1984. "The Ideology of 'Holy Men' Revolts in North East Thailand." In *History and Peasant Consciousness in South East Asia*, edited by Andrew Turton and Shigeharu Tanabe, 111–34. Osaka: Senri Ethnological Studies 13.

Cheesman, Nick. 2017. "How in Myanmar 'National Races' Came to Surpass Citizenship and Exclude Rohingya." *Journal of Contemporary Asia* 47(3): 461–83.

Chen Can. N.d. [ca. 1908]. *Huan Dian cun gao* [Collected writings from an official stationed in Yunnan]. Guiyang: Wentong shuju.

Chen Didan. 1985. "Weile paishe Wazu renmin ziji de xi: Dianshiju *Buluo mugusheng* paishe qiongying" [To film the Wa people's own drama: Glimpses from the filming of the TV drama *The sound of the tribal log drum*]. *Washan* 4: 58–59, ends on 29.

Ch'en Fa-Ch'in. 1964. "Wazu shangwei Chen Xingwu" [The Wa captain Chen Xingwu]. *Minzu huabao* [Nationalities Illustrated] 1(91): 20–21.

Chen, Han-sheng. 1949. *Frontier Land Systems in Southernmost China. A Comparative Study of Agrarian Problems and Social Organization among the Pai Yi People of Yunnan and the Kamba People of Sikang*. New York: Institute of Pacific Relations, International Secretariat.

Chen Meiwen. 2003. *Cong Mingming tan Guangxi Tianlin Pangu Yao ren de Goucheng yu Shengming de Laiyuan* [The formation of the Pangu Yao people of Tianlin, Guangxi, and the origin of life as seen from the perspective of naming practices]. Taipei: Tangshan.

Chen Ronghua. 2001. *Wa shan quan / Rom mgong Ba Raog* [The Wa mountain spring]. Kunming: Yunnan minzu.

Chen Weidong and Wang Youming. 1993. *Nbeen Oud Mgrong Goui Gon Ba Raog* [Customs and manners of the Wa (Baraog) people]. Kunming: Yunnan minzu.

Chen Yuke et al, ed. 1933. *Yunnan biandi wenti yanjiu* [Research on the problems of the border areas of Yunnan]. 2 vols. Kunming: Yunnan shengli Kunhua minzhong jiaoyuguan.

Chesnov, Ya. V. 1968. "Narod Kava" [The Kawa people]. In *Problemy etnografii i etniceskoi istorii narodov Vostocnii i yugo-vostocnoi Azii* [Issues in the ethnography and the ethnic history of the peoples of Eastern and Southeastern Asia], edited by G. G. Stratanovich, 137–82. Moscow: Isdatelstvo Nauka.

Cheung, Siu-Woo. 1995. "Millenarianism, Christian Movements, and Ethnic Change among the Miao in Southwest China." In *Cultural Encounters on China's Ethnic Frontiers*, edited by Stevan Harrell, 217–47. Seattle: University of Washington Press.

Chin, Ko-Lin. 2009. *The Golden Triangle: Inside Southeast Asia's Drug Trade*. Ithaca, NY: Cornell University Press.

Chit Hlaing (F. K. Lehman). 2007. "Introduction: Notes on Edmund Leach's Analysis of Kachin Society and Its Further Applications." In *Social Dynamics in the Highlands of Southeast Asia: Reconsidering Political Systems of Highland Burma, by E. R. Leach*, edited by François Robinne and Mandy Sadan, xxi–lii. Leiden: Brill.

———. 2009. "The Central Position of the Shan/Tai Buddhism for the Socio-political Development of Wa and Kayah Peoples." *Contemporary Buddhism* 10(1): 17–29.

Chit Phumisak. 1992. *Khwampenma khong kham Sayam Thai, Lao lae khom, lae laksana thang sangkhom khong chu chonchat chabap sombun phoemtoem, khothetching waduai chonchat Khom* [Comparative study on origins of Thai, Lao, and Khmer words, especially (the) word Siam, and social aspects of their personal names]. Bangkok: Samnakphim Sayam. In Thai.

Cholthira Satyawadhna.1990a. "A Comparative Study of Structure and Contradiction in the Austro-Asiatic System of the Thai-Yunnan Periphery." In *Ethnic Groups across National Boundaries in Mainland Southeast Asia*, edited by Gehan Wijeyewardene, 74–101. Singapore: Institute of Southeast Asian Studies.

———. 1990b. "Sir James George Scott and Wa Political Institutions." *Thai-Yunnan Project Newsletter 8*. Retrieved 20 January 2020 from http://chl-old.anu.edu.au/publications/typnewsletter/08.pdf. Also in *Tai World: A Digest of Articles from the Thai-Yunnan Project Newsletter*, edited by Andrew Walker and Nicholas Tapp, 218–26. Canberra: Research School of Pacific Studies, Australian National University, 2001.

———. 1991. "The Dispossessed: An Anthropological Reconstruction of Lawa Ethnohistory in the Light of Their Relationship with the Tai." PhD diss., Australian National University.

———. 2000. "Forced Village Relocations and the Story of Huuh Mah Akha." Retrieved 2 June 2014 from http://www.drugwar.com/akhalandtheft.shtm.

Chong, Key Ray. 1990. *Cannibalism in China*. Wakefield, NH: Longwood Academic.

Chouvy, Pierre-Arnaud. 2004. "Opium Ban Risks Greater Insecurity for Wa in Myanmar." *Jane's Intelligence Review* 16(2): 39–41.

———. 2009. *Opium: Uncovering the Politics of the Poppy*. London: I. B. Tauris.

Clastres, Pierre. 1987 [1974]. *Society against the State*. Translated by Robert Hurley. New York: Zone Books.

Colquhoun, Archibald Ross. 1970 [1885]. *Amongst the Shan: With . . . An Historical Sketch of the Shans by Holt S. Hallett, . . . Preceded by an Introduction on the Cradle of the Shan Race by Terrien de Lacouperie*. Repr. New York: Paragon Book Reprint [London: Field].

Condominas, Georges. 1977. *We Have Eaten the Forest: The Story of a Montagnard Village in the Central Highlands of Vietnam*. New York: Hill and Wang.

Connelly, F. 2003. "Introduction." In *The Grotesque and Modern Art*, edited by F. Connelly, 1–19. Cambridge: Cambridge University Press.

Cooke, Allyn B. 1930. "Always advancing." *China's Millions* [U.K. edition] 56(2): 29.

Couchman, G. H. H. 1897. *Report of the I.O. [Intelligence Officer] Accompanying the Superintendent, N.S.S. [Northern Shan States] on His Tour in 1896–1897 (Southern Wa States—Gold Tracts, Hsipaw, N. & S. Hsenwi)*. Rangoon: G.B.P.C.O. British Library, Oriental & India Office Collections, W2127.

Coulouma, Sarah. 2019. "Une ethno-histoire des Wa-Paraok de Wengding (Yunnan, Chine): pratiques, représentations et espace social face au tourisme." Thèse de doctorat, Aix-Marseille Université, France.

Covell, Ralph. 1995. *The Liberating Gospel in China: The Christian Faith among China's Minority Peoples*. Grand Rapids, MI: Baker Books.

Crossman, Eileen. 1994 [1982]. *Mountain Rain: A Biography of James O. Fraser, Pioneer Missionary of China*. Wheaton, IL: H. Shaw.

Dacos, Nicole. 1969. *La découverte de la Domus Aurea et la formation des grotesques à la Renaissance*. London: Warburg Institute.

Dai, Yingcong. 2004. "A Disguised Defeat: The Myanmar Campaign of the Qing Dynasty." *Modern Asian Studies* 38(1): 145–89.

Dakung Wadan. 2000. "Hu Shi de fuqin ye kanjian Hanren chi Fanrou" [Hu Shi's father also saw the Han Chinese eating "aboriginal flesh"]. *Taiwan yuanzhumin yuekan* [Taiwan's aborigines monthly] 3. Retrieved 2 June 2014 from http://redmedia034.so-buy.com/front/bin/ptlist.phtml?Category=245333.

Dalton, John. 2000. "The Incredible Journey of the Wa from 1949 to 2005." *Journal of the Siam Society* 88(1–2): 218–21.

Daly, Lieutenant H. 1891. *Report on the Administration of the Northern Shan States for the Year 1890–91*. Rangoon: Government Printing.

Da Matta, Roberto Augusto. 1971. "Myth and Anti-myth among the Timbira." In *Structural Analysis of Oral Tradition*, edited by Pierre Maranda and Elli Köngäs Maranda, 271–91. Philadelphia: University of Pennsylvania Press.

Damrong Tayanin, and Kristina Lindell. 2012 [1991]. *Hunting and Fishing in a Kammu Village: Revisiting a Classic Study in Southeast Asian Ethnography*. 2nd ed. Copenhagen: NIAS Press.

Dang Meng. 1968 [1905]. *Xu xiu Shunning fu zhi* [New edition of the Gazetteer of Shunning Prefecture]. Kunming: n.p. [Repr. Taipei: Xuesheng shuju].

Davin, Delia. 1999. *Internal Migration in Contemporary China*. New York: St. Martin's Press.

Davis, Anthony. 2014. "Wardrums in Myanmar's Wa hills." *Asia Times*, 23 April. Retrieved 2 June 2014 from http://www.burmanet.org/news/2014/04/23/asia-times-wardrums-in-myanmars-wa-hills-anthony-davis/.

De Genova, Nicholas. 2005. *Working the Boundaries: Race, Space, and "Illegality" in Mexican Chicago*. Durham, NC: Duke University Press.

Descola, Philippe. 1996. "Constructing Natures: Symbolic Ecology and Social Practice." In *Nature and Society: Anthropological Perspectives*, edited by Philippe Descola and Gísli Pálsson, 82–102. London; New York: Routledge.

———. 2013. *Beyond Nature and Culture*. Chicago: University of Chicago Press.

Dessaint, Alain Y. 1980. *Minorities of Southwest China: An Introduction to the Yi (Lolo) and Related Peoples and an Annotated Bibliography*. New Haven, CT: HRAF Press.

Diederich, Inga Kim. 2008. "Grotesque." Chicago: The Chicago School of Media Theory, Keywords. Retrieved 20 January 2020 from https://lucian.uchicago.edu/blogs/mediatheory/keywords/grotesque/.

Dietler, Michael. 1990. "Driven by Drink: The Role of Drinking in the Political Economy and the Case of Early Iron Age France." *Journal of Anthropological Archaeology* 9: 352–406.

———. 2006. "Alcohol: Anthropological/Archaeological Perspectives." *Annual Review of Anthropology* 35: 229–49.

Diffloth, Gérard. 1980. "The Wa Languages." *Linguistics of the Tibeto-Burman Area* 5(2): 1–182.

Diffloth, Gérard, and Norman Zide. 1992. "North Mon-Khmer Languages." In *International Encyclopedia of Linguistics*, edited by William Bright, 125–42. New York: Oxford University Press.

Dikötter, Frank. 2010. *Mao's Great Famine: The History of China's Most Devastating Catastrophe, 1958–1962*. New York: Walker & Co.

Dillabough-Lefebvre, Dominique. 2019. "The Wa Art of Not Being Governed." *The Diplomat*, 28 May. Retrieved 16 November 2020 from https://thediplomat.com/2019/05/the-wa-art-of-not-being-governed/.

Dirlik, Arif. 1978. *Revolution and History: The Origins of Marxist Historiography in China, 1919–1937*. Berkeley: University of California Press.

Douglas, Mary. 1987. "A Distinctive Anthropological Perspective." In *Constructive Drinking: Perspectives on Drink from Anthropology*, edited by Mary Douglas, 3–15. Cambridge: Cambridge University Press.

Doutriaux, Sylvie, et al. 2008. "Competing for Coffee Space: Development-Induced Displacement in the Central Highlands of Vietnam." *Rural Sociology* 73(4): 528–54.

Dove, Michael. 1988. "The Ecology of Intoxication among the Kantu of West Kalimantan." In *The Real and Imagined Role of Culture in Development: Case Studies From Indonesia*, edited by Michael Dove, 139–82. Honolulu: University of Hawaii Press.

Du, Shanshan. 2002. *Chopsticks Only Works in Pairs: Gender Unity and Gender Equality among the Lahu of Southwest China*. New York: Columbia University Press.

Duan Shilin and Zhao Mingsheng. 1991. "Li Dingguo dui kaifa Awashan de gongxian" [The contributions of Li Dingguo toward the development of the Awa mountains]. *Sixiang zhanxian* 5: 90–93.

Duckett, Jane. 2011. *The Chinese State's Retreat from Health: Policy and the Politics of Retrenchment*. London: Routledge.

Ebrey, Patricia. 1996. "Surnames and Han Chinese Identity." In *Negotiating Ethnicities in China and Taiwan*, edited by Melissa J. Brown, 19–36. Berkeley: Institute of East Asian Studies, University of California.

Economist, The. 2018. "Methamphetamines from Myanmar Are Causing Problems across Asia: As Poppy Cultivation Dwindles, Meth-Making Is Booming." 13 December. Retrieved 12 January 2020 from https://www.economist.com/asia/2018/12/15/methamphetamines-from-myanmar-are-causing-problems-across-asia.

Ehlers, Otto Ehrenfried. 1901. *Im Sattel durch Indo-China*. 2 vols. Berlin: Allgemeiner Verein für Deutsche Litteratur.

Enriquez, C. M. H. 1924. *Handbooks for the Indian Army: Races of Burma*. Calcutta: Government of India, Central Publication Branch.

Enwall, Joakim. 1994. *A Myth Become Reality: History and Development of the Miao Written Language*. Vols. 1–2. Stockholm: Stockholm University, Institute of Oriental Languages, East Asian Monographs, nos. 5, 6.

Etkind, Aleksandr. 2011. *Internal Colonization: Russia's Imperial Experience*. Malden, MA: Polity Press.

Evans-Pritchard, E. E. 1940. *The Nuer: A Description of the Modes of Livelihood and Political Institutions of a Nilotic People*. Oxford: Oxford University Press.

Evrard, Olivier, and Yves Goudineau. 2004. "Planned Resettlement, Unexpected Migrations and Cultural Trauma in Laos." *Development and Change* 35(5): 937–62.

Fang Guoyu. 1943a. *Dianxi bianqu kaocha ji* [Notes on investigations in the Western Yunnan borderlands]. Kunming: Guoli Yunnan daxue. First published in *Xinan bianjiang* 1 (1938): [91–106] (Part I); 2 (1938): [187–200] (Part II). (Partly repr. in Li Genyuan 1941; again repr. Kunming: Yunnan renmin, 2008).

———. 1943b. "Lufang yinkuang gushilu" [Accounts of the early history of the silver mine at Lufang]. In *Dianxi bianqu kaocha ji*, fo. 18. Kunming: Guoli Yunnan daxue.

———. 1943c. "Banhong fengtuji" [Account of customs and conditions of Banhong]. In *Dianxi bianqu kaocha ji*, fos. 1–50. Kunming: Guoli Yunnan daxue.

———. 1943d. "Kawashan wenjian ji" [Record of things seen and heard in the Kawa mountains]. In *Dianxi bianqu kaocha ji*, leaves 1–38. Kunming: Guoli Yunnan daxue. Preface dated first month of 1937; originally in *Xinan bianjiang* 10 [1940]: 897–907; partly reprinted in Li Genyuan 1941 (*Jizai* 32, *Min* 6, 12b–21b).

———. 1943e. "Luoheishan lüxingji" [Notes on a journey in the Lahu mountains]. In *Dianxi bianqu kaocha ji*. Kunming: Guoli Yunnan daxue. Originally in *Xinan bianjiang* 15 (1942): 1259–65 (Part I); 16 (1942): 1306–13 (Part II).

———. 1984a *Yunnan shiliao mulu gaishuo* [Yunnan historical materials: General annotated bibliography]. Vols. 1–3. Beijing: Zhonghua.

———. 1984b. "Wu Shangxian kaiban Maolong yinchang muqi" [Wooden records of Wu Shangxian launching and operating the Maolong silver mines]. In *Yunnan shiliao mulu gaishuo* [Yunnan historical materials: General annotated bibliography], 3:1273–76. Beijing: Zhonghua.

———. 1994. [On the names of countries and cities neighboring Nanzhao]. In *Fang Guoyu wenji* [Collected works of Fang Guoyu], edited by Lin Chaomin, 1:615–38. Kunming: Yunnan jiaoyu.

Fan Zhuo. 1961. *Man shu: Book of the Southern Barbarians*. Translated by Gordon H. Luce. Edited by Giok-Po Oey. Based on the 1774 Wuyingdian edition. Southeast Asia Program data paper 44. Ithaca, NY: Cornell University Press.

———. 1962 [ca. 860 CE]. *Man shu* [Book of the (southern) barbarians]. Annotated by Xiang Da. Beijing: Zhonghua.

Faure, David, and Ho Ts'ui-p'ing, eds. 2013. *Chieftains into Ancestors: Imperial Expansion and Indigenous Society in Southwest China*. Vancouver: UBC Press.

Feingold, David A. 2000. "The Hell of Good Intentions: Some Preliminary Thoughts on Opium in the Political Ecology of the Trade in Girls and Women." In *Where China Meets Southeast Asia: Social & Cultural Change in the Border Regions*, edited by Grant Evans, Chris Hutton, and Kuah Khun Eng, 183–203. New York: St. Martin's Press.

———, dir. 2002. *Trading Women*. 77 min. Watertown, MA: Documentary Educational Resources; Philadelphia: Ophidian Films.

Fei Xiaotong. 1955. "Kawa shehui gaikuang" [Outline of Kawa society]. In *Zhongguo minzu wenti yanjiu jikan* [Chinese nationalities issues and research quarterly] 2: 103–40.

Feinman, Gary M., and Joyce Marcus, eds. *Archaic States*. Santa Fe, N.M.: School of American Research Press, 1998.

Fife, Eric S. 1981. *Against the Clock: The Story of Ray Buker, Sr., Olympic Runner and Missionary Statesman*. Grand Rapids, MI: Zondervan.

Finley, Moses I. 1979. *Ancient Slavery and Modern Ideology*. London: Chatto and Windus.

Fiskesjö, Magnus. 1992. "The Ritual Celebration of Military Victories in Forty-Nine Bronze Inscriptions from the Western Zhou Period, with Special Reference to the Guoji Zibo *Pan* Inscription." Unpublished manuscript.

———. 1999a. "On the 'Raw' and the 'Cooked' Barbarians of Imperial China." *Inner Asia* 1(2): 139–68.

———. 1999b. "Review of *Leshi yanjiu* [Studies on the History of the Le Kingdom] and *Daizu shenling chongbai mizong* [Dai spirits worship] by Zhu Depu." *Crossroads—An Interdisciplinary Journal of Southeast Asian Studies* (Center for Southeast Asian Studies, Northern Illinois University) 12(2): 115–18.

———. 2000. "The Fate of Sacrifice and the Making of Wa History." PhD dissertation, joint degree in the Departments of Anthropology and East Asian Languages and Civilizations, University of Chicago.

———. 2001. "The Question of the Farmer Fortress: On the Ethno-archaeology of Fortified Settlements in Northern Southeast Asia." *Bulletin of the Indo-Pacific Prehistory Association* 21; *The Melaka Papers* V: 124–31.

———. 2002. "The Barbarian Borderland and the Chinese Imagination—Travellers in Wa Country." *Inner Asia* 4(1): 81–99.

———. *The Thanksgiving Turkey Pardon, the Death of Teddy's Bear, and the Sovereign Exception of Guantánamo*. Chicago: Prickly Paradigm Press, 2003.

———. 2006. "Rescuing the Empire: Chinese Nation-Building in the Twentieth Century." *European Journal of East Asian Studies* 5(2): 15–44.

———. 2007. "Barbarians Don't Wash: Dirt as Accusation in Chinese Interethnic Relations." Paper presented at the American Anthropological Association annual meeting, Philadelphia.

———. 2009a. "The Autonomy of Naming: Kinship, Power and Ethnonymy in the Wa Lands of the Southeast Asia-China Frontiers." In *Personal Names in Asia: History, Culture and Identity*, edited by Zheng Yangwen and Charles J-H Macdonald, 150–74. Singapore: NUS Press.

———. 2009b. "History Erased: Headhunting as Primitive Custom and the 'Overwriting' of Wa History." Paper presented at the Society for East Asian Anthropology conference, Taipei, Taiwan, 2009.

———. 2010a. "Mining, History, and the Anti-state Wa: The Politics of Autonomy between Burma and China." *Journal of Global History* 5(2): 241–64.

———. 2010b. "Participant Intoxication and Self-Other Dynamics in the Wa Context." *Asia Pacific Journal of Anthropology* 11(2): 111–27.

———. 2010c. "The Politics of Cultural Heritage." In *Reclaiming Chinese Society: The New Social Activism*, edited by Lee Ching Kwan and Hsing You-tien, 225–45. London: Routledge.

———. 2011a. "Slavery as the Commodification of People: Wa 'Slaves' and Their Chinese 'Sisters.'" *Focaal: Journal of Global and Historical Anthropology* 59: 3–18.

———. 2011b. "The Animal Other: Re-naming the Barbarians in Twentieth-Century China." In "China and the Human," special issue, no. 109, *Social Text* 29(4): 57–79.

———. 2012. "The Extraordinary Collaborative Research on Khmu Culture of Damrong Tayanin and Kristina Lindell." In *Hunting and Fishing in a Kammu Village: Revisiting a Classic Study in Southeast Asian Ethnography*, by Damrong Tayanin and Kristina Lindell, with contributions by Håkan Lundström, Olivier Évrard, and Magnus Fiskesjö, 195–207. Copenhagen: NIAS Press.

———. 2013a. "Introduction to Wa Studies." *Journal of Burma Studies* 17(1): 1–27.

———. 2013b. "Gifts and Debts: The Morality of Fieldwork in the Wa Lands on the China-Burma Frontier." In *Red Stamps and Gold Stars: Fieldwork Dilemmas in Upland Socialist Asia*, edited by Sarah Turner, 61–79. Vancouver: UBC Press.

———. 2014. "Review of Mandy Sadan, *Being and Becoming Kachin: Histories Beyond the State in the Borderworlds of Burma*." Thailand-Laos-Cambodia [TLC] network/ New Mandala Review LXX (16 May).

———. 2015. "Wa Grotesque: Headhunting Theme Parks and the Chinese Nostalgia for Primitive Contemporaries." In "Primitivist Tourism," special issue, *Ethnos* 80(4): 497–523.

———. 2017a. "People First: The Wa World of Spirits and Other Enemies." *Anthropological Forum* 27(4): 340–64.

———. 2017b. "The Legacy of the Chinese Empires: Beyond 'the West and the Rest.'" *Education about Asia* 22(1): 6–10. Retrieved 20 January 2020 from http://aas2.asian-studies.org/EAA/TOC/index.asp.

———. 2020a. "Research Ethics, Violated." *Allegra Lab*, May 7. Retrieved 20 November 2020 from https://allegralaboratory.net/research-ethics-violated/

———. 2020b. "China's 'Re-education'/Concentration Camps in Xinjiang/East Turkestan and the Wider Campaign of Forced Assimilation Targeting Uyghurs, Kazakhs, etc.: Bibliography." Uyghur Human Rights Project. Updated frequently. Website changed in April 2021 to https://uhrp.org/bibliography.

———. 2021. "Forced Confessions as Identity Conversion in China's Concentration Camps." *Monde Chinois* 2020/2 (No. 62), 28-43.

———. Forthcoming, 2022. "Agamben and the Chinese Forced-Confession Ritual." In *Philosophy on Fieldwork*, edited by Nils Ole Bubandt and Thomas Schwarz Wentzer. 2022). London: Routledge.

Fiskesjö, Magnus, and Y. C. Hsing, eds. 2011. "Rice and Language across Asia: Crops, Movement, and Social Change." *Rice* 4(3–4): 75–77.

Fitzgerald, John. *Awakening China. Politics, Culture and Class in the Nationalist Revolution.* Stanford University Press, 1992.

Forbes, Andrew. 1988. "History of Panglong, 1875–1900: A Panthay (Chinese Muslim) Settlement in the Burmese Wa States." *Muslim World* 78(1): 38–50.

Formoso, Bernard. 2001. "Des sacs charges de mémoire: Du jeu des tambours à la résistance silencieuse des Wa de Xuelin (Yunnan)." *L'Homme* 160: 41–66.

———. 2004. "A l'unisson des tambours: Note sur l'ordre social et la chasse aux tetes parmi les Wa de Chine." *Anthropos* 99(2): 353–63.

———. 2013. "To Be at One with Drums: Social Order and Headhunting among the Wa of China." *Journal of Burma Studies* 17(1): 121–39.

Fournier, Dominique, and Salvatore D'Onofrio, eds. 1991. *Le ferment divin*. Paris: Maison des sciences de l'homme.

Frake, C. O. 1964. "How to Ask for a Drink in Subanun." *American Anthropologist* 66(6): 127–32.

Frangville, Vanessa. 2014. "Négocier les identités ethniques dans 'Le Projet sur le cinéma non-han': Le cas du micro-film de Yang Rui sur les Wa du Yunnan." *Cahiers d'Extrême-Asie* 23: 201–35.

Frazer, J. G. 1911. *The Golden Bough: A Study in Magic and Religion*. 3rd ed., rev. and enlarged. London: Macmillan.
Friedman, Jonathan. 1987. "Generalized Exchange: Theocracy and the Opium Trade." *Critique of Anthropology* 7(1): 15–31. (Repr. in *System, Structure and Contradiction in the Evolution of 'Asiatic' Social Formations*. 2nd ed. 1998. Walnut Creek, CA: Altamira-Sage, Appendix 2, 341–56).
———. 1994. "Civilizational Cycles and the History of Primitivism." In Jonathan Friedman, *Cultural Identity and Global Process*, 42–66. London: Sage.
———. 1998 [1979]. *System, Structure and Contradiction in the Evolution of "Asiatic" Social Formations*. 2nd ed. Walnut Creek, CA: Altamira-Sage (orig. Copenhagen: The National Museum of Denmark; Social Studies in Oceania and South East Asia 2).
———. 2011. "States, Hinterlands, and Governance in Southeast Asia." Review of *The Art of Not Being Governed* by James Scott. *Focaal: Journal of Global and Historical Anthropology* 61: 117–22.
Fung, Christopher. 2000. "The Drinks Are on Us: Ritual, Social Status, and Practice in Dawenkou Burials, North China." *Journal of East Asian Archaeology* 2(1): 67–92.
Gaetano, Arianne. 2008. "Sexuality in Diasporic Space: Rural-to-Urban Migrant Women Negotiating Gender and Marriage in Contemporary China." *Gender, Place & Culture* 15(6): 629–45.
Gaetano, Arianne, and Tamara Jacka, eds. 2004. *On the Move: Women and Rural-to-Urban Migration in Contemporary China*. New York: Columbia University Press.
Gao Zhiqun. 1992. "Xianfuli yanjiu" [Research on the rite of presenting prisoners]. *Wenshi* 35: 1–20 (Part I); 36: 11–26 (Part II).
Garine, Igor de, and Valerie de Garine. 2001. *Drinking: Anthropological Approaches*. New York: Berghahn Books.
Gates, Hill. 1989. "The Commoditization of Chinese Women." *Signs* 14(4): 799–832.
———. 1996. "Buying Brides in China—Again." *Anthropology Today* 12(4): 8–11.
Gengma, Menglian, Shuangjiang: Wazu diaocha cailiao zhi wu [Gengma, Menglian, Shuangjiang: Wa research materials, vol. 5]. 1962. Beijing: Academia Sinica Nationalities Research Institute, Yunnan Investigative Committee and the Yunnan Province Nationalities Research Institute.
Gibson, Thomas. 1980. "Raiding, Trading and Tribal Autonomy." In *The Anthropology of War*, edited by Jonathan Haas, 125–45. Cambridge: Cambridge University Press.
Gibson, Thomas, and Kenneth Sillander. 2011. *Anarchic Solidarity: Autonomy, Equality and Fellowship in Southeast Asia*. New Haven, CT: Yale University Southeast Asian Studies Publications.
Giersch, Charles Patterson. 2006. *Asian Borderlands: The Transformation of Qing China's Yunnan Frontier*. Cambridge, MA: Harvard University Press.
———. 2013. "Across Zomia with Merchants, Monks, and Musk: Process Geographies, Trade Networks, and the Inner-East-Southeast Asian Borderlands." *Journal of Global History* 5(2): 215–39.
Gladney, Dru C. 1991. *Muslim Chinese: Ethnic Nationalism in the People's Republic of China*. Cambridge, MA: Harvard University Press.
Glanville, S. de. 1936. *Report on the Punitive Expedition from Lufang 10th April to 10th May 1936 (Confidential)*. Rangoon: Superintendent, Government Printing and Stationary. British Library, Oriental & India Office Collections L/PS/20/d235 (copy in Mss Eur E 252/30).
Global IDP Database. 2005. Profile of Internal Displacement: Myanmar (Burma). Compilation of the information available in the Global IDP Database of the Norwegian Refugee Council (as of 27 June 2005). Retrieved 2 June 2014 from http://www.inter

nal-displacement.org/assets/library/Asia/Myanmar/pdf/Myanmar-Burma-June-2005.pdf (link no longer available).

Global IDP Project. 2005. "Myanmar (Burma): Displacement Continues Unabated in One of the World's Worst IDP Situations." Report, 27 June 2005. Retrieved 20 January 2020 from http://www.reliefweb.int/rw/RWB.NSF/db900SID/LSGZ-6DSHCU?OpenDocument.

Glover, Denise M., Stevan Harrell, Charles McKhann, and Margaret Swain, eds. 2011. *Explorers and Scientists in China's Borderlands, 1880–1950*. Seattle: University of Washington Press.

Golas, Peter. 1999. "Mining." *Science and Civilisation in China*. Vol. 5, part 13. Cambridge: Cambridge University Press.

Gong Peihua et al. 1982. "Menglian Cangyuan liangxian Lahuzu jiating hunyin gaikuang" [Report on family and marriage arrangements among the Lahu nationality of Menglian and Cangyuan counties]. In *Lahuzu shehui lishi diaocha* [Investigations of the society and history of the Lahu nationality], edited by Yunnan Province editorial committee, 2:40–45. Kunming: Yunnan renmin.

Gong Yin. 1982. "Qingdai Dianxi bianqu de yinkuang ye" [Qing era silver mining in western Yunnan borderlands]. *Sixiang zhanxian* 2: 88–91.

———. 1988. *Ming shi Yunnan tusi zhuan jianzhu* [Commentary to the annals of Yunnan "native chiefs" in the *Ming History*]. Kunming: Yunnan minzu.

———. 1992. *Zhongguo tusi zhidu* [The *tusi* system in China]. Kunming: Yunnan minzu.

Gordon, Tamar (dir.). 2005. *Global Villages: The Globalization of Ethnic Display*. Film. New York: Tourist Gaze Productions.

Grabowski, Volker. 1999. "Forced Resettlement Campaigns in Northern Thailand during the Early Bangkok Period." *Journal of the Siam Society* 89(1–2): 45–86.

Graeber, David. 2006. "Turning Modes of Production Inside Out: Or, Why Capitalism Is a Transformation of Slavery." *Critique of Anthropology* 26(1): 61–85.

———. "Radical alterity is just another way of saying 'reality.'" *Hau: Journal of Ethnographic Theory* 5.2 (2015), 1-41.

Gravers, Mikael, ed. 2006. *Exploring Ethnic Diversity in Burma*. Copenhagen: NIAS.

Guo Dachang, Duan Hua, and Guo Shaorong. 1990–1997. *Si ndah baraog Joung gox/ Zhongguo Wazu yiyao* [Medicine of the Wa nationality, China]. 4 vols. Kunming: Yunnan minzu.

Guo Moruo. 1973. *Nulizhi shidai* [The slavery period]. Beijing: Renmin.

Guowuyuan renkou pucha bangongshi [State Council census office]. 1985. *Zhongguo 1982 nian renkou pucha ziliao* [The 1982 population census in China]. Beijing: Zhongguo tongji.

Hackett, William D. 1969. "Christian Approach to Animistic Peoples: Tribal Beliefs in the Shan State, Burma, and Their Meaning for the Proclamation of the Gospel." *South East Asia Journal of Theology* 10(4): 48–83.

Hanks, Lucien M. 1984. "A Heritage of Defeat: Hill Tribes Out of China." In *Change and Continuity in Southeast Asia*, edited by Robert A. Long and Damaris A. Kirchhofer, 83–101. Manoa: University of Hawai'i.

Hanna, A. C. 1922. "A Wonderful Story of Missionary Evangelism: How the Intrepid Missionary Triumphed over All Obstacles and Carried the Gospel Light to the Lahus and Was." *Missions* [American Baptist International Magazine] 13(9): 539–43.

Harrell, Stevan. 1996. "Being Poor, Peripheral, Outnumbered, and Han." Paper presented at the annual meeting of the Association for Asian Studies, Honolulu, Hawaii, April. (Also published as "The Majority as Minority," Ch. 14, in *Ways of Being Ethnic in Southwest China*. Seattle: University of Washington Press, 295–310.)

Harrell, Stevan, ed. 2001. *Perspectives on the Yi of Southwest China*. Berkeley: University of California Press.

Harrison, Simon. 2012. *Dark Trophies: Hunting and the Enemy Body in Modern War*. New York: Berghahn Books.

Harvey, Godfrey Eric. 1925. *History of Burma: From the Earliest Times until 10 March 1824, the Beginning of the English Conquest*. Bombay: Longmans & Green.

———. 1932. *Wa*. [Signed typescript memorandum, 5 March 1932]. British Library, Oriental & India Office Collections, Mss Eur E 252/27 (In "Clague papers;" pp. 56–63).

———. 1933. *1932 Wa Précis: A Précis Made in the Burma Secretariat of All Traceable Records Relating to the Wa States*. Rangoon: Office of the Superintendent, Government Printing and Stationery.

———. 1957. "The Wa People of the Burma-China frontier." *St. Anthony's Papers* 2:126–35. St. Anthony's College, Oxford; London: Chatto and Windus.

Haviser, J. B. 2005. "Slaveryland: A New Genre of African Heritage Abuse." *Public Archaeology* 4(1): 27–34.

He Jiren. 1992. "Lahuzu" [The Lahu nationality]. In *Zhongguoren de Xingming* [Surnames and names of China's people], edited by Zhang Lianfang, 343–53. Beijing: Shehui kexue.

He, Zhixiong. 2003. "Migration and the Sex Industry in the Hekou-Lao Cai Border Region Between Yunnan and Vietnam." In *Living on the Edges: Cross-Border Mobility and Sexual Exploitation in the Greater Southeast Asia Subregion*, edited by Muhadjir Darwin, Anna Marie Wattie, and Susi Eja Yuarsi, 1–44. Yogyakarta: Gadjah Mada University.

Healey, Christopher J. 1985. "Tribes and States in 'Pre-Colonial' Borneo: Structural Contradictions and the Generation of Piracy." *Social Analysis* 18: 3–39.

Hedén, Thomas. 1979. "The Evolution of Naga Society: A Development of a Hypothesis Outlined by Jonathan Friedman." Unpublished undergraduate thesis, Department of Social Anthropology, Stockholm University, 103 pages.

Hefright, Brook. 2012. "Language Contact as Language Ideology: The Case of Pǔtōnghuà and Bái." *International Journal of the Sociology of Language* 215: 141–58.

Heine-Geldern, Robert. 1976 [1914]. "Die Bergstämme des nördlichen und nordöstlichen Birma." In *Gesammelte Schriften*, Band 1. Vienna: Acta Ethnologica et Linguistica 35: 13–273.

Herman, John E. 1997. "Empire in the Southwest: Early Qing Reforms to the Native Chieftain System." *Journal of Asian Studies* 56(1): 47–74.

———. 2007. *Amid the Clouds and Mist: China's Colonization of Guizhou, 1200–1700*. Cambridge, MA: Harvard University Press.

High, Holly. 2008. "The Implications of Aspirations: Reconsidering Resettlement in Laos." *Critical Asian Studies* 40(4): 531–50.

Hill, Ann Maxwell. 1989. "Chinese Dominance of the Xishuangbanna Tea Trade: An Interregional Perspective." *Modern China* 15(3): 321–45.

———. 1998. *Merchants and Migrants: Ethnicity and Trade among Yunnanese Chinese in Southeast Asia*. New Haven, CT: Yale University Press.

———. 2001. "Captives, Kin, and Slaves in Xiao Liangshan." *Journal of Asian Studies* 60(4): 1033–49.

Holm, David. 2013. *Mapping the Old Zhuang Character Script: A Vernacular Writing System from Southern China*. Boston: Brill.

Hopple, Paulette. 1988. "In Their Own Language: Finding Communication Centers among Selected Dialects of Wa." In *Ekasan sammanaa thaang wichaakaan ruang Lawa nay laannaa, 7–8 Minaakhom 2531* [Seminar papers of different academic disciplines about Lawa in Lanna, 7–8 March 1988], 33–41. Chieng Mai: Faculty of Humanities and Social Sciences, Chieng Mai Teachers College, Lanna United Colleges.

Hoskins, Janet A., ed. 1996. *Headhunting and the Social Imagination in Southeast Asia.* Stanford, CA: Stanford University Press.

Howell, Signe, ed. 1996. *For the Sake of Our Future: Sacrificing in Eastern Indonesia.* Leiden: Research School CNWS.

Hu, Qingjun. 1986. "The Transition from Patriarchal Slavery to a Slave-Owning System: An Analysis." *Social Sciences in China* 1: 181–98.

———. 2004. "Several Major Issues in the Discussion on the Nature of Liangshan Yi Society." *Chinese Sociology and Anthropology* 36(1): 11–33.

Hu, Zheng-dong. 1985. "Diffusion of Bronze Drums (Yunnan-Type) and the Ethnohistory of the Pu." *Bulletin: Ancient Orient Museum* [Tokyo] 7: 135–53.

Hua Qiyun. 1937. "Chongkan Dian-Mian nan duan jiewu de renshi" [The present situation regarding the delimitation of the Yunnan-Burma south section]. *Xin yaxiya* [New Asia] 13.2:31-36.

Huang Qielin. 1934. "Ying ren qinzhan Banhong wenti" [The question of the invasion and occupation of Banhong by the English]. *Waijiao yuebao* [Diplomacy monthly] 4(5): 219–35.

Hubert, Henri and Marcel Mauss. 1964 [1898]. *Sacrifice: Its Nature and Function.* Chicago: University of Chicago Press.

Hung, Po-Yi. 2013. "Tea Forest in the Making: Tea Production and the Ambiguity of Modernity on China's Southwest Frontier." *Geoforum* 47: 178–88.

Hutton, John Henry. 1968 [1921]. *The Sema Nagas.* 2nd ed. London: Oxford University Press.

———. 1969 [1921]. *The Angami Nagas. With Some Notes on Neighboring Tribes.* London: Macmillan.

Institute of History and Philology, Academia Sinica (Taipei, Taiwan). n.d. "Zhongguo xinan shaoshu minzu ziliaoku" [Storehouse of materials on Southwestern China's ethnic minority peoples]. Retrieved 28 October 2012 from http://ndweb.iis.sinica.edu.tw/race_public/index.htm. (In Chinese only: select the first bar from the left; the Wa are the first people listed among a total of thirty-plus pages with twelve images each, a total of over four hundred photographs).

Internal Displacement Monitoring Centre (Geneva). 2004. "Shan State: Resettlement of 128,000 Wa Caused Further Displacement (February 2004)." In *Myanmar (Burma): No End in Sight for Internal Displacement Crisis.* IDMC report, 2008, 48–50. Retrieved 28 October 2012 from http://www.internal-displacement.org/assets/library/Asia/Myanmar/pdf/Myanmar-Burma-February-2008.pdf (no longer available online).

International Crisis Group. 2019. *Fire and Ice: Conflict and Drugs in Myanmar's Shan State.* Report 299, 8 January 2019. Retrieved 20 January 2020 from https://www.crisisgroup.org/asia/south-east-asia/myanmar/299-fire-and-ice-conflict-and-drugs-myanmars-shan-state.

Its, Rudolf Fernandovich. 1965. "Mon-Khmerskie narodi" [Mon-Khmer peoples]. In Cheboksarov, N. N. et als. ed. *Narody Vostochnoi Azii* [The peoples of Eastern Asia]. Moscow: Institut etnografii imeni N.N. Miklukho-Maklaia/Isdatelstvo Nauka.

Ivanoff, Jacques. 2000. "Oubli de soi, communication avec l'au-dela et remede exatique: L'omnipresence des substances de l'ivresse chez les Moken." In *Opiums: Les plantes du plaisir et de la convivialite en Asie*, edited by Annie Hubert and Philippe Le Failler, 365–90. Montreal: L'Harmattan.

Izikowitz, Karl Gustav. 1951. *Lamet: Hill Peasants in French Indo-China.* Göteborg: Etnografiska Muséet.

———. 1962. "Notes about the Tai." *Bulletin of the Museum of Far Eastern Antiquities* 34: 73–91. Retrieved 20 January 2020 from www.seasite.niu.edu/tai/TaiDam/article1.htm.

———. 1985 [1941]. "Fastening the Soul: The Lamet of French Indo-China." In *Compass for Fields: Essays in Social Anthropology*, edited by Göran Aijmer, 212–57. Gothenburg Studies in Social Anthropology 7. Gothenburg: Acta Universitatis Gothoburgensis.

Jablonski, Nina. 2012. "The Struggle to Overcome Racism." *New Scientist* 1017: 26–29. Retrieved 20 January 2020 from http://sites.psu.edu/ninajablonski/wp-content/uploads/sites/10224/2014/02/Jablonski.2012.New_.Sci_.26ff.pdf.

Jacka, Tamara. 2005. *Rural Women in Urban China: Gender, Migration, and Social Change*. Armonk, NY: M. E. Sharpe.

Jagan, Larry. 2005. "After Poppy Ban, Wa Face Tough Times Ahead." *Mekong News*. Retrieved 15 January 2010 from http://www.newsmekong.org/after_poppy_ban_wa_face_tough_times_ahead.

Jelsma, Martin, and Tom Kramer. 2005. *Downward Spiral: Banning Opium in Afghanistan and China*. Transnational Institute Briefing Series, No. 2005/2. Amsterdam: Transnational Institute.

Jenner, W. J. F. 1998. "China and Freedom." In *Asian Freedoms*, edited by David Kelly and Anthony Reid, 65–92. Cambridge: Cambridge University Press.

Jennings, J., K. L. Antrobus, S. J. Atencio, E. Glavich, R. Johnson, G. Loffler et al. 2005. "Drinking Beer in a Blissful Mood: Alcohol Production, Operational Chains, and Feasting in the Ancient World." *Current Anthropology* 46(2): 275–303.

Jensema, Ernestien, Martin Jelsma, Tom Kramer, and Tom Blickman. 2014. *Bouncing Back: Relapse in the Golden Triangle*. Amsterdam: Transnational Institute. Retrieved 20 January 2020 from http://www.tni.org/briefing/bouncing-back.

Jiang Yingliang. 1939. "Zhuge Liang yu Yunnan xibu bianmin" [Zhuge Liang and the border peoples of Western Yunnan]. *Xinan bianjiang* 6. Repr., Taipei: Chengwen; Zhongguo qikan huibian 40: 546–59.

———. 1983. *Daizu shi* [A history of the Dai/Tai nationality]. Chengdu: Sichuan minzu.

Johannesson, Jan-Endy. 1996. *Dokumentation av Svensk Pingstmission i Kina* [Documentation of Swedish Pentecostal missions to China]. Kaggeholms Folkhögskola: Pingströrelsens Informationscentrum.

Johnson, Douglas Hamilton. 1994. *Nuer Prophets: A History of Prophecy from the Upper Nile in the Nineteenth and Twentieth Centuries*. New York: Clarendon Press.

Jónsson, Hjörleifur. 1996. "Rhetorics and Relations: Tai States, Forests, and Upland Groups." In *State Power and Culture in Thailand*, edited by E. Paul Durrenberger, 166–200. New Haven, CT: Yale Southeast Asia Studies.

Kachin Women's Association Thailand (KWAT). 2008. *Eastward Bound: An Update on Migration and Trafficking of Kachin Women on the China-Burma Border*. Chiang Mai: KWAT.

Karlsson, Klemens. 2013. "The Songkran Festival in Chiang Tung: A Symbolic Performance of Domination and Subordination between Lowland Tai and Hill Tai." *Tai Culture* 23: 50–62.

Karp, Ivan. 1980. "Beer Drinking and Social Experience in an African Society: An Essay in Formal Sociology." In *Explorations in African Systems of Thought*, edited by Ivan Karp and Charles S. Bird, 83–119. Bloomington: Indiana University Press.

Kataoka, Tatsuki. 1998. "On the Notion of the Lost Book in the Early Mass Conversion to Christianity among the Lahu in Upper Burma." *Ajia Afurika gengo bunka kenkyū* [Journal of Asian and African studies, Tokyo] 56: 141–65. In Japanese.

———. 2013. "Becoming Stateless: Historical Experience and Its Reflection on the Concept of State among the Lahu in Yunnan and Mainland Southeast Asian Massif." *Southeast Asian Studies* 2(1): 69–94.
The Kawa. 1958. Beijing kexue jiaoyu dianying zhipianchang; Zhongguo kexueyuan Minzu yanjiusuo. Film (25 min.). Reissued (in Chinese and English): Institut für den Wissenschaftlichen Film (Göttingen, Germany). Göttingen: IWF, 1997. Series: Chinese Historical Ethnographic Film Series, 1957–1966.
Kawa zu diaocha cailiao [Kawa nationality research materials]. 1958. Vols. 1–4. Beijing: Quanguo renmin daibiao dahui, Minzu weiyuanhui bangongshi [National People's Congress, the Secretariat of the Nationalities Committee]. Vols. 5–7 issued separately, later, as *Wazu diaocha cailiao* [Wa nationality research materials]; see also *Wazu shehui lishi diaocha*.
Kerketta, Kushal. 1960. "Rice Beer and the Oraon Culture: A Preliminary Observation." *Journal of Social Research* [Ranchi, India] 3(1): 62–67.
Keyes, Charles F. 1993. "Why the Thai Are Not Christians: Buddhist and Christian Conversion in Thailand." In *Christian Conversion in Cultural Context*, edited by Robert Hefner, 259–84. Berkeley: University of California Press.
Knapp, Keith. 2014. "Chinese Filial Cannibalism: A Silk Road Import?" In *China and Beyond in the Mediaeval Period: Cultural Crossings and Inter-regional Connections*, edited by Dorothy C. Wong and Gustav Heldt, 135–49. Amherst, NY: Cambria Press.
Kneebone, Susan, and Julie Debeljak. 2012. *Transnational Crime and Human Rights: Responses to Human Trafficking in the Greater Mekong Subregion*. London: Routledge.
Kokubu, Shozo. 1944. *Wazoku no jisso* [The real situation of the Wa people]. Tokyo: Nanyo Keizai Kenkyu. Series: Nanyo shiryo; 465.
Kong, Lingyuan. 2013. "Ethnoarchaeology in China." In *Contesting Ethnoarchaeologies: Traditions, Theories, Prospects*, edited by Arkadiusz Marciniak and Nurcan Yalman, 173–88. New York: Springer.
Kramer, Tom. 2005. "A Downward Spiral." *BurmaNet News*, 19 October. Retrieved 2 June 2014 from http://www.burmanet.org/news/2005/10/19/irrawaddy-a-downward-spiral-tom-kramer/.
———. 2007. *The United Wa State Party: Narco-Army or Ethnic Nationalist Party?* Washington, DC: East-West Center.
———. 2009a. *Burma: Neither War nor Peace. The Future of the Cease-Fire Agreements in Burma*. Amsterdam: Transnational Institute (TNI).
———. 2009b. *From Golden Triangle to Rubber Belt? The Future of Opium Bans in the Kokang and Wa Regions*. Amsterdam: Transnational Institute.
Kramer, Tom, Martin Jelsma, and Tom Blickman. 2009. *Withdrawal Symptoms in the Golden Triangle: A Drug Market in Disarray*. Amsterdam: Transnational Institute.
Kramer, Tom, and Kevin Woods. 2012. *Financing Dispossession: China's Opium Substitution Programme in Northern Burma*. Amsterdam: Transnational Institute. Retrieved 20 January 2020 from http://www.tni.org/briefing/financing-dispossession.
Krasdolfer, Sabine. 2006. "Drinking and Eating: The Field-Test." *Journal des Anthropologues* 106–7: 287–305.
Kristeva, Julia. 1982 [1980]. *Powers of Horror: An Essay on Abjection*. New York: Columbia University Press.
———. 2012. *The Severed Head: Capital Visions*. New York: Columbia University Press.
Kumar, Vivek, and R. R. Rao. 2002. "Some Interesting Indigenous Beverages among the Tribes of Central India." Paper presented to the International Society of Ethnobiology (ISE), 8th International Congress, 16–20 September, Addis Abeba, Ethiopia.

Lahu National Development Organisation. 2002. *Unsettling Moves: The Wa Resettlement Program in Eastern Shan State (1999–2001)*. Web-based report. Retrieved 2 June 2014 from http://www.shanland.org/resources/bookspub/humanrights/wa/.

Lahuzu jianshi [A brief history of the Lahu nationality]. 1986. "Lahuzu jianshi" editorial committee. Kunming: Yunnan renmin.

Lahuzu shehui lishi diaocha [Investigations of the society and history of the Lahu nationality]. 1981–82. Vols. 1–2. Edited by the Yunnan Province Editorial Committee for the five series on nationalities issues. Kunming: Yunnan renmin.

Lambrecht, Curtis W. 2004. "Oxymoronic Development: The Military as Benefactor in the Border Regions of Burma." In *Civilizing the Margins: Southeast Asian Government Policies for the Development of Minorities*, edited by Christopher Duncan, 150–81. Ithaca, NY: Cornell University Press.

Lancang Lahuzu zizhixian zhi [Gazetteer of Lancang Lahu Autonomous County]. 1996. Edited by Yunnan Sheng Lancang Lahuzu zizhixian, editorial committee. Kunming: Yunnan renmin.

Langford, Jean M. 2009. "Gifts Intercepted: Biopolitics and Spirit Debt." *Cultural Anthropology* 24(4): 681–711.

Lau, Ting Hui. 2020. "Colonial Development and the Politics of Affliction on the China-Myanmar Border." PhD dissertation, Cornell University.

Launay, Robert. 1977. "Joking Slavery." *Africa* 47(4): 413–22.

Law-Yone, Wendy. 2010. *The Road to Wanting*. London: Chatto & Windus.

Law-Yone, Wendy, with Leslie Bow. 2002. "Beyond Rangoon: An Interview with Wendy Law-Yone." *MELUS* 27(4): 183–200.

Leach, Edmund R. 1970 [1954]. *Political Systems of Highland Burma: A Study of Kachin Social Structure*. London: Athlone Press, University of London. London School of Economics Monographs on Social Anthropology, No. 44.

———. 1960. "The Frontiers of 'Burma.'" *Comparative Studies in Society and History* 3(1): 49–68.

Lee, James Z. 1982. "The Legacy of Immigration in Southwest China, 1250–1850." *Annales de démographie historique* (1982): 279–304.

———. 1984. "State-Regulated Industry in Qing China, the Yunnan Mining Industry: A Regional Economic Cycle, 1700–1850." Paper presented at the conference "Spatial and Temporal Trends and Cycles in Chinese Economic History, 980–1980," Bellagio, Italy.

———. 2012. *Zhongguo Xinan bianjiang de shehui jingji, 1250–1850* [The political economy of a frontier: Southwest China, 1250–1850]. Translated by Lin Wenxun and Qin Shucai. Beijing: Renmin chubanshe.

Lehman, F. K. (Chit Hlaing). 1963. *The Structure of Chin Society: A Tribal People of Burma Adapted to a Non-Western Civilization*. Urbana: University of Illinois Press.

———. 1967a. "Ethnic Categories in Burma and the Theory of Social Systems." In *Southeast Asian Tribes, Minorities and Nations*, edited by Peter Kunstadter, 1:93–124. Princeton, NJ: Princeton University Press.

———. 1967b. "Burma: Kayah Society as a Function of the Shan-Burma-Karen Context." In *Asian Rural Societies*, edited by Julian Steward, 2:1–104. Contemporary Change in Traditional Societies. Urbana: University of Illinois Press.

———. 1984. "Freedom and Bondage in Traditional Burma and Thailand." *Journal of Southeast Asian Studies* 15(2): 233–44.

———. 1989. "Internal Inflationary Pressures in the Prestige Economy of the Feast of Merit Complex: The Chin and Kachin Cases from Upper Burma." In *Ritual, Power and Economy: Upland-Lowland Contrasts in Mainland Southeast Asia*, edited by

Susan Russell, 89–102. DeKalb: Center for Southeast Asian Studies, Northern Illinois University.

Leibold, James. 2007. *Reconfiguring Chinese Nationalism: How the Qing Frontier and Its Indigenes Became Chinese*. New York: Palgrave Macmillan, 2007.

———. 2013. *Ethnic Policy in China: Is Reform Inevitable?* Honolulu: East-West Center. Retrieved 20 January 2020 from http://www.eastwestcenter.org/publications/ethnic-policy-in-china-reform-inevitable.

———. 2019a. "Planting the Seed: Ethnic Policy in Xi Jinping's New Era of Cultural Nationalism." *China Brief* 19: 22. Retrieved 20 January 2020 from https://jamestown.org/program/planting-the-seed-ethnic-policy-in-xi-jinpings-new-era-of-cultural-nationalism/.

———. 2019b. "The Spectre of Insecurity: The CCP's Mass Internment Strategy in Xinjiang." *China Leadership Monitor*, 1 March 2019. Retrieved 20 January 2020 from https://www.prcleader.org/leibold.

Le Roux, Pierre. 2002. "Des hommes aux dieux: Boissons fermentees, rituelles et festives d'Asie du Sud-Est et au-dela." *Journal of the Siam Society* 90(1–2): 161–78.

Lévi-Strauss, Claude. 1969 [1949]. *The Elementary Structures of Kinship*. Boston: Beacon Press.

Li Daoyong. 1992. "Wazu" [The Wa nationality]. In *Zhongguoren de xingming* [Surnames and names of China's people], edited by Zhang Lianfang, 334–342. Beijing: Shehui kexue.

Li Daoyong, ed. 1996. "Meng-Gaomian yuzu qunti juan" [Mon-Khmer ethnolinguistic groups section]. In *Zhongguo ge minzu yuanshi zongjiao ziliao jicheng* [Collected materials on primitive religion among China's nationalities], edited by Lü Daji and He Yaohua, 4:510–83; plates 155–83, Beijing: Zhongguo shehui kexue.

Li Genpan and Lu Xun. 1985. *Daogeng huozhong yu chugeng bingcun de Ximeng Wazu nongye* [The agriculture of the Wa nationality at Ximeng, with coexistence of swiddening and hoeing]. *Nongye kaogu* [Agricultural archaeology] 1: 358–70.

Li Genyuan, ed. 1941. *Yongchang fu wenzheng* [Collected documents on the prefecture of Yongchang]. Kunming: Tengchong chuban gongsi.

Li Guo-ming and Yang Bao-kang. 2006. "Wazu yanjiu zongshu 1990-2005" [Review of the research on the Wa people, 1990–2005]. *Wenshan shifan gaodeng zhuanke xuexiao xuebao* [Journal of Wenshan Teachers College] 3: 8–13.

Li Jiarui and Li Yaoping. 2011. "Ershi shiji wushi niandai Yunnan Ximeng Awashan Wazu yuanshi shenghuo lao zhaopian—Yige lishixuejia de tianye diaocha" [Old photos of the primitive life of the Wa people of the Awa mountains in Ximeng, Yunnan, in the 1950s—A historian's field research]. *Minzu xuekan* 3: 9–18, 90.

Li Jiaxin. 1988. "Hanren liesha Taiwan yuanzhumin dang shibu mishi da gongkai" [Exposing how Han Chinese hunted and killed aboriginal Taiwanese and used them as a food supplement]. *Taiwan yuanzhumin yuekan* [Taiwan's aborigines monthly] (1). Retrieved 20 January 2020, from http://redmedia034.so-buy.com/front/bin/ptlist.phtml?Category=244771.

Li Jingsen. 1933. "Hulu wangdi gaikuang" [Overview of the land of the Bottle Gourd King]. In *Yunnan biandi wenti yanjiu* [Researches on the Yunnan border area problems], edited by Chen Yuke et al., 2:239–70, and map. Kunming: Yunnan shengli Kunhua minzhong jiaoyuguan.

Li, Quanmin. 2008. "Identity, Relationships and Difference: The Social Life of Tea in a Group of Mon-Khmer Speaking People along the China-Burma Border." PhD dissertation, Department of Anthropology, Australian National University.

———. 2010. "Tea and Ang: The Market Economy of a Group of Mon-Khmer-Speaking Tea Planters in Yunnan." *Asia Pacific Journal of Anthropology* 11(2) (June): 177–90.

Li Shengzhuang. 1933. "Yunnan diyi zhibian quyu nei zhi renzhong diaocha" [Investigation of the races of the first Yunnan border colonization area]. In *Yunnan biandi wenti yanjiu* [Research on the problems of the border areas of Yunnan], edited by Chen Yuke et al., pt. 1: 95–205. Kunming: Yunnan shengli Kunhua minzhong jiaoyuguan.

Li Shirao [Shiyao]. 1931 [1778]. "Yun-Gui zongdu zouchen xunyue bianjing qingxi" [Report of Yunnan-Guizhou governor general Li Shiyao regarding border inspections]. In *Shiliao xunkan* (22), fo. 802. Beijing: Gugong bowuyuan.

Li, Tseng Hsiu (Carol). 1987. "The Sacred Mission: An American Missionary Family in the Lahu and the Wa Districts of Yunnan, China." M.A. thesis, Baylor University, Waco, Texas.

Li Yangsong. 1983a [1957]. "Brewing and Betel-Nut Preparation by the Wa Nationality of the Damasan Village, Ximeng County." In *Wazu shehui lishi diaocha* [Investigations of the history and society of the Wa nationality], edited by the Yunnan Province Editorial Committee for the five series on nationalities issues, 2:99; 148–49. Kunming: Yunnan renmin. Translated by Irene Bain, *Thai-Yunnan Project Newsletter* 6 (September 1989). Retrieved 20 January 2020 from http://chl-old.anu.edu.au/publications/typnewsletter/06.pdf.

———. 1983b [1957]. "Ximeng Wenggake Wazu shehui jingji diaocha [Investigations of the society and economy of the Wa nationality at Wenggake in Ximeng]." In *Wazu shehui lishi diaocha* [Investigations of the history and society of the Wa nationality], edited by the Yunnan Province Editorial Committee, 2:85–115. Kunming: Yunnan renmin.

———. 1983c [1957]. "Ximeng Wazu xisu diaocha ziliao [Investigations of the customs and habits of the Wa nationality in Ximeng]." In *Wazu shehui lishi diaocha* [Investigations of the history and society of the Wa nationality], edited by the Yunnan Province Editorial Committee, 2:132–57. Kunming: Yunnan renmin.

———. 2006. "Xunzhao jiekai kaoguxue zhong yami de yaoshi" [Searching for the key to unlocking the silent mysteries of archaeology]. In *Kaoguren yu tamen de gushi* [Archaeologists and their stories], 1–54. Anonymous editorial committee; with texts by Wang Ningsheng, Wang Xueli, and Li Yangsong. Beijing: Xueyuan.

Liang, Yongjia. 2011. "Stranger-Kingship and Cosmocracy; or, Sahlins in Southwest China." *Asia Pacific Journal of Anthropology* 12(3): 236–54.

Lieberman, Victor. 2003. *Strange Parallels: Southeast Asia in Global Context, c. 800–1830*. Vol. 1. Cambridge: Cambridge University Press.

Lim, Janet. 1985 [1958]. *Sold for Silver: An Autobiography*. Singapore: Oxford University Press.

Lin, Kai-shyh. 1999. "The Frontier Expansion of the Qing Empire: The Case of Kavalan Subprefecture in Nineteenth Century Taiwan." PhD diss., University of Chicago.

Lincang diqu Daizu shehui lishi diaocha [Investigations of the society and history of the Dai nationality of Lincang district]. 1986. Edited by the Yunnan Province Editorial Committee. Kunming: Yunnan renmin.

Lindell, Kristina, and Damrong Tayanin. 1978. "Kammu Hunting Rites." *Journal of Indian Folkloristics* 1(2): 53–62.

Lindenbaum, Shirley. 2004. "Thinking about Cannibalism." *Annual Review of Anthropology* 33: 475–98.

Ling Shun-sheng [Ling Chunsheng]. 1938. "Tangdai Yunnan Wuman yu Baiman kao" [A study of the U-man and the Pei-man in the T'ang dynasty]. *Renleixue zazhi* [The anthropological journal of the Institute of History and Philology, Academia Sinica] 1.1:57–86.

———. 1953. "Yunnan Kawazu yu Taiwan Gaoshanzu de lietouji" [The headhunting ceremony of the Kawa tribe and that of the Formosan aborigines]. *Bulletin of the Institute of Archaeology and Anthropology* [Guoli Taiwan daxue kaogu renleixuekan, National Taiwan University] 2: 1–9.

———. 1957. "Kava-Drinking in China and East Asia." *Bulletin of the Institute of Ethnology*, (4): 1–30; pl. I–VIII.

———. 1958. "A Comparative Study of Kava-Drinking in the Pacific Regions." *Bulletin of the Institute of Ethnology* 5: 45–86.

———. 1960. "Guoshang Lihun yu guoshou jixiao" [Kuo shang and Li hun of the nine songs and the ceremonies of headhunting and head feast]. *Minzuxue yanjiusuo jikan* [Bulletin of the Institute of Ethnology, Academia Sinica] 9: 411–49.

Lintner, Bertil. 1990. *The Rise and Fall of the Communist Party of Burma (CPB)*. Ithaca, NY: Cornell University Southeast Asia Program.

———. 1992. "Heroin and Highland Insurgency in the Golden Triangle." In *War on Drugs: Studies in the Failure of U.S. Narcotics Policy*, edited by Alan A. Block and Alfred W. McCoy, 281–317. Boulder, CO: Westview Press.

———. 1994. *Burma in Revolt: Opium and Insurgency since 1948*. Boulder, CO: Westview Press.

———. 2003. *Blood Brothers: The Criminal Underworld of Asia*. New York: Palgrave Macmillan.

———. 2010. "UN Ignores Burma Junta's Drugs Role." *Democratic Voice of Burma*, 28 June 2010. Retrieved 20 January 2020 from http://www.dvb.no/analysis/un-ignores-burma-juntas-role-in-drugs/10460.

———. 2014. "Who Are the Wa?" *The Irrawaddy*, 2 June. Retrieved 20 January 2020 from http://www.irrawaddy.org/burma/magazine-politics/wa.html.

———. 2017a. "China Uses Carrot and Stick in Myanmar: China Professes Its Support for Myanmar's Peace Drive While Simultaneously Shipping Weaponry to Anti-government Forces." *Asia Times*, 28 February. Retrieved 20 January 2020 from http://www.atimes.com/article/china-uses-carrot-stick-myanmar/

———. 2017b. "Wa Rebel Group Torpedoes Suu Kyi's Peace Drive." *Asia Times*, 28 February. Retrieved 20 January 2020 from http://www.atimes.com/article/wa-rebel-group-torpedoes-suu-kyis-peace-drive/

———. 2018. "Why China Fears Myanmar's Christians." *Asia Times*, 17 September. Retrieved 20 January 2020 from http://www.atimes.com/article/why-china-fears-myanmars-christians/

———. 2021. *The Wa of Myanmar and China's Quest for Global Dominance*. Bangkok: Silkworm Books.

Liu, Li, and Chen Xingcan. 2001. "Cities and Towns: The Control of Natural Resources in Early States, China." *Bulletin of the Museum of Far Eastern Antiquities* 73: 5–47.

Liu, Shao-hua. 2010. *Passage to Manhood: Youth Migration, Heroin, and AIDS in Southwest China*. Stanford: Stanford University Press.

Liu, Tzu-k'ai (Liu Zikai). 2009. "Living with Hierarchies: Religion, Language, and Personhood among Wa Buddhists in Postsocialist China." PhD diss., University of Illinois at Urbana-Champaign.

———. 2013. "Re-constructing Cultural Heritage and Imagining Wa Primitiveness in the China/Myanmar Borderlands." In *Cultural Heritage Politics in China*, edited by Tami Blumenfield and Helaine Silverman, 161–84. New York: Springer.

Lone, Sai. 2008. *The Political Economy of Opium Reduction in Burma: Local Perspectives from the Wa Region*. M.A. thesis, Chulalongkorn University.

Longacre, William A., and Li Yungti. 1999. *Pottery among the Highland People of Western China*. Weston, CT: Pictures of Record, Inc.

Lorenz, Andreas. 2007. "Slavery in China: Combing the Brickyards for the Disappeared." *Spiegel Online*, 15 August. Retrieved 20 January 2020 from https://www.spiegel.de/international/world/slavery-in-china-combing-the-brickyards-for-the-disappeared-a-499877.html.

———. 2010. "As Profitable as the Drug Trade: China's Child-Trafficking Epidemic." *Spiegel Online*, 21 May. Retrieved 20 January 2020 from https://www.spiegel.de/international/world/as-profitable-as-the-drug-trade-china-s-child-trafficking-epidemic-a-696129.html.

Lu Guofan. 1933. "Pu-Si zhibian zhi xianjue wenti." [Basic prerequisites for the colonization of the border areas of Pu/er and Si/mao]. In *Yunnan biandi wenti yanjiu* [Research on the problems of the border areas of Yunnan], edited by Chen Yuke et al., pt. 2:1–12. Kunming: Yunnan shengli Kunhua minzhong jiaoyuguan.

Lu, Hui. 1998. "Les esclaves Yi des Montaignes Fraîches, entre 'os blancs' et 'os noirs.'" In *Formes extrêmes de dépendance: Contributions à l'étude de l'esclavage en Asie du Sud-Est*, edited by Georges Condominas, 235–82. Paris: EHESS.

Lu, Tina. 2008. *Accidental Incest, Filial Cannibalism, & Other Peculiar Encounters in Late Imperial Chinese Literature*. Cambridge, MA: Harvard University Press.

Luce, Gordon H. 1925. "Chinese Invasions of Burma in the Eighteenth Century." *Journal of the Burma Research Society* 15:115–28.

———. 1969–70. *Old Burma, Early Pagan*. Locust Valley, NY: Published for *Artibus Asiae* and the Institute of Fine Arts, New York University [by] J. J. Augustin. *Artibus Asiae*, Supplementum 25.

———. 1985. *Phases of Pre-Pagan Burma, Languages and History*. Vols. 1–2. Oxford: Oxford University Press.

Lundström, Håkan (with Kam Raw [Damrong Tayanin]). 2010. *I Will Send My Song: Kammu Vocal Genres in the Singing of Kam Raw*. Copenhagen: NIAS Press.

Luo Shipu. 1974. "Dianxi ershinian qian lüxingji" [Report from a journey to Western Yunnan twenty years past]. *Zhanggu* 29: 12–23; 30: 17–21; 31: 47–53; 32: 48–55 [Parts I–IV].

Luo Zhiji. 1985. "Wazu de renji jiqi gechu" [Human sacrifice among the Wa and its abolishment]. *Minzuxue yanjiu* [Research in ethnology] 6: 260–70.

———. 1995. *Wazu shehui lishi yu wenhua* [The society, history, and culture of the Wa nationality]. Beijing: Zhongyang minzu daxue.

———. 2001. *Ximeng Xian Wa zu juan* [Ximeng County: Wa section]. Beijing: Minzu.

Luo Zhiji, and Tian Jizhou. 1980. "Ximeng Wazu jiefang qian de jiazhang nuli zhi" [Patriarchal slavery system of the Wa minority nationality in Ximeng prior to Liberation]. *Sixiang zhanxian* 6: 53–59.

Luo Zhiji, et al. 1986. "Ximeng Wazu Xingshi diaocha baogao" [Report on investigations of Wa nationality lineage names at Ximeng]. In *Wazu shehui lishi diaocha* [Investigations of the society and history of the Wa nationality], edited by the Yunnan Province Editorial Committee, 4:20–50. Kunming: Yunnan renmin.

Ma Changshou. 1961. *Nanzhao guonei de buzu zucheng he nuli zhidu* [On the internal ethnic make-up of the Nanzhao state and its slavery system]. Shanghai: Shanghai renmin.

Ma Jianxiong. 1997. *Lahuzu de jingshen shijie yu shehui zhuanxing: Miandui xiandaihua de wenhua xuanze* [The world of the Lahu mind and the change of society: Cultural choices facing modernization]. Kunming: Yunnan minzu xueyuan.

———. 2007. "Ethnic Politics in the Ailao Mountains: Reforms to the Native Chieftain System in the Early to Mid Qing Dynasty and the Mobilization of the Lahu Identity." *Bulletin of the Institute of History and Philology* (Academia Sinica) 78(3): 553–602. In Chinese.

———. 2011. "Shaping of the Yunnan-Burma Frontier by Secret Societies since the End of the Seventeenth Century." *Moussons* 17: 65–84.

———. 2012a. *The Lahu Minority in Southwest China: A Response to Ethnic Marginalization on the Frontier*. London: Routledge.

———. 2012b. "Bianfang sanlao: Qing mo Min chu nanduan Dian-Mian bianjiang shang de guojia dailiren" [Three elders of frontier defense: State agents and the formation of Yunnan-Burma frontier in late Qing and early Republic]. *Lishi renleixue xuekan* [Journal of History and Anthropology] 10(1): 87–122.

———. 2013a. "Clustered Communities and Transportation Routes: The Wa Lands Neighboring the Lahu and the Dai on the Frontier." *Journal of Burma Studies* 17(1): 81–119.

———. 2013b. *Xinan bianjiang de zuqun dongyuan yu Lahuzu de lishi jiangou* [The mobilization of ethnicity on the Southwestern borders and the historical formation of the Lahu nationality]. Hong Kong: Zhongwen daxue.

Macdonald, Charles J-H. 2009. "Toward a Classification of Naming Systems in Insular Southeast Asia." In *Personal Names in Asia: History, Culture and Identity*, edited by Zheng Yangwen and Charles J-H Macdonald, 77–100. Singapore: NUS Press.

Macquoid, C. E. 1896. *Report of the Intelligence Officer on Tour with the Superintendent, Northern Shan States, 1895–1896*. Rangoon: Government Printers.

Maganza, Giuseppe. 1975. *Kengtung: 60 anni tra i monti della Birmania; Profilo biografico di p. Francesco Portaluppi del Pontificio Istituto Missioni Estere*. Milano: Tip. PIME [Pontificio Istituto Missioni Estere].

Malinee Gumperayarnont. 1987. "Neolithic Rock Art at Cangyuan in Yunnan Province." *Muang Boran* [Bangkok] 13(2): 95–101.

March, Kathryn. 1998. "Women, Hospitality and Beer." In *Food and Gender: Identity and Power*, edited by Carole M. Counihan and Steven L. Kaplan, 45–80. New York: Gordon and Breach.

Marshall, Andrew. 2002. *The Trouser People: Burma in the Shadow of the Empire*. Washington DC: Counterpoint.

Marshall, Mac. 1979. *Beliefs, Behaviors, and Alcoholic Beverages: A Cross-Cultural Survey*. Ann Arbor: University of Michigan Press.

Marshall, Mac, ed. 1982. *Through a Glass Darkly: Beer and Modernization in Papua New Guinea*. Boroko, Papua New Guinea: Institute of Applied Social and Economic Research.

Maule, Robert. 1992. "The Opium Question in the Federated Shan States, 1931–36: British Policy Discussions and Scandal." *Journal of Southeast Asian Studies* 23(1): 14–36.

———. 2002. "British Policy Discussions on the Opium Question in the Federated Shan States, 1937–1948." *Journal of Southeast Asian Studies* 33(2): 203–24.

Mauss, Marcel. 1985 [1938]. "A Category of the Human Mind: The Notion of Person; the Notion of Self." In *The Category of the Person: Anthropology, Philosophy, History*, edited by Michael Carrithers, Steven Collins, and Steven Lukes, 1–25. Cambridge: Cambridge University Press.

———. 2006 [1934]. "Techniques of the Body." In *Techniques, Technology and Civilisation: Marcel Mauss*, edited and introduced by Nathan Schlanger, 77–96. New York: Durkheim Press/Berghahn Books.

McAllister, Patrick. 2003. "Culture, Practice and the Semantics of Xhosa Beer-Drinking." *Ethnology* 42(3): 187–207.

———. 2004. "Domestic Space, Habitus, and Xhosa Ritual Beer Drinking." *Ethnology* 43(2): 117–35.

McCoy, Alfred W. 1992. "Heroin as a Global Commodity: A History of Southeast Asia's Opium Trade." In *War on Drugs: Studies in the Failure of U.S. Narcotics Policy*, edited by Alan A. Block and Alfred W. McCoy, 238–80. Boulder, CO: Westview Press.

———. 2003. *The Politics of Heroin: CIA Complicity in the Global Drug Trade; Afghanistan, Southeast Asia, Central America, Colombia*. Rev. ed. Chicago: Lawrence Hill.

McGrath, Thomas. 2002. "Provincial Militarism and Foreign Relations in China: Yunnan Province and the Western Powers, 1910–1937." PhD diss., Department of History, Cornell University, Ithaca, NY.

McKhann, Charles. 1992. "Fleshing Out the Bones: Kinship and Cosmology in Naqxi Religion." Unpublished PhD diss., Department of Anthropology, University of Chicago.

———. 1995. "The Naxi and the Nationalities Question." In *Cultural Encounters on China's Ethnic Frontiers*, edited by Stevan Harrell, 39–62. Seattle: University of Washington Press.

Means, Gordon P. 2000. "Human Sacrifice and Slavery in the 'Unadministered' Areas of Upper Burma during the Colonial Era." *SOJOURN: Journal of Social Issues in Southeast Asia* 15(2): 184–221.

Meehan, Patrick. 2011. "Drugs, Insurgency and State-Building in Burma: Why the Drugs Trade Is Central to Burma's Changing Political Order." *Journal of Southeast Asian Studies* 42(3): 376–404.

Meillassoux, Claude. 1991. *The Anthropology of Slavery: The Womb of Iron and Gold*. Chicago: University of Chicago Press.

Menglian xuanwu shi [History of the Menglian *Xuanwu* Office]. 1986. Yunnan sheng shaoshu minzu guji yicong [Selected translations of ancient books of the minority nationalities of Yunnan Province]. Vol. 5. Kunming: Yunnan minzu. In Dai (Northern Shan script), and Chinese.

Merleau-Ponty, Jules. 2003. *Homme a la tête de canard; ou les cannes du colonel Chuen Ling: Souvenirs d'un voyage en pays Wa*. Paris: Phileas Fogg.

Metro, Rosalie. 2011. "From the Form to the Face to Face: IRBs, Ethnographic Researchers, and Human Subjects Translate Consent." *Anthropology & Education Quarterly* 45(2): 167–184.

Miandian Wa Bang Mengmao Xian zhi/Phuk lai Been Meung Mau. 2002. Compiled by the Mengmao Xian zhi bianzuan weiyuanhui [The Committee for the Compilation of the Gazetteer of Mengmao County, Wa State, Burma]. N.p. [China].

Michaud, Jean. 2006. *Historical Dictionary of the Peoples of the Southeast Asian Massif*. Lanham, MD: Scarecrow Press.

———. 2010. "Editorial: Zomia and Beyond." *Journal of Global History* 5(2): 187–214.

Michelet, Jules. 1973 [1846]. *The People*. Translated by John P. McKay. Urbana: University of Illinois Press.

Midya, Dipak K. 2004. "Rice-Beer in Tribal Lore." *Oriental Anthropologist* 4(2): 198–203.

Miers, Suzanne. 1994. "Mui Tsai through the Eyes of the Victim: Janet Lim's Story of Bondage and Escape." In *Women and Chinese Patriarchy: Submission, Servitude, and Escape*, edited by Maria Jaschok and Suzanne Miers, 108–121. Hong Kong: Hong Kong University Press.

Milburn, Olivia. 2018. "Headhunting in Ancient China: The History of Violence and Denial of Knowledge." *Bulletin of the School of Oriental & African Studies* 81(1): 103–20.

Miller, E. 2001. "The UWSA: Guns, Drugs and Power Politics." *Burma Issues* 11(4): 1–3, 7. Retrieved 2 June 2014 from http://www.burmalibrary.org/docs13/BI2001-04-percent28V11-04 percent29.pdf.

Mills, James Phillip. 1922. *The Lhota Nagas*. London: Macmillan.

———. 1937. *The Rengma Nagas*. London: Macmillan.

Milsom, Jeremy D. 2005. "The Long Hard Road Out of Drugs: The Case of the Wa." In *Trouble in the Triangle: Opium and Conflict in Burma*, edited by Martin Jelsma, Tom Kramer, and Pietje Vervest, 61–93. Chiang Mai: Silkworm Books.

———. 2010. "Conflicting Agendas: Illicit Drugs, Development and Security in the Wa Special Region of Myanmar." PhD diss., University of Melbourne, Department of Resource Management and Geography.

Min, Benjamin. 1995. "The Bondage of Opium: The Agony of the Wa People." *Burma Debate* (New York) 2(1): 14–17.

U Min Naing. 1967. *Doh thwe doh tha tain yin bwa / U Min Naing le la tin pya thi* [Our blood, our people, the indigenous: Researched and presented by U Min Naing]. Yangon, Myanmar: Pyi-daun-zu yin-ce-hmu pya-gan kaw-ma-ti.

Mitchell, Timothy J. 2004. *Intoxicated Identities: Alcohol's Power in Mexican History and Culture*. New York: Routledge.

Mitton, Geraldine Edith [Lady Scott]. 1913. *In the Grip of the Wild Wa*. London: Adams and Charles Black.

———. 1936. *Scott of the Shan Hills: Orders and Impressions*. London: John Murray.

Mueggler, Erik. 2002. "Dancing Fools: Politics of Culture and Place in a 'Traditional Nationality Festival.'" *Modern China* 28(1): 3–38.

Mullaney, T., J. Liebold, and S. Gros, eds. 2012. *Critical Han Studies: The History, Representation, and Identity of China's Majority*. Berkeley: University of California Press.

Myan-ma nain-ngan ba-tha-pyan sa-pe a-thin. 1954. *Myan-ma sweh-soun-jan: sa-pe-be-man i youq-pya ba-hu-thu-ta ban* [Encyclopedia Myanmar]. Vol. 12. [Articles on "The Wa Area" and "The Wa People," by Mya Wa Di Yie Khaong et al.] [Also later editions; partial translation into Chinese by Li Xiaoji in *Dongnanya ziliao* (Southeast Asian Materials), 3 (1982).]

Na Jinhua, ed. 2009. *"Sigangli" yu chuantong wenhua xueshu yantaohui* [Siganglih and traditional culture: Academic conference]. Kunming: Yunnan chuban jiyuan gongsi.

Nari, Bilige [Bilik, Naran]. 2000. *Xingming* [Naming]. Beijing: Zhongyang minzu daxue.

Naw Seng. 2004. "Burma to China: One-Way Ticket." In *Exploring Borders: Reportage from Our Mekong*, 90–98. Bangkok: Inter Press Service Asia Pacific.

Netting, Robert McC. 1964. "Beer as a Locus of Value among the West African Kofyar." *American Anthropologist* 66(2): 375–84. (Also in Marshall 1979: 351–62).

Ni Tui [1668–ca. 1743]. 1992 [1737]. *Dian Yun linian zhuan* [Chronological annals of Dian and Yunnan]. 12 *juan*. 1914; Kunming: Yunnan tushuguan; repr. 1992; Kunming: Yunnan daxue.

Nonini, D. M. 2008. "Is China Becoming Neoliberal?" *Critique of Anthropology* 28(2): 145–76.

Notar, Beth. 2007. *Displacing Desire: Travel and Popular Culture in China*. Honolulu: University of Hawai'i Press.

Nugent, Stephen. 1988. "The Peripheral Situation." *Annual Review of Anthropology* 17: 79–98.

Nyi Ga [See also Wei Deming]. 1988. *Si Ngian Rang Mai Si Ngang Lih* [Myths and historical tales of the Wa nationality]. Kunming: Yunnan minzu.

Nyiri, Pál. 2006. *Scenic Spots: Chinese Tourism, the State, and Cultural Authority*. Seattle: University of Washington Press.

Oakes, Tim. 2013. "Heritage as Improvement: Cultural Display and Contested Governance in Rural China." *Modern China* 39: 380–407.

Obayashi, Taryo. 1966. "Anthropogonic Myths of the Wa in Northern Indo-China." *Hitotsubashi Journal of Social Studies* 3(1): 43–66.

O'Connor, Richard. 1989. "Cultural Notes on Trade and the Tai." In *Ritual, Power and Economy: Upland–Lowland Contrasts in Mainland Southeast Asia*, edited by Susan D. Russell, 27–65. DeKalb: Northern Illinois University, Center for Southeast Asian Studies.

Ogden, L.R., Asst. Superintendent, Burma Frontier Service. 1936. *Report on the Expedition to the Wa States for the Period 23rd December 1934 to 18th April 1936 (Confidential)*. Rangoon: Superintendent, Government Printing and Stationary. British Library, Oriental & India Office Collections L/PS/20/D228.

Ong, Andrew. 2018a. "Engaging the UWSA: Countering Myths, Building Ties." *Tea Circle, An Oxford Forum for New Perspectives on Burma/Myanmar*. 20 August. Retrieved 8 January, 2019 from https://teacircleoxford.com/2018/08/20/engaging-the-uwsa-countering-myths-building-ties/.

———. 2018b. "Producing Intransigence: (Mis)understanding the United Wa State Army in Myanmar." *Contemporary Southeast Asia* 40(3): 449–74.

———. 2018c. "Navigating Liminality: Region-Making and Political Practice on the Myanmar-China Border." PhD diss., Department of Anthropology, Harvard University, Cambridge, MA, May 2018.

Oppitz, Michael. 2008a. *Die verlorene Schrift: Abschiedsvortrag, gehalten am 20. Dezember 2007 im Völkerkundemuseum der Universität Zürich*. Zürich: VMZ.

———. 2008b. "The Log Drum." In *Naga Identities: Changing Local Cultures in the Northeast of India*, edited by Michael Oppitz et al., 169–98. Gent: Snoeck Publishers.

Oppitz, Michael, Thomas Kaiser, Alban von Stockhausen, and Marion Wettstein, eds. 2008. *Naga Identities: Changing Local Cultures in the Northeast of India*. Gent: Snoeck Publishers.

Paoli, Letizia, Victoria A. Greenfield, and Peter Reuter. 2009. *The World Heroin Market: Can Supply Be Cut?* New York: Oxford University Press.

Parker, Edward Harper. 1893. *Burma: With Special Reference to Her Relations with China*. Rangoon: Rangoon Gazette Press.

Parkin, David. 1989. "Politics of Naming among the Giriama." In *Social Anthropology and the Politics of Language*, edited by Ralph Grillo, 61–89. London: Routledge.

Parkinson, William, and Michael Galaty. 2007. "Secondary States in Perspective: An Integrated Approach to State Formation in the Prehistoric Aegean." *American Anthropologist* 109(1): 113–29.

Pasquet, Sylvie. 1989. "Entre Chine et Birmanie: Un mineur-diplomate au royaume de Hulu, 1743–1752." *Études chinoises* 8(1): 41–68 (Part 1); 8(2): 69–98 (Part 2).

———. 2010. "*Lawa* (*Wa*) in Burmese Historical Sources: A Preliminary Survey." Paper presented at the International Burma Studies Conference, Marseille.

Patterson, Orlando. 1982. *Slavery and Social Death*. Cambridge, MA: Harvard University Press.

Pearson, Thomas. 2009. *Missions and Conversions: Creating the Montagnard-Dega Refugee Community*. New York: Palgrave Macmillan.

Pedersen, Susan. 2001. "The Maternalist Moment in British Colonial Policy: The Controversy over 'Child Slavery' in Hong Kong, 1917–1941." *Past and Present* 171: 161–202.

Peng Gui'e (a.k.a Pen, or Peng, Kuei-Erh). 1926. *Shuangjiang yi pie* [A Glance at Shuangjiang]. Shuangjiang: Shuangjiang Normal College.

———. 1940. Shun-Zhen yanbian de Puman ren [The Puman people of the Shunning-Zhenkang border area]. *Xinan bianjiang* 7. Repr., Taipei: Chengwen; *Zhongguo qikan huibian* 40: 651–56.

Pitchford, V.C. (Senior Civil Officer-in-Charge). 1936. *Report on the Wa States Expedition Column of 1935-36 (Confidential)*. Rangoon: Superintendent, Government Printing and Stationary. British Library, Oriental & India Office Collections L/PS/20/d234; Mss Eur E 252/32g.

Pitchford, V.C. 1937. "The Wild Wa States and Lake Nawngkhio. " *Geographical Journal* 90: 223–32.

Prestre, W.-A [Willy-A]. 1938. "Rites étranges d'un pays inconnu: Au pays des coupeurs des têtes." *Illustration* [Paris], 15 January 1938, 78–81.

Prestre, Willy-A. 1946. *La piste inconnue; au pays des chasseurs de têtes*. Neuchatel and Paris: Victor Attinger.

Proschan, Frank. 1996. "Who Are the 'Khaa'?" In *Proceedings of the 6th International Conference on Thai Studies* 4(1): 391–414. Chieng Mai, Thailand, 14–17 October.

Proschan, Frank, ed. 1999. *Bamboo on the Mountains: Kmhmu Highlanders from Southeast Asia and the United States*. Washington, DC: Smithsonian Institution, Smithsonian Folkways CD, No. SFW40456. Retrieved 20 January 2020 from http://www.folkways.si.edu/albumdetails.aspx?itemid=2657.

Pun, Ngai. 2003. "Subsumption or Consumption? The Phantom of Consumer Revolution in 'Globalizing' China." *Cultural Anthropology* 18(4): 469–92.

Qian, Ning. 1997a. "Gui'sha, Fozu, Yesu: Lahuzu de zongjiao xinyang yu shehui bianqian" [Gui'sha, Buddha, and Jesus: religious beliefs and social change among the Lahu nationality]. *Sixiang zhanxian* [Thought front] 1997.4: 30–37.

———. 1997b. "Jindai jidujiao de chuanbo yu shaoshu minzu shehui de duanque" [The spread of Christianity in modern times and the shortcomings of the minority nationality societies]. *Sixiang zhanxian* [Thought front] 1997.1: 78–86.

Qing shi gao [Draft history of the Qing period]. 1938. ["Compiled 1914–27".] Edited by Zhao Ersui et al. Academia Sinica electronic edition, Scripta Sinica database. Retrieved 20 January 2020 from http://hanchi.ihp.sinica.edu.tw/ihp/hanji.htm.

Qu Ming'an. 1985. "Yuesong Wazu biaoniu lishi de yanbian ji xin wenti" [Historical transformations and new problems of cattle-spearing among the Wa nationality at Yuesong]. *Minzu yu xiandaihua* [Nationalities and modernization] 1: 38–41.

Radio Free Asia. 2018. "Bride and Birth Surrogate Ads in Northern Myanmar Spark Local Anger, Government Investigation." 12 December. Retrieved 20 January 2020 from https://www.rfa.org/english/news/myanmar/bride-and-birth-surrogate-ads-in-northern-myanmar-12122018160211.html.

Rao, S. V. A. S., and C. R. Prasad Rao. 1977. "Drinking in the Tribal World: A Cross-Cultural Study." *Man in India* 57(2): 97–120.

Raymond, Catherine. 2013. "An Ethnographic Illustration of Wa People in British Burma during the Early Twentieth Century: Notes on a Shan Album from the NIU Burma Collection, with Reference to Similar Illustrations from Other Sources." *Journal of Burma Studies* 17(1): 221–41.

Rehfish, Farnham. 1987. "Competitive Beer Drinking among the Mambila." In *Constructive Drinking: Perspectives on Drink from Anthropology*, edited by Mary Douglas, 135-45. Cambridge: Cambridge University Press.

Reichart, P. A., and H. P. Philipsen. 1989. *Betel and Miang: Vanishing Thai Habits*. Bangkok: White Lotus.

Reid, Anthony. 1982. "'Closed' and 'Open' Slave Systems in Pre-colonial Southeast Asia." In *Slavery, Bondage, and Dependency in Southeast Asia*, edited by Anthony Reid, 156–81 New York: St. Martin's Press.

———. 1985. "From Betel-Chewing to Tobacco Smoking in Indonesia." *Journal of Asian Studies* 44(3): 529–47.

Reid, R. M. 1992. "Cultural and Medical Perspectives on Geophagia." *Medical Anthropology* 13(4): 337–51.
Ren, Hai. 2005. "Theme Parks." In *Encyclopedia of Contemporary Chinese Culture*, edited by Edward L. Davis, 591–92. New York: Routledge.
———. 2007. "The Landscape of Power: Imagineering Consumer Behavior at China's Theme Parks." In *The Themed Space: Locating Culture, Nation, and Self*, edited by S. Lukas, 97–112. Lanham, MD: Lexington Books.
Renard, Ronald D. 2013. "The Wa Authority and Good Governance, 1989–2007." *Journal of Burma Studies* 17(1): 141–80.
Renard, Ronald D., and Xavier Bouan. 2016. *The Wa of Myanmar.* Paris: Indigo.
Report on the Administration of Burma for the Year 1934. 1935. Rangoon: Government Printing.
Report on the Administration of the Shan and Karenni States for the Year 1920. 1920. Rangoon: Government Printing.
Roberts, Sean R. 2020. *The War on the Uyghurs: China's Campaign against Xinjiang's Muslims.* Manchester: Manchester University Press.
Robinne, François, and Mandy Sadan, eds. 2007. *Social Dynamics in the Highlands of Southeast Asia: Reconsidering Political Systems of Highland Burma, by E.R. Leach.* Leiden: Brill.
Rocher, Émile. 1880. *La province chinoise du Yün-nan.* Vols. I–II. Paris: Ernest Leroux.
Rong Ruoxi. 1988. "Wazu lishi yanjiu zongshu." [General overview of research on the history of the Wa nationality]. *Minzu yanjiu dongtai* 3: 13–20.
Room, Robin. 2005. "Multicultural Contexts and Alcohol and Drug Use as Symbolic Behaviour." *Addiction Research & Theory* 13(4): 321–31.
Rooney, Dawn F. 1993. *Betel Chewing Traditions in South-East Asia.* Kuala Lumpur: Oxford University Press.
Roque, Ricardo. 2010. *Headhunting and Colonialism: Anthropology and the Circulation of Human Skulls in the Portuguese Empire, 1870–1930.* New York: Palgrave Macmillan.
Ruey Yih-fu [Rui Yifu]. 1948. "Yunnan xinan bianjing de Luohei ren" [The Luohei (Lahu) people of the southwestern borders of Yunnan]. *Guoji wenhua* [International culture] 1(3): 1–2.
Sadan, Mandy. 2008. *A Guide to Colonial Sources on Burma: Ethnic and Minority Histories of Burma in the India Office Records, British Library.* Bangkok: Orchid Press.
———. 2013. *Being and Becoming Kachin: Histories beyond the State in the Borderworlds of Burma.* Oxford and London: Oxford University Press and the British Academy.
Sahlins, Marshall. 2008. "The Stranger-King, or, Elementary Forms of the Politics of Life. *Indonesia and the Malay World* 36(105): 177–99.
Sai Kham Mong. 1996. "The Wa State (1945–60): Problems of Emergence into the Modern World." *Ajia Afurika gengo bunka kenkyū / Journal of Asian and African Studies* [Tokyo] 51: 209–64.
———. 1997. "A Supplement" [to Sai Kham Mong 1996]. *Ajia Afurika gengo bunka kenkyū / Journal of Asian and African Studies*] 53: 155–62.
Salemink, Oscar. 2003. *The Ethnography of Vietnam's Central Highlanders: A Historical Contextualization, 1850–1990.* Honolulu: University of Hawai'i Press.
Samarasinghe, Vidyamali. 2008. *Female Sex Trafficking in Asia: The Resilience of Patriarchy in a Changing World.* New York: Routledge.
Sangren, P. Steven. 2017. *Filial Obsessions: Chinese Patriliny and its Discontents.* Cham, Switzerland: Springer International Publishing/Palgrave Macmillan.
Sao Saimong Mangrai. 1965. *The Shan States and the British Annexation.* Ithaca, NY: Cornell University Southeast Asian Studies Program Data Paper 57.

Sao Saimong Mangrai, ed. 1981. *The Padaeng Chronicle and the Jengtung State Chronicle Translated*. Ann Arbor: University of Michigan, Center for South and Southeast Asian Studies.

Schendel, Willem van. 2002. "Geographies of Knowing, Geographies of Ignorance: Southeast Asia from the Fringes." *Environment and Planning D: Society and Space* 20(6): 647–68.

Schneider, D. M., with R. Handler. 1995. *Schneider on Schneider: The Conversion of the Jews and Other Anthropological Stories*. Durham, NC: Duke University Press.

Schafer, Edward H. 1967. *The Vermilion Bird: T'ang Images of the South*. Berkeley: University of California Press.

Schoenhals, Michael. 2004. "Cultural Revolution on the Border: Yunnan's 'Political Frontier Defence.'" *Copenhagen Journal of Asian Studies* 19: 27–54.

Scott, James C. 1998. *Seeing like a State: How Certain Schemes to Improve the Human Condition Have Failed*. New Haven, CT: Yale University Press.

———. 2009. *The Art of Not Being Governed: An Anarchist History of Upland Southeast Asia*. New Haven, CT: Yale University Press.

Scott, James C., John Tehranian, and Jeremy Mathias. 2002. "The Production of Legal Identities Proper to States: The Case of the Permanent Family Surname." *Comparative Studies in Society and History* 44(1): 4–44.

Scott, James George. 1893. "The Pacification of West Mang Lün, with Notes on the Wild Wa Country [. . .] Lashio, 13th June 1893." British Library, Oriental & India Office Collections (henceforth BL, OIOC), MS Eur F 278/78.

———. 1896. "The Wild Wa: A Headhunting Race." *Asiatic Quarterly Review* (3rd series) 1: 138–52.

———. 1911. *Burma: A Handbook of Practical, Commercial, and Political Information*. London: Alexander Moring.

———. 1918. "Indo-Chinese Mythology." In *The Mythology of All Races*, ed. Louis Herbert Gray. Boston: Marshall Jones Co. [Wa myths in Vol. 12: 247–357; 429–30; 448–50].

———. 1911 [1906]. *Burma: A Handbook of Practical Information; With Special Articles by Recognized Authorities on Burma*. Rev. ed. London: Alexander Moring, Ltd. and The De La More Press.

Scott, James George and J. P. Hardiman. 1983 [1900]. *Gazetteer of Upper Burma and the Shan States. Compiled from official papers by J. George Scott . . . assisted by J.P. Hardiman*. Part 1. Vols. I–II. New York: AMS Press. First published Rangoon: Printed by the Superintendent, Government Printing, Burma.

———. 1983 [1901]. *Gazetteer of Upper Burma and the Shan States. Compiled from official papers by J. George Scott . . . assisted by J.P. Hardiman*. Part 2. Vols. I–III. New York: AMS Press. First published Rangoon: Printed by the Superintendent, Government Printing, Burma.

Senior Commissioner, Sino-British Boundary Commission. n.d. [mid-1936?]. *Note on Chinese activities. Secret*. British Library, Oriental & India Office Collections, in Mss Eur E 252/30.

Shackley, Ted, and Richard A. Finney. 2005. *Spymaster: My Life in the CIA*. Dulles, VA: Potomac Books.

S.H.A.N. (Shan Herald Agency for News). 2003. "Sickness and Death Hit Wa—Again." 7 December. http://www.shanland.org/articles/drugs/2003/sickness_and_death_hit_wa.htm, accessed January 15, 2010 (removed from the internet?).

———. 2006a. "New Wave of Wa Settlers Reach Border." 21 April. Retrieved 15 January 2010 from http://www.shanland.org/index.php?option=com_content

&view=article&id=1443:new-wave-of-wa-settlers-reach-border&catid=87:human-rights&Itemid=285.

———. 2006b. "No More Wa Exodus." 9 May. Retrieved 2 June 2014 from http://www.burmanet.org/news/2006/05/09/shan-herald-agency-for-news- no-more-wa-exodus/.

Shang Zhonghao, Guo Sijiu, and Liu Yunti, eds. 1989. *Wazu minjian gushi xuan* [Selected Wa nationality folktales]. Shanghai: Shanghai wenyi.

Shorto, H.L. 2013 [1957]. *Wa-Praok Vocabulary*. Canberra: Asia-Pacific Linguistics.

Shorto, H.L., Paul Sidwell, Doug Cooper, and Christian Bauer. 2006. *A Mon-Khmer Comparative Dictionary*. Canberra: Pacific Linguistics, Research School of Pacific and Asian Studies, Australian National University.

Schiller, Anne. 1997. *Small Sacrifices: Religious Change and Cultural Identity among the Ngaju of Indonesia*. New York: Oxford University Press.

Shryock, Andrew. 2008. "Thinking about Hospitality, with Derrida, Kant, and the Balga Bedouin." *Anthropos* 103(2): 405–21.

Shuangjiang Lahuzu Wazu Bulangzu Daizu zizhixian gaikuang [Overview of the Shuangjiang Lahu, Wa, Bulang, and Dai nationalities' autonomous county]. 1990. Edited by the Shuangjiang Lahuzu Wazu Bulangzu Daizu zizhixian gaikuang editorial committee. Kunming: Yunnan minzu.

Shuangjiang Lahu zu Wa zu Bulangzu Daizu Zizhi xian zhi [Gazetteer of Shuangjiang Lahu, Wa, Bulang, and Dai nationalities' autonomous county]. 1995. Edited by Zhao Chenglong and Shuangjiang Lahu zu Wa zu Bulangzu Daizu Zizhi xian zhi bian zuan wei yuan hui. Kunming: Yunnan minzu.

Simao Yuxi Honghe Daizu shehui lishi diaocha [Investigations of the society and history of the Dai nationality of Simao, Yuxi, and Honghe]. 1985. Edited by the Yunnan Province Editorial Committee. Kunming: Yunnan renmin.

Sixiang zhanxian [Thought front] editorial dept., ed. 1981. *Xinan shaoshu minzu fengsu zhi* [The customs of minority nationalities of the southwest]. Kunming: Zhongguo minjian wenyi.

Smith, Martin. 1999. *Burma: The Insurgency and the Politics of Ethnicity*. Dhaka: University Press.

Sprenger, Guido. 2005. "The Way of the Buffaloes: Trade and Sacrifice in Northern Laos." *Ethnology* 44(4): 291–312.

———. 2006. "Out of the Ashes: Swidden Cultivation in Highland Laos." *Anthropology Today* 22(6): 9–13.

———. 2008. "The Problem of Wholeness: Highland Southeast Asian Cosmologies in Transition." *Zeitschrift für Ethnologie* 133(1): 75–94

Stanley, N., and S. K. Chung. 1995. "Representing the Past as the Future: The Shenzhen Chinese Folk Culture Villages and the Marketing of Chinese Identity." *Journal of Museum Ethnography* 7: 25–40.

Steinmüller, Hans. 2019. "Conscription by Capture in the Wa State of Myanmar: Acquaintances, Anonymity, Patronage, and the Rejection of Mutuality." *Comparative Studies in Society and History* 61: 508–34.

———. 2020. "The Moral Economy of Militarism: Peasant Economy, Military State and Chinese Capitalism in the Wa State of Myanmar." *Social Anthropology* 28(1): 121–35.

Stern, Theodore. 1968. "Ariya and the Golden Book: A Millennarian Buddhist Sect among the Karen." *Journal of Asian Studies* 27(2): 297–328.

Stevenson, H. N. C. 1943. *The Economics of the Central Chin Tribes*. Bombay: Times of India Press.

Sturgeon, Janet. 2005. *Border Landscapes: The Politics of Akha Land Use in China and Thailand*. Seattle: University of Washington Press.

———. 2007. "Pathways of 'Indigenous Knowledge' in Yunnan, China." *Alternatives: Global, Local, Political* 32(1): 129–53.

Summers, D. 2003. "The Archaeology of the Modern Grotesque." In *The Grotesque and Modern Art*, edited by F. Connelly, 20–46. Cambridge: Cambridge University Press.

Svantesson, Jan-Olof, Wang Jingliu, and Chen Xiangmu. 1981. "Mon-Khmer Languages in Yunnan." *Asie du Sud-Est et Monde Insulindien* 12(1–2): 91–100.

Takano, Hideyuki. 2002. *The Shore beyond Good and Evil: A Report from Inside Burma's Opium Kingdom*. Tokyo: Kotan.

Tambiah, Stanley Jeyaraja. 1969. "Animals Are Good to Think and Good to Prohibit." *Ethnology* 8(4): 423–59.

———. 1976. *World Conqueror and World Renouncer: A Study of Buddhism and Polity in Thailand against a Historical Background*. New York: Cambridge University Press.

———. 1985. "The Galactic Polity in Southeast Asia." In *Culture, Thought, and Social Action: An Anthropological Perspective*, by S. J. Tambiah, 252–86. Cambridge, MA: Harvard University Press.

Tapp, Nicholas. 1989. *Sovereignty and Rebellion: The White Hmong of Northern Thailand*. Singapore: Oxford University Press.

———. 1993. "Folk Culture Villages in Shenzhen." *Anthropology Today* 9(3): 23–24.

———. 2002. "In Defence of the Archaic: A Reconsideration of the 1950s Ethnic Classification Project in China." *Asian Ethnicity* 3(1): 63–84.

———. 2005. *Sovereignty and Rebellion: The White Hmong of Northern Thailand*. Rev. ed. Bangkok: White Lotus.

———. 2010. *The Impossibility of Self: An Essay on the Hmong Diaspora*. Berlin: Lit; London: Global [distributor]; Piscataway, NJ: [Distributed in North America by] Transacton Publishers.

Telford, James Haxton. 1937. "Animism in Kengtung State." *Journal of the Burma Research Society* 27(2): 85–238.

Teramoto, Y. S., S. Yoshida, and S. Ueda. 2000. "An Indigenous Rice Beer of Nagaland, India." *Ferment* (April/May): 39–41.

———. 2002. "Characteristics of a Rice Beer (zutho) and a Yeast Isolated from the Fermented Product in Nagaland, India." *World Journal of Microbiology and Biotechnology* 18(9): 813–16.

Terwiel, B. J. 1992. "Laupani and Ahom Identity: An Ethnohistorical Exercise." In *Patterns and Illusions: Thai History and Thought*, edited by Gehan Wijeyewardene and E. C. Chapman, 127–66. Singapore: Institute of Southeast Asian Studies, and the Department of Anthropology, Australian National University (Canberra).

———. 2003. *Shan Manuscripts: Compiled and edited by Barend Jan Terwiel with the assistance of Chaichuen Khamdaengyodtai*. Stuttgart: F. Steiner.

Than Sein Thit, Min Nwe Swe, San Lwin, and Mya-Wa-Ti Ye Khaung. 1962. *Wa-do hta-ni* [About Wa people of Burma: A study.] [Rangoon]: Myan Sa Pyan a-thin.

Thum, Rian. 2020. "The Spatial Cleansing of Xinjiang: Mazar Desecration in Context." *Made in China*, 24 August. Retrieved 30 August 2020 from https://madeinchinajournal.com/2020/08/24/the-spatial-cleansing-of-xinjiang-mazar-desecration-in-context/.

Tian Jizhou. 1983a. "Wazu jianjie" [Introduction to the Wa nationality]. In *Wazu shehui lishi diaocha* [Investigations of the society and history of the Wa nationality], edited by the Yunnan Province Editorial Committee, 1:1–6. Kunming: Yunnan renmin.

———. 1983b. "Banhong Wazu yuanshi shehui fazhan wei fengjian lingzhu zhi" [The development from primitive society to a feudal lord system among the Banhong Wa]. *Minzu yanjiu* (5): 39–43.

Tin Nyunt. 2016. *Myan-ma tha-te-ji-mya nauq-kweh-ga piq-yaq-hman-mya hnin wa-de-tha a-dwin-ye* [On social relations between Burmese tycoon(s) and Wa people, in Burma]. Ma-yan-koun Yangon, Myanmar: A-pyu-yaun sa-pe.

Tin Yee, Daw. 1999. *Wa tain-yin-dha-mya i lu-hmu si-bwa-ye bawa* [The socioeconomic life of the Wa nationality]. Yangon, Myanmar: Department of Anthropology, Yangon University.

Tin Yee, Daw. 2004. *The Socio-Economic Life of the Wah National.* Yangon, Myanmar: National Centre for Human Resource Development, Ministry of Education.

Ting, C. K. 1921. "On the Native Tribes of Yunnan." *China Medical Journal* 35: 162–67.

Tinker, Hugh. 1956. "Burma's Northeast Borderland Problems." *Pacific Affairs* 29(4): 324–46.

———. 1967. *The Union of Burma: A Study of the First Years of Independence.* London: Oxford University Press.

Tinker, Hugh, et al., eds. 1983–84. *Burma: The Struggle for Independence 1944–1948: Documents from Official and Private Sources.* 2 vols. London: HMSO.

Tong Enzheng. 1989. "Morgan's Model and the Study of Ancient Chinese Society." *Social Sciences in China* 10: 182–205

Took, Jennifer. 2005. *A Native Chieftaincy in Southwest China: Franchising a Tai Chieftaincy under the* tusi *System of Late Imperial China.* Leiden: Brill.

Torigoe Kenzaburo. 1993. "Wazoku to kodai Nihon" [The Wa people and ancient Japan]. In *Wazoku to kodai Nihon* [The Wa people and ancient Japan], edited by Suwa Haruo, 7–52. Tokyo: Yuzankaku.

Torigoe Kenzaburo, and Hiroko Wakabayshi. 1998. *Yayoi bunka no genryu ko: Unnansho Wazoku no seisa to shinhakken* [Investigations of the origins of Yayoi culture: Research and new discoveries with regard to the Wa people of Yunnan]. Tokyo: Taishukan Shoten.

Torigoe Kenzaburo, Hiroko Wakabayashi, and Miyoka Kawano, eds. 1983. *Unnan kara no michi: Nihonjin no rutsu o saguru* [The road from Yunnan: Exploring the route taken by the Japanese people]. Tokyo: Kodansha.

Tsintjilonis, Dimitri. 2004. "The Flow of Life in Buntao: Southeast Asian Animism Reconsidered." *Bijdragen tot de taal-, land- en volkenkunde* 160(4): 425–55.

Turchin, Peter. 2009. "A Theory for Formation of Large Empires." *Journal of Global History* 4: 191–217.

Turner, Terence S. 1986. "Production, Exploitation and Social Consciousness in the 'Peripheral Situation.'" *Social Analysis* 19: 91–119.

———. 1988a. "Commentary: Ethno-Ethnohistory; Myth and History in Native South American Representations of Contact with Western Society." In *Rethinking History and Myth: Indigenous South American Perspectives on the Past*, edited by Jonathan D. Hill, 235–81. Urbana: University of Illinois Press.

———. 1988b. "History, Myth, and Social Consciousness among the Kayapo of Central Brazil." In *Rethinking History and Myth: Indigenous South American Perspectives on the Past*, edited by Jonathan D. Hill, 195–213. Urbana: University of Illinois Press.

———. 2009. "The Crisis of Late Structuralism: Perspectivism and Animism: Rethinking Culture, Nature, Spirit, and Bodiliness." *Tipití: Journal of the Society for the Anthropology of Lowland South America* 7(1): 3–42.

Turton, Andrew. 1998. "Thai Institutions of Slavery." In *Formes extrêmes de dépendance: Contributions à l'étude de l'esclavage en Asie du Sud-Est*, edited by Georges Condominas, 411–57. Paris: EHESS.

———. 2004. "Violent Capture of People for Exchange on Karen-Tai Borders in the 1830s." In *The Structure of Slavery in Indian Ocean Africa and Asia*, edited by Gwyn Campbell, 69–82. London: Frank Cass.

UN Wire. 2003. "UNICEF Official Cites 'Largest Slave Trade in History.'" 20 February. http://www.unwire.org/UNWire/20030220/32139_story.asp, accessed June 2, 2014. (Removed from the Internet?)

US Department of State. 2006. *International Narcotics Control Strategy Report*. Retrieved 20 January 2020 from https://2009-2017.state.gov/j/inl/rls/nrcrpt/2006/index.htm.

Valeri, Valerio. 1994. "Wild Victims: Hunting as Sacrifice and Sacrifice as Hunting in Huaulu." *History of Religions* 34(2): 101–31.

———. 2000. *The Forest of Taboos: Morality, Hunting, and Identity among the Huaulu of the Moluccas*. Madison: University of Wisconsin Press.

———. 2001 [1994]. "'Our Ancestors Spoke Little': Knowledge and Social Forms in Huaulu." In *Fragments from Forests and Libraries: Essays by Valerio Valeri*, edited by Janet Hoskins, 349–68. Durham, NC: Carolina Academic Press.

Wa Notes A. 1936. "History of Manglun and Connected States as Abridged by Hsin Ta, Clerk to Manglun Sawbwa and Translated by Maung Shwe Mein, from a Poetical Record in Shan Kept at the Panghsang Monastery. The Present Manuscript Was Made from Memory about 1925 AD" (19). Rangoon: Office of the Supdt., Government Printing. British Library, Oriental & India Office Collections, Mss Eur E 252/26, pp. 104a–107b.

Wade, Geoff. 2009. "The Polity of Yelang and the Origins of the Name 'China.'" *Sino-Platonic Papers* 188: 1–26.

———. 2015. "The 'Native Office' System: A Chinese Mechanism for Southern Territorial Expansion over Two Millennia." In *Asian Expansions: The Historical Experiences of Polity Expansion in Asia*, edited by Geoff Wade, 69–91. New York: Routledge.

Walker, Anthony R. 1974. "Messianic Movements among the Lahu of the Yunnan-Indochina Borderlands." *Southeast Asia: An International Quarterly* 3(2): 699–712.

———. 2003. *Merit and the Millennium: Routine and Crisis in the Ritual Lives of the Lahu People*. New Delhi: Hindustan Pub. Corp.

———. 2009. "A Mahayanist Movement in the Luohei Shan (Lahu Mountains) of Southwestern Yunnan." *Inner Asia* 11(2): 309–33.

———. 2014. *Sakyamuni and G'ui Sha: Two Essays on Buddhism in the Lahu and Wa Mountains*. Fribourg: Academic Press.

Walker, Anthony R., ed. 1992. *The Highland Heritage: Collected Essays on Upland North Thailand*. Singapore: Suvarnabhumi.

Walton, M. J. 2013. "The 'Wages of Burman-ness': Ethnicity and Burman Privilege in Contemporary Myanmar." *Journal of Contemporary Asia* 43(1): 1–27.

Wang, Jianmin. 1997. *Zhongguo minzuxue shi* [History of ethnology in China]. Vols. I–II. Kunming: Yunnan jiaoyu.

Wang Jingliu. N.d. [ca. 1980]. "Maolong yinchang dieshi" [Historical notes on the Maolong silver mine]. Manuscript.

———. 1990. "Wazu mugu kao" [Research on the Wa wooden drum]. *Minzu yishu yanjiu* [Studies in National Art] (3): 42–46.

Wang Jingliu, ed. 1994. *Nbeen loux Vax* [Studies in the Wa language]. Kunming: Yunnan minzu.

———, ed. 2007. *Washan jishi* [Historical events in the Wa mountains]. Kunming: Yunnan minzu.

Wang Jingliu et al. 1992. *Loux gab Vax* [Collected Wa idioms]. Kunming: Yunnan minzu.

Wang Ming-ke. 2008. "Xunfang Ling Chunsheng, Rui Yifu liang wei xiansheng de zuji: Shiyusuo zaoqi Zhongguo xinan minzu diaocha de huigu" [Retracing the steps of Ling Shun-sheng and Ruey Yifu: Looking back at the early ethnographic investigations carried out in the Chinese Southwest by the Institute of History and Philology]. *Gujin lunheng* [Disquisitions on the past and present] 18: 17–32.
Wang Ningsheng. 1985. *Yunnan Cangyuan yanhua de faxian yu yanjiu* [The discovery and study of the rock paintings of Cangyuan, Yunnan]. Peking: Wenwu.
———. 1985/87. "Yangshao Burial Customs and Social Organization: A Comment on the Theory of Yangshao Matrilineal Society and Its Methodology." *Early China* 11–12: 6–32.
———. 1989. "Wazu tonggu" [Bronze drums of the Wa People]. In *Minzu kaoguxue lunji* [Essays in ethnoarcheology], edited by Wang Ningsheng, 259–71. Peking: Wenwu.
———. 1992. *Yunnan kaogu* [Archeology of Yunnan]. 2nd ed. Kunming: Yunnan renmin.
———. 1996. "A Forgotten Kingdom in Highland Southwest China." Paper presented at the 6th International Conference of the European Association of Southeast Asian Archaeologists, Leiden, 2–6 September 1996.
———. 1997. *Xinan fanggu sawu nian* [Thirty-five years exploring antiquity in the southwest]. Jinan: Shandong huabao.
———. 2001. *Gusu xin yan* [New research on old customs]. Taipei: Lantai.
———. 2006. "Li jiuzhou zhi fengsu kao xianmin zhi shiji" [Pursuing the customs of the Nine Continents in order to trace the history of our forebears]. In *Kaoguren yu tamen de gushi* [Archaeologists and their stories], 1–54. Anonymous editorial committee; with texts by Wang Ningsheng, Wang Xueli, and Li Yangsong. Beijing: Xueyuan.
———. 2008. *Minzu kaogu tansuo* [Explorations in ethnoarchaeology]. Kunming: Yunnan renmin.
———. 2010a. "Changes in Ethnic Identity among Han Immigrants in the Wa Hills from the Seventeenth to Nineteenth Centuries." *Asia Pacific Journal of Anthropology* 11(2): 128–41.
———. 2010b. *Wang Ningsheng cang Xinan minzu laozhaopian* [Old photographs of southwestern nationalities in the collection of Wang Ningsheng]. Edited by Li Yujie and Kong Lingyuan. Chengdu: Ba-Shu shushe, 2010.
Wang, Zhusheng, Tan Chee-Beng, Sidney C. H. Cheung, and Yang Hui, eds. 2001. *Tourism, Anthropology and China: In Memory of Professor Wang Zhusheng*. Bangkok: White Lotus Press.
Warren, James. 1982. "Slavery and the Impact of External Trade: The Sulu Sultanate in the Nineteenth Century." In *Philippine Social History: Global Trade and Local Transformations*, edited by Alfred W. McCoy and Edilberto C. de Jesus, 415–44. Quezon City: Ateneo de Manila University Press.
Warry, W. "Confidential from W. Warry, Esq., Political Officer, to the Chief Secretary to the Chief Commissioner, Burma, No. 9, dated Bhamo, the 15th June 1891." British Library, Oriental & India Office Collections, Mss Eur Photo Eur 384.
Washburne, Chandler. 1961. *Primitive Drinking: A Study of the Uses and Functions of Alcohol in Primitive Societies*. New York: College and University Press.
Watkins, Justin (Ai Sēng). 2002. *The Phonetics of Wa: Experimental Phonetics, Phonology, Orthography and Sociolinguistics*. Canberra: Australian National University, Research School of Pacific and Asian Studies (Pacific Linguistics 531).
———. 2007. "Burma/Myanmar." In *Language and National Identity in Asia*, edited by Andrew Simpson, 263–87. New York: Oxford University Press.
———. 2009. "Wa." In *Concise Encyclopedia of Languages of the World*, edited by Keith Brown and Sarah Ogilvie, 1155–57. Oxford: Elsevier Ltd..

———. 2013a. "A Themed Selection of Wa Proverbs and Sayings." *Journal of Burma Studies* 17(1): 29–60.

———. 2013b. *Dictionary of Wa: With Translations into English, Burmese and Chinese = Phuk lai toe: Dee bleeh lox Vax lox Hawx—lox Man—lox Enggalang = Pug lai doui: Ndee nbleeih loux Vax loux Hox—loux Man—loux Eing Ga Lang*. Boston: Brill.

Watkins, Justin, et al. 2006. SOAS Wa Dictionary Project. Incl. "A Bibliography of Materials in or about Wa Language and Culture." Retrieved 20 January 2020 from http://www.humancomp.org/wadict/.

Watson, James L. 1980. "Transactions in People: The Chinese Market in Slaves, Servants, and Heirs." In *Asian and African Systems of Slavery*, edited by James L. Watson, 223–50. Berkeley: University of California Press.

Watson, Rubie. 1986. "The Named and the Nameless: Gender and Person in Chinese Society." *American Ethnologist* 13(4): 619–31.

"*Wazu jianshi*," editorial committee. 1986. *Wazu jianshi* [A concise history of the Wa people]. Kunming: Yunnan jiaoyu.

Wazu diaocha cailiao. 1980 [1962]. Vols. 5–7. Beijing: Zhongguo Kexueyuan Minzu yanjiusuo Yunnan minzu diaocha zu [Yunnan nationalities research team, Nationalities research Institute, Chinese Academy of Sciences]. (Vols. 1–4 were issued as *Kawa zu diaocha cailiao*; see too *Wazu shehui lishi diaocha*.)

Wazu shehui lishi diaocha [Investigations of the society and history of the Wa nationality]. 1983–87. Edited by the Yunnan Province Editorial Committee for the five series on nationalities issues. Vols. 1–4. Kunming: Yunnan renmin. (See also *Kawa zu diaocha cailiao, Wazu diaocha cailiao*.)

———. 1983a [1957]. Ximeng Wazu shehui jingji diaocha baogao [Report on the investigations of the economy and society of the Wa people of Ximeng]. In *Wazu shehui lishi diaocha* [Investigations of the society and history of the Wa nationality], edited by the Yunnan Province Editorial Committee, 1:7–58. Kunming: Yunnan renmin.

———.1983b [1957]. "Ximeng Damasan Wazu shehui jingji diaocha baogao" [Report on the investigations of the economy and society of the Wa people of Damasan, Ximeng]. In *Wazu shehui lishi diaocha* [Investigations of the society and history of the Wa nationality], edited by the Yunnan Province Editorial Committee, 1:59–176. Kunming: Yunnan renmin.

Wei Deming [also see Nyi Ga, or Nyiga]. 1988. "Han di, Sigangli, Muyiji: Wazu wenhua san da yaosu" [Dry fields, the Si Ngang Lih myth, and the Moik sacrifice—three major constituents of Wa culture]. *Minzu diaocha yanjiu* (4): 49–55.

———. 1995. "Puzu yanjiu" [Research on the Pu nationality]. *Yunnan shehui kexue* (2): 68–74.

———. 1999. *Wazu lishi yu wenhua yanjiu* [Research in the culture and history of the Wa people]. Dehong, Mangshi: Dehong minzu chubanshe, 1999.

———. 2001. *Wazu wenhua shi* [A cultural history of the Wa nationality]. Kunming: Yunnan minzu.

Wechsler, Maxmilian. 2004. "Uncertainty over Pang Sang." *Bangkok Post*, 1 February 2004. Retrieved 20 January 2020 from http://www.mapinc.org/drugnews/v04/n220/a09.html.

Weng, Naiqun. 2006. "The Flows of Heroin, People, Capital, Imagination and the Spread of HIV in Southwest China." In *Translocal China: Linkages, Identities and the Reimagining of Space*, edited by Tim Oakes and Louisa Schein, 315–87. London: Routledge.

Werner, David, with Carol Thuman and Jane Maxwell. 1992. *Where There Is No Doctor: A Village Health Care Handbook*. Palo Alto, CA: Hesperian Foundation.

Wilson, T. M. 2005. "Drinking Cultures: Sites and Practices in the Production and Expression of Identity." In *Drinking Cultures: Alcohol and Identity*, edited by Thomas M. Wilson, 1–23. New York: Berg.

Winnington, Alan. 1959. *The Slaves of the Cool Mountains: The Ancient Social Conditions and Changes Now in Progress on the Remote South-Western Borders of China*. London: Lawrence & Wishart.

———. 1986. *Breakfast with Mao: Memoirs of a Foreign Correspondent*. London: Lawrence & Wishart.

Woods, Kevin. 2011. "Ceasefire Capitalism: Military-Private Partnerships, Resource Concessions and Military-State Building in the Burma-China Borderlands." *Journal of Peasant Studies* 38(4): 747–70.

———. 2016. "'China in Burma': A Multi-scalar Political Economy Analysis." In *Chinese Encounters in Southeast Asia: How People, Money and Ideas from China Are Changing a Region*, edited by D. Tan & Pál Nyiri, 227–55. Seattle: University of Washington Press.

———. 2019. "Rubber Out of the Ashes: Locating Chinese Agribusiness Investments in 'Armed Sovereignties' in the Myanmar-China Borderlands." *Territory, Politics, Governance* 7(1): 79–95.

Wright, Ashley. 2014. *Opium and Empire in Southeast Asia: Regulating Consumption in British Burma*. Houndmills, Basingstoke, Hampshire: Palgrave Macmillan.

Wyatt, David K. 2004. *Thailand: A Short History*. 2nd ed. New Haven, CT: Yale University Press.

Xiao Zegong. 1990. "Wazu xingshi de xingcheng" [The Formation of Wa surnames]. In *Wazu Minjian Gushi Jicheng* [Collected Wa nationality folktales], edited by Shang Zhonghao et al. Kunming: Yunnan minzu.

Xiao Zisheng et al. 1986. "Banhong shijian, yichang kangying de douzheng" [The Banhong incident, an anti-British struggle). In *Cangyuan wenshi ziliao xuanji* [Cangyuan history and culture, select materials], edited by Cangyuan Wazu zizhixian zhengxie. Yunnan, Cangyuan, 1:1–40.

Ximeng Wazu zizhixian zhi [Gazetteer of Ximeng Wa Autonomous County]. 1997. Edited by Yunnan sheng Ximeng Wazu zizhixianzhi bianzuan weiyuanhui. Kunming: Yunnan renmin.

Xu Zhiyuan. 2009. *Wa Shan xing: Yunnan Ximeng Wazu shehui diaocha jishi: 1956–1957* ["Journey to the Wa mountains": A record of the social investigations of the Wa nationality at Ximeng, Yunnan, in 1956–57]. Kunming: Yunnan daxue.

Xu Yunnan tongzhi gao [Further materials for a comprehensive account of Yunnan]. 1966 [1898] Compiled by Wang Wenshao et al., 2:28. Repr. Taipei: Wenhai. Zhongguo bianjiang congshu.

Yamada, Atsushi. 2007. *Parauk Wa Folktales/Wa zu (Baraoke) de minjian gushi*. Tokyo: Research Institute for Languages and Cultures of Asia and Africa (ILCAA), Tokyo University of Foreign Studies. In English, Chinese, and Wa [Parauk]; colophon in Japanese)

———. 2013. "Phonological Outline of the Vo Dialect." *Journal of Burma Studies* 17(1): 61–79.

Yan Qixiang. 1981. "Wa wen" [The Wa writing system]. *Minzu yuwen* [Nationalities' languages and writing systems] 4: 77–78.

Yan Qixiang and Zhou Zhizhi. 2012 [1995]. *Zhongguo Meng Gaomian yuzu yuyan yu Nan-Ya yuxi* [The Mon-Khmer languages in China and Austro-Asiatic languages]. Beijing: Zhongyang minzu daxue. Repr., Beijing: Social Sciences Academic Press.

Yan, Yunxiang. 2006. "Girl Power: Young Women and the Waning of Patriarchy in Rural North China." *Ethnology* 45(2): 105–23.

Yang, Bin. 2009a. *Between Winds and Clouds: The Making of Yunnan (Second Century BCE to Twentieth Century CE)*. New York: Columbia University Press.

———. 2009b. "Central State, Local Governments, Ethnic Groups and the Minzu Identification in Yunnan (1950s–1980s)." *Modern Asian Studies* 43(3): 741–75.

Yang Guanghai. 2009. *Minzu yingzhi tianye jilu* [Collected records of nationalities visual field research]. Kunming: Yunnan jiaoyu.

Yang, Li. 2011. "Minorities, Tourism and Ethnic Theme Parks: Employees' Perspectives from Yunnan, China." *Journal of Cultural Geography* 28(2): 311–38.

Yang Rui (dir.). 2009. *Crossing the Mountain* (Fanshan). Film, 98 mins.

Yang Shen [fl. ca. 1550]. 1969. *Nanzhao yeshi*. Vols. I-II. Repr., Taipei: Huawen shuju.

Yao, Alice. 2016. *The Ancient Highlands of Southwest China: From Bronze Age to the Han Empire*. Oxford: Oxford University Press.

Yasuda, Yoshinori. 2013. *Water Civilization: From Yangtze to Khmer Civilizations*. New York: Springer.

Yin Shaoting. 2001. *People and Forests: A Human-Ecological History of Swidden Agriculture in Yunnan*. Translated by Magnus Fiskesjö. Kunming: Yunnan Education.

———. 2009. *Yunnan shandi minzu wenhua shengtai de bianqian* [Cultural-ecological changes among the hill ethnic groups in Yunnan]. Kunming: Yunnan jiaoyu.

Yin Shaoting, Christian Daniels, et al., eds. 2005. *Zhongguo Yunnan Gengma Daiwen guji bianmu / A synopsis of Dai old manuscripts in Gengma County of Yunnan, China*. Kunming: Yunnan minzu.

———. 2010. *Zhongguo Yunnan Menglian Daiwen guji bianmu / A synopsis of Dai old manuscripts in the Menglian County of Yunnan, China*. Kunming: Yunnan minzu.

Yoshida, Shuji, Yuji Teramoto, and Seinosuke Ueda. 2000. "An Indigenous Rice Beer of Nagaland, India." *Ferment* (April/May): 39–41.

Young, Gordon. 1991 [1967]. *Tracks of an Intruder*. Bangkok and Chiengmai: Trasvin Publications.

Young, Rev. Harold [Mason] [= Yong Hengluo, sometimes Yong Hengle]. 1933. "The Reverend Harold Young's Deposition, Maymyo, March 1932." In Barton, *Barton's 1929 Wa Diary* 106–16.

———. N.d. [ca. 1946]. "Comments on the Wa tribe." Typescript, British Library, Oriental & India Office Collections, IOR Mss Eur C 710/1.

Young, Harold Mason, and Debbie Young Chase. 2015. *Burma Headhunters: The History and Culture of the Ancient Wa, A Mountain Tribal People*. Bloomington, IN: Xlibris.

Young, Sera L. *Craving Earth: Understanding Pica, The Urge to Eat Clay, Starch, Ice and Chalk*. New York, Columbia University Press, 2011.

Young, Rev. W[illiam] M[arcus] [= Yong Weili] (d. 1936). 1905a. *Cutting the Cords—A New People Strangely Prepared for the Missionary—A Trumpet Call to Baptists—Work among the Hill People of Burma-China*. Published by the Literature Department, American Baptist Missionary Union, Boston, Massachusetts. "No. 407." 4 pp. Files of the American Baptist Historical Society.

———. 1905b. "Shan Mission, Kengtung." *The News* (Rangoon) 18(3): 11.

———. 1906. "The Awakening of Keng Tung." *Missionary Review of the World*, N.S., 19 (March): 213–17.

———. 1926 [1925]. "Border Tribes: A Review of the Work on This Field, for the Year Ending March 31, 1925." In *The Evangel in Burma: Being a Review for the Quarter*

Century 1900–1925 of the Work of the American Baptist Foreign Mission Society in Burma, edited by Lizbeth B. Hughes, 124–29. Rangoon: ABM Press.

———. N.d. [1927]. "A Brief Review of the Work on Bana and Mong Mong Fields, during the First Four Months of 1927." File at the American Baptist Archives, Valley Forge, Pennsylvania.

———. 1933. "The Reverend W. M. Young's Deposition, Maymyo, 28 February 1932." In Barton, *Barton's 1929 Wa Diary*, 98–105.

You Zhong. 1979. *Zhongguo xinan minzu shi* [History of the nationalities of China's Southwest]. Kunming: Yunnan renmin.

———. 1980. *Zhongguo xinan de gudai minzu* [The ancient nationalities of China's Southwest]. Kunming: Yunnan renmin.

———. 1993. "Qingchao dui xinan minzu de shezhi he jingying" [The construction and exercise of government by the Qing dynasty in the nationalities areas of the Southwest]. *Yunnan shehui kexue* [Yunnan social sciences] 3: 68–77.

Yuan Jianqi, et al. 1940. *Yunnan kuangchan zhilüe* [Brief account of Yunnan mining production]. Vol. 1. General editor Wong Wen-hao. Kunming: Yunnan Daxue Congkan.

Yuan Yuliu. 1994. *Zhongguo Xingmingxue* [The study of Chinese surnames and given names]. Beijing: Guangming ribao.

Yun Yao-tsung. 1973. "Kang Ying yingxiong Li Xizhe" [The anti-English hero Li Xizhe]. *Yunnan wenxian* 13: 129–33, 147.

Yunnan Institute for Cultural Relics and Archaeology. 2010. *Gengma Shifodong* [The stone Buddha cave at Gengma]. Beijing: Wenwu.

Yunnan Wazu shehui diaocha cailiao: Wazu diaocha cailiao zhi liu [Yunnan Wa nationality research materials: Wa research materials, vol. 6]. 1962. Edited by Yunnan shaoshu minzu shehui lishi diaochazu, and Yunnan sheng minzu yanjiusuo. Beijing: Academia Sinica.

Zeng, Shicai. 1995. "Christianity in Southwestern China: Mass Conversion among the Miao and Yi." In *Perspectives on Chinese Society: Anthropological Views from Japan*, edited by Suenari Michio, J. S. Eades, and Christian Daniels, 248–64, eds. Tokyo: Tokyo University of Foreign Studies.

Zhang Chengyu. 1941 [1891]. "Lujiang xiayou yidong zhi Jiulongjiang xingji" [Journal of a journey downstream on the Lu River and east to the River Jiulong]. In *Yongchang fu wenzheng*, edited by Li Genyuan (*jizai* 23, Qing 12), 6a–12b. Kunming: Tengchong chuban gongsi.

Zhang, Jijiao. 2003. "Ethnic Minority Labor Out-Migrants from Guizhou Province and Their Impacts on Sending Areas. In *China's Minorities on the Move: Selected Case Studies*, edited by Robyn Iredale, Naran Bilik, and Fei Guo, 141–54. Armonk, NY: M. E. Sharpe.

Zhang Lianfang, ed. 1992. *Zhongguoren de Xingming* [Surnames and names of China's people] Beijing: Shehui kexue.

Zhang, Shiliang. "Nanwang de suiyue — chujin Washan de gongzuo huiyi" [A time hard to forget — The early days of work in the newly entered Wa areas]. *Washan wenhua* [Wa mountains culture] 1992.1:35-36.

Zhang, Yuqing. 2018. *Mystifying China's Southwest Ethnic Borderlands: Harmonious Heterotopia*. Lanham, MD: Lexington Books.

Zhao Furong. 2005. *Zhongguo Wazu wenhua* [China's Wa culture]. Beijing: Minzu.

Zhao Mingsheng. 2013. "Guanyu Wazu zhixi Benren den hanyi, renkou fenbu jiqi xingcheng yu fazhan [About the connotation, distribution and development of the "Ben people," a branch of the Wa nationality]. *Lincan shifan gaodeng zhuanke xuexiao xuebao* [Journal of Lincang Teachers' College] 4: 9–15.

Zhao, Yanshe [Aishe]. 2000. "A Tentative Research on the Culture of the Wooden Drum of Wa Ethnic Group." In *Dynamics of Ethnic Cultures across National Boundaries in Southwestern China and Mainland Southeast Asia: Relations, Societies and Languages*, edited by Hayashi Yukio and Yang Guangyuan, 233–45. Chiang Mai: Lanna Cultural Center, Rajabhat Institute Chiang Mai; Kyoto: Center for Southeast Asian Studies, Kyoto University.

Zheng, Chantal. 2000. "Bière de millet ou de riz: La technique brassicole des Austronesiens de Taiwan." In *Opiums: Les plantes du plaisir et de la convivialite en Asie*, edited by Annie Hubert and Philippe Le Failler, 391–400. Paris; Montreal: L'Harmattan.

Zhou Gengxin. 1984. "Wazu renkou de fenbu he suzhi" [Distribution and quality of the Wa population]. *Sixiang zhanxian* [Thought front] 6: 48–51; ends on 41.

Zhou Guangzhuo. 1935. *Dian-Mian nanduan weiding jie diaocha baogao* [The undecided southern portion of the Yunnan-Burma border: Investigation report]. Reprint, Taibei: Chengwen, 1967.

Zhou, Yongming. 2004. "Suppressing Opium and 'Reforming' Minorities: Antidrug Campaigns in Ethnic Communities in the Early People's Republic of China." In *Dangerous Harvest: Drug Plants and the Transformation of Indigenous Landscapes*, edited by Michael K. Steinberg; Joseph J. Hobbs, and Kent Mathewson, 231–45. New York: Oxford University Press.

Zhou Zhizhi. 1992. "Wawen" [The Wa writing system]. In *Zhongguo shehui kexueyuan Minzu yanjiusuo and Guojia minzu shiwu weiyuanhui Wenhua xuanchuan si*, edited by Zhongguo shaoshu minzu yuyan [The writing systems of the national minorities of China], 200–207. Beijing: Zangxue.

Zhou Zhizhi, Yan Qixiang, and Chen Guoqing. 2004. *Wayu fangyan yanjiu* [Research on dialects of the Wa language]. Beijing: Minzu chubanshe.

Zhu Depu. 1993. *Leshi yanjiu* [Studies in Le history]. Kunming: Yunnan renmin.

———. 1996. *Daizu shenling chongbai mizong* [Dai spirit worship: In pursuit of traces of the spirit-worship of the Dai nationality]. Kunming: Yunnan minzu.

Zhuge Yuansheng [fl. ca.1581–ca.1617]. 1994 [1618]. *Dian shi* [A history of Yunnan]. Reprinted with annotation by Liu Yachao. Luxi: Dehong Minzu.

Index

accidents, 60, 170, 182, 197, 203, 208–209
addiction (to drugs), 88, 225, 255
　See also opium, *blai* (liquor)
agency, 23, 75, 98, 114, 116–18, 126, 145, 150, 199, 200
　See also fate
agriculture, 2, 30, 33, 50n1, 74, 103, 115, 118, 129, 132, 189
　See also swiddening
ai (elder brother; the Wa people as the world's elder brother), 31, 54, 57, 141n22
Akha (Hani; ethnic group present in several countries), 217, 230
American Baptist Foreign Mission Society (ABFMS), 20, 88, 102, 222–43
ancestor spirits (*ge meang*), 69n4, 78–79, 82, 86, 90n20, 91n26, 152–53, 162, 197–200, 208
　See also spirits
animism. See spirits
annexation. See *wu ba nian* (the 1950s Chinese annexation of the Wa lands)
a nog (head-posts in 'skull avenues'), 148–50, 155, 157–58, 162–63
anti-chiefs, 98, 120n11
　See also chiefs, *o lang*, politics
anti-myth, 56, 191n13, 208, 218, 220n15, 220n22, 264
　See also myth
archaeology, 6–7, 24n6
assimilation, 238, 254, 262, 263–64, 267–68
autonomy (Wa), 3, 8, 14, 31, 56–57, 66–67, 85, 89–90n4, 95, 98–99, 108, 113, 123–24, 130, 135, 138, 188, 210–12, 219, 234
　See also social reproduction

bamboo, 38, 42, 56, 77, 207
bamboo cup. See *lei*
Banhong, 99–103, 106–111, 113–14, 117, 180–81, 188, 234
Banlao, 101, 103, 110

Baraog. See *Parauk*
barbarians, 49, 62, 105, 111, 126, 164–65, 177–180, 186, 190n5, 249
Bawdwin (Burmese silver mine), 100, 106, 120n18
Benren ("original people;" northern Wa), 4, 67–68
Benglong. See Palaung (Ta'ang or De'Ang, Mon-Khmer speaking people)
beer. See *blai*
betel (*bao*; betel chewing), 40, 44–45, 50n9, 77–78, 84 (Figure 3.2), 179
blai (*blai num*, rice beer), 33, 40, 44, 47–48, 73–91, 154, 158, 251, 269
blai Houx (hard liquor; Chinese liquor), 44, 75, 83, 87–89, 241n9, 245n55
Blang. See Bulang
Bloch, Maurice, 72n34, 90n21
border (China/Burma international border), 3–5, 9, 12–13, 18, 30, 59, 74, 85, 102, 104–109, 172n11, 174n35, 176, 180, 182–83, 187–89, 195, 212
Britain (incl. as colonial power in Burma), 3, 5–6, 8, 17–20, 22, 35–36, 47, 74, 85, 87, 92, 97, 99–112, 144–46, 157, 176, 178, 180–84, 187–188, 225–29, 232, 238–40, 245n49, 247n67, 250, 293
bronze drums, 7, 24n9, 56, 70n8, 93 (Figure 4.1)
　See also drums (*kroug*, log drums)
Buddhism, 15, 21, 26n31, 94, 101–103, 108, 110, 224, 234, 241n7
buffalo, 7 (Figure 0.3), 16, 69, 82, 135, 141n21, 142, 154, 158–59, 160–63, 168–70, 173n28, 174, 193, 207, 209, 216, 229, 249–52, 255, 257, 259, 261
　See also cattle; Chicago Bulls gear
Bulang (Blang, Mon-Khmer speaking people), 1, 10, 90n16, 243n38
Burling, Robbins (author of *Learning a Field Language*), 38

310 | *Index*

Burma (Myanmar), 1, 3–4, 8–20, 22, 25n17, 35–36, 39, 57, 63, 69, 74-76, 85, 92, 96, 100, 104–105, 108–110, 114–115, 175–78, 180–83, 186, 191n20
Burma Frontier Areas Committee of Enquiry, 8, 19, 247n67
Burmese Communist Party (BCP), 22, 25n17, 63, 195, 210, 212–13, 217, 251

Cangyuan (county), 4, 6–7, 9, 230, 235, 240, 255–57, 260
cannibalism, 131, 177–80, 191n10–13
cardinal directions, *See* spatial organization
cattle, 6, 33, 56, 69, 117, 135, 156–61, 168–70, 193, 208, 226, 237
ceasefire agreements (in Burma), 5, 17
ceramics, 24n8
Chen Can (Qing Chinese government official), 121n54, 122n59, 165
Chicago Bulls gear, 257
  See also buffalo, cattle
chicken, 69, 153, 155, 158, 201, 209, 216
  See also, chicken bone oracle
chiefs (*o lang*; *a meang*), 54–55, 90n15, 97–99, 101–102, 107, 109–110, 113–16, 118, 154, 163, 256
  See also politics, anti-chiefs, *o lang, tusi*
children, 9, 38, 48, 52, 58–62, 77–78, 112, 123–24, 127–139, 159–60, 196, 216, 220n19, 255, 264, 267
China, xiii, 3–5, 7, 8–11, 14–17, 22–23, 36, 54, 56, 62–63, 66, 74, 88–89, 92, 100, 104, 106–109, 124–28, 137–39, 145, 163–68, 175–83, 186–87, 195–96, 208, 211–212, 224, 249–65, 267–70
  See also empire (Chinese); headhunting (Chinese origins of); headhunting (Chinese myths about); *wu ba nian* (Chinese annexation of the Wa lands)
Chinese annexation of the Wa lands, See *wu ba nian*
Chinese genocide (in Xinjiang), see Uyghurs
Cholthira Satyawadhna, 23, 222n40
circle. *See jaig'qee*
civilization (as project, etc.), ix, xiv, 15, 62, 87, 94, 103, 105, 145, 168, 177, 179–180, 184–87, 190n5, 238, 240, 247n69, 254, 262–64
  See also primitivism, evolutionism
Clastres, Pierre, 115–116, 120n11
cleanliness, 44, 60, 73, 86–87
conversation (*a peag*), 48, 77–78
cotton, 95, 101, 119n6, 135, 178
culture (*hlag oud eix gon A Vex*), 18, 20, 36–37, 39, 46, 49, 145, 200, 210, 250–54, 262, 265
custom, 85, 103, 129, 136, 142, 144–46, 167, 184, 211
cutting the calf's tail (*maog si dah mui*), 156–61

Damasan village. *See* Yong Ou
dance, 42, 253, 258 (Figure 10.1), 259
Dax Jadie (Zhadie, Wa-Lahu prophet), 165, 229
De'Ang. *See* Palaung (Ta'ang, Mon-Khmer speaking people)
death, 131–32, 152, 193–222
debt, 29, 32–33, 45, 81, 117, 136
development, 3, 14, 31–35, 168, 189, 193, 251, 218, 262
disease (*saix*, illness), 29, 45, 60–62, 75, 83–84, 105, 112, 131, 193–222, 236
  See also medicine; geophagia (pica)
drinking. *See* social drinking; participant intoxication; *blai* (beer, liquor); tea
drums (*kroug*, log drums), 7, 14, 55–56, 154, 211, 256–57, 260
  See also Bronze drums
drum-shrine, 14–15, 21–22, 55–56

egalitarianism, x, 23, 56, 74–75, 82–83, 96–99, 112, 116, 126, 128, 133–35, 141n20, 194, 202, 219, 251, 264
  See also politics; hierarchy
eggs (chicken), 152–53
empire (British), 19, 75, 115, 144–45, 180, 240
  See also Britain
empire (Chinese), 11–12, 15, 25n20, 56, 62, 75, 94–96, 99, 104–105, 115, 118, 121n48, 133–34, 144–45, 164–67, 175–77, 180, 186, 222n46, 208, 224–27, 237, 240, 262–63, 267–68
  See also China; *wu ba nian* (Chinese annexation of the Wa lands)
empire (Burmese), 26n29, 180
  See also Burma
empire (Mongol), 5, 25n13
encompassment, 262–63
  See also "grammar"
envy, 207, 220n20
ethnic classification (Chinese state project), 13, 63, 127–28, 177–78
  See also naming, re-naming
ethnoarchaeology, 7, 24n8
ethnography, 13, 20–21, 37, 39
  See also jeep ethnography, fieldwork
ethnonymy (system of ethnonyms), 30, 36, 56–57, 63, 182–83
  See also naming
evolutionism, 96, 115–17, 128, 184, 189
  See also primitivism
exchange (trade), 44, 61, 69, 74, 88, 98, 100, 104–105, 113, 115–17, 123–28, 131–38, 156, 175–76, 180, 186, 214, 217, 260, 264
Evans-Pritchard, E.E., 74, 89n2, 167, 224, 263

fake (*jia*, Chinese loanword), 46, 81, 211, 240, 261, 265
fate (destiny), ix, 118, 131, 148, 269

fieldwork and fieldwork ethics, 29–51
feast of merit, 82, 133
film, 23–24
food, 44–46, 74–76, 82, 85, 87, 103, 111, 136, 152–54, 159–160, 167, 174n39
Fang Guoyu, 3, 12–13, 103, 108, 173n20, 179, 188–189
forced relocations (in Burma and China), x, 21, 211–19
fortifications, 3, 6–7, 23, 24n7, 75, 150, 163
Friedman, Jonathan, 21, 74–75, 94, 98, 114–18, 126, 133, 138–39, 263–64
Frontier Areas Committee of Enquiry, *See* Burma Frontier Areas Committee of Enquiry
funerals, 40–41 (Figure 1.4), 45, 75, 77, 81–83, 158, 197, 219n5

gaifangcao ('Liberation grass,' an invasive plant, *Eupatorium adenphorum*), 33
gaur (Asian forest bison), 129, 139, 168
ge muah (wild plantain), 67, 71n30
genealogy. *See ndax ntoung*
Gengma (county and former seat of a Shan kingdom), 4, 24n6, 104, 120n28, 220n21, 224–26, 230
geophagy (geophagia, or pica; eating clay or earth), 219n8
gifts, 33, 45, 85, 102, 162, 204, 226, 231, 234, 237–39
Glieh Neh (culture hero/trickster), 9, 132, 141n15
gold, 99–101, 110, 139, 193
grammars (of interethnic interaction), 252, 262–64
   See also encompassment, orientalism
Grax (foreigner: Indian, British, or Westerner), 30, 36, 57, 182–83, 191n21
grotesque, 250
Gui. *See* Lahu

headhunting, ix–x, 14–15, 18, 62, 74, 103, 112, 117, 119, 129–33, 142–74, 184, 188–89, 223, 228–30, 233–34, 238, 240, 244n40, 249, 252, 255, 262, 264
   headhunting (Chinese origins of), 163–66
   headhunting (Chinese myths about), 166–68
heritage, 261, 264, 267
hierarchy, x, 4, 75, 87, 92–119, 127–28, 133, 203, 251
   See also politics, egalitarianism
history, 31, 46, 93, 96, 103, 117, 124, 126–27, 129, 133, 142, 144–50, 167, 184, 213, 223, 251
   See also writing
Hmong (Miao, ethnic minority people in China), 23, 72n32, 268
hospitality, xii, 77–83, 87, 237, 250

house, 21, 38, 42–43, 46, 78, 103, 108, 129, 142, 151, 153, 160, 210–11, 250, 256
house, new (construction, associated rituals), 42–43, 48, 81, 253, 256
Houx (ethnic Chinese, Han Chinese; incl. Panthay, Muslim Hui Chinese), 30, 35, 57
Hulu (Ch. "gourd") Kingdom (Banhong), 99, 101, 103–109
   See also Banhong
human trafficking, 124

ideology, 56, 62, 94, 112, 123–34, 136–39
India, 30, 35–36, 57, 96, 116
India Office Records, *See* Oriental & India Office Collection, British Library
indigenous (autochthonous) peoples, 2, 15, 23, 62, 124, 179, 195, 224, 256, 261, 267
indigenous, as prohibited term, 261
Izikowitz, Karl Gustav, 20, 50n1

jaig'qee (Wa "circle," "realm"), 32, 53, 69, 86, 251
jeep ethnography, 46
   See also ethnography, fieldwork

Kachin (Kang; Jingpo, Tibeto-Burman speaking people), 30, 57, 114, 133, 138, 183
Karen (Tibeto-Burman speaking people, in Burma and Thailand), 127, 140n8, 230
Kawa (Shan and Chinese term for the Wa), 12, 176
Kengtung (Jaingtung; Jengtung, former Shan kingdom now within Burma), 1, 26n31, 101, 230
Khaa (barbarian/slave, mountain tribe, in Tai languages), 12, 26n31, 63, 120n27, 176
Kammu (Khmu), Mon-Khmer speaking people (in Laos), 173n26
Kazakhs (Turkic-speaking people, in Kazakhstan and China), 269
kitsch (Wa culture as Chinese kitsch), 249, 256, 262
Kuomintang (KMT), 13, 17, 27n36, 50n7

lah (public arena; market), 129, 156–157, 230
Lancang (county), 4, 102, 225–27, 235, 239–40, 244n42
Lahu (Gui, Muhso, Luohei; Tibeto-Burman speaking people), 1, 16, 20–21, 23, 30–31, 36, 43, 54, 57, 63, 65, 71n26, 84, 88, 94, 112, 143–44, 151, 166, 208, 223–40
Lashio (Burmese city), 1, 106, 109
Lawa (Burmese term for Mon-Khmer speaking people), 16
Lawa (Lua; Tai term for Mon-Khmer speaking people), 15–16, 26n30
Leach, Edmund, 21, 23, 96, 98, 114, 116, 120n8, 133

lead, 105–106, 110–111, 180
Lehman, F.K.L. (Chit Hlaing), 21, 108, 116, 133
lei (bamboo cup), 6, 73, 76–83, 87, 89
leopard, 168, 170 (Figure 6.5)
Lévi-Strauss, Claude, 70n10, 98, 116–17, 207
Li Dingguo, 101–103
Lindell, Kristina, 173n26
Ling, Shun-sheng (Ling Chunsheng), 148–151, 153, 157, 171n4, 188–89
Lintner, Bertil, 21, 27n36, 47, 211–212
liquor. *See blai*
Lisu (Tibeto-Burman speaking people), 226–27, 242n25
Liu Zikai (Liu Tzu-k'ai), 15, 21
Lusiades (the *Os Lusiadas* by Camões), 19, 179, 191n12
Luo Zhiji, 14, 50n10, 173n23, 173n25

Ma Jianxiong, 21, 208, 241n2, 4
Macdonald, Charles (theory of naming systems), 58
Man (the majority Burmese people), 30, 36, 57
Mangleng (Manglün mines), 99, 108–111, 118, 121nn54–55
Maolong (silver mine), 100–102, 105ff.
martial (warrior) prowess and ethos, 129, 130–31, 142, 149–50, 152–54, 161–62, 165, 170, 261
masculinity, *See* martial (warrior) prowess
Mauss, Marcel, 70n10, 90n21, 158, 171n8, 185
McKhann, Charles, xii
medicine, 10, 44–45, 195–98, 210–11, 213, 215–19, 219n4
Menglian (Mong Lem; county and former seat of a Shan kingdom), 15–16, 26–27n32, 88, 109–111, 224–25, 230, 233, 244n42
Meillassoux, Claude (theory of slavery), 134, 139
migrant workers, 124–26
mining, x, 3, 12, 18, 35, 63, 75, 92–122, 124, 127, 135, 167, 240, 251
minorities (under Chinese rule), 4, 8–9, 17, 32, 62–64, 67–68, 124, 214, 267
See also barbarians; re-naming the barbarians
missionaries, 9, 20, 88, 102, 222–43
See also Wa Christians
Mon-Khmer languages, 1, 6–7, 11, 15–16, 23, 67, 76, 94, 182
Möng Hka. *See* Ximeng
Muhso. *See* Lahu
muid' (moik; muit, important deity or spirit), 31, 154, 172n16, 200–201, 204
museums, 23
music, 21–22, 48, 246n59
Myanmar. *See* Burma
myth (origin myths), 7, 30–32, 54, 56, 93, 148–49, 191n13, 192n26, 201–202, 208, 251–52, 264
See also anti-myth

Naga (people of northern Burma and Northeast India), 90n12, 96, 98, 114–16, 133, 173n22
names and naming, 31, 52–62, 67–69, 130, 136
See also re-naming
Naxi (Tibeto-Burman speaking people, in China), xii
ndax ntoung, geneaology (lit. "footprints/tracks of the clan"), 53–54, 56
njouh ndoung, head-pole (storing severed heads), 146–48, 154, 250, 255–54
ntoung (patriclan, lineage), 3, 52–60, 63–68, 96, 109, 127, 129, 133–34, 138, 146, 150–51, 158, 162, 195, 210, 250–51
Nuer (African people), 3, 74, 97–98, 167, 224
Nuosu. *See* Yi

o lang (ritual village chief), 55, 90n15, 97–98, 149, 151, 154, 254
opium, ix–x, 2, 12, 14, 17, 22, 33, 63, 74, 85, 88, 90, 95, 111–13, 116–17, 135, 241n10
oracles, 203–204, 209
chicken bone oracle, 171n8, 172n14, 201, 203–207
Oriental & India Office Collection, British Library, xiv, 19
orientalism, 252, 262–64
See also grammars, encompassment
Ox Ag (silver mine, Ch. Xinchang), 111

Palaung (Benglong; Ta'ang; De'Ang, Mon-Khmer speaking people), 1, 10, 30
Panghsang (Pang Kham, capital of Wa State, Burma), 4
Panglong Agreement, 19
Panthay (Muslim Chinese trading communities), 105–106, 119n6, 234
Parauk (Baraog; Praok), 9
patriclans. *See ntoung*
participant intoxication, x, 39, 44, 73, 89, 91n31
periphery, *See* Wa periphery
peripheral situation, 68–69, 74, 86–89, 99, 102, 107, 113, 124, 177, 186, 193, 210, 223–25, 228, 236–37
photography, 13, 19, 24, 45, 47, 146, 148, 193
pigs, 61, 69, 71n30, 77, 153, 158, 168, 203, 209, 216, 227, 237
politics (Wa self-governance), 3, 22–23, 55–56, 68, 75, 85, 96, 108, 113–19, 195, 212, 229, 238, 256
See also autonomy
pottery. *See* ceramics
predatory polities, 75, 96, 115, 118, 120n14, 126–27, 264
Prestre, Willy-A., 154, 157, 172n10, 187–88
primitivism (as a corollary of evolutionism), 123, 128, 249, 255–56
See also evolutionism

prophets (Lahu and Wa), 102, 223–29, 231–33, 240
  See also Dax Jadie
Pu-Man (ancient peoples), 10–11
pumpkin (*a gie*), 143

Qing Dynasty (China), 104–105, 144, 164, 231

raw and cooked barbarians (Chinese terminology), 12, 94, 104, 145, 164, 180, 186–87, 244n43
reciprocity, xiii, 29, 45–46
  See also hospitality; social drinking
re-naming (minorities, barbarians etc.), 52, 62–67, 69
rice. *See* agriculture, swiddening, blai (beer)
rice beer. *See blai*
rock art (rock paintings, incl. fake art for tourist purposes), xiii, 5–7, 254

sacrifice, 16, 31, 54–55 (Figure 2.1), 60, 75, 78, 82, 88, 96, 117, 131, 136, 142, 145–46, 151, 153–163, 169–71, 185, 192n26, 193–96, 198–212, 218–19, 226, 229, 235, 250–51, 257
sacrifice, home, 171n9, 153, 209–10
sao mu ("sweeping tombstones"), 45–46
Sahlins, Marshall, 37–38
Schneider, David, 41–42
Scott, James C., 22–23, 33, 35, 53, 62, 74, 97–99, 108, 118, 219
Scott, Sir James George, 7, 17, 19, 27n40, 47, 97, 146, 157, 199, 227, 250–51
secondary state formation, 11, 95–96, 98, 115, 165
  See also state, empire
self and other, 47, 49, 57, 166, 206–207, 243n34, 243n35; 260, 263–64
Shan (Siam; Tai; Dai, ethnicity present in several countries), 1, 15–16, 30, 57, 88, 101, 114, 230
Shan conquest of Wa areas, 26n31, 220n21
Shenzhen (Chinese city), 249, 254, 258–60
si aob (destructive force), 152, 155–56, 169
Siam. *See* Shan
Sigang lih (location of humanity's emergence; origin myth), 5, 30, 56, 201–202
silver, 99, 101, 180
Simao (Szemao; Puer, Chinese city), 1, 244n44
skin color, 258–59
skull avenue, see *a nog*
slavery, 52, 111–13, 123–41
slavery in China, comparative, 137–38
social drinking, 44–47, 73–89, 193–94
  See also liquor; *blai* (beer); participant intoxication
social reproduction, 52–53, 62, 66, 126, 264
  See also autonomy
spatial organization, 153, 172n14

spirits, 31, 60–61, 136, 141n22, 142, 153, 156, 194, 197–202, 205–11, 215–16, 252
state, x, xii, 3–5, 8, 11, 22–23, 26n29, 33, 35, 62–66, 74–75, 86, 92–119, 124, 128, 133–34, 137–38, 144, 164–66, 168, 177, 180–81, 186, 196, 208, 211–19, 237, 249, 251, 262, 264–65
  See also empire; secondary state formation
Su-siu (Chinese "Su-xiu;" "Soviet-Revisionist;" Russian), 181–83
  See also Winnington, Alan
swiddening (swidden farming, shifting agriculture, slash-and-burn), 2, 30, 33, 50n1, 53, 103, 111, 118, 129, 155, 160, 174n36, 221n36

Ta'ang. *See* Palaung
Tai. *See* Shan
Tapp, Nicholas, 72n32, 266n7–8
tea, 32, 34, 74, 77, 86, 90n16, 124, 175, 189, 214, 241n4, 251
Telford, James Haxton, 219n7
Terwiel, Barend Jan, 76, 90n12
theme parks (Chinese ethno-cultural theme parks), xi, 23, 49, 175, 195, 249–63, 265
tiger, 87, 168–170, 174n39, 192n26, 202, 208, 220n15, 228
tiger rack (*ndaig'a vi*), 156, 168–70, 202
tobacco (cigarettes, cigars), 44–45, 50n9, 77, 88
Tong Enzheng, 123, 140n12
Torigoe, Kenzaburo, 21, 23, 191, 192n25
tourism, 6, 14–15, 23, 89, 195, 210–11, 250–51, 253–60, 265, 269
trade, *See* exchange
tribute, 15–16, 99, 101, 104–106, 110–115, 117, 119, 180, 226–27
  Also see exchange
trophy-taking, *See* headhunting
Tujia (Tibeto-Burman speaking people, in China), 71n28
Turner, Terence S., 74, 220n12, 264
tusi (Chinese imperial native-chief system), 11, 15–16, 25n18–19, 26–27n32, 62–63, 104, 106, 120n24, 28, 225, 233, 239, 241n3, 242n19
TV (television), 14, 23, 39, 48–49, 255

United Wa State Army (UWSA), 4–5, 21, 24n3–4; 39, 50n7, 107, 213–19, 229
United Wa State Party, 24n3
Uyghur (Turkic-speaking people), genocide 267–68, 270

Valeri, Valerio, xii, 158, 161–62, 171, 173n26–27, 191n21, 261
video (VCD, DVD, etc.), 14, 23, 48–49, 210, 252, 254–55, 260
virgins, 159

Wa as pretend Africans (in theme parks), 259–60
Wa Buddhists, 22, 95, 101–103, 229, 234
Wa Christians, 88, 101–102, 171n2, 213, 232–41, 245n49, 247n68, 248n70
Wa Küt ("Wa ged," "remaining Wa"), 230, 243n26
Wa periphery, 9, 113, 117, 185, 231
Wa State (Special Region 2, in Burma), *See* United Wa State Army (UWSA)
Wang Ningsheng, xiii, 6–7, 13–14, 24n8–9, 124, 140n12, 141n17, 178, 229
war, 38, 55, 63, 129–30, 142ff., 150, 209
  See also headhunting
war captives, 62, 112, 123, 130–31
warriors, *See* martial prowess and ethos
wealth (in Wa society), x, 1, 63, 74–75, 83–83, 92–94, 98–99, 104, 111, 114–17, 126–27, 130–31, 135, 141n20, 161, 165–66, 186, 193, 209, 214, 220n23, 251
Wenggake (district in Ximeng county), 82
Winnington, Alan, 19, 24, 36, 47, 140n9, 148, 172–73n20, 181–184, 191n16
women, 16, 38, 57, 59, 96, 108, 124–26, 132, 152–53, 159, 166, 211, 252
writing (in Wa history and myth), 9, 14, 56, 66, 71n21, 118, 132, 144, 146, 150, 220n22, 231, 233, 243nn34–35
wu ba nian (1958 Wa uprising and Chinese annexation of the Wa lands), 14, 35, 38, 42, 127, 130, 157, 163, 195, 212, 250
Wu Shangxian, 103–105

Ximeng (Möng Hka, Chinese trading and county town), 4–5, 24, 30, 36, 71n25, 82, 99, 101, 110, 112, 128, 157, 172n19, 174n36, 195, 208, 223, 226–28, 235, 249–51, 255–57, 265
Xinjiang (East Turkistan) genocide (2017-), 267–68, 270

Yelang (historical kingdom in Southwest China), 94–96, 113
Yi (Nuosu; Tibeto-Burman speaking people, in China), 36, 126–27, 146, 183
Yin Shaoting, 13, 14, 33, 174n36
yong dax (ancestral village of within a Wa *jaig' qee*, or circle), 129
yong guan (descendant village), 129, 154
Yong Ou (Damasan or Masan; village in Ximeng County), 34, 36–37, 40–42, 49, 54–55, 58, 60–61, 65, 67–69, 82, 84, 125, 128–30, 143, 148–49, 151, 154, 161, 168, 194–95, 205–206, 226–28, 230
Yong Soi (Aishuai / Aihsoi, village in Cangyuan county), 9, 36, 168, 225, 234
Young, Harold (Baptist missionary), 20, 152, 226, 236, 242n25, 246n61, 247n67
Young, William (Baptist missionary), 20, 230–31
Yunnan Province, 6, 10–11, 16, 23, 94, 99, 100, 104–107, 165–66, 176, 178–79, 187–88, 224, 233, 236, 239–40, 257

Zhuge Liang, 166–68, 174n35, 187
Zomia, 1, 22, 74, 76, 110, 118

www.ingramcontent.com/pod-product-compliance
Lightning Source LLC
Chambersburg PA
CBHW051527020426
42333CB00016B/1807